☆

☆

☆

☆

IWO JIMA:

AMPHIBIOUS EPIC

HISTORICAL BRANCH

G-3 DIVISION

HEADQUARTERS

U. S. MARINE CORPS

Lt. Col. Whitman S. Bartley, USMC

1954

Marine Corps Monographs
In This Series

The Defense of Wake
The Battle for Tarawa
Marines at Midway
Bougainville and the Northern Solomons
The Guadalcanal Campaign
The Assault on Peleliu
Saipan: The Beginning of the End
The Seizure of Tinian
Marine Aviation in the Philippines
The Campaign on New Britain
Marines in the Central Solomons
The Recapture of Guam
The Marshalls: Increasing the Tempo

Reprinted by
The Battery Press, Inc.
P. O. Box 3107, Uptown Station
Nashville, TN 37219
Thirteenth in the Elite Unit Series
1988
ISBN: 0-89839-108-3
Printed in the United States of America

COVER PICTURE: Mount Suribachi forms background as Marines struggle through
loose volcanic ash to move inland D-Day morning.

Foreword

The assault on Iwo Jima came as a smashing climax to the 16-month drive that carried the amphibious forces of the United States across the Central Pacific to within 660 miles of Tokyo. Striking first at Tarawa in November 1943, American forces had swept rapidly westward, seizing only those islands essential for support of future operations. Many powerful enemy strongholds were bypassed and neutralized. By the fall of 1944 the small but heavily fortified island of Iwo Jima, lying midway between the Marianas and the heart of the Japanese Empire, had assumed such strategic importance that its rapid seizure became imperative. Neutralization would not suffice; Iwo must become an operational United States base.

At Iwo Jima the amphibious doctrines, techniques, weapons, and equipment which had proven so effective during the three previous years of World War II received the supreme test. On that island more than 20,000 well-disposed and deeply entrenched Japanese troops conducted an intelligent and dogged defense. There, more than anywhere else in the Central Pacific, terrain and enemy defense preparations combined to limit the effectiveness of American supporting arms, placing a premium on the skill and aggressive fighting spirit of the individual Marine.

There can be no more fitting tribute to the men of all services who engaged in this bitter 36-day assault than the well-known words of Admiral Chester W. Nimitz, "Among the Americans who served on Iwo Island uncommon valor was a common virtue."

LEMUEL C. SHEPHERD, Jr.
GENERAL, U. S. MARINE CORPS
COMMANDANT OF THE MARINE CORPS

Preface

IWO JIMA is the thirteenth in a series of historical monographs prepared by the Historical Branch, G–3 Division, Headquarters U. S. Marine Corps, to present a factual account of Marine operations during World War II. Upon completion of this series, the individual monographs will be integrated into a final, definitive operational history of World War II.

Grateful acknowledgment is made to the many individuals who read and commented on the preliminary drafts of this monograph, and to the historical offices of the Departments of the Army, Navy, and Air Force for the helpful services rendered.

Mr. John M. Wearmouth prepared the appendices and made an outstanding contribution to this study by his painstaking research and editorial work. Captain Lawrence C. Switzer, a participant in the operation, wrote the preliminary drafts of Chapters III, IV, and V. Maps and sketches were prepared by the Reproduction Section, Marine Corps Schools, Quantico, Virginia. All photographs are official Marine Corps unless otherwise credited.

T. A. WORNHAM
BRIGADIER GENERAL, U. S. MARINE CORPS
ASSISTANT CHIEF OF STAFF, G–3

Contents

CHAPTER I

Background

STRATEGIC SITUATION

By February 1945 American forces had knifed their way across the Pacific and into well buttressed positions along the Luzon-Marianas Line. Admiral Chester W. Nimitz' Pacific Ocean Areas (POA) Forces were poised now for a deeper thrust.

Marianas-based B–29's were conducting heavy raids against important industrial and military targets in the Japanese home islands. Southwest Pacific Forces under General Douglas MacArthur were consolidating positions in the Central Philippines and had gained a strong foothold in Luzon. Japanese air power in the Philippines had been crushed and the exhausted Imperial Fleet driven from Philippine waters, leaving the large immobilized land force to wage a stubborn but losing fight.

As never before, the United States had blasted whatever hopes the Japanese held for victory in the Pacific. Moreover, the homeland itself was now in peril.

The relentless precision of the conquests of Saipan, Tinian, and Guam had stunned the Japanese Empire.[1] The initial landing by Central Pacific Forces in the Marianas had precipitated the highly significant naval and air battle of the Philippine Sea on 19–20 June 1944. For the enemy this was a fiasco from which their naval aviation never fully recovered.

The seizure of the Southern Marianas was completed by 10 August 1944, and in September troops of the III Amphibious Corps were occupying positions in the Palau Islands and Ulithi.[2] The right flank of our line was now secure for operations against the Philippines. (See Map I).

While conducting covering operations preliminary to the assault on the Palaus, Admiral William F. Halsey's Third Fleet had encountered surprisingly light resistance from Japanese land-based air power in the Central Philippines. Sensing that the time was ripe to strike this apparently vulnerable area, Admiral Halsey so informed Admiral Chester W. Nimitz, Commander in Chief, Pacific Fleet (CinCPac).[3] Halsey recommended that the projected Yap and Mindanao operations be abandoned, and that troops thus released be made available to Southwest Pacific Forces for an early attack on the Central Philippines. Nimitz concurred in this recommendation and

---

[1] Maj C. W. Hoffman, *Saipan: The Beginning of the End,* and *The Seizure of Tinian;* Maj O. R. Lodge, *The Recapture of Guam,* MarCorps Historical Monographs (U. S. Government Printing Office, 1950, 1951, and 1954).

[2] Maj F. O. Hough, *The Assault on Peleliu,* MarCorps Historical Monograph (U. S. Government Printing Office, 1950).

[3] Nimitz was also Commander in Chief, Pacific Ocean Areas (CinCPOA).

forwarded it to the Joint Chiefs of Staff.[4] Agreement on this plan was reached quickly in a remarkable demonstration of joint action and administrative flexibility.[5]

On 20 October 1944 the U. S. X and XXIV Corps went ashore at Leyte in the Central Philippines, having bypassed Mindanao in the south. The Japanese reacted to this landing just as they had in the Marianas. On 23 October they threw strong naval surface and carrier-based air forces against our vulnerable amphibious shipping in an all-out attempt to smash the invasion before it could commence. The ensuing naval engagement, however, proved disastrous to the Japanese sea power.[6] By the 26th, our Leyte beachhead was secure from enemy naval intervention.

Leaving the consolidation of Leyte to troops of the Eighth Army, the Sixth Army made a swift amphibious leap to the north and landed on beaches of the Lingayen Gulf in Luzon, 9 January 1945. The fate of the Philippines was now sealed.

The next step was to be an advance from the Marianas through the Bonins to the Ryukyus. This monograph deals with the first step: the amphibious assault on Iwo Jima.

---

[4] Maj C. W. Boggs, Jr., *Marine Aviation in the Philippines*, MarCorps Historical Monograph (U. S. Government Printing Office, 1951), hereinafter cited as *Boggs*.

[5] Biennial Report of The Chief of Staff of the United States Army, 1Jul43 to 30Jun45, 71–73.

[6] A report by the Joint Intelligence Subcommittee of the Combined Chiefs of Staff called, "Possibility of Japanese Withdrawal from the Outer Zone," (London, 8Dec44) states in part:

> As a result of their misguided intervention in the Philippines, the effective strength of the Japanese major naval units has now been reduced to 4 battleships, 3 fleet and converted operational carriers, 2 escort carriers, 7 heavy cruisers. Repairs to damaged ships may increase this strength within the next few months by 2 battleships, 2 carriers and 7 heavy cruisers. In addition 2 new fleet carriers may be ready.
>
> Although the 2 battleship carriers and some effective cruisers are still in the South China Sea Area, the Japanese Navy is unlikely again to intervene in strength until the allies launch their final assault on Japan. Japanese Naval policy will be to conserve their remaining strength for the defense of the Inner Zone.

HISTORY

Iwo Jima is an infinitesimal piece of land located within the Nanpo Shoto, a chain of islands extending 750 miles in a southerly direction from the entrance of Tokyo Bay to within 300 miles of the Marianas. Comprising the Nanpo Shoto are three major island groups. From north to south these groups are: the Izu Shoto, the Ogasawara Gunto (Bonin Islands), and the Kazan Retto (Volcano Islands). Iwo Jima lies within the third group, some 660-nautical miles from Tokyo.[7]

Detailed early history of the Nanpo Shoto is somewhat obscure. Although Japanese fishermen were familiar with the islands of the Izu Shoto, using them for bases as early as 1500, there is no indication that they operated as far south as the Bonins. A Spanish captain, Bernard de Torres, sighted the Volcano Islands in 1543; yet, despite Spanish activity in the nearby Marianas, it was some 250 years before white men gave attention to islands of the Nanpo Shoto.

The Bonins, however, were discovered in 1593 by a Japanese, Sadayori Ogasawara. This group was found to be uninhabited, and Ogasawara chose to call them *munin*, meaning "empty of men." Their present popular name, Bonin, is a corruption of that Japanese word.

Beginning a half-century of unprecedented activity, the early 1800's found an increasing number of whaling ships sailing into the waters surrounding the Bonin Islands. Captain Reuben Coffin, of the whaler *Transit* from Nantucket, landed at Haha Jima in 1823 and claimed it for the United States. Four years later Captain Frederick William Beechey, RN, commanding H. M. S. *Blossom*, dropped anchor at Chichi Jima and claimed the entire Bonin group in the name of King George IV.

Shortly afterward, as a result of Beechey's visit to Chichi Jima, a strangely mixed company of colonists set out from Hawaii under

---

[7] *Shoto* is a Japanese word meaning chain of islands; *Gunto*, several islands in a group; *Retto*, several islands in a line; *Shima* or *Jima*, an island. *Iwo* is a Japanese word meaning Sulphur. *Kazan* means volcano.

the auspices of the British Consul. They settled on Chichi Jima and claimed British sovereignty. This group included Englishmen, Portugese, Italians, Hawaiians, and one American, Nathaniel Savory of Massachusetts.

Commodore Matthew Perry of the United States Navy stopped at Chichi Jima in 1853. Impressed with the potential importance of the entire Bonin group as coaling stations along the route to China, Perry urged the purchase of a strip of beach at Chichi Jima from Nathaniel Savory—the only remaining white member of the original Hawaiian contingent. Perry's intent was to construct warehouses there dependent on ultimate approval of the United States Government. At that time, however, American foreign policy did not admit Pacific obligations, and the commodore's plan was abandoned.

In the passing of some three hundred years since their discovery, the Volcano Islands and little Iwo Jima did not go entirely unnoticed. An Englishman named Gore had visited this group in 1673 and given Iwo Jima a new name, calling it Sulphur Island for obvious reasons. The next visitor was a Russian explorer named Krusenstern, who came in 1805. Yet not a man who had observed these islands recommended to his parent country that they be colonized.

Some years after Perry's visit of 1853 had opened Japan to the west, the Japanese dispatched two officials with 40 colonists to hold the Bonins for Japan. They renamed the islands "Ogasawara" and based their claims on the assumption that they had been discovered by Sadayori, Prince of Ogasawara, in 1593. In 1861 the Japanese made formal claim to the Bonins and were never seriously challenged.

In 1887 the Japanese started colonizing the Volcano Islands and by 1891 had incorporated them into the Ogasawara Branch Administration. Thereupon, all the islands of the Nanpo Shoto came under the jurisdiction of the Tokyo Prefectural Government and were administered as an integral part of Japan. Never very strong, American and European influence in this area died out almost entirely. With in-

NO TRESPASSING sign dated 1937 indicates Japanese attitude toward visitors at Iwo.

creased Japanese colonization in the early 1900's and a ban on foreign settlement, the entire Nanpo Shoto became completely Nipponese. On Chichi Jima, however, descendants of Nathaniel Savory and the other original settlers, who called themselves "Bonin Islanders," celebrated Washington's Birthday and the Fourth of July each year by displaying Old Glory and refused to associate with individuals of Japanese blood.[8]

The civilian population on Iwo Jima numbered 1,091 in 1943, all of whom were of Japanese descent. These people were centered in and around Motoyama, Nishi, Kita and Minami. Their homes were typically Japanese—flimsy one-story frame dwellings, often built a foot off the ground. Livelihood was derived from working in a small sugar mill and a sulphur refinery. Small scale agriculture was carried on, with vegetables, sugar cane, and dry grains being grown for local consumption. Although rice was a staple, it had to be obtained from the homeland, as did all manufactured articles needed for a bare existence. The Iwo inhabitants also fished to piece out their meager diet.

---

[8] Interview Maj J. N. Rentz with author 29Nov51.

3

AERIAL VIEW illustrates pork chop shape of Iwo Jima.   Suribachi, in right foreground, is at southern end of island. (Navy Photo)

In the main, potable water was obtained by catching rain in concrete cisterns.[9]

GEOGRAPHY

The island of Iwo Jima lies slightly south and west of the midpoint of a line drawn between Tokyo and Saipan: 625 nautical miles north of Saipan and 660 miles south of Tokyo.

[9] The foregoing account of the historical background is a synthesis of the following sources: CinCPac-Cin-CPOA Bulletin No. 126–44 (August 1944); Osborn, *The Pacific World* (New York, 1944), 157–159; Encyclopedia Britannica, articles "Ogasawara Jima" and "Volcanic Islands"; F. R. Dulles, *America in the Pacific* (Boston and New York, 1932), 68–73; T. Terry *Terry's Japanese Empire* (Boston and New York, 1914), 105–106; W. Price, *Japan's Islands of Mystery* (New York, 1944) 31–36.

Viewed from the air this desolate looking piece of land resembles a pork chop, while in profile from the sea it has the appearance of a half-submerged whale.   An extinct volcano, Mount Suribachi, forms the narrow southern tip of the island and rises 550 feet to dominate the entire area.   Suribachi is linked to a dome-shaped northern plateau by land that fans out broadly to the north and northeast.   The entire island measures only 4⅔ miles along its northeast-southwest axis, while the width varies from about 2½ miles to slightly less than one-half mile at the narrow base of the volcano. The surface area of Iwo Jima is 7½ square miles.   (See Map II.)

The "shank" of the island between Suribachi and the plateau is covered with a deep layer of coarse, black volcanic ash. The particles of grit are light enough to be shifted by the wind. Progress over this soft, drifted surface is difficult both on foot and in vehicles.

The northern plateau is roughly one mile in diameter and the ground sloping to the coast from this elevation is rough, steep, and broken by rocky cliffs. The plateau itself is interlaced with chaotic gorges and ridges, the elevation being between 340 and 382 feet. Here the ground is rough and rocky, a jumble of scarred stone, with scattered clearings in the rock. In many places the ground is hot. Steam hangs in ghostly veils over the gray-brown sulphur vents that emit their characteristic fumes.

From the northern tip, Kitano Point, along the shoreline for a distance of about two miles southeastward to Tachiiwa Point, the beach is narrow and steep with many rocky shoals obstructing approach. Just behind these northeastern beaches the ground rises sharply to the northern plateau with few beach exits. The remainder of the northern coast is rough, with abrupt cliffs ascending directly from the water's edge.

To the south, on either side of the narrow part of the island, the beaches are generally unobstructed by offshore rocks and vary from 150 to 500 feet in depth. Sand terraces of varying heights and widths hinder movement inland even for tracked vehicles. These terraces are caused by perpetual wave action and tend to change from time to time in size and location. Violent storms cause radical changes.

Surf conditions at Iwo, even in normal weather, are difficult for all classes of landing craft. There is no anchorage or protected area, and ships must discharge their cargo into lighters to be transferred to the shore. The steep beaches cause the waves to come close inshore before breaking, so that most of their force is expended in a downward blow on the bows of incoming or beached small boats. An onshore wind greatly increases the severity of the surf, often making unloading on the windward side of the island precarious.

Because Iwo lies just north of the Tropics (24° 44′ north latitude—141° 22′ east longi-

tude), the weather is subtropical, with a cool season lasting from December through April and a hot season from May through November. Average temperatures range from 63° to 70° in the cool period to 73° to 80° during May-November. Annual rainfall averages 60 inches; February is the driest month and May the wettest. The path of Pacific storm centers includes this area from December through June and although the normal typhoon track passes to the north, Iwo is a typhoon danger area.

An absence of potable water supply, other than rain, presents an acute problem. Since the soil and rock are highly permeable, use of cisterns remains the only effective means to catch and retain the rain. Distillation of sea water and the occasional use of tankers supplement the supply.

Natural cover on Iwo Jima is sparse. So sterile is the soil that coarse grasses and gnarled bushes and trees appear in a constant struggle to exist. Major Yokasuka Horie, Imperial Japanese Army, writes of Iwo: ". . . But we had no special product on this island and it had been written on the geographical book as only an island of sulphur, no water, no sparrow and no swallow. . . ." [10]

Such was Iwo Jima: so economically insignificant as to be largely unknown even to the Japanese, yet having a potential strategic importance of such magnitude that it became the most heavily fortified and stubbornly defended real estate in the Pacific.[11]

JAPANESE PREPARATIONS

Military activity in the Volcano-Bonin Islands area began in 1914 when the Japanese General Staff decided to fortify Chichi Jima.

---

[10] Y. Horie, "Explanation of Japanese Defense Plan and Battle of Iwo Jima," Chichi Jima, 25Jan46, hereinafter cited as Horie. Maj Horie, a staff officer of the Japanese 109th Division (commanded by LtGen Kuribayashi), was commanding officer of the Chichi Jima Detached Headquarters.

[11] The foregoing section on geography is a synthesis of the following sources: CinCPOA Joint Staff Study, DETACHMENT, 7Oct44, hereinafter cited as DETACHMENT; Intelligence Section, Amphibious Forces Pacific "Information on Iwo Jima (Kazan Retto)," undated; Assistant Chief of Staff, G–2, U. S. Army Forces, Pacific Ocean Areas, "Study of Iwo Jima," undated.

A small amount of heavy artillery was emplaced, and in 1917 a naval radio station and a weather station were established. No major development was attempted, however, and in 1941 when hostilities between Japan and the United States broke out the total Japanese garrison in the area was only about 1,400 men, all on Chichi Jima. A naval force of about 1,000 manned the Chichi Jima Naval Base and a small seaplane base in addition to the radio and weather stations. The army garrison consisted of a Fortification Headquarters and one company of about 400 men under command of the Eastern Army Headquarters in Japan.

In 1943 the major portion of the Japanese military strength in the Volcano-Bonin Island area was still located at Chichi Jima, but the army strength had increased to about 3,800 men. Chidori Airfield (Airfield Number 1) had been constructed on Iwo Jima, and about 1,500 naval air force personnel with 20 planes were stationed there.

With the invasion of the Marshalls, early in February 1944, followed by the crippling strikes against Truk in the same month, it became clear to Japanese Imperial Headquarters that the Marianas-Carolines area was threatened. Steps were taken to strengthen the defenses of the "inner line" (Carolines, Marianas, and the Volcano-Bonins), and in March the 31st Army was organized with its headquarters on Saipan and charged with the responsibility for the over-all defense of the area. The Chichi Jima Fortress Commander was ordered to take charge of all army and navy units in the Volcano-Bonin Islands.

During March and April the army-navy buildup on Iwo began in earnest. Some units were sent from Japan directly to Iwo while others were transferred there from Chichi Jima. A naval guard force was organized with about 500 men from Chichi and another 500 from the Yokosuka Naval Base, and this unit was given the responsibility for fixed antiaircraft and coast defenses on the island.

By the end of May 1944 army strength on Iwo was listed as 5,170 men, 13 artillery pieces, over 200 light and heavy machine guns, and 4,652 rifles. In addition, 14 coast-defense guns of 12cm or larger, 12 heavy antiaircraft guns and 30 25mm twin-mount antiaircraft guns [12] were operated by the Iwo Naval Guard Force. This buildup was not without some friction, however, and the commanding officer of the Iwo Jima Guard Force sounded a note of warning when he wrote:

On this narrow island where water and other necessities of life are very scarce, there are concentrated over 7,000 Army and Navy personnel. If the Army and Navy are especially careful to act as one harmonious unit, there will result a determination which will increase the fighting strength on this island.[13]

Late at night on 13 June the troops on Iwo were alerted to the fact that Saipan had been under heavy attack by naval forces. On 15 June "Condition 1" was set on Iwo, and by the time the men had reached their shelters a dogfight was in progress overhead and dive bombers pounded the airfields. Those not busy manning the antiaircraft guns watched this show with awe. The American pilots soon had complete control of the skies, and one Japanese witness told his diary, "Somehow, my faith in Navy air groups has been somewhat shaken." [14]

When United States troops seized Saipan the headquarters of the Japanese 31st Army fell with the island, and Imperial General Headquarters in Tokyo reorganized the command structure for their dwindling island holdings. On 26 June the enemy high command sent out an order removing troops in the Volcano-Bonin area from the 31st Army and placing them under direct control of headquarters in Tokyo.[15] By the end of June a new command, the 109th Infantry Division, had been organized, with

[12] CinCPac-CinCPOA Item No 9652 "A Report from the Chief of Staff of the 31st Army to the Chief of Staff, Central Pacific Fleet," a Japanese report dated 31May44.

[13] CinCPac-CinCPOA Item No. 9512, "Report on Present Conditions by Iwo Jima Guard Unit Commander." Unless otherwise cited, material contained in the preceding section was based on the following sources: CinCPac-CinCPOA Bulletin No 2–46, 15Feb46, "Field Survey of Japanese Defenses on Chichi Jima Retto," 5; Fifth Amphibious Corps C–2 Study of Enemy Situation, 6Jan45, 1–3, hereinafter cited as *VAC C–2 Study*.

[14] CinCPac-CinCPOA Bulletin No 161–45, 27Jun45, "The Japanese on Iwo Jima," extracts from a series of diaries, 2May44–11Mar45, hereinafter cited as *Japanese Extracts*.

[15] *VAC C–2 Study*, 7.

headquarters on Iwo, and entrusted with the defenses in the area.

Troops and equipment that had been hastily assembled in Japan for the relief of Saipan were now reassigned to the 109th Division, and Japanese planners concerned themselves with making Iwo Jima impregnable.[16] The emphasis had switched from Chichi Jima to Iwo Jima because it was the only island in the area suitable for airfield construction. Chichi Jima's importance from this time on lay only in its function as a supply base for Iwo, and the 109th Division maintained a "detached headquarters" there for the express purpose of handling supplies.[17]

With American planes and submarines harassing convoys, the task of reinforcing Iwo Jima was not easy.[18] Most shipments were sent first to Chichi Jima where ships were unloaded at night as protection against air attack. Material destined for Iwo was loaded into smaller craft for the final perilous 150-mile leg of the journey. Cargo and troops making the trip direct to Iwo from Honshu were carried in destroyers or light high-speed transports. Air attacks, rough seas, and the lack of harbor facilities combined to make unloading at Iwo difficult and hazardous.

An idea of the difficulties involved in reinforcing Iwo can be drawn from the experiences of the 26th Tank Regiment as related by Superior Private Hisao Nakada of the 3d Company. His regiment was in Manchuria during

LIEUTENANT GENERAL KURIBAYASHI, senior Japanese officer on Iwo, planned and directed astute defense of the island.

all of 1943, but in April of 1944 the unit received orders to proceed to Saipan. After a reorganization, the regiment left Manchuria, but by the time it reached Pusan, Korea, news of Saipan's fall arrived and it was ordered to Iwo. Upon reaching Japan, all but one company and 13 tanks of the regiment embarked in the *Nisshu Maru* and sailed from Yokohama on 14 July. When only 30 hours out from Chichi Jima the ship was struck by two torpedoes and sank in about half an hour. Most of the personnel were rescued and taken to Chichi, but the 28 tanks were lost. In August, 46 men from the regiment returned to Japan for replacement tanks, but, for reasons unknown, it wasn't until 18 December that they left Yokohama with 22 tanks, arriving at Iwo on 23 December. Before they could be unloaded, three of these tanks were destroyed during a naval bombardment of the island.[19]

[16] One desperate solution advanced involved complete destruction of the island to keep it out of enemy hands. Major Y. Horie voiced this plan as follows: "Now we have no fleet and no air forces. If American forces will assault this island it will fall into their hands in 1 month. Therefore it is absolutely necessary not to let the enemy use this island. The best plan is to sink this island into the sea or cut the island in half. At least we must endeavour to sink the first airfield." *Horie*, 4.

[17] *Horie*, 5; CinCPac-CinCPOA Bulletin No 2–46, 15Feb46.

[18] A Japanese source states: "The number of ships damaged by enemy submarines and planes gradually increased after August 1944, especially in the area between Chichi Jima and Iwo Jima. Over 1,500 persons were killed and over 500 tons of supplies lost." Japanese studies in World War II, No. 61, "Operations on Iwo Jima," hereinafter cited as *Japanese Studies*.

[19] CinCPac-CinCPOA Bulletin No 170–45, 7Jul45, 139. Another example is the 17th Mixed Regiment, which left Japan for Iwo in July 1944. The ship that carried the 1st and 2d Battalions was sunk and the survivors taken to Chichi. The 3d Battalion reached Iwo but was never joined by the other two. CinCPac-CinCPOA Bulletin No 2–46, 15Feb46, 5.

MAJOR GENERAL SENDA commanded 2d Mixed Brigade, the major army unit on the island.

In spite of these difficulties, during the 3-month period from June through August of 1944, fighting strength on Iwo more than doubled. Additions during this period numbered more than 9,600 troops: 7,350 army and about 2,300 navy.

The 109th Infantry Division was commanded by 53-year-old Lieutenant General Tadamichi Kuribayashi. Kuribayashi had seen combat in Manchuria in 1938 and 1939 as a colonel commanding the 7th Cavalry Regiment. In 1940 he was promoted to Major General (the lowest general officer rank in the Japanese Army) and given command of the 1st Cavalry Brigade. He was transferred to the Canton area in 1942 where he served as Chief of Staff of the 23d Army. In 1943 he was called to Tokyo to reorganize the Guards Brigade into the 1st Imperial Guards Division.

While on duty in Tokyo he attained the ambition of every Japanese when he was given the singular honor of an audience with the Emperor. In June 1944, he went to Iwo Jima and a rendezvous with death and renown. A Japanese major captured on Iwo revealed that the general was ". . . sternly disciplined and very strict with his subordinates . . . the troops disliked the general possibly because of these very

attributes." During the fighting for this island Radio Tokyo described him as a man ". . . whose partly protruding belly is packed full of strong fighting spirit." [20]

The major army units of Kuribayashi's command on Iwo were the 2d Mixed Brigade commanded by Major General Sadasue Senda,[21] Colonel Masuo Ikeda's 145th Infantry Regiment, and the 3d Battalion, 17th Mixed Infantry Regiment under Major Tamachi Fujiwara. All the artillery on the island was organized into a Brigade Artillery Group under Colonel Kaido. This included the artillery battalion of the 2d Mixed Brigade, the 145th Infantry's artillery battalion, the 1st and 2d Medium Mortar Battalions, and the 20th Independent Artillery Mortar Battalion.[22] The Brigade was reinforced further by five independent antitank battalions, the remnants of the 26th Tank Regiment,[23] two independent machine-gun battalions, and three rocket companies.[24]

Over-all command of the naval forces fell to Rear Admiral Toshinosuke Ichimaru, the senior naval officer on the island and one of the foremost airmen in the Japanese Navy. He was commanding officer of the 27th Air Flotilla, a joint command with the 2d Air Attack Force of the Eastern District (Tokyo Area), under the 3d Air Fleet. The next ranking naval officer was Captain Samaji Inoue, also a naval airman, who commanded the Nanpo Shoto Naval Air Group. In October, Captain Inoue was given

[20] This thumbnail sketch of Kuribayashi is based on information contained in: *VAC C–2 Study*, Section 1, j; VAC C–2 Special Interrogation Report of Major Hara, Mitsuaki, CO of 1st Bn, 145th Infantry Regiment, 22Mar45, hereinafter cited as *Hara; The New York Times*, 3Mar45.

[21] Major General Osuka, first commanding officer of this organization, was relieved by General Senda in December 1944 when hospitalized on Iwo for paratyphus. *Horie*, 3.

[22] The Brigade Artillery Group also exercised operational control over all naval coast defense guns. CinCPac-CinCPOA Bulletin No. 122–45, 1Jun45, 29.

[23] LtCol Takeo Nishi, who commanded the 26th Tank Regiment on Iwo, was a champion of "Olympic Horse Games." *Horie*, 3.

[24] Fifth Amphibious Corps Landing Force, Assistant Chief of Staff, G–2, Special Action Report, Iwo Jima Campaign, 20Apr45. Hereinafter cited as *VAC Intel-Rpt*. For enemy order of battle see Appendix VI.

REAR ADMIRAL ICHIMARU, senior naval officer on Iwo, was one of Japan's foremost airmen.

additional duties as Commander of the Iwo Jima Naval Guard Force. The 204th Naval Construction Battalion, composed of Japanese, Koreans, and about 400 natives of Iwo, was commanded by Lieutenant Fujiro Iida. During 1944 a second airfield (Motoyama) became operational and construction was begun on a third field north of Motoyama. Airbase Unit Number 52 operated these fields for the planes of the 901st Air Group, the 252d Air Group, and the 2d Independent Army Air Unit based on the island.

For defense, all naval units other than the coast defense and antiaircraft batteries of the Naval Guard Force were organized into the Naval Land Force and trained and equipped for infantry action. Aviation specialists and ground crews were integrated with the construction battalion personnel in this defensive setup. As commanding officer of the Nanpo Shoto Naval Air Group and the Naval Guard Force, Inoue commanded this Land Force.[25]

The chain of command was quite complicated. Nominally, all army forces were under General Kuribayashi and all naval forces under Admiral Ichimaru, but actually there were three major headquarters operating more or less autonomously. These were the headquarters of the 109th Division, the 2d Mixed Brigade, and the Naval Land Force. In addition, the island was divided into five defense-sector subcommands with one army battalion (plus supporting units) commanded by the senior army officer in the sector. Also in each sector was one group of naval troops independently commanded by the senior naval officer of the sector. While there was no real unity of command in such an organization, Kuribayashi and Ichimaru "cooperated" and directed their subordinates to do likewise.[26]

The five defense sectors with troop allocations as indicated on a captured map were as follows:

Sector	Troops
Mount Suribachi Sector.	312th Ind. Inf. Bn. (Army). AA and CD Units (Navy).
Southern Sector	309th Ind. Inf. Bn. (Army). Naval Land Force Unit. AA and CD Units. (Navy).
Western Sector	311th Ind. Inf. Bn. (Army). 1st Co., 26th Tank Regt. (Army). Naval Land Force Unit. AA and CD Units (Navy).
Eastern Sector	314th Ind. Inf. Bn. (Army). 3d Co., 26th Tank Regt. (Army). AA and CD Units (Navy).
Northern Sector	3d Bn., 17th Ind. Mixed Regt. (Army). 2d Co., 26th Tank Regt. (Army). Naval Land Force Unit. AA and CD Units (Navy).[27]

Although not assigned to a defense sector by any of the Japanese documents found on the island, the 1st Battalion, 145th Infantry occupied the area of Airfield Number 1.[28] (See Map 1.)

---

[25] The preceding information on enemy naval forces and commands was derived from the following sources:

CinCPac-CinCPOA Bulletin No 79–45, 27Mar45, 56, 79; CinCPac-CinCPOA Bulletin No 124–45, 1Jul45, 32, 37; *VAC IntelRpt*, 10.

[26] *Vac IntelRpt*, 14.

[27] CinCPac-CinCPOA Bulletin No 140–45, 7Jun45, 81–90.

[28] *Hara.*

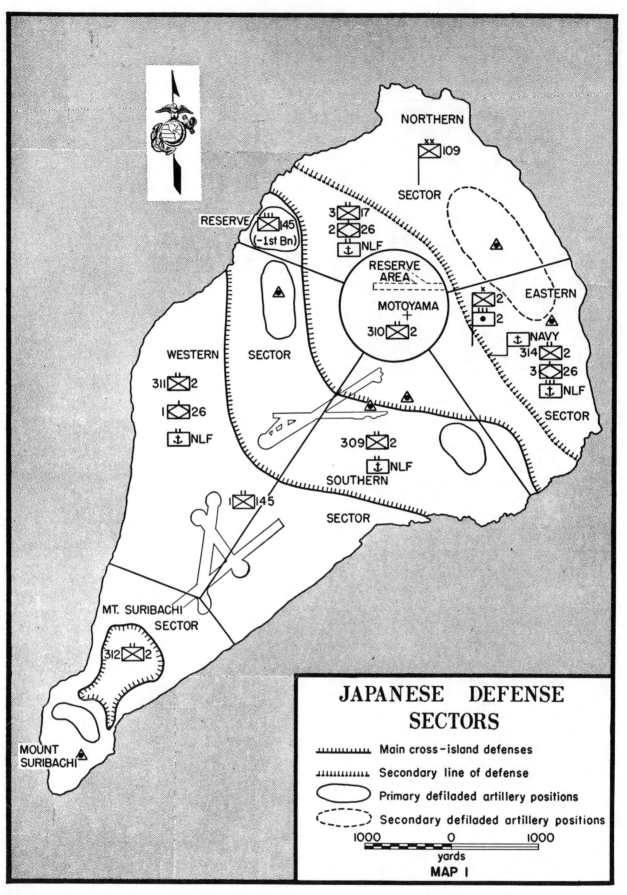

NORTHERN

SECTOR

NORTH 109

3 | 17
2 | 26
NLF

RESERVE 145
(-1st Bn)

RESERVE
AREA

MOTOYAMA
+

310 | 2

EASTERN

2
2

NAVY
314 | 2
3 | 26
NLF

WESTERN   SECTOR

311 | 2

1 | 26

NLF

SECTOR

309 | 2

NLF

SOUTHERN

1 | 45

SECTOR

MT. SURIBACHI
SECTOR

312 | 2

MOUNT
SURIBACHI

JAPANESE DEFENSE SECTORS

⊥⊥⊥⊥⊥⊥⊥⊥ Main cross-island defenses

⊥⊥⊥⊥⊥⊥⊥⊥ Secondary line of defense

◯ Primary defiladed artillery positions

⬭ Secondary defiladed artillery positions

1000   0   1000

yards

MAP I

In drawing up early plans for the defense of Iwo, Kuribayashi and his staff recognized that the naval surface and air power thrown against them would make positions on the beaches and around Airfield Number 1 untenable. Their plan, therefore, called for fortifying the Mount Suribachi and Motoyama Plateau districts, holding the beaches lightly but covering them by fire from the high ground. They would also have a large reserve force, including tanks, to counterattack and drive the invader back into the water should he gain a foothold.

Naval tacticians, however, held to the idea that the beach must be heavily defended and the decisive combat joined with the enemy at the water's edge. To this end a naval staff officer from 3d Fleet Headquarters visited Iwo to champion their cause. He urged that the navy be permitted to construct pillboxes on the east and west beaches and in the vicinity of Airfield Number 1. The army was far from enthusiastic about this plan of action, but in August Kuribayashi decided to permit the navy to construct the positions and designated one infantry battalion to man them.[29]

By January 1945 Kuribayashi had modified his concept of the defense.[30] His new plan was simple and well adapted to the terrain and size of the island. In a departure from traditional Japanese defensive doctrine he abandoned the idea of all-out counterattacks against the beachhead and costly *banzai* charges. Instead, strong, mutually supporting positions were to be occupied prior to D-Day and defended to the death. Large-scale counterattacks or withdrawals were not planned.

The Mount Suribachi area was made a semi-independent defense sector, its heavily fortified positions bristling with weapons of all types, ranging from casemated coast-defense guns and artillery to automatic weapons emplaced in mutually supporting pillboxes. The narrow isthmus connecting Suribachi to the rest of the island was lightly held by infantry, but heavily defended by enfilade fire from artillery, rockets, and mortars emplaced on both the high ground in the south (Suribachi area) and the northern portion of the island.

The main defense line was a belt of mutually supporting positions organized in depth, running generally northwest-southeast across the island. It stretched from the cliffs north of the western beaches south to include Airfield Number 2; then, turning eastward through Minami, terminated at the rugged coast north of the eastern beaches. Pillboxes, blockhouses, bunkers, and dug-in tanks strengthened the defenses in the naturally formidable terrain everywhere throughout this belt.

The second defense line generally bisected the remaining area in the northern portion of the island. It began several hundred yards below Kitano Point on the northwest coast, cut through Airfield Number 3 and the Motoyama area in the center, and terminated between Tachiiwa Point and the East Boat Basin on the eastern coast. Man-made emplacements were not as numerous in this second line, but natural caves and other covered positions afforded by the fantastically rugged terrain were skillfully organized for the defense.[31]

It is believed that this positional defense was Kuribayashi's own personal solution and was adhered to despite the contrary advice of Colonel Horie, his Chief of Staff.[32]

Although Kuribayashi's final plan of defense was basically static, the training annex to his operation order dated 1 December 1944, made it clear that he did not intend it to be entirely without movement and aggressive counteraction. He directed that troops occupying "main positions" should be trained for small unit counterattacks in front of cutoff positions, and that reserves should practice counterattacks and "movements inside positions," stressing cooperation with the artillery. He also emphasized

---

[29] *Japanese Studies; Horie.*

[30] *Ibid.*

[31] *VAC IntelRpt,* 16–17.

[32] *Ibid.,* 18. A Japanese major captured on Iwo, when asked whether Kuribayashi's tactics might be an indication of a new plan for defense of other strongholds, replied that, ". . . it was a matter of individual temperaments on the part of the various CO's and no conclusions should be drawn relative to operations." *Hara.* There is evidence to support the conjecture that this difference of opinion between Kuribayashi and his chief of staff became a major point of personal contention. In December Hori was ". . . discharged from this position [Chief of Staff, 109th Division] . . ." and replaced by Col Takaishi.

the training of tank units for participation in counterattack.[33]

The artillery plan was the brain child of Colonel Kaido, the Artillery Group Commander. In it he assumed that the attackers would have more artillery than the Japanese and stated that counterbattery duels should be avoided; but he added that full fire power should be used in an attempt to destroy enemy tanks. Detailed plans were made for displacement of observation posts and firing positions to secondary positions. As a general rule there was to be no adjustment of artillery fire as practiced by United States artillery units, and emphasis was given to surveys and preregistered fires. Airfields were mentioned re-

peatedly as important targets. A part of the firepower was to be prepared to cover each airfield in the event of landings by airborne forces.[34]

Dispersal and concealment were stressed:

We must strive to disperse, conceal, and camouflage personnel, weapons and materiel, and make use of installations to reduce damage during enemy bombing and shelling. In addition we will enhance the concealment of various positions by the construction of dummy positions to absorb the enemy shelling and bombing.[35]

A reserve force was held out "to take part in the long term resistance." [36]

Although the army exercised operational control over all artillery on the island, anti-

[33] 4th Marine Division, D-2 Language Section Translations, "TAN OpOrder A, No 43, Iwo Jima, 1Dec44," hereinafter cited as *TAN OpOrder.*

[34] CinCPac-CinCPOA Bulletin No 122–45, "Artillery Battle Plan for Iwo Jima," 1Jun45, 30.

[35] *Ibid.*, 31.

[36] *Ibid.*

127MM DUAL-mount antiaircraft guns protected the airfields. (AF Photo)

aircraft artillery was under the operational control of the navy. As the commanding officer of the 109th Division Antiaircraft Artillery Unit wrote in his battle plan:

The Iwo Jima AA Arty Unit will be under the single command of the Naval Guard Unit Hq for combat purposes and will cooperate with the other Naval Forces.[37]

The logic of this control is obvious when it is considered that more than three-fourths of the antiaircraft guns were naval. Moreover, Naval Guard Force units had originally been charged with responsibility for the antiaircraft defenses of Iwo. A large number of these weapons were emplaced to fire not only in their primary role but also to engage ground targets.

The Japanese defenders had 46 artillery pieces of 75mm or larger, including 12 artillery mortars of 320mm; 65 medium and light mortars (150mm and 81mm) ; 33 naval guns (80mm and above), many of which were dual purpose; 94 antiaircraft guns 75mm or larger, and over 200 20mm and 25mm antiaircraft guns. To this should be added 69 37mm and 47mm antitank guns and the 37mm and 57mm guns of the 12 light and 12 medium tanks on the island.

In addition to previously mentioned weapons, there were at least three different rocket-propelled projectiles. The largest was a 250kg (550-pound) bomb, less tail assembly, with rocket motor attached. Fired from a launching trough 22 feet long, it had a range of better than 7,500 yards. Similar, but smaller, was the 63kg bomb with rocket motor. Launching troughs for this projectile were from 13 to 15 feet in length, and its maximum range was about 2,000 yards.

The navy had a spin-stabilized 8-inch rocket weighing about 200 pounds with a range of 2,000 to 3,000 yards. This projectile was converted from a naval 200mm shell by cutting it off forward of the rotating band and threading it to receive a base plate and rocket motor. It was fired from a stovepipe-like barrel mounted on a steel carriage equipped with two wheels, giving it mobility. The three army rocket companies on Iwo were probably

equipped with the 63kg rocket-propelled bomb.[38]

The 320mm (spigot) mortars of the 20th Independent Artillery Mortar Battalion were crude and unusual. This defensive weapon consisted of a solid steel cylinder with a cavity in the upper end, seated on a steel base plate secured to a platform of wooden beams. For firing, the 320mm projectile (5-feet long, 12.8-inch diameter) fitted around and over the 250mm cylinder (31.7 inches long, 10.1 inches in diameter). The maximum range of this weapon was 1,440 yards with traverse of 20° to either flank, range adjustment effected by quantity of the charge. Deflection changes were made by the mortar crew shoving and pulling the ponderous platform by hand. This rather bizarre weapon had a life of only five or six rounds and this, plus constant fear of dropping the 675-pound shells on their own men, limited training of the gun crews.[39]

The Japanese active defense against United States air raids was only moderately successful, but passive defense measures were so effectively carried out that enemy fighting strength was conserved almost intact. As American bomber raids increased in intensity and frequency the Japanese dug deeper and camouflage discipline tightened.

An elaborate system of caves, concrete blockhouses, and pillboxes was commenced soon after the fall of Saipan, and construction work continued right up until the time of the Marines' landing. Blockhouses and pillboxes near the beach were sited to deliver flanking fire. These pillboxes were constructed of reinforced concrete with walls as much as four feet thick, and with sand piled as high as 50 feet in front of some of them for additional protection, leaving only a narrow fire lane. This construction sacrificed fields of fire for protection, but the number of such structures made up for this limitation.

[37] CinCPac-CinCPOA Bulletin No 140–45, "Iwo Jima AA Arty Unit Battle Plan," 7Jun45, 71.

[38] Weapons information in this paragraph was taken from CinCPac-CinCPOA Bulletin No 152–45, 1Jul45, 38, 76, 80, 84; CinCPac-CinCPOA Bulletin No 6–45, 4th Supplement, 4Jun45; VAC IntelRpt, 18.

[39] CinCPac-CinCPOA Bulletin No 152–45, 1Jul45, 76; CinCPac-CinCPOA Bulletin No 161–45, 27Jun45, 126; Expeditionary Troops (TF 56) Report of Intelligence, Iwo Jima Operation, 1Apr45, Encl C, Part III, 38. Hereinafter cited as TF 56 IntelRpt.

320MM SPIGOT MORTAR showing steel cylinder, base plate, and wooden platform.

In spite of a shortage of cement and reinforcing rods throughout enemy-held islands in the Pacific, Iwo received a large quantity of these items. After several Japanese defeats and island losses in late 1944, supplies intended for other garrisons were routed to Iwo, including vital building materials.

The main communication center for maintaining contact with Imperial Headquarters was a large blockhouse of reinforced concrete located just south of Kita. The roof was ten feet thick and the walls five feet. This fortress contained a single room 150 feet long and 70 feet wide that housed about 20 radios with one operator for every two or three sets. The entrance was a 500-foot tunnel about 75 feet underground with the tunnel opening located between small hills.[40]

Natural caves were improved, their entrances camouflaged and so planned that shelling could not hit them directly. From small caves that could accommodate only a few men, they ranged in size to some large enough to accommodate 300 to 400. Most of them were provided with multiple entrances to permit escape. The man-made caves were 30 to 40 feet deep and complete with stairways, interlacing corridors, and passageways. The brigade headquarters, located about 800 yards east of Airfield Number 2, consisted of circular tunnels capable of sheltering 2,000 troops. Further tunneling was planned to connect this cave installation with the command posts in the several defense sectors.

The alternate command post for the Naval Land Force and the 109th Division CP were dug in the northern part of the island about 500 yards northeast of Kita. Because of hard ground and sulphur fumes, the men had to work in shifts and were expected to dig three feet during a 3-hour shift. Construction continued "round the clock:" three hours on and five off, but if workers did not accomplish the allotted three feet, they were required to dig until completed. In one place the ground was so hot that the Japanese could cook a pan of rice in 20 minutes.[41]

A Japanese account mentions a plan to dig an underground passageway (total length 38,000 meters) to connect all the various defense sectors. About 25 percent of the garrison was employed daily in these projects. The work was extremely tiring, and workers were only able to labor from five to seven minutes at a time, wearing gas masks because of the sulfur fumes. Only 5,000 meters of the passageway had been completed when the American troops landed on Iwo Jima.[42] A captured survey

sketch of the air defense shelter plan of the Suribachi sector, covering about half of the northern slopes, shows the lower portions of these honeycombed with tunnels connecting gun positions, observation posts, and command posts. Entrances were in close proximity to storage areas and ammunition dumps. In this one section the sketch shows more than 7,000 yards of tunneling.[43]

To protect the airfields, antitank ditches were prepared in a broken line of segments 20 to 30 feet in length with 20-foot intervals between trenches. In this, as in other phases of the construction of defenses, excellent use was made of the terrain. Natural tank routes were mined, with and without pattern. Extensive use also was made of antipersonnel mines and booby traps in these mined areas.[44]

Not all construction effort was expended on fortifications. Men and equipment were kept busy in large numbers repairing airfield damage caused by the B–24 raids. Typical were the activities of 624 men, 11 trucks, three rollers, and two bulldozers employed in repairing Number 1 Airfield after a raid by 14 B–24's on 2 January 1945. Twelve hours were required to put the field back into operation. This work interfered with fortification and training, but it was necessary.

United States air and submarine attacks on Japanese shipping were making it increasingly difficult to supply Iwo by surface craft. Logs kept by the Nanpo Shoto Naval Air Group Transport Office indicate that many items normally supplied by ship (such as food, automotive parts, and munitions) were flown in. The log makes repeated reference to mortar shells and shows that, during the few weeks just prior

[40] 3d Marine Division, G–2 Language Section. "Aggregate Report from POW's who worked on Communication Center Pillbox and Tunnels leading thereto from various units," 2Mar45.

[41] 4th MarDiv D–2 Language Section, Preliminary POW Report No. 13.

[42] *Japanese Studies.*

[43] *VAC IntelRpt*, Encl H. Although this captured enemy survey sketch bears the notation, "Completed 6 February 1945," it is not known whether these planned defenses actually reached completion prior to 19Feb45.

[44] The foregoing account of Japanese defense construction was derived from the following sources: *VAC IntelRpt;* Military Intelligence Service, War Department, Washington, D. C., *Tactical and Technical Trends*, No. 58, May 1945 (U. S. Government Printing Office, 1945), 1–15.

to the invasion, air shipments of armor-piercing shells were received.[45]

At this time Iwo was also used as a base to stage planes from Kisarazu, Honshu for attacks on Saipan. A captured list of planes using Airfield Number 1 indicates that the last such flight consisted of two planes that landed on 3 January. There is no time of departure shown, however, and the following note appears in the log: "Both planes were defective and the attack was abortive." [46]

Kuribayashi's primary mission was to defend Iwo, and he became somewhat impatient with the expenditure of time and effort in airfield construction. While he must have been keenly aware of the importance of the existing fields and their maintenance, he expressed himself rather strongly on the subject:

Long period of time and enormous number of men used for the extension work of the first and "Motoyama" airfield have impeded the defense, fortification, and drill greatly.

We must avoid constructing hopeless airfield.[47]

Training was not neglected. Colonel Kaido's artillery group conducted extensive maneuvers and exercises during November. In his critique Kaido commented on all phases of the maneuvers. The following remarks are quoted as being of special interest:

It is necessary to eliminate completely the idea that firing results are satisfactory if shells merely fall in the enemy area. We must without fail score direct hits on the targets. On this island, where the amount of ammunition is small and there is no hope of replenishment, this is especially true. Accordingly, it is necessary to perfect the various activities of the gun crews and observation and communication [personnel], as well as firing preparations and fire control.

Protection and camouflage are still incomplete. This is particularly true of embrasures, covered gun positions, observation posts, and entrances.

The dispersion and location of ammunition dumps is good, . . . but they might easily be damaged by shells landing nearby.

It is necessary to rush the construction of reserve positions and OP's and to make plans for facilities for moving to reserve positions.

It is desirable that attention be given to the prevention of dust in front of gun muzzles. Some arrangements such as spreading straw matting or sprinkling water must be made.[48]

In his operations order of 1 December, Kuribayashi directed all units to ". . . plan for absolutely thorough training and for further strengthening of fortifications." He instructed that existing fortifications should be tested as to practicality and improved when found lacking:

Matters to be kept in mind when considering improvements in existing fortifications are as follows:

1. Increasing AT obstacles, such as ditches, terraces, obstructions (piles of rocks).

2. Strengthening connecting and escape trenches.

3. Establishment of "waiting" trenches for use in close combat and raiding.

4. Setting up of combat installations for the defense of billeting areas.[49]

Setting 11 February as the deadline for completion, he specified that 70 percent of the time should be devoted to training and 30 percent to fortification.

The major personnel buildup was effected by the middle of 1944, but reinforcements continued to arrive until February 1945. Early in 1945 rumors among the troops suggested that the Japanese Army promised no further aid to Iwo and that it was up to the defenders to repulse any major landing attempt with the men and materials at hand, or to hold out as long as possible. There was more optimism, however, in the belief that the navy would resist strenuously any United States fleet venture into the Volcano-Bonin area.

Morale was good, although there were malcontents who complained about the food and lack of beer, *sake*, and women, and the general

[45] CinCPac-CinCPOA Bulletin No 122–45, 1 June 45, "Air Transport at Iwo Jima, Nanpo Shoto Naval Air Group Transport Office August 1944-February 1945, 55–100." Other interesting items mentioned are a shipment of "Imperial Gifts (Sake)" for the Commander of the 27th Air Flotilla and three swords consigned to Rear Admiral Ichimaru.

[46] CinCPac-CinCPOA Bulletin No 75–45, 20Mar45, "List of Planes Using Motoyama Airfield #1, between 1 January and 14 February 1945," 108.

[47] Contained in Instructions of War telegraphed from LtGen Kuribayashi to Chief of the General Staff, as quoted from memory in *Horie*.

[48] CinCPac-CinCPOA Bulletin No 170–45, 7Jul45, "Japanese Criticism of Artillery Maneuvers on Iwo Jima," 27–42.

[49] *TAN OpOrder*.

WOODEN ROCKET LAUNCHERS like this were found after Marines landed. (AF Photo)

dreariness of life on this desolate outpost. A feeling of hopelessness and pessimism as to the outcome of the inevitable battle was countered by the resolve to fight bitterly to the end and die gloriously for the Emperor.

On 14 February Admiral Marc A. Mitscher's Fast Carrier Force (TF 58) was detected moving north. Interpreting this as a sign of impending assault on Iwo Jima, Army Group Headquarters ordered all units into the D-Day positions. The 1st Battalion of the 145th Independent Infantry Regiment moved into positions in the vicinity of Airfield Number 1, and other units left their bivouacs to take over their battle assignments. When the landing seemed imminent, the chief of staff of the garrison forces issued the following order:

All units, especially headquarters, will take the utmost precaution not to let our tables of organization, tables of equipment, strengths or very secret documents be compromised. Even persons in Headquarters must keep them to themselves and not let them be passed to the enemy.[50]

Another captured document stated that certain key officers in the Iwo Jima Naval Guard Force were to be responsible for the destruction of all classified documents when so ordered by the highest naval command, or when it was apparent to the custodian that such destruction was necessary.[51] These instructions revealed a growing security consciousness among the Japanese.

---

[50] *TF 56 IntelRpt*, 41.
[51] *Ibid.*

Final preparations were hastily made. Time was precious, and much remained to be done. Camouflage had to be repaired, mines armed, and positions strengthened. On 17 February, word was passed to complete demolition of roads. At about 1030 the Japanese in the East Boat Basin area observed "twenty-odd large and small landing craft . . . approached as if to land." The description of this incident from a Japanese diary is given below:

> The position of myself and my buddies is untenable. We were immediately posted at our positions to make preparations for an attack, and at the same time our artillery laid down a fierce barrage. At first, both sides were firing and the continuous smoke and noise of the explosions were terrific. This lasted for 30 minutes after which the enemy without attaining its objective moved the attack to the west coast. The enemy made all of this sacrifice without attaining any results.[52]

The same day the chief of staff issued the following instructions:

> The time has come for the enemy to direct his attack upon the Ogasawaras. I fervently desire you and your unit who are charged with the defense of the first line to heroically fight with absolute confidence.[53]

Kuribayashi himself expressed his feelings in these words:

> All shout *Banzai* for the Emperor! I have utmost confidence that you will all do your best. I pray for a heroic fight.[54]

[52] 4th MarDiv D–2 Language Section Enemy Diary Translation, 28Feb45. This was actually the D-minus 2 UDT operations described later in this monograph.
[53] 4th MarDiv D–2 Language Section Translation, 26Feb45.
[54] *Ibid.*

CHAPTER II   Plans and Preparations

HIGH-LEVEL PLANNING

As early as September 1943, the Joint War Planning Committee in Washington formulated preliminary plans to seize the Bonin Islands.[1] Planners realized that after the fall of the Marianas the Bonins would constitute a vital point in the intermediate defense of the Japanese homeland. And since these islands were traditional Japanese territory, administered as part of the Tokyo Prefecture, their loss would be a tremendous psychological blow to the Empire. In spite of the dearth of intelligence information at that time, planners correctly foresaw that the terrain favored the defenders and that the operation would entail heavy losses for the attackers. Iwo Jima was singled out as being one of the most vital objectives in this group.[2]

These early plans were consonant with Army Air Force desires to seize Marianas bases for the new long-range bombers, which were then under discussion at high-level conferences. By March 1944 the Marianas operation was definitely scheduled for 15 June, and the over-all objective of the Central Pacific Forces became clearly outlined. This mission was now essentially twofold: (1) to secure control of sea com-munications by neutralizing the Carolines, and (2) to establish sea and air bases for operations against Japanese sea routes and for long-range air attacks against the home islands of the Empire. All Central Pacific Force planning was now predicated upon the decision to capture the Marianas.[3]

Lying midway between the Marianas and Tokyo, directly athwart the route to be followed by our very-long-range (VLR) bombers operating from the Marianas, the Volcano-Bonins became of major strategic importance. Consequently, the Army Air Force became intensely interested in an operation designed to seize objectives in this area. Such an operation, however, was not to be executed until the Marianas were secured for B–29 bases. Fighter strips would then be required from which long-range fighters could escort the big bombers in their sorties northward from the Marianas to Japan.[4]

By mid-1944 the conduct of Pacific operations reflected much more than an effort to seize

---

[1] JWPC 91/D, 13Sep43, "Seizure of the Bonins."

[2] Iwo Jima is located in the Volcano Islands (Kazan Retto) but early operations plans, as well as several that followed, refer to this island as being part of the Bonin Group.

[3] A new JCS directive, issued on 12Mar44, speeded up the Pacific war by assigning new operations and cancelling others. Air attacks on the Marianas, Palaus, and Carolines were to be intensified and seizure of the southern Marianas was firmly scheduled for 15Jun44. JCS 713 and 713/4, 12Mar44.

[4] Even before Saipan was secured, a plan was advanced advocating immediate occupation of Iwo. On 24Jun44 a paper prepared by one of the teams of the Joint War Plans Committee discussed immediate seizure of Iwo Jima, utilizing forces assembled for occupation of Guam. JWPC 244, 24Jun44, "Immediate Occupation of Iwo Jima."

islands, naval bases, and airfields. Campaigns were listed as follows:

Code Name	Operations	Tentative target date
FORAGER.....	Capture of Saipan, Guam, and Tinian.	15 June 44
STALEMATE..	Capture of Palau........	8 Sept 44
INSURGENT..	Occupation of Mindanao.	15 Nov 44
CAUSEWAY...	Capture of Southern Formosa and Amoy or	15 Feb 45
INDUCTION ..	Capture of Luzon.......	[5] 15 Feb 45

Seizure of these objectives would place American forces in position to tighten an iron vise around the heart of Japan. Then United States military and naval might would be poised to launch attacks on the home islands.

At the end of June a paper entitled "Operations Against Japan Subsequent to Formosa," listed an advance from the northern Marianas into the Bonins as a possible step following the Formosa operation, the tentative date being April 1945.[6]

In line with concepts contained in the above reference, the Joint War Planning Committee completed a plan for the seizure of the Bonins and submitted it to the Joint Staff Planners on 12 August 1944. This stated that seizure of the Bonins could be conducted as a highly desirable "operation of opportunity" for:

(1) Providing fighter cover for application of our air effort against Japan.[7]

(2) Denying these strategic outposts to the enemy.

(3) Furnishing air defense bases for our positions in the Marianas.

(4) Providing fields for staging heavy bombers against Japan.

Iwo Jima, planners contended, was the only practical objective in the group. It was the only island that could support a large number of fighter aircraft, and its topography appeared to render it unusually susceptible to preliminary softening by aerial and surface bombardment with full benefit of advance aerial and submarine reconnaissance.[8]

The seizure of the Marianas was executed as planned. Tinian and Guam had been taken by the end of August and the way cleared to construct B–29 bases on these islands. The heavy attrition suffered by enemy air power throughout the theater, as well as the reduction of once powerful garrisons, convinced the American high command that our forces could overcome enemy resistance on any island position in the Pacific. This confidence was based on the fact that we could now concentrate and coordinate the combined power of all available naval, amphibious, and shore-based air forces in any concerted operation that might be necessary.

An operation in the Volcano-Bonin Islands, which fitted neatly into the big picture, was now more than a mere possibility: the question became "when" rather than "if." In a study of naval personnel requirements for the Pacific Theater through 30 June 1945, the Joint Staff Planners presented the Joint Logistics Committee with a list of projected operations as well as the number of divisions needed in each instance. In this study three divisions were specified for the Volcano-Bonin operation. The target date was given tentatively as 15 April 1945.[9]

Admiral Nimitz, too, in planning for the projected Formosa invasion, pointed to the eventual Volcano-Bonin objective. In September 1944 he advised Lieutenant General Holland M. Smith, Commanding General, Fleet Marine Force, Pacific, that it was desirable to retain the 2d and 3d Marine Divisions in the Marianas as an area reserve for Formosa and

---

[5] CinCPOA, Campaign Plan GRANITE II, 3Jun44.

[6] JCS 924, 30Jun44.

[7] In July 1944 the AAF advised the Joint Planning Staff that Iwo was a potential base for fighter planes since Tokyo would be within the radius of action for P-51's (Mustangs) based on that island. Hence, in view of the predicted need for protecting B-29's over Nippon proper, it was recommended that "plans for the defeat of Japan include operations to capture and develop fighter bases on the Bonin Islands." AAF memorandum for JPS, 21Jul44, "Fighter Escort for VLR Bombers."

[8] JWPC 91/3, 12Aug44, "Plan for the Seizure of the Bonins," notes from JPS 163d meeting, 16Aug44.

[9] JLC 67/4/, 23Aug44, "Memorandum of Request, Naval Personnel Requirements."

CHICHI JIMA

FUTAMI KO

CHICHI JIMA had good harbor but was too rugged to accommodate extensive airfields.   (AF Photo)

as the major troop units for an impending attack on Iwo Jima.[10]

During September 1944, top Navy, Army, and Army Air Force commanders began to express doubt concerning the wisdom of an operation against Formosa. Early in the month Lieutenant General Millard F. Harmon, USA, Commanding General, Army Air Forces, Pacific Ocean Areas, advocated bypassing Formosa in favor of the Bonins and Ryukyus. Lieutenant General Robert C. Richardson, Jr., USA, Commanding General, Army Forces, Pacific Ocean Areas, saw "no advantage whatsoever in the capture of Formosa," and preferred striking through the Nanpo Shoto. Admiral Nimitz, in a communication to his top commanders, indicated that seizure of Formosa would only be in preparation for operations against the China coast. Recent Japanese military gains in that area caused Nimitz to question the value of such a move.[11]

Late in September Admiral Nimitz and Admiral Ernest J. King (CominCh and Navy member of the Joint Chiefs of Staff) met in San Francisco. Admiral Raymond A. Spruance (Commander, U. S. Fifth Fleet), who had been on leave in California, was ordered to attend this conference and his interesting account of that meeting and its preliminaries follows:

After the completion of the Marianas Operation I turned my command over to Admiral Halsey on 28 August 1944, and returned to Pearl Harbor early in September. On reporting to Admiral Nimitz, he advised me that my next operation would be the capture of Formosa and Amoy. I said that I thought Iwo Jima, followed by Okinawa, would be preferable, but was told that the orders from CominCh called for Formosa. . . .

At this Conference [San Francisco] Admiral Nimitz presented a paper—prepared, I believe, by Captain Forrest Sherman, USN, head of Fleet War Plans Division— recommending the substitution of Iwo Jima and Okinawa for Formosa and Amoy. The reason for this change was that Lt. Gen. S. B. Buckner, USA, Commander 10th Army, who was to command the Landing Force for Formosa, said that he had insufficient Service Troops for an objective so large as Formosa; but that he could take Okinawa. Admiral King, after considerable discussion, was convinced of the necessity for the change and so recommended to the J. C. S., who approved it.[12]

Immediately following the conference (2 October 1944) Admiral King returned to Washington and submitted a proposed directive for future operations. He indicated that there were not sufficient ground forces available in the Pacific to meet the minimum requirements for an invasion of Formosa and the southeast China coast. Furthermore, the War Department had revealed that there could be no increase in these troops until cessation of the war in Europe. The proposal stated, however, that occupation of positions in the Nanpo Shoto, specifically Iwo Jima in January 1945, would allow fighter support for the B–29's operating from the Marianas. Also, a move into the Nansei Shoto, particularly Okinawa, would sever Japanese air communications throughout the

[10] Ltr CinCPac, 000106, 11Sep44 to ComGenPOA and ComGen FMFPac.

[11] Ltr ComGenAAFPOA to CinCPac, 11Sep44; Ltr CinCPOA, 000113, to ComFifthFlt, ComGen Tenth Army, ComAmphForPacFlt, 16Sep44; Ltr ComGenPOA, 00013, to CinCPOA, 27Sep44.

[12] Ltr Adm R. A. Spruance, USN (Ret) to CMC, 5Jan52.

COMINCH WITH TWO OF HIS TOP ADMIRALS. From left to right: Admiral Spruance, in over-all command of Iwo operation; Admiral King, who advocated Iwo's capture to JCS; Admiral Nimitz, CinCPac-CinCPOA.

Ryukyus. Forces to accomplish these two operations were available.[13]

The Joint Chiefs of Staff accepted Admiral King's proposal almost immediately and issued a new directive on 3 October that guided the Pacific War to a conclusion. CinCPOA was directed to conduct the following operations:

(1) Provide fleet cover and support for the occupation of Luzon by Southwest Pacific Forces, target date 20 December 1944.

(2) *Occupy one or more positions in the Nanpo Shoto*, target date 20 January 1945, [Italics by author.]

(3) Occupy one or more positions in the Nansei Shoto, target date 1 March 1945.[14]

The same arguments that dictated the decision to take an objective in the Nanpo Shoto led inevitably to the final choice of the objective. Use of the airfields in the area must be denied

to the Japanese and quickly gained for United States forces. Only Iwo Jima could satisfy this requirement and justify a military operation of the magnitude necessary to assure success.

A top secret dispatch from Admiral Nimitz on 9 October 1944 informed General Holland M. Smith that Iwo Jima was definitely the objective.[15]

The Joint War Plans Committee, in the outline of "Operations for the Defeat of Japan," dated 18 October 1944, placed in proper perspective the part Iwo played on the Pacific stage. Its seizure was listed as a contributory operation in keeping with the over-all objective of the war. In effect, this operation would contribute toward lowering Japanese ability and will to resist by: (1) establishing sea and air blockades; (2) conducting intensive air bombardment; and (3) destroying enemy air and naval strength. The capture of this island

---

[13] JCS 713/18, 2Oct44, "Future Operations in the Pacific."

[14] JCS 713/19, 3Oct44, "Future Operations in the Pacific."

[15] Ltr CG FMFPac to CG VAC, 00059, 14Oct44.

would help make feasible ultimate invasion of the industrial centers of Japan.[16]

The decision to take Iwo Jima, like many strategic decisions, had been based on projected plans. Airfields in the Marianas, from which B–29's would operate against the Empire, were still under construction on 3 October when the Joint Chiefs issued their directive for the drive northward. But by D-Day, 19 February 1945,[17] B–29 attacks against Japan from Marianas bases had been a reality for nearly three months. Plane and crew losses over Japan and on the long return trip bore tragic testimony to the need for an intermediate base from which fighters could provide protection over the target and where damaged bombers could find secure haven. Never before in the Pacific War had troops engaged in amphibious assault been able to see so clearly the immediate importance of the objective. Long before the battle ended, fighting Marines saw huge crippled "Superforts" land safely on an airfield just recently cleared by costly, bitter fighting.

OPERATIONAL PLANNING

Planning for the Iwo Jima operation was affected by the Philippine operations which immediately preceded it. By mid-November it became evident that the 1-month interval between the Luzon operation (20 December) and the Iwo target date (20 January) would not allow sufficient time for reallocation of amphibious and support shipping from one operation to the other. For this reason Admiral Nimitz recommended that target dates for operations DETACHMENT (Iwo Jima) and ICEBERG (Okinawa) be deferred to 3 February and 15 March respectively.

Operations in the Philippines were unexpectedly prolonged. Attempting to hold Leyte at all costs, the Japanese had successfully reinforced their garrison by landing two divisions, one infantry regiment, and various supporting troops. In addition, rain and mud seriously impeded United States troop movement and

construction of airfields.[18] In the face of these delays General MacArthur was likewise caught in a time squeeze. Accordingly, the assault on Luzon was ordered postponed to 9 January 1945, again throwing Nimitz' Iwo and Okinawa plans out of kilter. Consequently, in early December JCS received from CinCPOA a recommendation that operations DETACHMENT and ICEBERG be further delayed to 19 February and 1 April 1945 respectively.[19] The Joint Chiefs concurred and the target dates were readjusted accordingly.

Initial planning for Iwo could not anticipate these changes in target dates. Upon receipt of the JCS 3 October directive with a target date of 20 January listed for taking Nanpo Shoto positions, CinCPOA and his Joint Staff immediately went to work. The result was a Joint Staff study published 7 October 1944 and issued to major subordinate commanders for use in preliminary planning. The document was not considered a directive, however, and did not commit the Commander-in-Chief, U. S. Pacific Fleet and Pacific Ocean Areas to any specific course of action.[20]

Purposes of the DETACHMENT operation were clearly designated in this study:

To maintain unremitting military pressure against Japan.

To extend our control over the Western Pacific.

To establish a base from which we may:

(1) Attack the Japanese Empire.

(2) Protect our bases in the Marianas.

(3) Cover our naval forces and conduct search operations in the approaches to the Japanese Empire.

(4) Provide fighter escort for very long range operations.

Specific tasks envisioned were:

(a) To reduce Japanese naval and air strength and production facilities in the Empire.

(b) To destroy enemy naval and air strength in the Bonins.

---

[16] JPS 404/15, 18Oct44, "Operations for the Defeat of Japan."

[17] D-Day had been twice postponed prior to final designation of the 19Feb45 date. See next subchapter.

[18] Boggs, 26–28.

[19] Disp CinCPOA to JCS, 030215, Dec44.

[20] DETACHMENT.

LIEUTENANT GENERAL HOLLAND M. SMITH commanded the Expeditionary Troops at Iwo Jima.

(c) To capture, occupy, and defend Iwo Jima and develop an air base on that island.[21]

On 9 October General Smith received this staff study along with Admiral Nimitz' directive ordering the seizure of Iwo Jima. The directive named these commanders for the operation:

(1) Operation Commander
Admiral Raymond A. Spruance, USN.

(2) Joint Expeditionary Force Commander
Vice Admiral Richmond Kelly Turner, USN.

(3) Commanding General Expeditionary Troops
Lieutenant General Holland M. Smith, USMC.

(4) Second in Command Joint Expeditionary Force
Rear Admiral Harry W. Hill, USN.

General Smith started planning immediately in conjunction with the Comander Fifth Fleet; Commander Amphibious Forces, Pacific; Commander Service Force, Pacific; Commander Air Force, Pacific; Commanding General,

Pacific Ocean Areas; and Commanding General, Army Air Forces, Pacific Ocean Areas.[22]

Within a few days General Smith issued a letter of instruction which designated Major General Harry Schmidt, Commanding General, V Amphibious Corps, as Commanding General of the Landing Force. General Schmidt and his experienced staff, headed by Brigadier General William W. Rogers, assumed responsibility for preparing and executing all Landing Force plans for the operation. The staff of Headquarters, Fleet Marine Force, Pacific, was at their disposal for any assistance they might require. Upon completion of Landing Force plans, General Schmidt was to submit them to General Smith for approval.[23]

Major units assigned to the Landing Force for planning, training, and operations were the 3d, 4th, and 5th Marine Divisions. Of these, the 3d and 4th Divisions, commanded by Major General Graves B. Erskine and Major General Clifton B. Cates, respectively, were veteran fighting units. Major General Keller E. Rockey's 5th Division, about to experience its first battle action as a unit, contained many seasoned and combatwise troops who had helped subdue other Pacific strongholds.

After participating in the highly successful Saipan and Tinian operations, the 4th Division had only recently returned to its camp site on Maui, T. H. The 5th Division had embarked from San Diego the previous August for a training area on the big island of Hawaii, T. H. With both of these major units in the Hawaiian area, close liaison could be affected between them and with various echelons at Pearl Harbor. The 3d Division, on the other hand, was encamped on Guam, having recently completed the liberation of that island. Similarly, General Schmidt had located his V Amphibious Corps command post on Guam.

To facilitate and speed planning for the Iwo operation, VAC Headquarters moved to Pearl Harbor on 13 October 1944. All major planning staffs, with the exception of the 3d Di-

---

[21] *Ibid.*

[22] TF 56 Report of Planning, Operations, Iwo Jima Operation, 27Mar45, Encl A. Hereinafter cited as *TF 56 OpRpt.*
[23] *Ibid.*

vision,[24] were now in the Hawaiian Area, so that intimate coordination of effort could be effected. All subordinate commanders—assault, support, and garrison—reported to the Landing Force Commander at an early date, and joint planning soon began.

Not only were the individuals of the various staffs well acquainted with their jobs; they were also, for the most part, well acquainted with one another. Previously the V Amphibious Corps had participated with the Fifth Fleet in operations for the capture of the Gilberts, Marshalls, and Marianas. With the proximity of these staffs affording immediate exchange of information between all echelons of command, the work proceeded smoothly and efficiently and plans were issued almost simultaneously.

The first tentative operation blueprint for the Landing Force was issued by General Schmidt on 19 October as a guide for subordinate commanders. One day later, CG, FMFPac issued a directive to CG, Landing Force in which troop assignments for training, planning, and operations were designated. Corps was directed to be ready for combat in all respects by 15 December.[25]

During the next two months General Schmidt's original plan went through many changes. The effect of increasingly complete intelligence was reflected in amendments to original concepts. Even the issuance of final operation plans did not prevent flexibility, and changes continued to be made up until D-Day.

In close sequence, final drafts for Operation DETACHMENT were published on the following dates:

25 November—CinCPOA Operation Plan 11–44.
23 December—VAC Operation Plan No. 3–44.

MAJOR GENERAL HARRY SCHMIDT commanded the V Amphibious Corps Landing Force at Iwo Jima. (From painting by Albert K. Murray, USNR)

27 December—Joint Expeditionary Force Operation Plan No. A25–44.
31 December—Fifth Fleet Operation Plan No. 13–44.

By 26 January 1945, when Admiral Spruance assumed command of all forces assigned to Central Pacific Task Force for the Iwo operation, CinCPOA's Plan 11–44 was fully in effect.[26]

That the landings at Iwo would have to be made over the southeast beaches was a near certainty. Predominant northerly or northwesterly winds caused hazardous swells almost continuously on the southwest side of the island. Preferred plans were drawn accordingly. On 8 January 1945, however, VAC issued an alternate plan to cover the possibility of adverse surf conditions along the southeastern beaches. Except that it prescribed using beaches on the western side of Iwo, this alternate plan differed little from the preferred plan.

---

[24] Of the three divisions, the 3d was the latest to emerge from combat at this time. Though Guam was called secure by 10 August 1944, savage and tenacious resistance by certain isolated Japanese elements required laborious, and many times costly mopping-up activities until mid-December. Maj O. R. Lodge, *The Recapture of Guam*, MarCorps Historical Monograph (U. S. Government Printing Office, 1954).

[25] For Task Organization of V Amphibious Corps Landing Force, see Appendix V.

[26] For task organization of forces supporting the V Amphibious Corps Landing Force see Appendix VII.

Designated for the beach assault were the 4th and 5th Division, less the 26th Marines, which was to remain in Landing Force reserve. For training purposes, however, the 26th Marines would remain with the 5th Division. After staging on Guam, the 3d Division was to be in Expeditionary Troops reserve and would be available afloat in the objective area on D-plus 3.

In anticipation of the possibility of a strong reaction by enemy planes, the 138th Antiaircraft Artillery Group (Army), commanded by Colonel Clarence E. Rothgeb, was attached to the assault force to land on order and provide antiaircraft protection for the beachhead and the airfields when secured. [27]

Commanders decided that corps artillery should be kept at a minimum, since there was limited space for emplacement on the island. It was reasoned that air and naval gunfire would compensate for this lack. Corps artillery was restricted, therefore, to two battalions of 155mm howitzers organized as the 1st Provisional Field Artillery Group, under Colonel John S. Letcher.

A reevaluation of enemy strength and misgivings as to the effectiveness of the short (3-day) period of naval gunfire preparation, coupled with the importance of rapid seizure of the commanding Mount Suribachi area by the 5th Marine Division, brought about an 11th-hour amendment to the assault task organization. On 14 February General Schmidt released one battalion of the 26th Marines (1/26) to the 5th Division,[28] and requested that one RCT of the 3d Marine Division be made available at Iwo on D-Day to replace RCT 26 as corps reserve. This would permit release of the 26th Marines to its parent organization (5th Marine Division) for use in the assault if necessary.[29]

The request was approved and TransDiv 32 (carrying the 21st Marines) ordered to leave Guam on 16 February to report to Admiral Turner at the objective at 1000 D-Day.[30]

SCHEME OF MANEUVER

The corps scheme of maneuver for landing was not complicated. The 4th and 5th Divisions would land abreast on the southeastern beaches with the 5th on the left. As Expeditionary Troops Reserve, the 3d Division, when released to corps would land over the same beaches on or after D-plus 1, prepared to assist in the attack or occupy defensive positions as ordered. Infantry RCT's [31] and their assigned beaches were as follows:

3D DIVISION (EXPEDITIONARY TROOPS RESERVE)

3d Marines (Division Reserve)	To be ordered later as necessary.
9th Marines	Yellow 1 and Yellow 2.
21st Marines	Red 1 and Red 2.

4TH DIVISION

23d Marines	Yellow 1 and Yellow 2.
24th Marines (Division Reserve)	Blue or Yellow, as ordered.
25th Marines	Blue 1.

5TH DIVISION

27th Marines	Red 1 and Red 2.
28th Marines (less 3d Bn)	Green 1.
3d Bn, 28th Marines (Division Reserve).	Red or Green.
1st Bn, 26th Marines (Division Reserve).	Red or Green.
26th Marines (less 1st Bn) (Corps Reserve)	As ordered.

Colonel Harry B. Liversedge's 28th Marines would attack on the extreme left of the corps, cut straight across the narrow neck of Iwo, then turn southwest to secure the Mount Suribachi area. On the immediate right of the 28th Marines, Colonel Thomas A. Wornham's 27th would attack to the opposite shore, then turn

[27] 138th AAA Group (USA) Special Action Report, Iwo Jima Campaign, 17Mar45, hereinafter cited as *138th AAA Group SAR*. The group included the 483d AA/AW Bn (automatic weapons) and the 506th AA Gun Bn (90mm Guns).

[28] 5th Marine Division Action Report, Iwo Jima, 28Apr45, Sec III, 5, hereinafter cited as *5th MarDiv SAR*. The 5th Div reserve was now composed of 3/28 and 1/26, leaving the 26th Marines (less 1/26) in VAC reserve until released on 19 Feb.

[29] Disp CTG 56.1 CTF 56, 0018, 14Feb45.

[30] Amphibious Forces U. S. Pacific Fleet (CTF 51), Report of the capture of Iwo Jima, 19May45, hereinafter cited as *TF–51 Rpt.*

[31] Regimental Combat Team. The 5th MarDiv called its reinforced regiments Combat Teams (CT's), while the 3d and 4th MarDivs used the term Regimental Combat Teams (RCT's). In this monograph RCT is used for all reinforced regiments.

northeast and seize the 0–1 [32] line in its zone. The action on these two RCT's would clear the enemy from the dominating heights at the southern end of the island and secure the corps' left flank and rear. (See Map III.)

The 4th Division would employ Colonel Walter W. Wensinger's 23d Marines first to seize Motoyama Airfield Number 1, then to turn northeast and clear that portion of Motoyama Airfield Number 2 and the 0–1 line in its zone of action. Colonel John R. Lanigan's 25th Marines, on the corps' right flank, was to assist in the capture of Airfield Number 1 and seize Beach Blue 2 and the 0–1 line in its zone of action.[33] These 4th Division objectives included the southern portion of Airfield Number 2 and the rugged southern edge of the Motoyama Plateau. It was foreseen that this cliff line dominating the Blue Beaches must be captured as quickly as possible.

Commanding the 24th Marines, Colonel Walter I. Jordan would stand ready in 4th Division reserve to support the assault as ordered. Similarly, the 26th Marines, commanded by Colonel Chester B. Graham, was prepared to support the 5th Division after release from corps reserve on D-Day.

Division artillery would move into selected positions upon order from the respective division commanders; Colonel Louis G. DeHaven's 14th Marines in the 4th Division and Colonel James D. Waller's 13th Marines in the 5th Division.

At H-Hour 68 LVT(A) 4's of the first wave would hit the beach and proceed inland to the first terrace or bluff beyond the high-water mark. Here they would deploy to bring their maximum fire power to bear, affording covering protection to the succeeding waves of infantry debarking from LVT's.

Initially the VAC operation plan prescribed tanks of the 4th and 5th Tank Battalions to land in a scheduled wave at H-plus 30 minutes. Later studies of the beach terrain and anticipation of congestion at the water's edge, however, convinced division planners that the tanks should be "on call." Regimental commanders would be permitted to use their discretion as to the appropriate times.[34]

As previously indicated, the alternate scheme of maneuver to employ the western beaches was little different from the preferred plan. It did, however, include an interesting addition, centered around Kangoku Rock, a 600-yard long bit of volcanic cast-off lying some 2,250 yards off the northwestern shores of Iwo. At H-minus 50 minutes a company of the 24th Marines, reinforced by a platoon of armored amphibians from the 2d Armored Amphibian Battalion, was to seize this spot as a possible artillery site. The 105mm howitzers of the 4th Battalion, 14th Marines were to be prepared to land on Kangoku Rock on order.

INTELLIGENCE

When the V Amphibious Corps began planning for the Iwo operation in October, a considerable amount of excellent intelligence information was already available. Documents captured on Saipan in June provided a fairly complete picture of the enemy forces and dispositions in the Volcano-Bonin area. Enemy maps, U. S. Hydrographic Office charts, and aerial photos taken in conjunction with carrier strikes in June and July [35] were used to compile

---

[32] The 0–1 line as drawn on the map indicated initial objectives. It was delineated along commanding or conspicuous terrain features where units could be halted for control, coordination, and further orders. This line was designated in the Corps Operation Plan.

[33] The VAC LANFOR plan originally called for the use of Beach Blue 2 as a landing beach in the assault. Because of the proximity of Blue 2 to the commanding high ground on the right, and in order to provide a safety factor while maintaining adequate neutralization fires on this high ground during the initial landing, the 4th Division requested permission to confine the landing of the 25th Marines to Blue 1. This permission was granted. The 25th Marines was directed to land on Blue 1 and seize Blue 2 rapidly to permit the early use of this beach for succeeding units and supplies. 4th Marine Division Operations Report, Iwo Jima, 18May45, Sec I, 2, hereinafter cited as *4th MarDiv OpRpt*.

[34] There was one exception to this plan. Company A, 5th Tank Battalion, attached to the 27th Marines, was scheduled to land on the Red Beaches at H-plus 30 minutes. *5th MarDiv SAR*, Sec VII, 10.

[35] Navy photo work done over Iwo Jima during these strikes was never excelled in later efforts to gain coverage of the target. Aerial photographs taken during the 15Jun44 raids furnished planners with complete

situation maps and beach studies of remarkable accuracy. But information concerning the enemy order of battle was incomplete because it did not reflect changes that occurred subsequent to the fall of Saipan, and the hydrographic and terrain data, while good as far as it went, needed amplification.

The corps intelligence section was responsible for collection, evaluation, and dissemination of intelligence for all elements of the landing force. The G–2 section, FMFPac rendered valuable assistance in procuring maps, photographs, bulletins, and maintaining essential liaison between VAC and the Joint Intelligence Center, Pacific Ocean Areas (JICPOA). Intelligence officers from FMFPac formed the 2-section of the Expeditionary Troops (TF 56) staff for the operation but did not function in that capacity until embarkation for the rehearsals in December.[36]

Aerial photographs were a major source of information, and during the planning phase of the operation 371 photo sorties were flown. Navy Photographic Squadrons 4 and 5 and the 28th Photographic Reconnaissance Squadron of the Army Air Force contributed most of the coverage. This was augmented by strike photos taken by Seventh Air Force bombers during their bombardment missions. Ample periodic coverage permitted constant checking of the enemy's defense efforts.[37]

One of the highlights of preassault intelligence was the extent of cooperation in this effort. In October 1944 officers of Admiral Turner's staff coordinated information disseminated by Amphibious Forces, Pacific and Fleet Marine Force, Pacific. Direct liaison was maintained between photo interpretation units of both echelons. This resulted in the production of a Joint Situation Map on 6 December. The scope of these joint activities extended to all naval and Marine units involved in the Iwo Jima operation.

Out of this consolidation of effort evolved a decision to publish a single Joint Enemy Installation Map to issue to all organizations making or supporting the assault. Late in January 1945, photo interpretation officers from each major participating unit assembled on Guam. These representatives from FMFPac, VAC, 3d, 4th, and 5th Marine Divisions, Joint Expeditionary Force, and Amphibious Group Two, examined all photographs that accumulated in the forward area after 5 January and with the receipt of excellent pictures taken during the 2–10 February period they were ready to produce the final Enemy Installation Map.[38]

Previews of the target were not limited to aerial observation. Early in December 1944, a United States submarine, the *Spearfish*, snooped just off the coast of Iwo and through his periscope the sub commander watched the activities of enemy troops. His observations were recorded and given wide circulation along with periscope photos of beach areas. Most of this data proved valuable as substantiation of previous information.[39]

Beach studies indicated that movement over the loose sand would be difficult for wheeled vehicles but that tractors would find it somewhat easier. Partially buried gasoline drums were observed at the water's edge on both the east and west beaches. Their regular pattern led intelligence experts to believe that they might be some kind of beach obstacles. This belief was strengthened by capture of Japanese documents giving detailed instructions for employment of burning gasoline to check hostile landing forces.[40]

Analysis of the organization of ground forces on Iwo Jima indicated that the Japanese garrison was applying lessons learned from defensive failures on other islands. Their beach defenses appeared to be organized in depth with open areas covered by extensive antitank defenses and machine guns laid on final protective

and clear pictures of the entire island. They were of special value to intelligence personnel as the enemy did not begin intensive fortification of Iwo until after Saipan fell, and the progress of the Japanese defense build-up could be noted through comparison of mid-1944 aerial shots of Iwo with those taken up to D-Day. Ltr Col G. A. Roll to CMC, 15Dec52, hereinafter cited as *Roll*.
  [36] *TF 56 IntelRpt.*
  [37] *TF 51 Rpt*, Pt V, Sec A.

  [38] *TF 56 IntelRpt* 3.
  [39] *Ibid.*, 2.
  [40] 1st Supplement to Nanpo Shoto Information Bulletin No. 122–44, 10Oct44, CinCPac-CinCPOA Bulletin No. 9–45, 10Jan45.

B–24's HIT IWO and other islands in the Volcano-Bonins for 74 consecutive days beginning 8 December 1944. (AF Photo)

lines. The light artillery of infantry units was also emplaced to bring flanking fire against the beaches. It appeared that the Japanese were learning how to fight without adhering to the rigid perimeter defense that had marked their earlier tactics.

Intelligence officers took particular note of the fact that field works seemed adequate for only four of the nine infantry battalions known to be on the island. This left five battalions in reserve, held out to execute a counterattack. But, it was pointed out, the enemy might now see the folly of beating uselessly against our well established beachheads. Preassault studies indicated that if the enemy should fail in his first full-scale attack against our positions, he would in all probability fall back to high ground in the center of the island to hole up, and resist fanatically to the last man.

Although enemy antitank defenses and weapons had proved inadequate in the past, Marines were warned to expect extensive use of antitank mines and obstacles, combined with "close quarter attack units" using hand-placed charges. It was cautioned also that infiltration tactics designed to knock out tanks as well as command posts, communications, artillery, and mortars were likely.

No change was anticipated in the enemy's artillery tactics. Although many artillery pieces were reported on the island, there did not seem to be any indication that massed fires would be encountered in larger than battery concentrations. Reference was made to the fact that Japanese infantry had always been reluctant to forego close support in favor of general support.[41]

Study of aerial photographs and captured documents showed that Iwo was probably divided into four defense sectors with one infantry battalion manning the defenses in each sector. The principal concentration of entrenched forces provided maximum strength in the southern part of the island to defend the vulnerable east and west coasts. These positions consisted of pillboxes and fire trenches. Here lines of fortification were known to be strengthened by extensive employment of antitank and beach mines. Lack of noticeable activity in the north led intelligence officers to assume that enemy fortification in that locality held less attention, and for good reason. There nature allied herself with the Japanese. The steep cliffs would all but prohibit invasion over northern beaches. Even so, one battalion was reported to be in defensive position along this northern coastal area with its companies deployed along the rocky heights overlooking the ocean.

Aerial photos taken during early 1945 revealed that the number of field fortifications,

[41] The foregoing remarks on the expected Japanese defensive tactics were taken from Supplement No. 1 to CinCPac-CinCPOA Bulletin No. 122–44, 10Oct44.

pillboxes, and covered artillery positions increased despite air bombardment. The most significant development noted in photographs was the construction of a defensive line traversing the island from coast to coast. These fortifications stretched from a point near Hiraiwa Bay on the northwest coast to high ground north of the East Boat Basin. This line appeared to be a chain-like series of centers of resistance and was obviously established in depth. A study of these changes resulted in a sharp upward revision in estimates of enemy strength on Iwo. Relative to this adjustment, intelligence authorities stated that:

Photographic coverage of Iwo Jima to 24 January 1945, indicates that damage to installations resulting from bombing strikes between 3 December 1944, and 24 January 1945, was, on the whole, negligible. These strikes have apparently not prevented the enemy from improving his defensive position and, as of 24 January 1945, his installations of all categories had notably increased in number. The island is now far more heavily defended by gun positions and field fortifications than it was on 15 October 1944, when initial heavy bombing strikes were initiated.[42]

A comparative tabulation of enemy installations issued 13 February illustrated the progress of Japanese defensive preparations:

Gun positions

Type	To 3Dec44	To 10Feb45	Increase
			Percent
Coast defense............	3	6	100
Dual purpose............	16	42	162
Dual purpose (empty)...	4	8	100
Automatic AA..........	151	203	41
Automatic AA (empty)...	2	16	700
Covered artillery........	39	67	71
Open artillery...........	40	5	−87
Antitank-antiboat.......	18	3	−83
Machine guns...........	352	292	−17
Total............	626	642	....

Commenting on the apparent decrease in number of some types of gun positions the G–2, Expeditionary Troops, stated:

. . . the apparent reduction in observed MG's may be offset by the heavy increase in field fortifications, including blockhouses and pillboxes. The blockhouses

may contain fixed artillery and, in many instances, their construction is such as to permit mobile artillery pieces to be wheeled into them. It is also considered that each pillbox provides emplacements for one or more heavy or light MG's. But even if the figures given above were to be accepted as showing no important change in totals, they do reveal significant increases in the number of heavy caliber weapons: CD's, DP's, and Auto. AA's.[43]

Intelligence officers estimated that Iwo's defenders numbered between 13,000 and 14,000 troops. In the *C–2 Study of Enemy Situation*, issued 6 January 1945, the Japanese order of battle is given as follows: [44]

2d Mixed Brig:	
Hq and 6 IndInfBn's_____	3,700
Arty Bn_____	400
Engr Bn_____	500
Fld Hosp_____	120
Total Brig_____	4,720
145th Inf Regt:	
Hq and 3 InfBn's_____	3,475
Sig Co_____	150
Regt Gun Co_____	150
AT Gun Co_____	125
Total regt (estimated)_____	3,900–4,000
2 AT Gun Bn's_____	1,000
Mortar Bn_____	600–700
Detachment, 26th Tk Regt_____	350
Br, 59th Anchorage_____	25
Army Fort Section_____	20
Iwo Jima Naval Guard Force_____	1,500–2,000
Naval Airbase Personnel_____	400
Construction Personnel_____	700
Total Army_____	10,600–10,800
Total Navy_____	1,900–2,400
Total construction_____	700
Total Iwo Jima_____	13,200–13,900

It was known that the backbone of this force was the 2d Mixed Brigade of the 109th Division, believed to be commanded by Major General Koto Osuka, and Colonel Masuo Ikeda's 145th Infantry Regiment. A detachment of the 26th Tank Regiment with about 30 medium and ten light tanks were reported on Iwo, but the whereabouts of Colonel Takeichi Nishi, the regimental commander, and the bulk of his troops was uncertain.

Order of battle experts assumed that Lieutenant General Tadamichi Kuribayashi exer-

---

[42] *TF 56 IntelRpt*, 4.

[43] *TF 56 IntelRpt*, Appendix A.
[44] *VAC C–2 Study*, 3.

cised over-all command of the Volcano-Bonin Defense Sector from his 109th Division Headquarters on Chichi Jima, and that Major General Osuka was in charge of Iwo's defenses.

Information on the Japanese naval guard and air base units on Iwo was noticeably lacking in preassault intelligence. It was pointed out, however, that as a rule naval guard units such as the one thought to be on Iwo were usually commanded by a commander or a captain.[45]

Early in January, after careful study and evaluation of all enemy information, the Corps C–2 issued a statement of enemy capabilities:

a. To defend initially by a combination of an active and passive defense with the mission of repelling or destroying our forces in the water and on the beach.

b. To counterattack our beachhead with all available reserve strength under the cover of darkness.

c. To reinforce and improve his defensive positions prior to D-Day.

d. To attack our assault shipping with submarines, suicide-plane squadrons, and other special attack units—with carriers and transports as priority.

e. To withdraw or abandon Iwo Jima.[46]

In modification of (e) above, C–2 believed that the enemy should not be expected to abandon Iwo without a fight. Being only three air hours from the homeland, Iwo was considered a keystone in Japan's inner defense system.

A D-minus 2 reconnaissance by underwater demolition teams (UDT's) would provide naval and troop commanders with up-to-date information on beach conditions. For liaison, specially trained Marines from the reconnaissance companies of the two assault divisions were attached to these units to make the trip to the beach. After the reconnaissance these liaison personnel would transfer at sea to the headquarters of their respective commands and furnish beach information to supplement official reports of the UDT Commander.[47]

In spite of efforts to maintain secrecy concerning the objective, some breaches of security did occur. For example, on 22 December 1944 the *Honolulu Advertiser* printed two excellent "Bombs Away" pictures with captions identifying the island target as Iwo Jima. The similarity between these pictures and the map of "Island X," which had been issued by VAC for training, was obvious.[48]

To offset possible serious consequences of such breaches of security, VAC ordered counterintelligence measures taken. Prior to leaving Hawaii, C–2 permitted information to leak out that all the buildup and activity was in preparation for an attack on Formosa in the near future.[49]

While the ships of Task Force 51 assembled in the Marianas and at Ulithi, Japanese submarines kept Imperial Headquarters in Tokyo fully informed of their movements. Thus, the enemy was well aware of the impending attack. Ten days before the assault, Tokyo advised the Volcano-Bonin command that an American attack would be launched soon, but the Imperial Chiefs could only guess as to whether the target would be Iwo Jima or Okinawa.[50] The Formosa ruse does not appear to have affected Japanese estimates of United States intentions.

Although the Japanese intelligence experts in Tokyo were not able to predict exactly where the huge United States task force would strike, there seems to have been little doubt on Iwo. In fact, that garrison had a pretty good idea of when the attack would come and what units would make the assault.[51]

LOGISTICS AND ADMINISTRATION

The major responsibility for logistical planning fell to the VAC staff. Even before the

---

4th MarDiv Support Group Rpt; 5th MarDiv SAR, Annex B, Intelligence, 34, hereinafter cited as *5th MarDiv IntelRpt.*

[48] *Ibid.,* 12.

[49] *Ibid.*

[50] CinCPac-CinCPOA Bulletin No 2–46, 15Feb46, 5.

[51] A notebook found on the body of an unidentified enemy soldier on Iwo contained the following information: "The task force will take four days to arrive at Iwo Jima from Saipan. One battleship, 18 cruisers and destroyers, 40 transports left Hawaii. (? and the 5th Marine Division) 3d and 4th Marine Divisions, one brigade." As quoted in *TF 56 IntelRpt,* Sec III, 9.

---

[45] *Ibid.* The foregoing estimates of Japanese strength may be compared with the actual enemy situation by referring to Chapter I and Appendix VI of this monograph.

[46] *Ibid.*

[47] 4th MarDiv Support Group, Operation Report, Iwo Jima Operation, 4Apr45, Sec III, hereinafter cited as

arrival of V Corps staff planners in Pearl Harbor on 13 October, however, such planning was underway.

The special staffs of FMFPac conducted preliminary conferences and drew tentative plans for logistical operations essential to the Iwo assault. Also, prior to General Schmidt's arrival in the Hawaiian area, the FMFPac staff handled all lower echelon correspondence and information requests regarding Iwo and logistics. The harmonious interworking at all levels of command paid real dividends. Within a short time, logistical planners issued directives that detailed exactly who would do what, where, when, and how.

The Quartermaster, U. S. Army Forces, Pacific Ocean Areas, would supply rations for all participating troops; also all clothing, special equipment, supplies, and ammunition for Army troops at Iwo. The Navy's Service Force, Pacific, would provide the necessary fuels and lubricants. Ammunition, special supplies, and equipment for the Marine troops, were to be provided by the Supply Service, FMFPac.[52] These latter supplies were to be distributed initially by the 6th Base Depot through the 1st and 2d Service and Supply Battalions in Hawaii, and by the 5th Field Depot through the 3d Service Battalion on Guam.

Tending to complicate the supply problem was the 3d Marine Division's role as Expeditionary Troops reserve. To predetermine the amount of combat participation of this division and the time of its battle commitment was, of course, impossible. For this reason supplies earmarked for the 3d were loaded separately, so that, if the division were not used on Iwo, these materials would be available for future operations.

Stocks of ready packaged supplies were to be maintained at the 7th Field Depot on Saipan by the Air Delivery Section, VAC, for emergency delivery by air. The Expeditionary Troops Commander was also at liberty to draw from other stockpiles in the Marianas and Hawaiians.

Prior to the establishment of supply dumps ashore, vital materials were to be furnished from preloaded LST's. Using the shore party communication channels, requests for such supplies would be transmitted to logistical personnel on control vessels. They, in turn, would dispatch LVT's, DUKW's, or other craft to the LST's to pick up the desired items and deliver them to the beach.

The 8th Field Depot was organized by VAC for the Iwo operation and as such was to be the nucleus of the shore party organization. Commanding this depot was Colonel Leland S. Swindler, also designated as the Landing Force Shore Party Commander. His responsibility on the beach was to coordinate the activities of the division shore parties.

Absence of reefs off the shores of Iwo Jima offered obvious advantages to the ship-to-shore movement. All types of landing craft would be able to make the run from the transport area to the beach without the time-consuming reef transfer operations that had marked previous Central Pacific landings. Because of this, V Corps units were authorized to palletize [53] supplies up to 50 percent when practicable.

It was foreseen, however, that the soft sand along the beaches, plus the steep gradient and high inshore banks, would render all movement of wheeled vehicles difficult. As a partial solution, runner sleds were supplied that could be loaded with necessary items and hauled across the beaches to inland points by tracked vehicles.

Marston matting, it was determined, would also be invaluable on Iwo's beaches. Designed originally for use in making airstrips, this material had been found ideally suited for use by assault troops in construction of temporary roadways over soft, yielding beach terrain. It came in plank-shaped lengths, ten feet long and 14 inches wide, each weighing 65 pounds. The shore party developed a means of hinging these lengths into 50-foot "accordion-pleated" units. Seven of them were bound together and lashed on sleds to be towed by tracked vehicles. As

---

[52] TF 56 Report of Logistics, Iwo Jima Operation, 31Mar45, 1., hereinafter cited as *TF 56 Logistics Rpt*; VAC Assistant Chief of Staff, G–4, Special Action Report, Iwo Jima Campaign, 30Apr45, 4, hereinafter cited as *VAC Logistics Rpt*.

[53] *TF 56 Logistics Rpt*, 5. Materials strapped or fastened on wooden platforms (pallets). Palletization facilitates loading and unloading operations when cranes and other special lifting devices are available to handle these convenient but heavy loads.

it was pulled along, the matting would unfold neatly and quickly over the sand. Altogether, 8½ miles of this hinged matting was prepared at the Pearl Harbor Navy Yard for the operation.

In earlier operations the Sherman M4A2 (medium) tanks had been landed from landing craft, mechanized (LCM's) or landing craft, tank (LCT's). When the M4A2's were replaced by the newer, heavier M4A3 tanks for this campaign, tests revealed that LCM's carrying them rode dangerously low at the bow. As a result, landing ships, medium (LSM's) were used in lieu of the LCM's.[54] For the Iwo operation all tanks went ashore in LSM's except those of Company A, 5th Tank Battalion, which were carried from a landing ship, dock (LSD) to the beach in three tank landing craft (LCT's).

Among the great variety of amphibious equipment available for landings, two items were new to the VAC: the Clever-Brooks 3½-ton amphibian trailer, and the light cargo carrier M-29C (weasel), capable of hauling a half-ton load. The amphibian trailers, two-wheeled towed vehicles, reached the 3d Division in November 1944, while the 4th and 5th Divisions received their allotments later in December. Training exercises revealed these trailers to be difficult to handle but, nevertheless, they were utilized as "one-way" carriers to lift high priority preloaded cargo.

The weasels were received and distributed to the three divisions in November. Outstanding performance in tests and training exercises disclosed that these boatlike tracked vehicles resembling miniature LVT's without ramps, were valuable equipment. Critical shortages of repair parts, however, caused doubts as to the advisability of embarking the vehicles for Iwo. An air shipment of urgently needed parts erased these doubts, and all divisions loaded weasels. Additional parts were received by surface shipment in time to be distributed before the divisions sailed.[55]

Five amphibian truck (DUKW) companies were assigned to VAC units for the operation. Of these, three were Army and the 4th and 5th Marine Divisions had one each, known as Provisional Amphibian Truck Companies, FMFPac. During training, Army personnel who had many months of experience with the vehicles, rendered valuable assistance to the Marines. Spare parts again became a problem: 200 propeller shafts and 100 propellers were needed, and neither Army nor Marine procurement agencies could obtain them. To meet this emergency, the Pearl Harbor Navy Yard manufactured these items, but delivery was not made until 23 January 1945.

For engineer support, the divisions had their organic engineer battalions plus the 133d and 31st Naval Construction Battalions ("Seabees"), attached to the 4th and 5th Divisions respectively. In addition, the following units were assigned to VAC and placed under the Corps Engineer for operational control:

2d Separate Engineer Battalion (Marine).
2d Separate Topographic Company (Marine).
2d Bomb Disposal Company (Marine).
156th Ordnance Bomb Disposal Squad (Army).
62d Naval Construction Battalion (Navy).[56]
Engineer missions would include clearing of mine fields, bomb disposal, road building and maintenance, water supply, and early repair and improvement of airfields. One of the most common of all combat engineering missions—bridge building—was not assigned. Only minor culvert installation would be needed.

The 62d Naval Construction Battalion received orders to commence repairs and improvements on Airfield Number 1 as early as possible after the beach assault. The specific mission of this unit was to prepare air strips for OY-1's

---

[54] *4th MarDiv OpRpt*, Annex D, Logistics, 2, hereinafter cited as *4th MarDiv Logistics Rpt*. The LSM's were oceangoing ships of 165-ton capacity and were about 200 feet long. They could carry five medium tanks each or other heavy vehicles direct to a hostile beach.

[55] The fast, maneuverable weasel, with its low silhouette, pulled trailers and artillery pieces over terrain that wheeled vehicles could not negotiate. Of great value on land, they did not prove very seaworthy. *VAC Logistics Rpt*, 45.

[56] VAC Engineer Special Action Report, Iwo Jima Campaign, 17Apr45, hereinafter cited as *VAC EngRpt*.

(light observation planes) and fighter aircraft. Similarly, the 31st Seabees would repair and extend Airfield Number 2 to 7,000 feet for accommodation of B-29's. Target dates for completing these assignments were D-plus 7 and D-plus 10.[57]

With three divisions, plus corps troops and other supporting units committed in a heavily fortified area of less than eight square miles, high casualties were expected.[58] The 3d, 4th, and 5th Medical Battalions were integral parts of the divisions. Corps had its organic medical battalion, Evacuation Hospital Number 1, and the 38th Field Hospital. The latter, an Army unit, originally was slated to participate only as a part of the Garrison Force. Mounting concern regarding casualties, however, caused assignment of this hospital to the Landing Force.

After the Marianas operation, the Marine medical battalions were each authorized a 100-percent increase in patient facilities and equipment, from 72 to 144 beds. The three divisions of VAC thus could accommodate 432 casualties. Corps, with the attached Army hospital, could care for 3,160. The 8th Field Depot carried cots, tents, blankets, and mess gear for an additional 1,500.[59]

Two hospital ships, the *Samaritan* and the *Solace*, and one APH (Auxiliary Personnel, Hospital), the *Pinkney*,[60] were originally assigned for the operation, as was the LSV (Landing Ship, Vehicle) *Ozark*,[61] which would serve as an auxiliary hospital ship. One other hospital ship, the *Bountiful* was later scheduled for Iwo.

In addition, four hospital LST's [LST(H)] were to be stationed 2,000 yards off the beaches to serve as evacuation control centers. This was planned as the first step in the process of evacuation from the beach. There casualties would be logged, given additional emergency treatment, then transferred to other ships for further care. LCVP's would be available as ambulance boats to carry patients to the transports (which provided limited hospital facilities) and hospital ships. Casualties were to be taken to Saipan and Guam, where a total of 5,000 beds were available. Air transportation was scheduled as soon as air strips were ready to accommodate transport planes.[62]

In early Pacific operations whole blood for transfusions in a combat area had been obtained from on-the-spot personnel. However, with the establishment of a whole-blood distribution center on Guam it was now possible to provide for a vitally important mobile blood bank at the target area. Early in January a mobile blood bank facility, consisting of one medical officer and two corpsmen, was attached to the corps medical battalion. Operating on an evacuation control LST, this bank was to act as a local blood distribution center for ships receiving casualties and for medical units ashore. When the situation ashore permitted, this bank, complete with refrigerating equipment, would move in and function until regular air delivery of whole blood from Guam[63] could be established.

Paralleling the problem of care and evacuation was the accurate reporting of casualties.

[57] VAC OpPlan 3-44, 23Dec44, Annex M, Engineer Plan.

[58] For the computation of casualties, it was assumed that: "fourteen (14) days would be required to complete the seizure of the objective; that 5 percent of the entire force would become casualties on each of the first and second days; 3 percent on the third and fourth days; and 1½ percent on each of the remaining ten days; that 20 percent of all casualties would be dead or missing." VAC Surgeon, Special Action Report, Iwo Jima Campaign, 24Mar45, 1, hereinafter cited as *VAC MedRpt.*

[59] TF 56 Medical Report, Iwo Jima, 28Mar45, 1–2, hereinafter cited as *TF 56 MedRpt.*

[60] There were only three APH's commissioned during the war. These craft were designed to accommodate the wounded brought offshore direct from combat. As contrasted with the regular hospital ships, they carried troops and armament; they were not painted white and claimed no immunity under the Geneva Convention. They were named for deceased Surgeons General of the Navy (Pinkney, Tryon, Rixey). Maj F. O. Hough, *The Island War* (Philadelphia, 1947), 214.

[61] The *Ozark* (LSV2) was converted in 1944 from a mine layer and equipped with a stern ramp. This vessel of 6,000 tons (455 ft. long), could carry 21 LVT's, 44 DUKW's, or 800 troops. The *Ozark* lifted 50 preloaded amphibian trailers to Iwo. J. C. Fahey, *The Ships and Aircraft of the United States Fleet* (Washington, 1950), 33–35.

[62] VAC Assistant Chief of Staff, G-1, Special Action Report, Iwo Jima Campaign, 1Mar45, 13, hereinafter cited as *VAC Personnel Rpt.*

[63] *TF 56 MedRpt,* 2. *VAC MedRpt,* 16.

In some past operations many wounded were long carried as missing in action because their whereabouts remained unknown for several months. VAC took steps to prevent this situation at Iwo. The four LST(H)'s, as the first link in the chain of shore-to-ship evacuation, were to maintain complete records of receipt and disposition of casualties. Troop commanders on each transport were to assign a clerical NCO to record and report all casualties brought on board. All ships were requested to submit reports of casualties to corps headquarters; air evacuees were to be reported by the air evacuation officer. A casualty section of one officer and two NCO's was provided at corps to process these reports. Detailed plans were issued concerning the collection and interment of friendly dead, burial of enemy dead, establishment of cemetery sites, and graves registration.[64]

During the closing months of 1944, six replacement drafts embarked from the United States destined for duty with VAC. Each consisted of approximately 1,250 officers and men. Two of these contingents went to each of the three divisions, where some of the personnel were absorbed prior to departing staging areas for Iwo. For the most part, however, these units were kept intact for use with shore parties for employment on the beaches until needed to replace combat losses.[65]

Painstakingly, corps G–4 and G–1 sections worked out the many other details of logistical and administrative planning. As the target date for Iwo drew near, these plans meshed smoothly with the over-all operational scheme.

TRAINING AND REHEARSAL

For troops in the Pacific during the war years, life boiled down to a very simple formula: training for combat, combat, more training, followed by more combat. At the lower echelons, where the intensive troop training programs were conducted, knowledge of the identity of the next objective was not necessary: sufficient the certainty that "another rock" had to be taken.

It was at the higher levels that the training program dealt with preparation for specific targets. The Commanding General, Fleet Marine Force, Pacific, assumed responsibility for training and equipping all forces under his command. A primary function of FMFPac in connection with this duty was the distribution to all subordinate commands of information concerning new developments and changes in amphibious techniques.

Following his assignment as Commanding General, VAC Landing Force, Major General Harry Schmidt assumed direct responsibility for the preparation and training of all units assigned to him for the operation. In addition to the routine training program, units of V Corps participated in tests and demonstrations of new types of amphibious vessels, craft, vehicles, weapons, and techniques developed in anticipation of revised enemy defensive doctrines.[66]

As the nature of the Iwo operation became better known, the division training programs placed added emphasis on attacking fortified positions, reduction of pillboxes, detection, marking, and removal of mine fields, and the use and coordination of supporting arms.

During the period 15 to 30 November, the 4th Division conducted amphibious exercises in the Maalea Bay area of Maui, followed by a division field exercise based on the scheme of maneuver for the Iwo Jima operation. Two command post exercises were later held in the camp area.[67]

The 5th Division began specialized instruction and exercises as soon as initial plans for the operation were distributed. Special emphasis placed on the mission of the 28th Marines resulted in an effort to utilize terrain similar to southern Iwo Jima. Each battalion of that regiment received the benefit of exercises that involved landing on beaches thought to resemble Iwo's, and enveloping a hill mass remarkably like Mount Suribachi. In an area marked off to represent the objective, elements of the division actually executed the scheme of maneuver. This unit held three command post ex-

---

[64] *VAC Personnel Rpt*, 13–15.
[65] *Ibid.*, 15.

[66] *TF 56 OpRpt*, Encl C.
[67] *4th MarDiv OpRpt*, Sec I.

ercises in the Hawaiian area, including one problem employing coordination of air, naval gunfire, and artillery support.[68]

Preparation of the 3d Division for the operation followed a pattern dictated by its assigned mission. Training exercises emphasized the various phases a reserve unit passed through while landing and moving up to the assault. Particular attention was paid to methods used in executing a passage of lines in order to continue the attack. Because this division would not land in the assault, no assault landing rehearsals were held. The plan called for 3d Division use of shore party facilities of previously landed organizations. Nevertheless, the division and combat team shore parties engaged in training exercises on Guam prior to embarkation.[69]

Replacement drafts did not reach the divisions until late in November. Although these men had undergone basic infantry training before leaving the United States, there was still much preparation to be accomplished in the short period of time remaining. Exercises were sorely needed to integrate these troops with the units to which assigned as combat replacements. It was necessary further to acquaint them with the shore party duties they were to perform prior to their commitment as infantrymen.

Training of the newly activated amphibian truck companies was delayed by the late delivery of the DUKW's. Tank-infantry maneuvers were handicapped by the necessity of considerable retraining of tank crews and maintenance personnel in operation of the new M4A3 tank.

The loading of assault elements staged in the Hawaiian Islands began on 24 December, following completion of amphibious training exercises. By 9 January, embarkation of all troops was concluded in preparation for initial rehearsals. As individual units completed loading, transport divisions carried them independently to Oahu where they assembled with other elements of the Joint Expeditionary Force.[70]

Dress rehearsals, conducted in the Hawaiian area from 12 to 18 January, involved major elements of the Landing Force scheduled for the assault. These mass exercises, based on the actual scheme of maneuver, took place at Maalea Bay, Maui, and Kahoolawe Island. During the entire time, emphasis was placed on communications and control.[71]

The absence of several assault organizations from Hawaiian rehearsals detracted somewhat from the over-all value of these exercises. Only two of the five LVT battalions assigned to the Iwo operation participated. The other three, which staged in the Marianas, sent liaison officers to observe the exercises and carry back information relative to changes in plans and procedures.[72] During landing exercises, training tractors and landing craft replaced the missing units and provided Marines with the necessary practice in loading and landing. Another unit, the 4th Tank Battalion, was not present at rehearsal because of the delayed loading of LSM's.

Participation of V Corps Artillery was limited to part of group headquarters, the 2d 155mm Howitzer Battalion, and half of the 473d Amphibian Truck Company, USA. The only operations performed by the group involved testing primary radio circuits; the corps landed no equipment. No DUKW's were launched because of need to prevent corrosion and deterioration of preloaded ammunition, and LST's were not beached because of reefs off rehearsal landing beaches.[73]

In spite of these deficiencies, participating units felt that rehearsals were of definite value, especially to the 5th Division, then operating

---

[68] 28th Marines Action Report, Iwo Jima, undated, Pt IV. Hereinafter cited as *28th Mar SAR.*

[69] 3d Marine Division Action Report, Iwo Jima Operation, 30Apr45, Pt. 2, hereinafter cited as *3d MarDiv SAR.*

[70] *TF 56 OpRpt*, Encl C.

[71] *Ibid.*

[72] The 2d Armored and the 3d and 5th Amphibian Tractor Battalions did not participate. These three units had supported Marianas operations and remained in that area during Hawaiian rehearsals for rehabilitation, re-equipping, and training. They were assigned to assault divisions at Saipan before final exercises. The 10th and 11th Amphibian Tractor Battalions were present. All five LVT battalions participated in the Saipan rehearsals which followed. VAC LVT Officer, Special Action Report, Iwo Jima Campaign, 30Apr45, 2.

[73] *VAC Artillery Officer's Report*, 18Mar45, 9 hereinafter cited as *VAC ArtyRpt.*

for the first time as part of a corps. Experience gained while working with adjacent units proved valuable as weak links in control and communications came to light for subsequent correction.[74]

Final rehearsals in the Marianas during the second week of February included ships and aircraft of the Amphibious Support Force (TF 52) and the Naval Gunfire and Covering Force (TF 54), neither of which had engaged in the Hawaiian maneuvers. All assault shipping was now assembled at Saipan, including all LVT's embarked in LST's of the tractor groups. Troops of assault battalions were transferred from APA's to LST's just prior to rehearsals. These exercises were held primarily to test coordination between supporting arms and the Attack Force, with the emphasis again centered on communications and control. Marines were boated but did not land. Shore fire control parties did land on Tinian, however, and conducted drills and tests of communications in connection with simulated bombardment. During landing exercises troops executed a ship-to-shore feint in LVT's as assigned for D-Day.[75]

MOUNTING OUT

By late 1944 American shipyards, operating on record-breaking production schedules, began to catch up with almost overwhelming shipping demands in the Pacific. Newly constructed ships made possible a reorganization in the composition of transport divisions for the Iwo operation. Now each division contained five APA's (auxiliary personnel, attack; i. e., troop transports) and two AKA's (auxiliary cargo, attack). Of these seven transports, one APA and one AKA carried troops and cargo from corps rather than a division. Thus, each assault regiment had at its disposal for transportation four APA's and one AKA from a transport division. Three of these transdivs constituted a transport squadron capable of lifting a reinforced Marine division. Men and supplies of service elements were distributed among the ships of the transrons and the LST's and LSM's

assigned to carry assault infantry (and their LVT's), artillery (in DUKW's), tanks, and other mechanized equipment. The organization of transports for Iwo resulted in a minimum separation of units from their equipment when loading.[76]

The 4th Marine Division loaded for combat at Maui between 27 December and 8 January, the 5th Division at Hawaii between 25 December and 16 January, and elements of the 3d Division later at Guam. Although not destined for the assault, the 3d Division arrived off Iwo combat loaded. The wisdom of this later became evident when the 21st Marines received orders to disembark for combat before other units of the division. This regiment arrived prepared for battle, with its equipment and supplies readily available when needed. Corps and garrison troops loaded in the Hawaiian area at various times between 23 December and 25 January with six APA's and four AKA's employed for these elements.[77]

Of the 63 LST's and 31 LSM's assigned to the operation, the assault divisions necessarily drew the lion's share. Each of these units used 19 LST's while the 3d Division managed with two to lift machines of the 3d Tank Battalion. The remaining tank landing ships lifted supporting elements of V Corps. Allotment of LSM's gave 16 to the 4th Division and 12 to 5th Division, while the others became part of V Corps shipping. One LSD assigned to the 5th Division to carry tank landing craft balanced the disproportionate allotment of LSM's.[78]

In anticipation of early need, V Corps preloaded (in addition to the primary cargo) infantry LST's with vital initial landing supplies. These included such items as water,

[74] *4th MarDiv OpRpt*, Sec I. *5th MarDiv SAR*, Sec IV.

[75] *TF 56 OpRpt*, Encl C; *VAC OpRpt*.

[76] TF 56 Transport Quartermaster Report on Iwo Jima Operation, 1Apr45, 3, hereinafter cited as *TF 56 TQM Rpt*. APA's and AKA's embarked about 550 and 2,000 tons of cargo respectively, APA's loading this tonnage in addition to their primary cargo—personnel. VAC Transport Quartermaster Special Action Report, Iwo Jima Campaign, 27Mar45, hereinafter cited as *VAC TQM Rpt*.

[77] *VAC TQM Rpt; 3d MarDiv SAR*, 45. The 483d AA(AW) Bn (USA), 138th AAGp, loaded at Ulithi, where it had comprised part of the garrison force.

[78] *VAC TQM Rpt*, Encl A.

AIRFIELD NUMBER 2 and Japanese antiaircraft installations take 500-pound bombs from Seventh Air Force Liberators. Unfinished Airfield Number 3 is left center in picture. (AF Photo)

approximately two infantry battalion units of fire, 2,000 C and K rations, 1,200 D rations, concertina wire, gasoline, and lubricants.[79]

The primary purpose of preloading was to assure a balanced supply of rations, fuels and ammunition for assault troops on D-Day. Such provision and replenishment allowed Marines to continue the attack while the bulk of supplies filtered ashore through the hands of the shore parties. A total of 28 LST's arrived at Iwo thus preloaded or understowed.[80] In addition, 42 amphibian trucks (DUKW's) were preloaded at Pearl Harbor for early discharge on the beaches at Iwo. On the occasion of their introduction to V Corps operations, 50 of the new 3½-ton amphibian cargo trailers were preloaded at Guam with rations, fuels, and ammu-

nition. These loads, embarked in the LSV *Ozark*, would supply troops ashore on D-Day, and the *Ozark*, following discharge of her cargo, would serve as an evacuation hospital.[81]

The fleet that lifted the Landing Force included a variety of vessels carrying a great diversity of items essential to waging modern war. These ships sailed from many different ports but all gravitated toward a common goal: Iwo Jima. Assault shipping transported over one ton of supplies for every man in the assault force, amounting to approximately 98,000 tons.[82] A total of 485 ships of various types were employed by Task Force 51 during the operation. This includes combat vessels, assault shipping, and early Garrison Force echelons but not vessels from other forces that operated temporarily under the senior officer present afloat at the objective.[83]

---

[79] *VAC TQM Rpt. 3; 4th MarDiv Logistics Rpt.*

[80] Understowed, preloaded cargo consisted of items loaded in ships or craft in addition to the primary cargo, which might be tanks or vehicles. Supplies loaded in an LST tank deck would be covered with dunnage and primary cargo loaded on top. Preloaded supplies could be stowed in any available space from which they could be quickly discharged when landing ship or craft beached.

[81] *VAC Logistics Rpt.*

[82] *TF 56 TQM Rpt.*

[83] Commander in Chief United States Fleet, Amphibious Operations, Capture of Iwo Jima, 16Feb to 16Mar45, P–0012, 17Jul45, 1–5, hereinafter cited as *CominCh P–0012.*

MOVEMENT TO THE OBJECTIVE

Upon completion of final rehearsals, the Landing Force convoy anchored off Saipan on 14 and 15 February. By late 'afternoon of the latter date all elements of the creeping tractor groups had pointed clumsy bows northward toward the Volcano Islands. Slowly but surely they began to put distance between themselves and the Southern Marianas. The next day Transport Squadrons 15 and 16, lifting other elements of Major General Harry Schmidt's Landing Force, also weighed anchor and steered a northerly course toward Iwo. While en route to the objective, this assault force received cover and protection from a carrier unit and naval surface elements.[84]

Most of the Landing Force units that staged on Guam were not scheduled to arrive at the target on D-Day. Therefore, these troops sailed after the assault divisions left Saipan. Supporting units of the 3d Division and corps troops sailed in LST's on the 16th, followed by the main body of the division in the faster transports the next day. These ships from Transport Squadron 11, less TransDiv 32, would stand by approximately 80 miles off the southeast coast of Iwo Jima, with the 3d and 9th Marines in Expeditionary Troops reserve.[85] RCT 21 followed other plans. Leaving the 3d Division at Guam, it embarked in TransDiv 32 and departed a day earlier to arrive at the objective by 1000 on D-Day.

PRELIMINARY BOMBARDMENT

Before Marines set foot on Iwo Jima, that island had endured the longest and most intensive preparation given any objective in the Pacific during World War II. From the initial carrier raid of June 1944 to the pre-H–Hour bombardment on 19 February 1945, tons of explosives showered down on this small island until it seemed that means and will to resist must surely be smothered.

Air Activities

Regularly scheduled air strikes against the target began as early as August 1944. Air operations were divided roughly into two phases: those prior to 16 February (the strategic phase), and those conducted from then to D-Day. During this time the tempo of air raids increased steadily to the point where Marianas-based bombers hit Iwo with a daylight attack once every 24 hours. These strikes were accompanied by night harassing missions, fighter sweeps and photo reconnaissance flights.[86]

The workhorses of these air assaults proved to be the heavy bombers (B–24's) of the Seventh Air Force stationed in the Marianas. This campaign marked the greatest effort made by Seventh Air Force bombers in the Pacific. Commencing on 8 December, and continuing for 74 consecutive days, explosives from these aircraft rained on islands in the Volcano-Bonins, with particular attention given to Iwo Jima.[87]

Marine PBJ's (B–25 medium bombers) from VMB–612 participated in this bombing from early December 1944 until D-minus 20. These flying Marines operated from the Marianas under the VII Bomber Command and flew night sorties through the Volcano-Bonin Islands in an effort to disrupt enemy shipping activities. Because of omnipresent United States aircraft in this area during daylight hours the enemy made frantic attempts to supply their island outposts at night. Against this nocturnal logistics program Marines, using rockets and radar, operated with considerable success, reporting 23 Japanese ships sunk.[88]

All air missions on or after D-minus 20 were executed in compliance with provisions of the Iwo Jima Air Support Plan.[89] During this period Marianas-based Liberators flew 30 to 34 sorties a day against the Iwo defenses.[90] Although land-based aircraft missions over Iwo were controlled by Commander Task Force 93

---

[84] *VAC OpRpt*, 9.
[85] *Ibid.; 3d MarDiv SAR*, 4.
[86] TF 56 Report of Air Operations in Support of the Capture of Iwo Jima, 4Apr45, 1, hereinafter cited as *TF 56 Air Rpt.*
[87] These B–24's were from the 11th Group on Guam and the 30th Group on Saipan. Two squadrons hit Iwo daily, primarily with 500-pound general purpose bombs, from 8 December until D-Day. Army Air Forces, Pacific Ocean Areas, Report of Participation in the Iwo Jima Operation, 1945, 75.
[88] *Ibid.*, 76.
[89] CTF 51 OpPlan A25–44, Annex I.
[90] *TF 51 Rpt*, Pt V, Sec E, 17–18.

(Lieutenant General Millard F. Harmon, USA), after D-minus 20 they were conducted according to requests of Commander Joint Expeditionary Force. Bombing missions were planned to accomplish the following:

(a) Neutralization of the airfields and installations on Iwo Jima.

(b) Destruction of gun positions and fixed defenses.

(c) Unmasking of additional targets.[91]

Naval Activities

The initial plan for preliminary naval gunfire bombardment provided for one cruiser division to shell Iwo beginning on D-minus 8, to be joined on D-minus 3 by seven old battleships (pre-World War II) and six more cruisers.[92]

Planning for naval preliminary fires at Iwo was marked by three unsuccessful attempts by Marine naval gunfire specialists to lengthen the period of shore bombardment. Efforts to gain more time for preassault destruction of enemy defenses were based upon previous experience of Marines at Tarawa, Saipan, and Peleliu. In these operations prelanding naval activities left much to be desired, and the corps wanted to ensure more adequate softening of the target at Iwo. Requests for more than three days of fires were made in consideration of the known nature and number of defenses at the objective. The naval gunfire officers of V Corps believed that only a long period of deliberate destructive fire could properly prepare the target.

The first Marine request called for a 10-day bombardment by one cruiser division and three

battleships. This proposal was turned down by naval commanders, and General Schmidt then asked for nine days. After failing a second time, the VAC commander made sweeping concessions and submitted a third letter requesting only four days of preliminary bombardment. But naval planners still insisted that their schedule would provide adequate preparation without even one more day.

In his fourth and final effort, General Schmidt asked for additional firing time. Realizing, however, that the Navy would probably continue firm in its decision to devote only three days to the task, he proposed as an alternative that shelling on those days be concentrated on and adjacent to the preferred landing beaches. This request received the same strong support from General Smith as all former attempts, but Admirals Turner and Spruance again held to the original plan.[93]

The Navy's major considerations in turning down Marine requests may be summarized as follows:

(a) The initial surface bombardment must be simultaneous with the first carrier attack upon the Tokyo area by the Fast Carrier Force (TF 58). The carrier attacks were to continue for three days but unforeseen conditions might force TF 58 to withdraw earlier. Therefore, if preparation fires at Iwo commenced on D-minus 4 and the carriers were forced to abandon their operations against the Empire in two days or less, the enemy would have sufficient time to recover and launch air attacks against United States invasion shipping off Iwo Jima.

(b) The limitations on the availability of ships, difficulty in replenishing ammunition, and loss of surprise interposed serious obstacles to a protracted preparation.

(c) The Navy plan for three days of firing would accomplish all the desired objectives.

(d) The prolonged air bombardment might be considered at least as effective as one day of additional surface bombardment.[94]

[91] *CominCh P-0012*, 3-1.

[92] TF 56 Preliminary Report on Naval Gunfire Support in Operations against Iwo Jima, 1Apr45, 4, hereinafter cited as *TF 56 Preliminary NGF Rpt; DETACHMENT*. On 15Nov44 Admiral Turner informed V Corps that CinCPOA's initial plan for preparation fires was changed. Instead, one cruiser division would shell Iwo on 15 December and at irregular intervals thereafter. This was the substitute for five continuous days of bombardment by a cruiser division. Then, on D-minus 3, the Amphibious Support Force, including seven battleships, would commence a "methodical and thorough bombardment." Ltr ComPhibsPac to CG VAC, 000209, 15Nov44.

[93] Ltr CG VAC to ComPhibsPac 0009B, 2Jan45, 1st endorsement, 6Jan45; 2d endorsement, 9Jan45; Ltr ComFifthFlt to CG FMF Pac, 00036, 12Jan45.

[94] Ltr ComFifthFlt to ComPhibsPac, 00066, 2Dec44; Ltr ComPhibsPac to ComGenVAC, 000209, 15Nov44.

TOP COMMANDERS AT IWO. From left to right: Vice Admiral Turner, Expeditionary Force Commander; Major General Schmidt, Landing Force Commander; Lieutenant General Smith, Expeditionary Troops Commander.

The Amphibious Support Force of Rear Admiral William H. P. Blandy (TF 52), first of the American forces to arrive at the target, experienced serious setbacks and revisions during preparations. Task Force 52 was composed as follows:

> Gunfire and Covering Force (TF 54), RAdm Bertram J. Rodgers, USN.[95]
> Support Carrier Group (TG 52.2), RAdm Calvin T. Durgin, USN.
> Mine Group (TG 52.3), RAdm Alexander Sharp, USN.
> Underwater Demolition Group (TG 52.4), Capt B. Hall Hanlon, USN.
> Gunboat Support Units One and Two (TU's 52.5.1 and 52.5.2), Capt Theodore C. Aylward, USN.
> Air Support Control Unit (TU 52.10), Capt Elton C. Parker, USN.[96]

Late in January it became evident that certain major support vessels would not be ready in time to take part in the preparatory bombardment as planned. These ships still supported General MacArthur's forces in the Philippines and could not be released while needed

there. Others, damaged in recent operations, could not be repaired in time. Extensive changes in the gunfire support plan became necessary, and Navy commanders began scouring the Pacific ocean areas for replacement battleships and cruisers for Iwo. New schedules of ships' bombardment duties, based on a revised naval task organization, were ready by 28 January [97] and included the battleships *North Carolina* and *Washington* (BB's—new battleships). Admiral Spruance now indicated that

[95] Vessels of TF 54 were assigned to TF 52 for execution of shore bombardment at the objective. Gunfire and Covering Force (TF 54) Report of Operations of Task Force 54 in the Iwo Jima Campaign, 10Mar45, hereinafter cited at *TF 54 OpRpt.*

[96] Amphibious Support Force (TF 52) Action Report, Iwo Jima, 23Feb45, 3–4, hereinafter cited as *TF 52 SAR.*

[97] Heavy support vessels for this revised naval gunfire plan came from great distances and many stations. In November 1944, the *Nevada, Texas, Arkansas,* and *Tuscaloosa* reached the Pacific through the Panama Canal after supporting landings in North Africa, Normandy and Southern France. The *New York,* after supporting North African landings and operating on Atlantic convoy duty, also reached the Pacific by way of the Panama Canal in November and joined 5th Fleet units at Ulithi. The *Idaho* and *Tennessee* both joined Iwo Jima bombardment units directly from West Coast shipyards where each had undergone badly needed repairs after extensive prior Pacific operations. The *Vicksburg,* commissioned in June 1944, participated in her first combat operation at Iwo. The *Pensacola, Chester* and *Salt Lake City* (CruDiv 5, RAdm Allen E. Smith, USN) had been shelling Volcano-Bonin Islands intermittently since November 1944. Office of Naval Records and Library, Ships' Histories Branch, Navy Department, U. S. Navy Ships' Histories. Hereinafter cited as *Ships' Histories.*

these two heavy bombardment vessels with their powerful 16-inch guns would not arrive off the target until D-Day. A second revision of gunfire support plans now became necessary, and firing schedules and sector assignments were again altered.[98]

Other naval commands were also active toward the end of January in preparing to support the coming operation. At midnight, 26 January, Admiral Spruance relieved Admiral William F. Halsey at Ulithi, and the U. S. Third Fleet thereby became the Fifth Fleet. Concurrently, command of the Fast Carrier Force passed from Vice Admiral John S. McCain to Vice Admiral Marc A. Mitscher, and it became Task Force 58, soon to strike the Empire in support of the Marine attack in the Volcanos.[99]

Task Forces 52 and 54 arrived in the Marianas from Ulithi on 12 February and engaged in final rehearsals with the invasion fleet. Shore bombardment units left the Saipan-Tinian area on 14 February and arrived at the objective early in the morning of 16 February.[100]

The decision to limit pre-D-Day preparation fires to 3 days (16–18 February) imposed a tremendous task on the heavy support ships of Rear Admiral Bertram J. Rodgers' Naval Gunfire and Covering Force (TF 54). The mission of these vessels was to knock out or neutralize the most powerful and threatening enemy defense installations prior to D-Day. Target priorities for the preliminary bombardment were as follows:

Priority A—Installations that threatened ships, aircraft, and UDT operations (coast defense and antiaircraft guns, artillery emplacements, antitank guns).

Priority B—Installations threatening the Landing Force in the ship to shore movement (blockhouses, covered artillery, pillboxes, machine guns, command posts).

Priority C—Installations such as caves, ammunition and fuel dumps, bivouac areas.

Shore bombardment ships assumed the responsiblity for dealing with a total of 724 A and B priority targets. And the job would have to be accomplished by six old battleships, four heavy cruisers and one light cruiser.[101]

Admiral Blandy and a large staff, on board the *Estes* (AGC 12), controlled all activities at the target during the preassault period. Assisting the Amphibious Support Force commander at this time were Lieutenant Colonel Donald M. Weller, USMC, V Corps Naval Gunfire Officer; and Captain Elton C. Parker, USN, commanding the Air Support Control Unit of TF 52.[102]

Upon arrival at the objective, heavy support units came under direction of Admiral Blandy for shore bombardment. Firing commenced at 0800, with support vessels following mine sweepers that swept shoreward from the 100-fathom mark. Initial ranges for gunfire were therefore great, making airborne spotters and observers indispensable. All fire support units received orders to shell Iwo only when specific targets could be identified and impacts observed from the air.[103]

---

[98] *TF 52 SAR*, 3–4.

[99] Fast Carrier Force (TF 58) U. S., Fifth Fleet, Report of Combat Operations from 10Feb45 to 4Mar45, 13Mar45. The Fast Carrier Force was designated TF 38 when operating under the Third Fleet, and TF 58 while operating under Fifth Fleet command. This dual designation of TF 38/58 paralleled that of the Third and Fifth Fleets, of which Admiral Halsey later wrote, "Instead of the stagecoach system of keeping the drivers and changing the horses, we changed drivers and kept the horses." Fleet Admiral W. F. Halsey, USN, and Lieutenant Commander J. Bryan, III, USNR, *Admiral Halsey's Story*, (New York, 1947), 197, 247.

[100] *TF 54 OpRpt*, 6.

[101] *Tennessee, Idaho, Texas, New York, Nevada, Arkansas, Chester, Salt Lake City, Tuscaloosa, Pensacola, and Vicksburg.*

[102] *TF 52 SAR*, 11.

[103] Ltr Adm W. H. P. Blandy, (Ret), to CMC, 20Jan53; air observers from the 3d, 4th, and 5th MarDivs, assigned to fire support ships, spotted targets for Navy guns. Also, Navy VOC-1 (fighter-spotter squadron) flew from the CVE *Wake Island* to locate targets for TF 54. The Iwo operation saw the first employment of VOF (Navy fighter planes) aircraft for spotting assignments in the Pacific area. Organization of VOC-1 was prompted by experience in use of fighter-type planes for spotting during invasions of Africa, Sicily, and Italy. Composite Spotting Squadron One, Participation of VOC-1 in Iwo Jima Operation, 18Mar45, 1; Naval Gunfire Officer, Expeditionary Troops, Fifth Fleet, Report on Naval Gunfire Support in Operations Against Iwo Jima, 9Jun45, 2, hereinafter cited as *TF 56 Final NGF Rpt*.

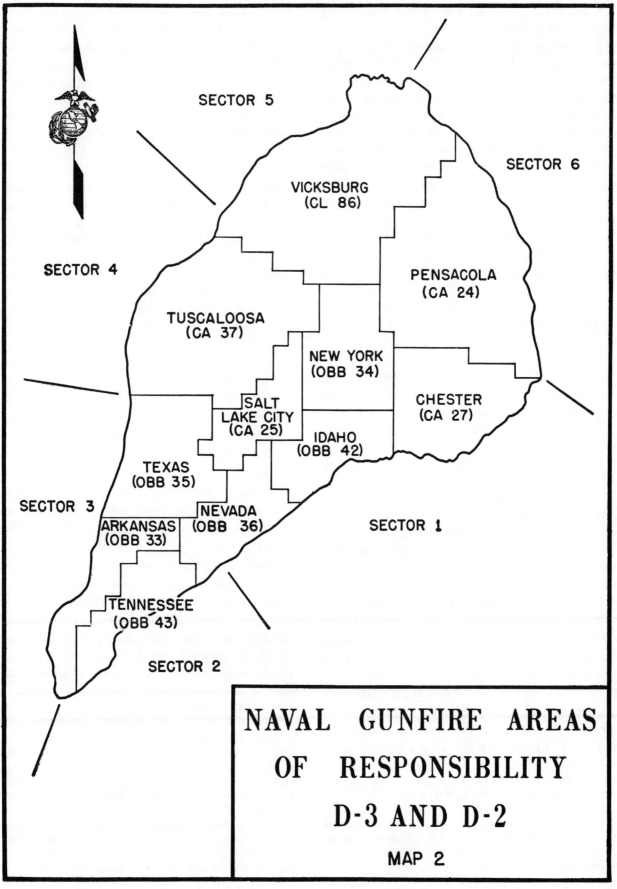

SECTOR 5

SECTOR 6

VICKSBURG
(CL 86)

SECTOR 4

PENSACOLA
(CA 24)

TUSCALOOSA
(CA 37)

NEW YORK
(OBB 34)

SALT
LAKE CITY
(CA 25)

CHESTER
(CA 27)

IDAHO
(OBB 42)

TEXAS
(OBB 35)

SECTOR 3

NEVADA
(OBB 36)

SECTOR 1

ARKANSAS
(OBB 33)

TENNESSEE
(OBB 43)

SECTOR 2

NAVAL GUNFIRE AREAS
OF RESPONSIBILITY
D-3 AND D-2

MAP 2

Observers and spotters found their task almost impossible because of a low ceiling that caused poor visibility. Planned firing schedules could not be carried out, and each ship fired in its assigned sector whenever the weather permitted.[104] During rare moments when Iwo became visible from the air, intensive antiaircraft fire forced United States observation planes to remain at altitudes above 3,000 feet, preventing accurate assessment of gunfire effects. At the end of firing on 16 February, damage to enemy installations appeared negligible.[105]

In spite of the unfavorable weather on D-minus 3, air operations continued, and a total of 158 sorties were flown that at least kept the enemy off balance. Airfield Number 1 was strafed and hit with rockets by eight Navy fighters. During periodic clearing of the skies carrier aircraft also managed to attack gun emplacements on Mount Suribachi. In the afternoon Army Air Force bombers arrived over Iwo but could not complete successful bomb runs because of the dense overcast.[106]

The bulk of the missions flown on 16 February were by Navy flyers from Rear Admiral Calvin T. Durgin's Support Carrier Group (TG 52.2). This included the escort carriers (CVE) *Sargent Bay*, *Natoma Bay*, *Wake Island*, *Petrof Bay*, *Steamer Bay*, *Makin Island*, *Lunga Point*, *Anzio*, *Bismarck Sea*, *Saginaw Bay*, *Rudyard Bay*. Until land-based aircraft could fly from Iwo airstrips, planes from these carriers would furnish nearly all the close air support for combat troops ashore.[107]

Simultaneous with the beginning of the Iwo bombardment on 16 February, Admiral Mitscher's Fast Carrier Force had smashed at the Tokyo area of Japan in a covering action to distract enemy attention from American forces attacking the Volcano-Bonins. This strike against the mainland continued through the 17th, when Mitscher withdrew his force

to a point from which its might could be brought to bear on Iwo Jima by 19 February.[108]

By morning of 17 February the weather had cleared and remained excellent throughout the day. At 0840 the *Nevada*, *Idaho*, and *Tennessee* moved in to 3,000 yards from shore to provide close support for the underwater demolition team operations scheduled to begin at 1100.[109] While UDT's awaited orders to head for the beach, the covering fire support vessels experienced stiff opposition from enemy shore batteries. At 0848 the *Tennessee* was hit and about an hour later the cruiser *Pensacola* rocked under the impact of several direct hits and near misses from heavy-caliber enemy shells. *Pensacola* suffered extensive damage and 115 casualties. Among the 17 killed was the ship's executive officer.[110]

At about 1045 the UDT swimmers headed toward the hostile island while LCI(G)'s covered their approach from positions 1,000 yards off shore flailing the beaches with rocket barrages and 40mm gunfire. Working under heavier mortar and small-arms fire than they had ever before experienced, these men proceeded with their assigned tasks in a "business as usual" manner. Their mission included checking beach and surf conditions, searching for obstacles on the beach, and in the water approaches. Obstacles were to be destroyed when found. Some of the swimmers actually crawled out of the water to collect soil samples for examination on board ship.[111]

As UDT men labored near the beaches, their 12 supporting LCI(G)'s ran into serious trouble. At about 1100 the gunboats suddenly began to receive extremely heavy fire from enemy mortars and previously hidden large-

---

[104] CominCh P–0012, 1–2.

[105] *TF 54 OpRpt*, 9; *VAC NGF Rpt*, 7.

[106] *TF 52 SAR*, Encl D, 3.

[107] USS *Makin Island* Action Report, Occupation of Iwo Jima, 10Feb45 to 11Mar45, undated; *Ships' Histories*, USS *Wake Island*, USS *Petrof Bay*, USS *Steamer Bay*.

[108] *TF 56 Air Rpt*, 2.

[109] *TF 52 SAR*, Encl (I), 1; *TF 54 OpRpt*, 10.

[110] *Ibid.* Damage to *Pensacola* included a burned observation plane, three compartments flooded, combat information center rendered inoperative, catapult damaged, one 5-inch gun out of action and sickbay flooded. This ship received six enemy shells, *TF 52 SAR*, 6–7, Pt G, 1.

[111] *TF 52 SAR*, Pt C, 1; Ltr Cdr D. L. Kauffman, USN, to author, 13Jan53. Cdr Kauffman commanded the UDT unit and served as chief of staff to Capt Hanlon, UDT Group Commander at Iwo Jima.

120MM GUN COMMANDING EASTERN BEACHES. This gun was knocked out prior to D-Day.

caliber fixed artillery.[112] Gunboat crews immediately answered these batteries with their own light armament, remaining on station until forced to retire by heavy casualties and severe

damage. Vessels most seriously hit withdrew and were replaced by others, thus maintaining constant 40mm fire on enemy batteries. In a 45-minute period beginning at 1100, nine of the 12 gunboats were put out of action and three less seriously damaged by Japanese shellfire.[113]

[112] An interesting opinion by a victim of these guns, who was brought aboard the *Nevada* from LCI(G) 441, throws some light on why the enemy revealed the location of his most powerful beach defenses prior to D-Day. His conclusions were that the guns opened fire as soon as rockets were launched and since this was the first time rockets were used in support of pre-D-Day UDT operations, the enemy assumed the reconnaissance to be an actual landing attempt. *TF 54 OpRpt*, 24.

[113] Damaged LCI(G)'s: 474, 441, 473, 438, 449, 457, 466, 471, 469, 450, 346, and 348. This LCI group suffered 170 casualties at Iwo—132 wounded and 38 killed in action. Shell fragments later recovered from these craft indicated that the heaviest enemy shore batteries firing on the group were guns of about 150mm. *TF 52 SAR*, Encl G, H. Of the officers commanding these 12 gunboats of LCI(G) Group

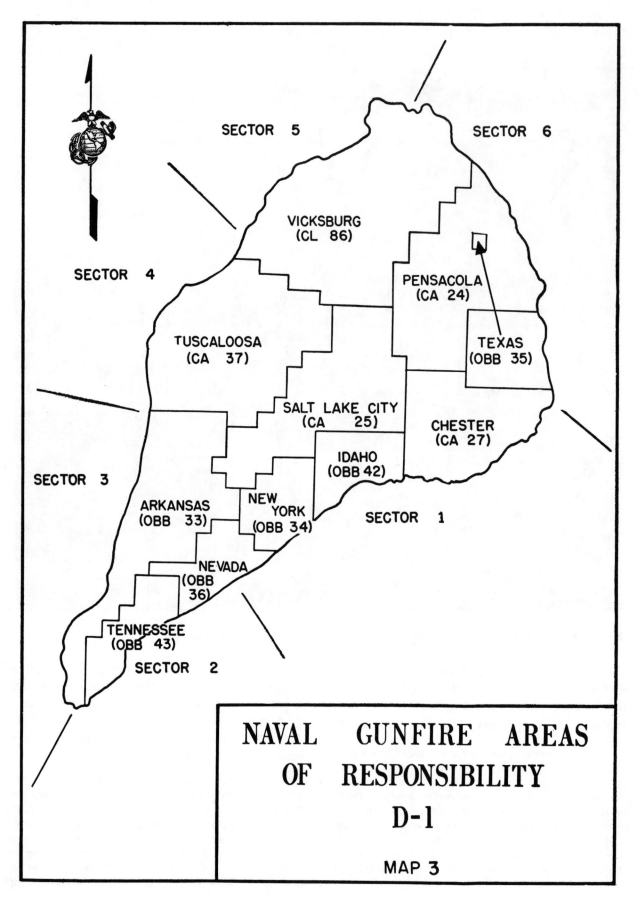

SECTOR 5

SECTOR 6

SECTOR 4

VICKSBURG
(CL 86)

PENSACOLA
(CA 24)

TUSCALOOSA
(CA 37)

TEXAS
(OBB 35)

SALT LAKE CITY
(CA 25)

CHESTER
(CA 27)

SECTOR 3

IDAHO
(OBB 42)

ARKANSAS
(OBB 33)

NEW
YORK
(OBB 34)

SECTOR 1

NEVADA
(OBB
36)

TENNESSEE
(OBB 43)

SECTOR 2

NAVAL GUNFIRE AREAS OF RESPONSIBILITY
D-1

MAP 3

The startling opposition offered by enemy guns did not long go unchallenged by large-caliber United States naval weapons. The old *Nevada*, standing close by to offer watchdog services during the beach reconnaissance, leveled powerful 14-inch rifles on these newly awakened shore batteries and continued heavy, concentrated counterbattery fire until 1240. To furnish much needed concealment to UDT's and stricken LCI(G)'s, the *Tennessee, Nevada,* and *Idaho* quickly put down a smoke screen along the entire eastern beach area. Under this protection and the additional covering fire of destroyers, the UDT's withdrew from the beach. By 1220 all members of these teams were recovered and back aboard their APD's (transport-destroyers) where they made their reports. Despite the continuous heavy opposition, they had suffered only one casualty.[114]

While elements of the four UDT's prepared to conduct a reconnaissance of west coast beaches during the afternoon of 17 February, heavy bombardment ships administered a thunderous pounding to top priority targets on the east coast. Ammunition allotments were revised upward by Admiral Blandy to permit heavier concentrations of fire on eastern beaches, and shells saturated the areas of recently revealed heavy Japanese coast-defense guns. Admiral Rodgers had recommended to Admiral Blandy that all available weapons now be employed in smashing top priority installations around Mount Suribachi and in the high ground north of the eastern beaches. Fire Support Units One and Two (including the *Nevada, Idaho, Tennessee, Vicksburg,* and *Salt Lake City*) executed close-range fire missions against these areas during the remainder of the day.[115]

The UDT examination of western beaches and their approaches, originally scheduled for 1500, did not begin until 1615 because of the unexpected opposition met off the eastern beaches earlier in the day. As during their morning activities, underwater demolition men worked under constant fire from Japanese automatic weapons and rifles.[116] At about 1800 the swimmers returned to their APD havens without incurring any casualties.

Results of the morning and afternoon reconnaissances were reassuring. Swimmers reported beach and surf conditions suitable for a landing on either the preferred or alternate beaches. No underwater or beach obstacles existed and the single mine found was destroyed.[117]

Reconnaissance company Marines (two officers and 20 enlisted men) from the two assault divisions accompanied UDT teams on both beach investigations and later reported to their units aboard command ships at sea. Three enlisted men from Company B, Amphibious Reconnaissance Battalion, Fleet Marine Force, served as observers during UDT operations. With information furnished by these Marines prior to 19 February, regimental and battalion commanders were acquainted with conditions existing on landing beaches assigned their units in the D-Day scheme of maneuver.[118]

Softening-up activities of aircraft on D-minus 2 accomplished considerably more than on the previous day. This second day of preliminary bombardment gave airmen perfect flying weather, and they took advantage of it by showering destruction on the island from sunrise to sunset. Carrier pilots flew a total of 226 sorties, excluding search and patrol missions. Flyers concentrated on dual-purpose guns and automatic antiaircraft weapons around the airfields, as well as both beach areas in support of UDT operations.

Eight Navy fighters dropped napalm with limited success during the day. Some of the napalm bombs did not release on the first attempts and several failed to ignite upon hitting

Eight, LCI(G) Flotilla Three, one received the Medal of Honor, ten received the Navy Cross, and the unit was awarded the Presidential Unit Citation for this action of 17 February. Navy Department Press and Radio Release, 5Sep45.

[114] *TF 54 OpRpt*, 10; *TF 52 SAR*, 7, Pt A, 38, Pt G, 2, Pt C, 4; *TF 51 Rpt*, Pt V, Pt G, 3, 5.

[115] *TF 54, OpRpt,* 10; *TF 51 OpPlan*, Change No Three, Annex H.

[116] *TF 51 Rpt* Pt V, G.

[117] *TF 52 SAR*, 7, 8.

[118] VAC Headquarters Commandant, Special Action Report, Iwo Jima Campaign, 30Mar45, Encl A; 4th MarDiv Support Group Rpt, Pt IV, 9; *5th MarDiv IntelRpt*, 34.

the ground. Planes also worked over pillboxes and strafed vehicles. Enemy opposition was intense all day, and heavy antiaircraft fire greeted 42 Army Air Force B–24's that arrived on station over Iwo. These craft dropped their bombs from 5,000 feet, achieving hits in the target area but actually inflicting no known damage to installations.[119]

The last day of preliminary naval gunfire bombardment began with the job far from finished. Negligible evidence of destruction wrought on enemy defenses during two days of bombardment suggested a modification of firing schedules and assignments. Accordingly, the V Corps Naval Gunfire Officer recommended that "a maximum concentration of bombardment be placed on and near the preferred landing beaches." This proposal received Admiral Blandy's immediate approval.[120]

A rearrangement of firing units now permitted four battleships and one heavy cruiser to concentrate their entire armament (5-, 8-, and 14-inch guns) in a blanket bombardment of landing areas (compare Maps 2 and 3). Ships received permission to fire all unexpended ammunition (less that needed for D-Day) weather allowing. Once more nature failed to cooperate during the softening phase. On D-minus 1 visibility was only fair with frequent light rains reducing it to poor.[121]

At 0745 Admiral Rodgers ordered his ships to "close beach and get going."[122] These units immediately moved in to within 2,500 yards of the shore (close range) and opened fire to commence the third day of bombardment. Admiral Blandy issued orders early in the day that the batteries nestled at the foot of Mount Suribachi must positively be destroyed. The same order applied to coast-defense guns emplaced on the rim of a quarry about 400 yards inland north of the East Boat Basin. The *Tennessee* and *Idaho* received this vital assignment. The *Tennessee* sent salvo after salvo into these positions for 4¾ hours, expending a total of 333 rounds.

The *Idaho*, not to be far outdone, fired a total of 280 rounds during the same period of time.[123]

Friendly aircraft again operated over Iwo Jima on D-minus 1 to assist the naval vessels in their all-out effort to prepare the island for assault the following day. As on the first day of preliminary fires, weather set the tempo of activity for carrier and land-based planes. In early afternoon Seventh Air Force bombers arrived over the island after a long trip from the Marianas, but the B–24's could just as well have remained grounded. Clouds effectively masked the objective and the strike was canceled. Navy flyers from Admiral Durgin's escort carriers directed 28 sorties against positions flanking the landing beaches.[124]

The last day of preparatory bombardment ended at 1821, 18 February, when close-range fires ceased along the east coast and heavy support ships moved out toward night deployment areas.[125] At 2130 the *Blessman* (APD 48), while en route to join her deployment unit for the night, received a bomb hit from a low-flying enemy plane; only one bomb, but it struck a vital area—the troop space above the forward fireroom. In addition to serious material damage, personnel loss was heavy and more tragic than usual. This vessel was carrying members of UDT 15 that had survived the hazardous beach reconnaissance missions of the previous day. Casualties included two killed and 20 wounded among UDT men. The *Blessman's* own crew suffered 11 wounded.[126]

Pre-H-Hour bombardment (D-Day fires in preparation for the landing) would give sup-

---

[119] *TF 52 SAR*, Encl I, 1.
[120] *VAC NGF Rpt*, 15; *TF 54 OpRpt*, 1.
[121] *VAC NGF Rpt*, 15.
[122] *TF 54 OpRpt* 11.

[123] *VAC NGF Rpt*, 15.
[124] During this 3-day period of activity carrier planes flew a total of 612 sorties against ground targets on Iwo Jima. Only three were lost to enemy ground fire, and the crewmen of these were rescued. *TF 52 SAR*, Encl D, 9.
[125] *TF 54 OpRpt*, 12.
[126] *TF 51 Rpt*, Pt IV, 13; *TF 52 SAR*, Encl H, 1. This attack on 18 Feb was the only raid by enemy aircraft to cause damage to American units at or near Iwo during the pre-D-Day operations. Other contacts resulted in the downing of one Zeke (single-engine Japanese fighter) over the island by an OS2U from the *Pensacola* (CA) at 0830 16 Feb, and destruction of one enemy twin-engine bomber by the antiaircraft guns of the *Halligan* (DD) on picket duty 80 miles north of Iwo. *TF 51 Rpt*, Pt IV, Sec B.

PRE-H-HOUR BOMBARDMENT pounds landing beaches and adjacent areas shrouding rest of island in smoke and dust (Navy Photo)

port ships another and final opportunity to pummel the enemy defenses before the assault. But the fact was that when heavy support units withdrew from Iwo the evening of 18 February, the softening-up phase had ended. At the close of this third day Admiral Blandy sent the following message to Admiral Turner:

> Though weather has not permitted complete expenditure of entire ammunition allowance and more installations can be found and destroyed with one more day of bombardment I believe landing can be accomplished tomorrow as scheduled if necessary. I recommend however special attention before and during landing to flanks and East Coast of island with neutralizing fire and white phosphorus projectiles immediately available if required. Amplifying report follows immediately.[127]

Admiral Turner deemed necessary the execution of assault plans without modification and D-Day for Iwo Jima remained 19 February 1945. The preliminary bombardment phase was finished.

Pre-H-Hour Bombardment

On the morning of D-Day emphasis shifted from painstaking fire for destruction to area neutralization and beach preparation. To accomplish this the heavy gunfire support ships were augmented by the gunboat and mortar support groups.[128] The big naval guns opened

up at 0640, having been reinforced by the 16-inch rifles on the *Washington* and *North Carolina*. Five minutes later nine LCI(R)'s commenced launching rockets toward the island. For the next 1½ hours the heavy support and rocket ships fired on targets of opportunity in assigned areas, giving priority to coast-defense and antiaircraft positions to cover the transports as they moved in to debarkation stations. The LCI(R)'s concentrated on the Motoyama Plateau throughout the morning, firing 9,500 5-inch spin-stabilized rockets into that heavily fortified area.

Other support craft added their weight to the bombardment at 0730, showering the slopes of Mount Suribachi and the high ground on the north flank of the beaches with rockets and mortar shells.

Between 0805 and 0825 (H-minus 55 to H-minus 35), while fire-support ships maneuvered into final positions, 120 fighter and bomber planes from Admiral Mitscher's Fast Carrier Force struck fiercely at the landing beaches and adjacent areas. When this air strike was completed, naval guns resumed firing.

Now the tempo increased, with neutralization of beaches as the primary mission. Initially, some air bursts were employed to cut down

---

[127] Message CTF 52 to CTF 51, NCR 60303, 18Feb45.

[128] This powerful flotilla of support craft totaled 42 vessels: 12 Landing Craft, Support (large) [LCS(L)'s] armed with 4.5-inch rockets and 40mm guns; three Landing Craft, Infantry (gunboat) [LCI(G)'s] with similar armament; 18 Landing Craft, Infantry (mortar ship) [LCI(M)'s] armed with 4.2-inch mortars; and nine Landing Craft, Infantry (rocket ship) [LCI(R)'s] armed with 5-inch rockets. *VAC NGF Rpt*, 25, 26.

defenders who might be in the open, but naval gunners shifted to impact rounds when troop-carrying LVT's passed through the line of firing ships stationed in the boat lanes. Rocket craft again seared landing areas, and the mortar boats shelled inland to a depth of about 1,000 yards. As assault troops neared shore, the naval bombardment shifted ahead and to the flanks and planes returned to give the beach a final pounding.

In previous Pacific assaults, naval gunfire had lifted too far inland when troops landed. The lack of adequate fires close to landing areas had resulted in heavy casualties early in the operation at Saipan. To correct this at Iwo a rolling barrage [129] technique was developed and used.

Five-inch batteries delivered this fire, maintaining a 400-yard margin of safety to the front of friendly troops by lifting inland in accordance with the best available estimate of troop advance. When the attack did not move forward as rapidly as expected, certain blocks (target areas) of prearranged fire were repeated.[130]

The effectiveness of preliminary bombardment remained little more than conjecture until after H-Hour. Even officers who conducted the softening-up attacks could not positively ascertain the amount of actual preassault damage inflicted on enemy defenses. Excellent camouflage plus unfavorable weather during most of the 3-day period seriously hampered all operations, including spotting and damage analysis. Naval commanders believed, however, that they had destroyed, or at least neutralized, enemy guns capable of placing observed fire on the eastern beaches and their seaward approaches.

[129] A true definition of the term rolling barrage, as used in WW I, is artillery fire in which the range increases regularly according to a definite time schedule. This schedule was adhered to rigidly and it was the responsibility of infantry commanders to keep their troops from advancing faster than the time allowed for lifting artillery fire to the next range. On Iwo Jima, however, although the fire was called a rolling barrage and set up on a time schedule, air observers reported troop progress and fire was adjusted in accordance with troop advances.

[130] VAC NGF Rpt. 23.

CHAPTER III D-Day—19 February 1945[1]

During the early morning hours of 19 February 1945, the assault shipping of Admiral Hill's Attack Force, carrying the 4th and 5th Marine Divisions, arrived off Iwo Jima and combined its huge convoy with Admiral Blandy's Amphibious Support Force, already lying close off the island's shores. As darkness gradually dissolved, the silhouettes over 450 ships of the United States mighty Fifth Fleet became sharpened in the dawn. This vast armada—larger than any ever before assembled for a Pacific operation—tended to dwarf the tiny island.

At 0640 guns of the heavy support ships boomed into action, and the pre-H-Hour bombardment got underway. Given this last chance to silence the heavy Japanese guns that dominated the boat lanes and beaches, gun crews turned-to with grim determination. The generally poor weather that had hampered the preliminary bombardment since D-minus 3 gave way to fair skies, unlimited visibility, and a gentle breeze from the north that did little more than ripple the surface of the placid sea.

As tons of hot, destructive steel tore into the island, LST's and transports eased slowly into assigned areas and made ready to disgorge their cargo of fighting men and machines. Bow doors yawned open and ramps dropped slowly to the water; APA's lowered landing craft, which circled monotonously as they waited to receive troops. On the tank decks of the LST's all was noisy activity as motors started and assault Marines clambered into their assigned LVT's to await the launching signal. This came at 0725, and 20 minutes later 482 amtracs that would carry eight battalions into battle were churning the water.

With only minor exceptions, all phases of pre-H-Hour preparation were going smoothly according to plan.[2] At 0805 naval guns lifted their fire as 72 fighter and bomber planes from Admiral Mitscher's Fast Carrier Force roared in to attack the eastern and northern slopes of Suribachi, the landing areas, and the menacing high ground on the north flank of the eastern beaches with rockets, bombs, and machine guns. Following on their heels, 48 additional fighters, including 24 Marine Corsairs (F4U's) led by Lieutenant Colonel William A. Millington, came in to ravage the same areas with napalm, more rockets, and machine-gun bursts. During these strikes gunfire support ships moved in closer and assumed the positions from which they would deliver final neutralization fires.

To the uninitiated spectator the scene may have appeared to be confusion unlimited. But

---

[1] Unless otherwise cited, material in this section is based on the following: *TF 51 Rpt; TF 53 OpRpt; TF 56 Air Rpt; TF 56 Preliminary NGF Rpt; 5th MarDiv SAR; 4th MarDiv OpRpt.*

[2] Only 15 of the 45 7th AAF heavy bombers were able to make their scheduled pre-H-hour strike, the remainder having been diverted or delayed because of bad weather between Iwo and the Marianas. *TF 56 Air Rpt, 2.*

TROOP-LADEN LVT'S churn shoreward under cover of intensive naval barrage. (Navy Photo)

observers on the command ships could see order emerging, and it was apparent that the 0900 H-Hour would be met. At 0830 the first wave (68 LVT(A)'s) crossed the line of departure and headed for shore behind gunboats that poured rockets and 40mm shells into the beach before turning right and left to positions from which they continued to support the flank battalions.

Thirty minutes were allotted for each assault wave to travel the 4,000 yards from the line of departure to the shore, and as hundreds of naval shells continued to pass overhead, successive waves crossed the line with 250 to 300 yards between them. Admiral Rodgers' battleships were now firing from close-in positions, and their devastating barrage smashed viciously at the eastern beaches to paralyze the enemy while Marines closed for action. At 0857, with the leading armored amphibs nearing their objective, naval gunfire shifted inland and to the flanks. Simultaneously, the planes returned, snarling down to strafe the beaches in a magnificent display of close support, continuing as the waves moved shoreward. Up from the south past Suribachi they roared, swooping low over the shore as they attacked,

then executed sweeping turns to the right to escape hostile ground fire. When the first LVT(A) hit the beach, the bullet impact area was shifted 500 yards inland.[3]

The LVT(A)'s of the first wave set their tracks down on Iwo Jima at 0902 and commenced grinding forward. They soon found, however, that the terrace immediately behind the beach (up to 15 feet high) masked the fires of many. Those that could not give effective support retracted from the beach and covered the landing of troops by engaging inland targets from the water. Three minutes later (0905) the second wave (first of the troop-carrying waves) waddled up out of the water, and as ramps were lowered all along the 3,500-yard strip of dark, repulsive looking beach, Marines of the 4th and 5th Divisions swarmed

[3] These were the same planes, led by LtCol Millington, that had executed the napalm and rocket strike against the beaches earlier. This low-level attack had been worked out by Millington with Col Vernon E. Megee, Commander of the Landing Force Air Support Control Unit and Deputy Commander, Aircraft, Landing Force. Sherrod, *History of Marine Corps Aviation in World War II* (Washington, 1952), 347, hereinafter cited as *Sherrod*.

out of their vehicles and hit the volcanic sand at a run that slowed almost immediately to a laborious walk as their feet sank ankle deep into soft, loose volcanic ash.

General Rockey's 5th Division and General Cates' 4th Division landed abreast on beaches Green, Red, Yellow, and Blue, each with two reinforced regiments in the assault. From left to right these were: 28th Marines (Colonel Harry B. Liversedge), 27th Marines (Colonel Thomas A. Wornham), 23d Marines (Colonel Walter W. Wensinger), and 25th Marines (Colonel John R. Lanigan). Still under cover of the naval barrage, these units hastily reorganized and commenced the inland push. During these first few minutes Japanese resistance was light. Both divisions reported only scattered mortar, artillery, and small-arms fire, and excepting a few land mines, no manmade obstacles were found on the beaches.

As the troops moved forward, stumbling and dragging themselves up the incline of the first terrace to clear the beach, some dared to entertain the optimistic thought that estimates of enemy strength had been considerably exaggerated or that the naval gunfire and air bombardment during the softening-up period had been even more effective than expected. As it turned out, however, the enemy garrison—even larger than intelligence reports indicated—was following General Kuribayashi's carefully made plan. During the terrific pre-H-Hour bombardment the Japanese defenders had waited in well-prepared underground positions, emerging only after the fire had lifted ahead of advancing troops. The beaches themselves were not heavily manned but enemy guns emplaced on Suribachi and in commanding positions on the northern plateau had been registered to execute prearranged fires on all landing beaches.

The enemy reacted quickly all along the line but particularly on the right, in the 4th Division zone of action. Beach Yellow 2 was subjected to moderate mortar fire within two minutes after the first wave landed, and by 0920 troops on both Yellow and Blue beaches were reporting heavy enemy fire. To the south, the 5th Division encountered lighter resistance initially, but by 0935 Green and Red beaches were under a brisk mortar barrage. As Marines advanced beyond

LVT'S pass through line of control craft on way to beach.

NAVAL GUNFIRE lifted inland and to the flanks as troops landed. Support ships can be seen in the foreground. (Navy Photo

protection of the first high terrace, they received intense machine-gun and rifle fire from well-concealed pillboxes, blockhouses, and caves.

Congestion along the shore mounted dangerously as LVT's and landing craft became casualties. Direct hits by mortars and artillery were not the only reasons for trouble on the beach. As jeeps and trucks rolled out of landing craft, they became bogged down in soft sand even before clearing the ramp. Unless a tractor was available to snake these vehicles free immediately, the small craft, with bow pinned to the beach, often broached and swamped, thus compounding the clutter at the water's edge. But, somehow, landings and the inland push continued. Confronted by stiffening resistance and mounting casualties, troop leaders led their men forward. Intrepid Navy coxswains continued to bring their craft in to the shore, skillfully maneuvering them into position. Many of those coxswains whose boats were hit, or had become stranded, immediately joined Marines ashore and assisted with any task necessary. By 1030, elements of all eight assault battalions were on the island. From left to right these were: 2/28, 1/28, 2/27, 1/27, 1/23, 2/23, 1/25, and 3/25.[4]

---

[4] These are abbreviated designations and will be used throughout this monograph. The battalion numeral precedes that of the regiment, i. e., 2d Battalion, 28th Marines is written 2/28.

MOUNT SURIBACHI ISOLATED [5]

On the corps' southern (left) flank the 28th Marines landed with the 1st and 2d Battalions in column. Lieutenant Colonel Jackson B. Butterfield's 1st Battalion, with Companies B and C abreast, led the way westward to clear the path so that the 2d Battalion could make a turn toward Suribachi after coming ashore.

The 2d Battalion, commanded by Lieutenant Colonel Chandler W. Johnson, started landing behind 1/28 at 0935 and attempted to move in off the beach in order to deploy facing Suribachi and cover the regiment's left flank. With heavy mortar and artillery fire now falling, companies had difficulty reorganizing as units became separated.

Although it was only 700 yards across this narrowest part of the island it soon became apparent that the drive to the opposite coast by 1/28 would be costly. The attack developed in such a manner that some elements were held up while others managed to slash through and con-

---

[5] Unless otherwise cited, material in this section is based on the following: 26th Marines, Action Report on Iwo Jima Operation, 20Apr45, hereinafter cited as *26th Mar SAR;* 27th Marines, Action Report on Iwo Jima Operation, 17Apr45, hereinafter cited as *27th Mar SAR;* 13th Marines, Action Report, Iwo Jima Campaign, 17Apr45, hereinafter cited as *13th Mar SAR;* 5th Tank Battalion, Action Report, Iwo Jima, 24Apr45, hereinafter cited as *5th TkBn SAR;* 5th MarDiv SAR; *28th Mar SAR;* 5th MarDiv War Diary, Feb45.

tinue westward. At 1035 a small group of men from Company B reached the western beach, followed soon after by Marines from Company C.

The island had been crossed, but bypassed enemy continued to resist fiercely. Company A, which had landed in 1/28 reserve and faced south to secure the battalion's left flank, was relieved by 2/28 and joined the rest of the 1st Battalion in mopping up. This battalion had become badly disorganized during its rapid advance and casualties were high. It was clear that another unit would have to be committed on the right of 2/28 facing south in order to launch an attack against Suribachi. Consequently, at 1039 General Rockey ordered Lieutenant Colonel Charles E. Shepard's 3/28, which had been division reserve, to revert to RCT 28 and land on order.

Shepard received the order to land his battalion at 1210, and ten minutes later his first boats crossed the line of departure headed for shore. Japanese shelling was furious during this landing, and 3/28 received many casualties and lost some of its equipment. All elements of the battalion were ashore by 1306, but, because of the volume of enemy fire, progress inland was very slow as Shepard struggled to get his units into position for the attack to the south. This assault by the 2d and 3d Battalions was scheduled to jump off at 1545, following a preparation by naval gunfire and air.

Meanwhile, Company C, 5th Tank Battalion, in direct support of RCT 28, was ordered to land. According to the scheme of maneuver, this company, composed of 14 Sherman tanks, two flame tanks, one tankdozer, and one retriever, was to land over Beach Red 1. How-

5TH DIVISION MARINES crawl slowly up the terrace of soft volcanic ash just in from Beach Red 1. Digging in was easy but forward progress difficult and tiring.

ever, Company A, supporting RCT 27, had landed earlier and reported that conditions were such that it was impracticable to bring tanks in on Red 1. Acting on this information, Lieutenant Colonel William R. Collins, commanding the 5th Tank Battalion, decided to send Company C in over Red 2, but officers on board the naval control vessels refused to permit this action. The tank battalion registered a protest and an argument ensued, but rather than waste time the tanks went ashore over Red 1 at 1130. They were then obliged to execute a lateral movement northward in order to find suitable routes of egress. Although soft soil, congestion, the steep terrace, and violent enemy fire combined to harass this operation, the company lost only one tank while getting off the beach.[6]

While two battalions attacked south, the 1st Battalion, with Company E attached, was to occupy recently won positions on the west coast and continue mopping up throughout the regimental zone. At about 1400, tanks of Company C crossed the shell-torn neck of Iwo to assist in these activities. Providentially, they arrived just when Colonel Butterfield's weary Marines were pinned down and receiving heavy casualties from enemy weapons still active in pillboxes and blockhouses bypassed during the morning.

Moving in single file to avoid enemy mine fields and obstructions, the column soon came under antitank fire, and four tanks received direct hits before the opposing gun could be located and silenced.[7] With this danger out of the way, armor and infantry cooperated in reducing enemy strong points. At 1600 the surviving Shermans commenced grinding their way toward the fighting fronts of the 2d and 3d Battalions, leaving the 1st Battalion engaged in preparations for its first night on Iwo Jima.

Colonel Shepard's attempts to get his 3d Battalion farther inland and in position to attack alongside the 2d Battalion proved futile. Very heavy enemy fire made movement almost impossible and it wasn't until late afternoon that the battalion was able to get on line in the center of RCT 28's zone of action. By that time it was too late to join the attack, and Shepard's men started digging in for the night with Company I on the left, G on the right, and H in reserve.

Colonel Johnson's 2d Battalion had been in position facing Suribachi since early afternoon, waiting for the southward push, but with the 3d Battalion unable to get on line, the 1545 attack was delayed. At 1645, however, 2/28, supported by tanks from Company C, jumped off without the 3d Battalion. Although 3/28 was now getting into position a gap developed as the 2d Battalion's right flank moved slowly ahead. By 1730 the assault had advanced only 150 yards toward the mountain and 2/28 had to relinquish even those slight gains when it withdrew to tie in with 3/28 for the night. The tanks, which had advanced about 200 yards, remained out in front to cover consolidation of the infantry's lines, and then they also moved back assuming positions 300 yards to the rear.

While RCT 28 was attacking over Green Beach, the 27th Marines landed on the 1,000-yard strip of beach designated as Red 1 and Red 2, with 2/27 and 1/27 abreast. Major John W. Antonelli's 2d Battalion, on the left, hit the beach with Companies E and F in the assault and after a hasty reorganization pushed inland against scattered resistance. The 1st Battalion, commanded by Lieutenant Colonel John A. Butler, encountered the same light opposition, and Company C, on the left, was able to make good initial progress. But the amtracs carrying Company B landed some 200 to 300 yards to the left of their assigned positions, and confusion and delay in reorganization resulted.

Although individuals and small units of misplaced Company B acted independently to move

---

[6] Other supporting arms units were not so fortunate. The regimental rocket section of RCT 28 landed during D-Day morning. Three of the four truck-mounted rocket launchers were smashed by enemy artillery fire immediately after landing, but the remaining launcher fired one ripple into the near slopes of Mount Suribachi that caused a terrific explosion. This was the only bright note on D-Day; it brought loud cheers from all Marines in the area. Ltr LtCol O. F. Peatross to CMC, 23Dec52.

[7] Two of these tanks received penetrations through the turret, wounding three crewmen in each, and a third was put out of action when a shell damaged, but did not go through the turret. *5th TkBn SAR*, Encl C, 1.

RESERVE UNITS reorganize quickly and move inland. LVT(A) stands by to give fire support with its 75mm and machine guns.

to the right into their proper company zone of action, it became clear by 1030 that they could not advance along with Company C. To maintain the forward momentum, the battalion reserve, Company A, was ordered to attack on the right while Company B reorganized.

Both battalions advanced rapidly despite mounting casualties bypassing many positions along the way. By 1130 Company A was infiltrating across the southern end of the airfield and building up along the western edge. Company C, on the left, had passed the field and held a line that extended about 250 yards in a northwesterly direction from the southwest end of the field. The 2d Battalion was generally abreast, with Company F maintaining contact with 1/27 on the right. Among the casualties at this time was the regimental executive officer, Colonel Louis C. Plain. While in the front lines he was hit in the arm, but continued his inspection and made his report before being evacuated.[8]

Anxious to push the attack, General Schmidt sent a message to the 5th Division at 1102, or-

dering it to exploit any weak points. At 1133 General Rockey passed this word along to both assault regiments,[9] and the 27th Marines continued to attack. The 1st Battalion, supported by tanks from the 3d Platoon, Company A, turned north against determined enemy opposition, while the 2d Battalion, with the 1st and 2d Platoons of tanks, drove to the west.[10] Aided by this armor, the Marines were able to reduce positions that had been stubbornly resisting, but the presence of the Shermans in the front lines attracted heavy Japanese anti-tank fire, which plagued the infantry. The 1st Battalion made little progress to the north but the 2d pushed on and reached the cliffs overlooking the west coast at about 1500. The 3d Battalion, commanded by Lieutenant Colonel

---

[8] H. M. Conner, *The Spearhead, The World War II History of the 5th Marine Division* (Washington, 1950), 54.

[9] Disp VAC to 5th MarDiv, 1102, 19Feb45; Messages, 5th MarDiv to RCT's 27 and 28, Nos. 25 and 26, 19Feb45.

[10] These tanks from Company A, 5th TkBn, were the first ashore at Iwo. Following closely behind the assault battalions, they landed on the Red Beaches at 0925, and although enemy shelling did not interfere with their movement, the sand did. Four tanks broke tracks and one was drowned out before they found an exit from the beach and headed for Airfield No. 1 to support RCT 27.

Donn J. Robertson, landed in RCT reserve at 1130 and followed 2/27 at 200 yards mopping up bypassed positions.

Lieutenant Colonel Daniel C. Pollock's 1st Battalion, 26th Marines, in division reserve, completed landing operations at 1500 and went into an assembly area about 300 yards inland from Red 1. At 1502 this battalion was attached to the 27th Marines and ordered into defensive positions behind 2/27.[11]

Company B, 5th Tank Battalion had been held offshore waiting for tanks of Company C to clear Red 1, but at 1300 it began landing. Beset by the same difficulties that had delayed their predecessors, these tanks took a long time getting off the beach, and it was 1600 before they reached the other side of the island to join RCT 27.

At 1744, when General Rockey ordered his regiments to consolidate,[12] the 0–1 line was still far distant, but the 5th Division was now firmly established ashore. With Mount Suribachi isolated from the rest of the island, the 28th Marines faced south from a line across Iwo's narrow waist, ready to resume the offensive in the morning. The 27th Marines had also advanced to the western shore, and held positions from which it could launch the drive northward up the coast.

26th AND 13th MARINES LAND

The 26th Marines spent most of D-Day waiting to land. At 0955 General Schmidt released Colonel Chester B. Graham's RCT 26 (less the 1st Battalion) to its parent 5th Division, and the 21st Marines, 3d Marine Division, newly arrived in the transport area, became corps reserve. This shift gave General Rockey the full strength of his division early on D-Day and at the same time reconstituted the corps reserve. In anticipation of early release, the 26th Marines commenced boating vehicles and other heavy equipment at 0750, and at 1106

received word to proceed to the line of departure. But because of crowded conditions on the beaches and limited space inland, it was after 1500 when Graham was directed to land his battalions. Crossing over Red 1 a battalion at a time, RCT 26 completed its landing at 1732, and moved into an assembly area along the southern tip of Airfield Number 1, where it took up defensive positions.

Also waiting to land were the four battalions of Colonel James D. Waller's 13th Marines (artillery). Reconnaissance parties had gone ashore as early as 1030 only to find that the previously selected battery positions were still in enemy hands. As those areas were uncovered by the advancing infantry the division artillery officer ordered his battalions to land. The first elements of Lieutenant Colonel Henry T. Waller's 3d Battalion crossed the beach at 1400, followed by Major Carl W. Hjerpe's 2d Battalion at 1430; the 1st, commanded by Lieutenant Colonel John S. Oldfield, at 1645; and the 4th Battalion, under Major James F. Coady, at 1930.

DUKW's of the 5th (Marine) and 471st (Army) Amphibian Truck Companies, which carried these units, had difficulty negotiating the deep sand and were unable to climb the steep incline behind the beaches unless towed by bulldozers or LVT's.

The first battalion ashore (3/13) went into position on the north end of Beach Green, and, since it did not have to struggle far inland, was able to fire before any of the others. Within 20 minutes after landing one section of the 105mm's was registered, and by 1745 all pieces were emplaced and ready to support RCT 28.

The 2d Battalion attempted to land on Red 2, but because of a terrific barrage that hit just as the first DUKW's reached the water's edge, the battalion commander ordered the rest to land on Red 1. As the trucks crawled out of the water their wheels sank in the soft sand and all progress stopped. But bulldozers of the 5th Engineer Battalion, standing by on the beach, snaked them out of trouble. This operation was carried out repeatedly, with each individual vehicle being hauled clear of the beach to a firing position or a point from which it could advance inland under its own power.

---

[11] Although ordered to back up 2/27, elements of 1/26 actually held front line positions on the extreme left of 2/27 and assisted in closing a gap between RCT's 27 and 28 during the night of 19/20Feb45. Ltr LtCol D. C. Pollock to CMC, 8Dec52, hereinafter cited as *Pollock.*

[12] 5th MarDiv D–3 Journal, Iwo Jima.

Battery E, the last to make shore, was unable to occupy its position until 0200 the next morning because its DUKW's were under constant pounding by the enemy. One of its 105mm howitzers was destroyed by fire and another slightly damaged during this period.

The 1st Battalion, in direct support of RCT 27, landed its first 75mm pack howitzer at 1645 and encountered the same adverse beach conditions that had made progress so difficult for preceding units. But within the first hour after reaching shore Battery B was in position ready to fire, and the entire battalion was set up for action by 2245.

There had been a definite reason for assigning this battalion in direct support of the 27th Marines for early operations ashore. The 75-mm pack howitzers could be manhandled into firing positions if the DUKW's carrying them became stuck. On the other hand, 105mm howitzers would be dependent upon tractors to extricate them. In spite of difficulties, however, it was not necessary to unload any of the 75's before they reached their positions because tractors were made available on the beach to haul the amphibious trucks clear of the terrace.

The 4th Battalion, in general support, was given last priority in going ashore. Its howitzers arrived at the beach between 1930 and 2030 and had to be hauled across the sand and up the incline in the same laborious manner as the others. Darkness and enemy fire seriously interfered with the work. Three DUKW's swamped in the darkness while waiting to be pulled out of the water, and two pieces as well as valuable communications gear were lost as a

JUST IN FROM BEACH BLUE 1 4th Division Marines watch their tanks (just below horizon) heading north toward Blue 2.

FLAME THROWERS go into action early as Marines burn their way to Number 1 airfield. Sand-covered bunkers such as one pictured here were hard to locate and destroy during preliminary bombardment. (Navy Photo)

result. Eight howitzers had been emplaced by 0400 on D-plus 1, but five vehicles carrying the two remaining 105's and some other equipment did not make it to the position area until 0800 because the road became blocked by crippled LVT's.

NARROW BEACHHEAD [13]

While the 5th Division struggled to cut across Iwo in the south, General Cates' 4th Division landed on Beaches Yellow 1 and 2 and Blue 1, and began its drive toward 0–1. In the 23d Marines' zone of action Lieutenant Colonel Ralph Haas' 1st Battalion landed over Yellow 1 with Company B on the left, Company A on the right, and C in reserve. The landing and initial advance were accomplished easily, but upon reaching the second terrace the two as-

sault companies came under heavy and accurate fire. Advancing through this, 1/23 gained 250 yards by 0930, but a devastating barrage from Airfield Number 1 blunted the attack.

On Haas' right, Major Robert H. Davidson's 2d Battalion made similar gains with Company E on the left and F on the right, but was slowed by the same deadly fire. With both battalions meeting increasingly stubborn resistance from pillboxes to their front and flanks, it became obvious that tanks were needed ashore.

Upon early requests from both infantry battalion commanders, Company C, from Lieutenant Colonel Richard K. Schmidt's 4th Tank Battalion, was dispatched from the line of departure at 0948, and three LSM's carrying 16 tanks hit the Yellow Beaches at 1005. The first tank off LSM 216 bogged down less than five feet from the ramp's end, blocking the remaining four tanks in that vessel.[14] The other LSM's

[13] Unless otherwise cited, material in this section is based on the following: 23d Marines, Operation Report, Iwo Jima, 9Apr45, hereinafter cited as *23d Mar OpRpt*; 24th Marines, Final Report on Iwo Jima Operation, 20Apr45, hereinafter cited as *24th Mar OpRpt*; 25th Marines, Operation Report, Iwo Jima, 15Apr45, hereinafter cited as *25th Mar OpRpt*; 4th Tank Battalion, Operation Report, Iwo Jima, 18Apr45, hereinafter cited as *4th TkBn OpRpt*.

[14] LSM 216 continued to have a hard time getting rid of its valuable cargo. After the first abortive attempt it retracted and beached again about 200 yards to the south where a foot reconnaissance showed that tanks would also bog down. The LSM, in the meantime, had broached on the beach and it took 30 minutes for it to retract the second time. At 1245 it beached on Yellow

discharged their loads successfully, but three of these tanks struck mines less than 150 yards in from the water. Grinding through loose ash and many shellholes, the remaining vehicles commenced their search for 1/23, but progress was slow and it became apparent that front line Marines would not get tank support for some time.

RCT 23, nevertheless, fought forward through the murderous hail of shells and small-arms fire, and though casualties mounted steadily with every yard gained, 1/23 was 500 yards inland by 1200; 200 yards short of Airfield Number 1. The 2d Battalion, having a rougher time, was about 100 yards less advanced and needed help.

At this juncture, Colonel Wensinger decided to bring in his reserve battalion, 3/23, (Major James S. Scales). At 1300 Scales was ordered to land his units along Beach Yellow 1, move inland about 200 yards, and support the 2d Battalion's attack with 81mm mortars. The battalion met intense mortar and artillery fire, but fortunately very few rounds fell in the water and none of the landing craft suffered hits while approaching the beach. Once ashore, however, the heavy pounding caused casualties and serious disorganization.

Supported by tanks that finally made their way to the front, the left flank of 1/23 reached the airfield at 1405, but intense antitank fire caused the tanks to make a quick withdrawal behind the revetted edge of the field. Thirty minutes later, in order to get 3/23 clear of the beaches, Colonel Wensinger ordered it to pass through 1/23 and continue the attack across the airfield. In spite of casualties and confusion on the beach, the 3d Battalion pressed forward, and, after some difficulty locating the front lines and flanks of adjacent units, passed through the 1st Battalion. By 1700 3/23 had completed the seizure of the near edges of the airfield and shortly thereafter consolidated for the night.

In the 2d Battalion's zone of action the soft volcanic ash combined with mines and enemy gunners to prevent the movement of tanks, and the infantry had to go it alone. At 1500 an attempt was made to move Companies E and F laterally northward around the strong point that had been holding them up since noontime. This maneuver, executed in the face of fierce resistance, became confused and disorganized, but by 1730 Company F, on the right, succeeded in reaching Airfield Number 1.

While the 23d Marines battled toward the airfield, General Cates at 1405 ordered ashore the 1st and 2d Battalions of Colonel Walter I. Jordan's 24th Marines, the division reserve. These battalions would be attached to RCT's 25 and 23, respectively, upon landing but could not be committed without clearance from division. At 1615 Lieutenant Colonel Richard Rothwell's 2d Battalion received orders to land over Beach Yellow 2 and relieve hard-pressed 2/23. The first wave crossed the line of departure at 1620 and half an hour later the entire battalion was ashore. Reorganizing rapidly after landing, 2/24 quickly moved inland about 700 yards to the front line, relieved 2/23 by 1800, and dug in for night defense just short of the airfield, holding the line between 3/23 and 1/25.

To solve the problem presented by the high ground of the quarry cliff line that dominated the Blue Beaches, Colonel John R. Lanigan's 25th Marines landed two battalions abreast over Beach Blue 1 and the southern edge of Blue 2. The regiment then attacked on a two-direction front. The 1st Battalion, on the left, struck directly inland, while the 3d Battalion drove to the right (northeast) to clear the remainder of Beach Blue 2 and envelop the threatening quarry area.

By 1130 Lieutenant Colonel Hollis U. Mustain's 1st Battalion had pressed forward about 600 yards and was abreast of the line of the airfield extended (northeast end of northeast-southwest strip). At this point Company B, on the right, began to turn for an attack to the north, but Company A, on the left, was unable to make a similar turn because to do so would have opened a dangerous gap between the 1st Battalion and 2/23 (the right flank unit of the 23d Marines). As a result, the 1st Battalion front began to spread, and Colonel Mustain ordered Company C to fill any holes that might

1, but the sand was too soft, so it withdrew for the third time, and at 1300 made a final try and was successful in discharging its vehicles.

develop. The turning movement was completed at 1330, and Company B occupied positions on the high ground east of the airfield facing generally north.

The 3d Battalion landed in a column of companies with Company I in the lead, K and L following. Company L and units of the battalion headquarters landed about 200 yards out of position to the south and became intermingled with 1/25, making reorganization on the beach difficult. Well-placed enemy fire added to the problem as men sought shelter in large bomb craters along the shore. Casualties, particularly among officers, aggravated the situation: Company K lost eight officers by 1530, Company I lost six by 1700, and Company L lost five by 1630.[15]

The tanks of Company A, 4th Tank Battalion attached to 3/25 began landing on Beach Blue 1 at 1020 and immediately became priority targets for mortars, artillery, and antitank weapons. The fire they drew made the situation even more miserable for men of 3/25 as they struggled to organize and move out in the assault. All three of the tank landing ships were hit and damaged [16] while unloading, but were able to retract from the beach and withdraw after all tanks had cleared. The tank dozer cut a road through the first terrace inland from Beach Blue 1 but was completely destroyed when it hit a large horned mine and became the helpless target for three large caliber shells. The rest of the tanks left the beach in column, picking their way slowly through the shell holes until, after proceeding about 100 yards, they ran into a mine field where they halted. From these positions they supported the infantry with their 75's, engaging the enemy in the cliffs to the north and pillboxes behind the beach while engineers attempted to clear the mine field.

---

[15] Ltr Col J. M. Chambers to CMC, 5Nov52.

[16] Marines had high praise for the crews of the LSM's that landed tanks on Beaches Yellow and Blue so soon after H-Hour. The division operation report takes special note of the ". . . high degree of courage and tenacity shown by these ships in beaching and accomplishing the landing of this vital equipment in the face of the heaviest enemy mortar and artillery fire yet seen in any operation." *4th MarDiv OpRpt*, Sec III, 8–9.

Advancing slowly against withering small-arms and machine-gun fire from the front and flanks, and under a relentless mortar barrage, Lieutenant Colonel Justice M. Chambers' 3d Battalion broke contact with 1/25 on its left. Company I was moving northeast along the beach with K and L extending the battalion front inland, but by noon a gap of 100 yards had developed between 3/25 and 1/25. Colonel Lanigan now decided to commit at least a part of his reserve battalion to help seize the high ground to the northeast of the regimental beach.

In view of the gap that existed between his two assault battalions, he directed 2/25, the reserve battalion, to land on Beach Blue 1 and attack in a column of companies astride the boundary between the 1st and 3d Battalions to take the high ground northwest of the quarry. The 2d Battalion, commanded by Lieutenant Colonel Lewis C. Hudson, landed at 1250 and moved into an assembly area about 300 yards in from Blue 1, and Company E prepared to take up a position between 1/25 and 3/25.

At 1400, RCT 25 launched a coordinated attack to the north. The 3d Battalion advanced about 200 yards along the beach and toward the quarry in the first hour and 45 minutes of this attack, but on its left Company E, 2/25 and Company B, 1/25 gained only a temporary 100 yards, which they had to relinquish after coming under intense small-arms fire. At 1630 Company L received orders to take the ridge line to its front, which included the quarry area. Company K, in reserve, was to favor the left and maintain contact with 2/25. Company I would continue along the beach in the area of the East Boat Basin. The 2d Battalion at this time committed two fresh companies; Company F passed through Company E, and G moved up on the left. The objective was that portion of the ridge line northwest of the troublesome quarry. By 1745, 2/25 had gained the high ground, and L/3/25 reached the top of the quarry at about 1830. Contact between the two battalions, lost during the attack, was reestablished at 1900.

Colonel Lanigan joined his advance CP group (established ashore at 1530) at about 1700 and set about strengthening positions for the night. He requested permission to commit one

BULLDOZER HAULS DUKW up onto beach. This was only one of the yeoman services performed along the shore by the invaluable dozers. DUKW pictured here is equipped with an A-Frame.

company of the 1st Battalion, 24th Marines (Major Paul S. Treitel), which completed landing by 1700. With permission granted, Company B was ordered to relieve Company L, 3/25 on position.[17]

This relief commenced at 1845, but when Lieutenant Colonel Chambers reported that the frontline strength of 3/25 was down to 150 Ma-

---

[17] 1/24 landed amid much confusion on beaches Yellow 2 and Blue 1. Upon receiving word to send one company to reinforce 3/25 the 1/24 commander ordered that Company A be dispatched. But, because of the confusion on the beaches, A/1/24 could not be located immediately and B/1/24 was ordered to report to 3/25. Company B proceeded to relieve L/3/25 in position atop the quarry, positions very lightly held by a handful of Marines. Company A, 1/24, reported to RCT 25 later and joined 3/25 prior to 2100. Ltr from LtCol H. C. Parks to CMC, 2Dec52; *24th Mar OpRpt*, 120.

rines, Colonel Lanigan requested the use of another company to beef up the right flank of his regimental line. In response, division ordered 1/24 to attach another company to 3/25, and at 2030 Company A started moving into the lines. The remaining company of the 1st Battalion took up a defensive position to the rear of 2/25. Relief of Chambers' battalion, executed after dark, and under sporadic enemy fire, was not completed until 2330, when the remnants of 3/25 pulled back and dug in behind 1/24.

The last battalion of RCT 24 (3/24, Lieutenant Colonel Alexander A. Vandegrift, Jr.) had landed by 1900 and moved to positions a short distance inland from Beach Blue 2. The 4th Division now had all infantry battalions ashore and prepared for a possible enemy counterattack. Although the D-Day penetration by the division was not as great as planned, by nightfall front lines included the eastern edge of the airfield and were of sufficient depth inland from the Blue Beaches to guarantee the successful holding of the beachhead.[18]

14th MARINES LAND[19]

The artillery regiment of the 4th Division, Colonel Louis G. DeHaven's 14th Marines, could furnish little assistance during the violent struggle of this first day of assault. By the time the 1st and 2d Battalions were ashore and ready to fire the division was consolidating for the night defense. The 3d and 4th Battalions, except for reconnaissance parties, did not land until the next day (D-plus 1).

Reconnaissance parties from the artillery battalions went ashore in the early afternoon to select positions for their batteries, but they encountered the same difficulties that faced the artillerymen of the 13th Marines on the beaches to the south: front lines had not advanced beyond the preselected position areas, nor had routes been cleared to permit DUKW's to carry artillery pieces inland from the beaches. Heavy enemy fire caused casualties among the men of these reconnaissance teams, one of the first being Lieutenant Colonel Robert E. McFarlane, commanding officer of the 3d Battalion.[20]

At 1405 the division ordered Colonel De-Haven to land his two direct support artillery battalions regardless of beach conditions: 1/14, Major John B. Edgar, Jr., in direct support of RCT 25; and 2/14, Major Clifford B. Drake, in direct support of RCT 23. When DUKW's of the 4th Amphibian Truck Company, carrying the 75mm Pack Howitzers of the 1st Battalion, hit Beach Blue 1 they bogged down immediately and even heavy tractors strained to pull them up the steep beach.[21] However, by unloading the vehicles where they stopped and manhandling the weapons into position, the 1st Battalion was able to get 11 howitzers set up by 1715.[22]

In the meantime, communication had been established with the forward observers and registration firing was underway. The difficulty in locating features on maps that could be identified on the ground made selection of registration points difficult, but by 1745 all batteries were ready to execute fire missions in support of the 25th Marines.

The 2d Battalion, landing on Yellow 1 with the heavier 105mm howitzers, could not solve its problems by manhandling weapons as 1/14 had done. Each howitzer had to ride to its position in the DUKW that brought it ashore. It was a long, grueling struggle to coax, push, and pull the vehicles out of the water and up over the terrace dunes. Only one amphibian truck at a time could land because of beach and surf conditions that combined to stall and almost halt forward movement of these usually versatile and dependable vehicles. Amazingly, none of them was hit, but the crews suffered casualties from near misses. After hours of unceasing efforts this battalion had moved its 12 pieces into position on the first terrace at the right flank of Beach Yellow 1 and was ready to fire.

The 3d Battalion, now commanded by Major Harvey A. Feehan, received orders to launch its DUKW's at 1505, and the first vehicle left the ramp at 1510. But failure of some of the DUKW's to start held up the operation, and it was 1630 before all trucks were in the water. By that time the situation ashore was such that

---

[18] *4th MarDiv OpRpt*, Sec III, 11, Sec IV, 3.

[19] Unless otherwise cited, material in this section is based on the following: 14th Marines, Operation Report, Iwo Jima, 13Apr45, Appendices 1–8. Hereinafter cited as *14th Mar OpRpt*.

[20] Shortly after this the fire on the beach became so heavy that when the regimental commander ordered the 3d Battalion's reconnaissance party back aboard the control ship the men were unable to get off the beach to comply. *14th Mar OpRpt*, Appendix 3, 9.

[21] In almost all cases beaches were too steep and soft for DUKW's and they had to be unloaded just clear of the surf. When tractors were immediately available, the amphibian trucks could be towed out of the water. But if there were as much as five minutes delay, they settled in the sand, filled with water, and nothing could pull them out. In one case during D-Day, two tractors and an LVT were hooked to a foundered DUKW, but only succeeded in pulling off the towing shackles. *14th Mar OpRpt*, Appendix 6, 3.

[22] One howitzer was lost when the DUKW in which it was loaded sank immediately after being discharged from the LST. *Ibid.*, 2.

the regimental commander saw that it would be impracticable to land his 3d and 4th Battalions, so he ordered 3/14 to reembark on board the LST.[23]

After ordering his 3d Battalion to land, Colonel DeHaven had ordered his CP on board the *Hendry* (APA 118) to move ashore. Upon receiving word that no more artillery could be landed that day, the command group, under Lieutenant Colonel Randall M. Victory, held up at LST 763 and operated from there until the following day.[24] Lieutenant Colonel Carl A. Youngdale's 4th Battalion spent the entire day on board its LST, and although not engaged with the enemy, suffered six casualties, including one man killed from enemy shells falling in the transport area.

DARKNESS D-DAY

D-Day at Iwo Jima had been an uneven struggle with advantage of terrain and troop disposition heavily in favor of the defenders. While the Marines battled to bring their mechanized equipment ashore across the difficult beach, Japanese gunners poured death and destruction on them from the high ground on both flanks. To enlarge their beachhead and close with this hard-fighting enemy, the Marines were forced to advance over open ground while subjected to a terrific pounding from positions that were difficult to locate and so well protected that naval gunfire and air support units could do little to silence them.

In the face of these tremendous obstacles, D-Day advances fell far short of the 0–1 objective, but by the end of the day six infantry regiments, an equal number of artillery battalions, and the two tank battalions had landed and were disposed for the defense of the narrow beachhead against the expected night counter-

attack.[25] Units were tied in with physical contact all along the corps' front except for two small gaps. One of these weak points was between RCT 23 and RCT 25 at the end of the northeast-southwest runway of the airfield where a 75-yard break existed. The other was created by a small pocket of Japanese entrenched on the edge of the airfield where a turning circle bulged out into the 23d Marines' zone. Both these areas were well covered by fire and observation.[26] (See Map 4.)

As it turned out the Japanese did not launch any large-scale counterattacks, and infantry action was limited to attempts at infiltration. At 2315 the 1st Battalion, 28th Marines repulsed an attempted barge landing on the west coast, killing 25 of the enemy,[27] and RCT 27 reported a counterattack developing 500 yards in front of 1/27 at 0345. The 1st and 2d Battalions of the 13th Marines took this enemy force under fire and dispersed it.[28]

Although enemy infantry remained strangely quiet this first night on Iwo, Japanese mortars and artillery pounded Marine lines relentlessly all along the front. Combat teams of the 4th Division in particular took serious losses. Hardest hit was the 1st Battalion, 23d. The commanding officer, Lieutenant Colonel Ralph Haas, and his operations officer were killed by artillery rounds falling in one of two large shellholes on the beach that served as the CP. The personnel officer received serious wounds and other staff members lesser injuries from this same blast. In an identical shell crater nearby, the executive officer, Lieutenant Colonel

---

[23] During this reembarkation one howitzer and DUKW were lost when the truck's motor failed as it started back up the ramp. *14th Mar OpRpt*, Appendix 3, 9.

[24] Colonel DeHaven, as division artillery officer, operated from the 4th Division Command Post on board the *Bayfield* (APA 33). The command group of the 14th Marines, under LtCol R. M. Victory (the executive officer), was embarked in the *Hendry*. Ltr LtCol R. M. Victory to CMC, 11Dec52.

[25] The belief was generally held that the Japanese would attack the beachhead on this its most vulnerable night. After noting that few enemy dead had been seen during the day, and that the enemy was known to have a large reserve force of infantry and tanks available for counterattack, the Corps Intelligence Officer listed this as the most probable course of action for Kuribayashi to take. VAC G–2 Periodic Report No. 1, 19Feb45, hereinafter cited as *G–2 Periodic Rpt*.

[26] *25th Mar OpRpt*, Appendix VI, 11; *5th MarDiv SAR* Annex F; 5th Shore Party Regiment Action Report, Iwo Jima, Sec. III, 12, hereinafter cited as *5th Shore Party Rpt*.

[27] TF 56 G–3 Journal 1800, 19Feb45 to 1800, 20Feb45.

[28] *Ibid.*; *13th Mar SAR*, Sec. II, 11.

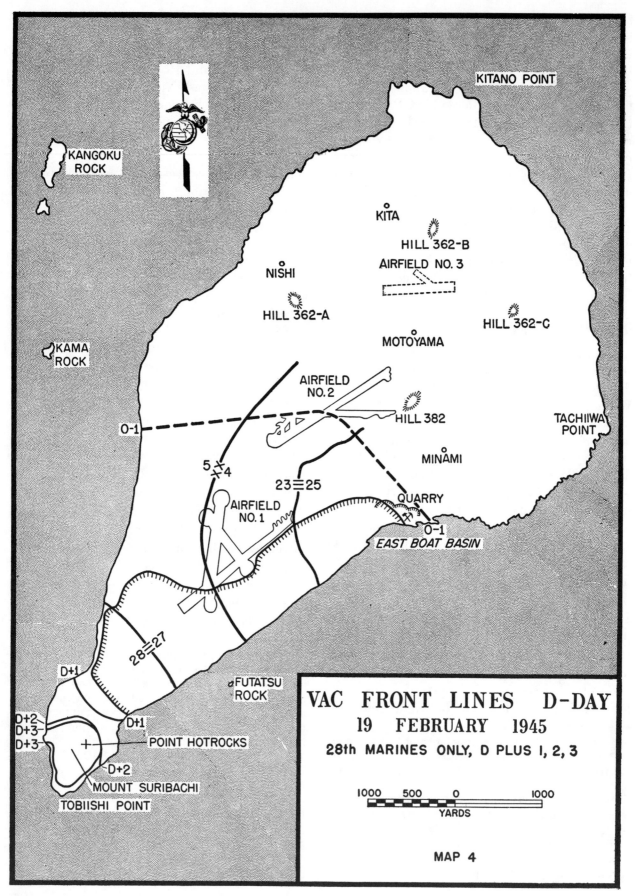

KITANO POINT

KANGOKU
ROCK

KITA

HILL 362-B

AIRFIELD NO. 3

NISHI

HILL 362-A

HILL 362-C

KAMA
ROCK

MOTOYAMA

AIRFIELD
NO. 2

TACHIIWA
POINT

O-1

HILL 382

MINAMI

5 4

23 25

QUARRY

AIRFIELD
NO. 1

O-1

EAST BOAT BASIN

28 27

D+1

FUTATSU
ROCK

VAC FRONT LINES D-DAY
19 FEBRUARY 1945
28th MARINES ONLY, D PLUS 1, 2, 3

D+2
D+3
D+3

D+1

POINT HOTROCKS

D+2

MOUNT SURIBACHI

TOBIISHI POINT

1000   500   0   1000
YARDS

MAP 4

Louis B. Blissard, and the intelligence officer plus several other Marines suffered no effects from this shelling. Lieutenant Colonel Blissard assumed command of 1/23 upon the death of Haas.[29] In the RCT 25 zone of action enemy fire harassed Marine lines continuously throughout the night. The 3/25 supply dump on the beach was destroyed by direct hits of enemy rockets prior to dawn.[30]

All infantry regiments had established CP's ashore during the day, but division and higher commanders remained on board ship. Brigadier General Leo D. Hermle, assistant commander of the 5th Division, was the only general officer ashore on D-Day. He landed at 1430 and established an advance CP just east of the southern end of the airfield, but advised General Rockey that heavy fire plus communication difficulties made it unwise for him to land.[31]

The assault infantry battalions of the Landing Force received assistance throughout D-Day from all the supporting arms available to the Amphibious Support Force. Carrier pilots of TF 58 and the escort carriers of TF 52 flew missions all day as airborne observers and spotters maintained constant vigilance over the target. Including pre-H-Hour strikes, 606 support aircraft flew 26 missions on 19 February and dropped 274,500 pounds of bombs. These planes also fired 2,254 rockets into the island defenses and dropped over a hundred napalm bombs. Air and naval gunfire liaison teams remained in communication with both air and sea supporting units through the hectic hours that followed the beach assault. Naval rifles from 5- to 16-inch caliber pounded enemy positions in response to Marine requests. Gunfire support vessels engaged enemy artillery that covered landing areas from high ground to the north, and concentrated on concealed Japanese mortars that shelled landing areas with deadly effect.[32]

Throughout this first day, the situation on the beaches prevented landing of any but the highest priority "hot cargo." This consisted of ammunition, rations, water, and signal equipment brought to the beach in LCVP's and LCM's. Shore party teams, working under extremely adverse conditions without sufficient trucks and other heavy equipment, could do little more than stack the supplies on the beach above the high water mark. LVT's and weasels made trips from the beach dumps inland carrying these supplies to the troops and returned bearing wounded men. The busy amtracs also made nonstop trips from LST's, ferrying critically needed items direct to Marines on the front lines.

Most of the transports and other vessels of the task force retired from the island at nightfall, but some command ships, preloaded LST's, and hospital LST's remained behind. Emergency items, especially 81mm mortar ammunition, were brought in during the night, but actually very little unloading was accomplished and many of the wounded spent this night on the beach because they could not be evacuated. Some progress was made cutting exits through the terrace and clearing mines, but enemy fire and the shortage of equipment limited this activity.[33]

Casualties on D-Day were high but not up to five percent of the entire landing force as had been expected.[34] Reports submitted at the close of operations the first day were exaggerated, particularly in the number of men reported

<hr>

[29] *23d Mar OpRpt*, Annex F, 4; Ltr LtCol L. B. Blissard to CMC, 13Jan53.

[30] *25th Mar OpRpt*, Appendix VIII, Sec. IV, 3.

[31] *5th MarDiv SAR*, Sec VII, 15.

[32] *TF 54 OpRpt*, 13; VAC Air Officer, Special Action Report, Iwo Jima Campaign, 30Apr45, Encl A, 1, hereinafter cited as *VAC Air Rpt*.

[33] The critical shortage of ammunition, especially 81mm mortar, remained serious throughout D-Day. Shells hand-carried ashore for these mortar lasted about one hour after the weapons opened fire. No other supply of 81mm rounds existed on the island, and mortar crews spent much of D-Day scouring the landing beaches in search of ammunition for their weapons. With the 81mm's out of action, assault battalions lost the services of their only high-trajectory supporting arm during most of the violent D-Day action. Ltr LtCol F. J. Mee to CMC, 15Dec52, hereinafter cited as *Mee*.

[34] *VAC MedRpt*, 2. Five percent of the entire force would have been 3,050. However, the really significant figure is the percent of casualties among the 30,000 troops actually landed on D-Day. This figure is eight percent, of which 20 percent were killed in action.

missing in action. These figures were reduced the following day when Marines who had been separated from their units on the beaches and fought with other organizations during the day returned to their own commands. Corps gave only a very incomplete estimate of losses in its dispatch summary for D-Day, but combat efficiency, which is closely related to numerical strength, was rated very good to excellent for the landing force as a whole.[35] Actual casualty

figures for this day were later determined to be:

Killed in action	501
Wounded in action	1755
Died of wounds	47
Missing in action	18
Combat fatigue	99
Total	2420 [36]

[35] VAC Dispatch Summary D-Day, Iwo Jima.

[36] These casualty figures were taken from statistics prepared by the Casualty Section, Headquarters Marine Corps. For a summary of casualties see Appendix III.

CHAPTER IV HOTROCKS[1]

(D-plus 1—D-plus 4)

The early morning of 20 February found units of VAC about to embark upon two distinct phases of the fight for Iwo Jima: the capture of formidable Suribachi in the south; and the long, exhausting drive to the north to clear the airfields and the remainder of the island.

TO THE BASE OF THE VOLCANO[2]

The job of securing the southern end of the island belonged to the 28th Marines. This unit, as a result of its D-Day progress, was positioned across the narrowest part of the island, isolating looming Mount Suribachi and its defenders from the rest of the Japanese garrison. But General Kuribayashi had foreseen that the American landing force would almost certainly split Iwo early in the operation and had designed his defenses accordingly. Severing Suribachi from the northern plateau had done little to damage the over-all defense system beyond partial disruption of communications between the mountain fortress and the other sectors. Mount Suribachi was one of several semi-independent sectors capable of continuing the battle with or without assistance.[3]

Colonel Liversedge planned to have his 28th Marines attack the mountain, surround its base while maintaining a steady pressure on all located positions in the cliffs, and search for suitable routes to the summit.[4]

Activity throughout the night had prevented much rest or sleep for men of the 28th Marines, and it was a weary group that waited for the preattack bombardment by supporting ships and aircraft to lift and allow them to move out in assault. With the 2d Battalion on the left, the 3d on the right, and the 1st in reserve, RCT 28 jumped off on schedule at 0830. Company E, held in reserve for the night defense, reverted to 2/28 just before K-Hour in order to strengthen the assault elements. Tanks did not participate in the early phases of this assault because they were unable to refuel and rearm in time as their maintenance section had not yet come ashore.[5]

---

[1] Point HOTROCKS, Lat. 24°45'11'' N; 141°17'28'' E, was designated by the navy as the reference point for reports of radar contacts in the Volcano Islands Area. Technically it was the name given to the highest peak of Mount Suribachi. In common usage, however, it came to refer to all of the mountain. *TF 51 OpPlan*, par 3 (x) (22) a.

[2] Unless otherwise cited, material in this and the following sections of this chapter is based on the following: *28th Mar SAR*; LtCol R. H. Williams, "Up the Rock on Iwo the Hard Way," *Marine Corps Gazette*, Aug45.

[3] *VAC IntelRpt*, 16, 17.

[4] *5th MarDiv*, Sec VIII, 19.

[5] The following quote from the Special Action Report of Company C explains this delay: "We had eight tanks to place in action, however, no fuel or ammunition was available. Salvaging from knocked out tanks and redistribution was started. A heavy mortar barrage was placed upon us and we were forced to move to another position. Work had no sooner started in the

37MM GUN fires against cave positions in north face of volcano in support of RCT 28. These light but extremely accurate weapons did some of their best work in the southern part of the island.

During the forenoon Marines gained only 50–70 yards. Aircraft and ships pounded Japanese positions and the 3d Battalion, 13th Marines fired mission after mission, but stiff enemy resistance continued, particularly from well-camouflaged pillboxes hidden in the brush to the front of the Marine lines. These emplacements, too close to friendly troops to be engaged by heavy support weapons, could only be silenced by coordinated attacks of assault

demolition teams using flamethrowers and explosive charges.

At 1100 the tanks came forward, and with this support the attack continued from pillbox to pillbox. The 37mm guns and 75mm half-tracks of the regimental weapons company were also brought close to the front and gave effective aid.

Behind the lines the 1st Battalion spent the day mopping up enemy positions bypassed during the D-Day assault. Although in reserve, it engaged in fierce close-quarter fighting and killed 75 of the enemy.

When the attack halted at 1700, the regiment had advanced 200 bloody yards closer to the

new position and the barrage was upon us again. This occurred three times as there was no place to which we could move where we would not be under direct observation by the enemy on Mount Suribachi." *5th TkBn SAR*, Encl C, 2.

objective. The casualties for the day included two officers killed and six wounded; 27 enlisted men killed and 127 wounded. (See Map 4.)

Naval illuminating shells filled the hours of darkness with an eerie light, and Marines strained tired eyes to the south to detect hostile activity. White and amber pyrotechnic signals fired from Suribachi called down enemy artillery from the north to augment harassing fires from the mountain, but for a second night the expected counterattack did not develop.

Although progress the first two days had been slow, it was felt that by the end of D-plus 2 the front lines would be so close to the base of the volcano that further support by aircraft would be impossible. For this reason K-Hour on 21 February was preceded by a 40-plane strike. Attacking to within 100 yards of the front lines, these aircraft hit enemy positions that had given so much trouble the previous day. Particular attention was given to areas inaccessible to tanks.

The 1st Battalion was assigned a one-company front on the right flank of the regimental zone and placed Company A on line next to the 3d Battalion. Otherwise, when the regiment moved out in the attack at 0825, units and boundaries were the same as the day before. Again tanks were unable to make the jump-off schedule because of delays in servicing.

Operating on the extreme right, with Company A attacking, followed by Companies B

TWO FLAME THROWER OPERATORS team up to send twin streams of burning liquid into well-concealed Japanese position at foot of Suribachi.

71

and C, the 1st Battalion advanced rapidly along the west beach to the base of the volcano. Although tanks could not be used in this sector, the attached 37mm platoon destroyed 11 enemy positions during the day. Companies B and C kept busy mopping up and clearing rear areas of snipers.

The 3d Battalion, in the center, met heavy opposition from the positions that had held up the advance the day before. Only small gains were registered until the tanks arrived. Then, with armor, 37mm guns, and halftracks mounting 75mm guns in support, the attack gained a momentum by 1100 that was only temporarily checked by an enemy counterattack that struck 3/28's front at 1145. By 1400 the battalion had advanced almost to the foot of the mountain,

and remained in position there for the rest of the day although part of Company H fell back about 15 yards when a second enemy thrust hit at 1800.

Tanks were unable to operate on the left of the 2d Battalion's zone, but they could be used in the center and on the right. Although 2/28's attack got underway slowly, good gains were made once the tanks joined in the fighting. Two platoons of Company D had been held out as a reserve when the assault opened, but by 1100 all platoons of all companies were engaged. At 1400, with the right of the battalion nearing the base of the mountain, Company F on the left started to swing around the east side in a sweep toward Tobiishi Point at the southern tip of the island. Units on the beach moved

PATROL FINDS ROUGH GOING as it picks its way up the side of Mount Suribachi. All paths up the volcano were obliterated by bombing and naval gunfire before the landing.

FIRST IWO JIMA FLAG RAISING. Small flag carried ashore by the 2d Battalion, 28th Marines is planted atop Mount Suribachi at 1020, 23 February 1945.   (Navy Photo)

ahead quite rapidly, but progress over the rugged terrain of the ledges 50–60 feet above the shore line was slow. Many positions were bypassed during this drive, but engineers and infantry with flame throwers were left behind to clean up.

About 1830 the 2d Battalion began the difficult job of consolidating for the night. Com-

FAMOUS FLAG RAISING pictured in this photo by Mr. Joe Rosenthal took place after an unknown Marine obtained a set of colors from LST 779 to replace the stars and stripes first raised over the volcano.

BLASTING CAVES on top of Suribachi. After securing the summit Marines of RCT 28 spent days sealing caves and mopping up stubborn defenders. Most caves had multiple entrances. Note smoke issuing from both mouths of this underground position.

pany E, which operated in the center during the day, was ordered to move to the left and relieve Company F. One platoon of Company D and 20 men from the 81mm mortar platoon filled the gap thus created. Heavy enemy fire from cliffs overlooking the east coast and throughout areas recently occupied held up the relief until after dark. Tying in was extremely difficult under these conditions, and it was 2300 before the Marines were settled for the night.

Company F reported that it had penetrated all the way to Tobiishi Point during the afternoon, but lines for the night did not extend that far south. Marines of RCT 28 now occupied positions that formed a semicircle in front of the north face of Suribachi, with 1/28 halfway around on the western shore and 2/28 a like distance along the eastern side. In the course of the day's action regimental lines had moved

650 yards on the left, 500 yards in the center, and 1,000 yards on the right.

During late afternoon and evening an estimated 50 enemy planes staged a 3-hour *Kamikaze* attack against shipping of the task forces assembled off Iwo.[6] Three carriers were hit during this attack. The *Bismarck Sea* (CVE) was sunk, the *Saratoga* (CV) so badly damaged that she had to return to Pearl Harbor for repairs, and the *Lunga Point* (CVE) was

---

[6] These were planes of the 2d Mitate Special Attack Unit. They took off from Katori Airbase (near Yokosuka, Honshu), stopped over at Hachijo Jima (an island about 125 miles directly south of Tokyo Bay) for necessary supplies, then, toward evening, attacked the shipping off Iwo Jima. There were no survivors from this unit. Japanese Studies in World War II, No. 57, "Air Operations on Iwo and the Ryukyus."

hit but continued operations. Two other ships, the *Keokuk* (AKN) and LST 477, were also damaged.[7] The LST, loaded with precious 3d Division tanks, was badly damaged but was able to unload on the beach before returning to Saipan.

Dug in close to the volcano's steep face, Marines of RCT 28 could hear the defenders moving restlessly above them. Enemy artillery and mortar fire fell in the area throughout the night but it was not so heavy now as during the day the regiment had moved to positions that were masked from most of the heavy weapons on the mountain. Two night infiltration attempts were repulsed. Men from the 81mm mortar platoon killed some 60 Japanese in front of 2/28 during one of these efforts, and Company C accounted for 28 who tried to move north along the western beach.

On 22 February (D-plus 3) the heaviest fighting occurred in the center of the regimental zone where 3/28 forced its way the remaining short distance to the base of Suribachi. Because of extremely rugged terrain and limited room for maneuver, it was impossible to use supporting fires of tanks and artillery to maximum advantage. Demolitions and flame throwers again proved the only way to silence enemy fortifications. On the right flank the 3d Battalion squeezed out 1/28 and a patrol from Company G worked its way on down the west coast toward the southern tip.

On the other side the 2d Battalion continued mopping up and sent a group from Company E south along the east coast to meet the patrol from 3/28. Both these patrols looked for routes up the steep sides of the mountain but found none, as naval gunfire and aerial bombardment had destroyed the few previously existing trails.

This was a miserable day. A cold rain, driven from the southeast by a 16- to 20-knot wind, soaked Marines to the skin and combined with volcanic ash to clog automatic weapons, reducing them to single shot effectiveness. But in spite of this temporary alliance between weather and enemy, RCT 28 had surrounded

HOTROCKS by 1630, except for 400 yards on the west coast, where friendly fire prevented patrol contact.

SCALING THE HEIGHTS

Since the only route to the top of Suribachi lay up the north face in the 2d Battalion's zone, the attack order for D-plus 4 directed 2/28 to secure and occupy the crest. The 1st Battalion would relieve 3/28 and attack south around the western side of the mountain. At 0900 Lieutenant Colonel Johnson sent out two 3-man patrols from Companies D and F to reconnoiter suitable routes and probe for enemy resistance. Surprisingly, no hostile fire was encountered and Marines reached the edge of the crater at 0940.[8]

In the meantime, 1st Lieutenant Harold G. Schrier, executive officer of Company E, and a 40-man detachment set out to follow the patrols and occupy the highest point of land on Iwo Jima. The number of live Japanese lurking in caves along this north face was unknown, so flankers were sent out to guard against ambush as Schrier's men clawed their way warily upward. Still there was a mysterious lack of enemy activity and the only Japanese encountered were the harmless dead.

Positions along the rim of the crater were reached at about 1015 and as Marines scrambled over the lip the tenseness was eased by action. A small defending force challenged the patrol and a short, hot fight developed. Even while this skirmish was in progress some of the men located a length of Japanese iron pipe, secured a small American flag to one end, and raised the Stars and Stripes at 1020. It was an inspiring sight for thousands of Americans on Iwo as the flag waved bravely from the summit.

Shortly after the mounting of this flag that measured only 54 inches by 28 inches an unidentified Marine went aboard LST 779, beached near the base of the volcano, to obtain a larger set of colors. As this second and larger (8 feet by 4 feet 8 inches) flag was being carried up the slopes of Suribachi, photographer Joe Rosenthal, who covered the Iwo

---

[7] *TF 51 Rpt*, Sec **IV**, 14.

[8] 5th MarDiv D-3 Journal, Iwo Jima.

operation for the Associated Press, noticed it and instantly started in close pursuit. His efforts that morning resulted in the now famous picture of the second flag raising.[9]

Among the many that gazed proudly at the National Colors on Suribachi that morning was a distinguished visitor, Secretary of the Navy James V. Forrestal. In company with General Holland Smith and party, the Secretary left the Expeditionary Troops Command Post on board the *Eldorado* to come ashore and observe the final stages of the battle for the mountain.

---

[9] Ltr Lt(jg) Alan S. Wood, LST 779, to BrigGen R. L. Denig, 7Jul45, along with other corroborating data retained in the archives of the Historical Branch, G–3, HQMC.

The American Colors were raised atop the mountain just as their craft touched the beach.[10]

During the afternoon 2/28 continued mopping-up actions. All accessible outer and inner slopes were covered as the Marines annihilated enemy snipers and blasted shut the many cave entrances, sealing in an uncounted number of Japanese. Much observation equipment was found, emphasizing the fact that this had been an excellent point of vantage from which hostile observers directed murderous fire against the entire beachhead. Marine artillerymen, ready and eager to seize this advantage, hastened to move flash-ranging equipment into position.

---

[10] Gen H. M. Smith, *Coral and Brass* (New York, 1949), 261–262.

AERIAL VIEW OF THE CRATER. This picture demonstrates the excellent observation of the landing beaches and southern portion of the island afforded by positions atop Suribachi. (Navy Photo)

While part of Company E scaled the heights, another group from the same company patrolled down around the eastern end of the island to contact a unit from 1/28, which advanced down the other side to complete the encirclement of HOTROCKS. These patrols made contact near the southern tip at 1015. Neither unit met enemy resistance, but two men from 1/28 were lost in a land mine explosion.

Engineers and demolition squads continued to assist the 1st and 2d Battalions in destroying enemy positions and sealing off caves around the bottom of Suribachi. Throughout the entire assault RCT 28 drew heavily on the resources and skill of these men from the 5th Engineer Battalion. Landing with assault troops, they constantly proved indispensable in blasting enemy fortifications, carving routes through the rock for tanks, and probing for land mines.

For the night defense on D-plus 4, 40 men from Company E remained on the crest, while the rest of the regiment manned positions around the base of Suribachi. During the hours of darkness 122 Japanese were killed trying to infiltrate the lines. Most of these had demolitions secured to their bodies and were probably trying to reach command posts and artillery positions before destroying themselves. A few rounds of high-velocity artillery fell in the area and several 320mm mortar shells passed overhead to land out at sea. These projectiles were at first thought to be P–61 night fighter aircraft because of the peculiar sound made while passing overhead.

The Japanese had conducted an effective defense. Making maximum use of their artillery, mortars, and automatic weapons, they did not waste themselves in costly all out counterattacks. Forcing the Marines to come to them, the enemy inflicted heavy casualties before being blasted or burned out of their fortifications.

During the battle for the volcano, the district commander of the Mount Suribachi Sector sent the following message to General Kuribayashi:

Enemy's bombardments from the air and sea and their assaults with explosions are very fierce and if we ever try to stay and defend our present positions it will lead us to self-destruction. We should rather like to go out of our position and choose death by *"banzai"* charges.[11]

General Kuribayashi's reply to this message is not available, if indeed he chose to reply. But the following excerpt from the enemy plan of battle seems to typify the doctrine employed in the defense of this fortress:

Even if the enemy does capture our positions we will defend Suribachi Yama to the utmost and, . . . even though all positions fall into enemy hands and organized resistance becomes difficult, we will continue fighting fiercely to the last man and inflict heavy casualties on the enemy.[12]

In the 4-day period (D-plus 1—D-plus 4) the 28th Marines lost 510 men. Added to the D-Day figure, this made a total of 895 casualties for the five days from beach to summit.[13] Japanese casualties for the same period were almost 2,000 killed or sealed in some of the more than 1,000 caves honeycombing the area.[14]

After five days of violent fighting, RCT 28's almost independent war on the southern end of Iwo Jima was marked with success, but the regiment remained in the south until D-plus 10, cleaning out die-hard Japanese, reorganizing, and reequipping. On D-plus 6 (25 February), at 0630, the 28th Marines reverted to corps reserve, and Colonel Liversedge, with his battalion commanders and staff officers, reconnoitered routes to the northern front where the rest of the corps was engaged in bitter fighting.

---

[11] *Horie*, 8.

[12] As quoted in *TF 56 IntelRpt*, 33.

[13] *5th MarDiv SAR*, Sec. VII.

[14] Approximately 1300 army and 640 naval troops were committed by Kuribayashi to the defense of the Suribachi area, *5th Mar Div IntelRpt*, Map.

CHAPTER V

Into the Main Defenses

(D-plus 1—D-plus 5)[1]

During D-Day and while subduing Mount Suribachi, Marines had encountered an alarming number of completely unscathed enemy positions. This disappointing revelation, however, was but a suggestion of the maze upon maze of intact strongholds that would confront American troops throughout the rest of the fight for Iwo Jima.

General Kuribayashi had concentrated the majority of his forces and installations in the central and northern part of the island, and had used every conceivable means to make his defenses in this sector impregnable. The entire area was a weird looking mass of cliffs, ravines, gorges, crevices, and ledges. Jumbled rock, torn stubble of small trees, jagged ridges, and chasms all sprawled about completely without pattern, and within this macabre setting the Japanese were deeply entrenched in hundreds of excellently constructed positions. From blockhouses, bunkers, pillboxes, caves, and camouflaged tanks, enemy guns jutted de-

---

[1] Unless otherwise cited, material in this chapter is based on the following: *3d MarDiv SAR;* 21st Marines Action Report, Iwo Jima Operation, 10Apr45, hereinafter cited as *21st Mar SAR;* 3d Tank Battalion Action Report, Iwo Jima Operation, 9Apr45, hereinafter cited as *3d TkBn SAR;* 12th Marines Action Report, Iwo Jima Operation, undated, hereinafter cited as *12th Mar SAR; 4th MarDiv OpRpt; 4th TkBn OpRpt; 14th Mar OpRpt; 23d Mar OpRpt; 24th Mar OpRpt; 25th Mar OpRpt; 5th MarDiv SAR; 5th TkBn SAR; 13th Mar SAR; 26th Mar SAR; 27th Mar SAR.*

fiantly. Every possible approach to the north was contested by weapons with well-integrated fields of fire.

The enemy had so deftly prepared this area that it had been impossible to neutralize or destroy an appreciable number of positions before troops landed. Masterful camouflage had prevented American ships and planes from detecting many of these positions, and of those that were spotted, as often as not a direct hit failed to put them out of business. Complete accomplishment devolved upon ground Marines.

D-PLUS 1—20 FEBRUARY

As the 28th Marines were preparing to attack Mount Suribachi on the morning of 20 February 1945, the bulk of General Harry Schmidt's V Amphibious Corps was getting set for the northern offensive. Front line battalions from left to right were 1/26, 3/27, 3/23, 2/24, 1/25, 2/25, and 3/25 (with two companies of 1/24 attached). These units were positioned along a 4,000-yard front that stretched in a northeasterly direction from the western side of the small neck of the island, up across the southern end of Airfield Number 1, along the eastern slopes of the field, and cut sharply down to the coast at the East Boat Basin. (See Map IV.)

Following intensive artillery, naval gunfire, and air preparation, the attack was launched at 0830 with the mission of seizing the 0–1 line. To complete the northward pivot, which had

MARINE AMTRACS AND SHERMAN TANKS litter the beaches. These vehicles were victims of the soft volcanic ash and heavy enemy fire. In the distance can be seen part of the vast armada that supported the operation.

begun on D-Day, VAC's left flank and center-most units were to sweep across the airfield and gain positions on an east-west line, generally abreast of RCT 25 on the right.

The attack in the 5th Division's zone was pushed along a regimental front of about 1,000 yards. With 1/26 attached to RCT 27, Colonel Wornham employed two battalions on line (1/26 and 3/27) and two in reserve (1/27 and 2/27). General Rockey held RCT 26 (less 1/26) in division reserve in positions along the southwestern tip of Airfield Number 1.[2]

The two assault battalions encountered many pillboxes and land mines as they moved forward on D-plus 1, but suffered most from well directed enemy mortar and artillery barrages. Since the route of advance led along the relatively open terrain west of the airfield, attacking units were exposed with little cover against the excellent observation and fields of fire enjoyed by the Japanese. The Marines pushed the attack, however, and with Companies A and B, 5th Tank Battalion in support, they gained 800 yards. When Colonel Wornham ordered his units to halt and consolidate, 1/26, on the left, had to drop back about 200 yards to more favorable ground for night defense. The two front line battalions dug in on an east-

west line from the northwest edge of Airfield Number 1 to the coast. The 2d Battalion, 27th backed up 1/26 for the night while 1/27 dug in behind the 3d Battalion to provide a defense in depth.

The 4th Division employed two regiments abreast for the D-plus 1 attack. On the left of the division zone RCT 23 (with 2/24 attached) jumped off at K-Hour and ran head-on into intense enemy machine-gun, mortar, and artillery fire. In attempting to locate and counter this fire, Colonel Wensinger's regiment temporarily lost contact with Lanigan's RCT 25. Though the going was tough in this area for tanks, one reinforced platoon from Company C, 4th Tank Battalion, got through to help push the 23d's advance, and by 1200 a determined attack had carried past the northern limits of Airfield Number 1. During this move an important part of the Japanese defensive positions was breached and a series of well-concealed pill-boxes and infantry strong points reduced.

Wensinger continued to push his units during the afternoon but the Shermans, slowed by mine fields and increasingly rough terrain, were unable to give much aid. The enemy directed deadly rocket, artillery, and mortar barrages against the front lines, and the Marine attack gained little after the morning advance.

---

[2] *VAC OpRpt,* 13, 14.

At 1630 the reserve of RCT 23 (1/23 and 2/23) displaced forward to positions along the seaward edge of the airfield to form a strong, secondary line of defense. Contact was established with RCT 27 on the left and regained with RCT 25 on the right, and by 1800 units were solidly tied in. The day's total advance was approximately 500 yards.

RCT 25's attack plan for D-plus 1 called for three battalions abreast. The 1st, on the left, would make the main effort, while the 2d, in the center, was to seize the high ground to its front and then assist the advance of 1/25 by fire. On the extreme right flank 1/24 (attached) was to remain in position until such time as the other two battalions could advance and come abreast. The 3d Battalion, 25th Marines, having sustained heavy casualties on D-Day, was removed from the lines and placed in regimental reserve.

At 0715 a mortar shell burst in the command post of 2/25, wounding the commanding officer, executive officer, and the operations officer. This blast also fatally wounded the commanding officer of Company B, 4th Tank Battalion as he conferred on tank support for the morning attack. Lieutenant Colonel James Taul, executive officer of 3/25, was ordered to relieve the wounded Lieutenant Colonel Hudson. Because of a shortage of officers in the 2d Battalion, Taul functioned throughout the operation without the assistance of an executive officer.

RCT 25 attacked on schedule, but made only slight advances as 1/25 struggled to come abreast of 2/25. Company B (tanks) supported the attack, but was of little value because of the exceptionally rough terrain. Each time a tank reached a firing position it immediately became the target for accurate enemy mortar and artillery fire. Crossfires of machine guns from

MARINE ENGINEERS in one of their most ticklish operations. Before supporting vehicles could move inland lanes had to be cleared through mine fields. The white tapes mark the safe path through the field.

concealed emplacements, coupled with intense and accurate rifle fire, seriously impeded the infantry advance and inflicted many casualties.

Not only the front lines encountered the severity of Japanese fire; there seemed more than adequate disposition of enemy guns to provide continued coverage of all the beaches and routes inland. Enemy gunners appeared particularly adept at searching out various supply dumps, evacuation stations, and command posts. LVT's were relied on heavily to get supplies to front lines, but the nature of the terrain in some parts of RCT 25's zone of action prevented even these workhorse vehicles from getting through, and carrying parties drawn from reserve units hurried forward with critical items.

At 1100, the battalion command post of 1/25 received a direct artillery hit, and six naval corpsmen were killed and seven others wounded.

Mercilessly, enemy shells singled out aid and evacuation stations along the entire corps front. It was not uncommon for a casualty awaiting treatment to receive a second and third wound, and the percentage of casualties among naval doctors and corpsmen was extremely high.

Throughout the afternoon, RCT 25 continued its dogged efforts. At 1600 friendly planes misdirected their fire adding terror to the situation. An air strike consisting of .50-caliber machine-gun strafing, rockets, and bombs fell on troops of Company B, 1/24, which was positioned on top of the quarry some 400 yards inland from the eastern shore. This strike was made without a preliminary "dry-run", and despite the fact that yellow front line panels were displayed prior to and during the aerial attack. The battalion suffered five killed and six wounded as a result of this misguided effort.

THIS SHERMAN TANK was disabled by a land mine and five hits by Japanese artillery but the crew escaped uninjured. Note heavy planking on side to protect against magnetic demolition charges.

Shortly after the planes left the area, this battalion reported that friendly artillery and naval gunfire was being registered on its lines.

By 1800 the two battalions on the left had gained an average of about 200 yards, but 1/24 on the right inched forward only a short distance. Heavy casualties throughout D-plus 1 further reduced the combat efficiency of Cates' 4th Division, but the capture of Airfield Number 1 was completed during the day, and the division front had advanced from 200 to 500 yards. (See Map IV.)

General Schmidt had ordered his corps reserve, RCT 21, commanded by Colonel Hartnoll J. Withers, to boat and report to its control station at 0800 on D-plus 1, prepared to land on order. But the situation along the beaches, instead of improving, became progressively worse. Congestion was everywhere, with wrecked landing craft, immobilized vehicles, and other gear littering the entire area. Also, during the early afternoon the wind rose, making landing operations hazardous. Schmidt, consequently, ordered RCT 21 to reembark and be prepared to boat on order.[3]

Desperately in need of all its organic artillery, the 4th Division landed the 3d and 4th Battalions of the 14th Marines on 20 February. By 1012, 3/14 had launched all its DUKW's, but enemy fire along the shore and in selected position areas inland delayed the landing. Over five hours later the amphibian trucks carrying 3/14 began to land over the south edge of Beach Yellow 1. The battalion's 105mm howitzers were then put into prepared gunpits (made ready by the 3/14 Reconnaissance Party) just inland from the boundary of Yellow 1 and Red 2. The 3/14 howitzers opened fire at 1728 to reinforce fires of the 1st Battalion of division artillery.[4]

The first DUKW's carrying 105's of 4/14 slipped into the rough water from LST 1032 at 1511. Disaster struck almost immediately when a DUKW sank as soon as it hit the water. Shortly after this accident seven others went down carrying with them as many 105mm howitzers, over half of the battalion's

weapons.[5] The remainder of the DUKW's headed for the beach where two more broached and were lost while landing at 2230. The surviving machines got ashore, however, and the remnants of 4/14 were set up in firing positions by midnight, inland from the Yellow Beaches.

Of the corps artillery, only Battery C, 2d 155mm Howitzer Battalion, managed to get ashore during the day. It was attached to the 13th Marines for operational control and fired supporting missions as required. This battery commenced landing over Beach Red 1 from LST 779[6] at 1630. In spite of unparalleled chaotic beach conditions, tractors pulled the four clumsy howitzers up steep, loose-sand bluffs and into position by 1840, in the 5th Division zone near the west coast. Batteries A and B of Major Earl J. Rowse's 2d 155mm Howitzer Battalion landed on 22 and 24 February respectively.[7]

During the night of 20–21 February gunfire support ships and mortar gunboats[8] delivered

---

[3] *VAC OpRpt*, 14.

[4] *14th Mar OpRpt*, Appendix 3, 8–10.

[5] *Ibid.*, Appendix 4, 5–8. The motors of the DUKW's failed within minutes after launching. In each case the reason was water in the gasoline, caused by insufficient freeboard resulting from extremely heavy loads and choppy water. All of these sank while attempting to return to the LST after their engines stopped. 4/14 thus lost seven of 12 howitzers before firing a round on Iwo Jima. *Ibid.*, Appendix 5, 3.

[6] The first LST to beach at Iwo, this ship remained in at Red 1 all night to unload but was forced to retract at 0430 the next morning when a heavy enemy barrage hit the vessel and nearby beach areas. At 0700 the 779 headed back into the beach but was ordered by Admiral Hill to remain at sea. The admiral extended a "Well done" to all hands of 779 for landing and supplying Battery C's 155's under extremely difficult conditions. From this ship came the now famous American Flag raised over Mount Suribachi on 23February45 to replace the first small flag. *VAC ArtyRpt*, Encl T, 3–5.

[7] *Ibid.* Artillery battalions continued to experience unusual problems after emplacement ashore. Until Marines knocked out enemy artillery on Mount Suribachi, artillerymen firing to the north received enemy fire from the south that proved more troublesome than Japanese rounds from the front. Ltr LtCol R. J. Spritzen to CMC, 7Nov52.

[8] LCI's mounting 4.2-inch mortars were employed for the first time in support of the V Amphibious Corps at Iwo Jima. The night harassing fires, their primary mission, proved very satisfactory. Although these craft operated without radar and with inade-

CARRIER PLANES ATTACKING ground targets in support of the Marines. Aircraft from escort carriers provided aggressive air support until 11 March when Iwo-based Army P–51's took over. (Navy Photo)

counterbattery and harassing fires while star shells from destroyers pierced the darkness with a ghostly, wavering light. About 2000 a counterattack of undetermined strength in the 5th Division zone was repulsed with the welcome assistance of the 13th Marines. At 0443 the enemy counterattacked in the 4th Division zone with an estimated 100 men, who were unsuccessful in penetrating Marine lines. Intermittently, 3- and 4-man enemy patrols attempted to infiltrate both division zones. Japanese guns harassed front lines and rear areas throughout the night.

---

quate navigation gear, night firing techniques developed prior to the operation were successful. The LCI's steamed in an elliptical track around a reference ship that kept station by radar, and fired during the leg on which they headed toward the island. *TF 53 OpRpt, Pt IV, 5, 6.*

D-PLUS 2—21 FEBRUARY

At 0740, 21 February, artillery, rockets and naval gunfire commenced blasting away at enemy-held territory in close proximity to friendly lines. Additional support arrived when 68 carrier-based planes bore in, sending rockets and bombs tearing into areas several hundred yards in front of Marines. The 4th and 5th Divisions jumped off in the attack at 0810 and the well-coordinated fires shifted northward to allow for anticipated troop advances. As Marines gradually gained yards, Japanese fire gained intensity. Automatic weapons and rifles spurted accurately from the tiny, well-concealed apertures of pillboxes and caves. Again it was tragically apparent to Marine leaders that human flesh would have to succeed where heavy armament failed.

On the corps' left front, the 5th Division found terrain suitable for tank employment, and throughout the morning substantial gains were made with armor spearheading the attack. By 1340, 1/26 on the left and 3/27 on the right had pushed almost 1,000 yards in their zone and were now just south of the 0–1 line. Casualties had been heavy during this advance, and units experienced more than usual difficulties maintaining contact. On the right, 3/27 had a particularly hard time keeping contact with the 23d Marines on its right. Resulting from the rapidity of the 5th Division attack and the intense enemy shelling, a sizable gap developed between divisions by early afternoon. To close this, Company B, 1/27 moved up from regimental reserve, and in order to establish proper contact this company had to extend a short distance into the 4th Division's zone of action.

Under heavy enemy fire, General Rockey's division spent the afternoon attempting to reorganize, get casualties to the rear, and consolidate lines. By 1600 firm contact had been made with the 4th Division, and units were ordered to start preparations for the night. Colonel Wornham again employed a tight defense, with three battalions on line (1/26, 1/27, and 3/27) and one battalion in immediate support. Colonel Waller's 13th Marines plus Battery C, 2d 155mm Howitzer Battalion provided on-calls fires as requested.[9]

General Rockey closed his division command post on board the USS *Cecil* (APA 96) in the early afternoon and by 1500 he and his staff arrived ashore and set up headquarters just off the southern end of Airfield Number 1.

General Cates' 4th Division, facing exceptionally rugged terrain and heavy fire, was able to advance only about half the distance covered by the 5th Division. As the 23d and 25th Regiments jumped off in the morning attack they met severe mortar, machine-gun, and artillery fire, and after only slight advances encountered a series of extremely well laid mine fields. Expertly covered by enemy fire, these fields further indicated the thoroughness with which General Kuribayashi had prepared his defenses.

With Marines assuming covering positions to add their support to the tanks' covering fire, engineer units went forward to remove the mines. The 23d Marines made some gains on the left flank where slightly defiladed areas permitted local and restricted envelopment, but the center and right flank units, despite maximum use of all supporting weapons, advanced only slightly. The 23d Marines' progress during the day averaged a little over 100 yards along its entire front.

After contact had been reconstituted with the 27th Regiment on its left, RCT 23 began digging in deeply at 1745. Because of extremely heavy casualties in assault elements, Colonel Wensinger committed one company from his reserve 1/23 to strengthen front line positions. Battalions 1/23 (less Company A) and 2/23 remained on the regimental reserve line along the eastern edge of Airfield Number 1 as a secondary line of defense directly behind 2/24 and 3/23.

Although enemy mine fields in front of the 25th Marines were skillfully laid, the terrain in this sector was so rocky and irregular that the Japanese were unable to cover all avenues of approach. With 1/25, 2/25, 1/24 in line from right to left, and 3/25 in reserve, RCT 25's attack gained some momentum. Tanks of Company A, 4th Tank Battalion supported the assault of 1/25 and 2/25, while Company B tanks delivered destructive fires on pillboxes and bunkers on the cliff line to the front of 1/24, driving the enemy out of these positions. The 1st Battalion, 14th Marines placed counterbattery and supporting fire across the regimental front. Air strikes and naval gunfire continued to work over troublesome areas, while the 25th Marines maintained constant pressure on obstinate enemy positions. Resistance gradually weakened in the center of the regimental zone and units made fair progress on the right flank along the shore of the East Boat Basin. Gains during the morning varied from 50 to 300 yards.

Inevitably, casualties continued to mount, with a high percentage occuring among unit commanders. Lieutenant Colonel Hollis U. Mustain, commanding 1/25, was one of these. He was checking his front line positions at 1000 when he was killed by enemy artillery or

---

[9] *VAC OpRpt*, 15.

mortar fire. Major Fenton J. Mee (battalion executive officer since D-Day) immediately assumed command.

Maintaining contact had been exceedingly difficult and when a serious gap developed between the 1st and 2d Battalions, 25th Marines, at 1430, Colonel Lanigan committed his 3d Battalion between the two. Company B, 1/25, was withdrawn from that battalion's right flank to make room for the 3d Battalion and committed on the left soon after dark. All units were under heavy enemy fire and 3/25 experienced considerable difficulty getting up into line. At 1700 the order was given to consolidate for the night and contact was established all along the front except for the extreme left flank of the RCT where physical contact with the 23d Marines had been a problem throughout the day.

With improved beach and weather conditions prevailing on the morning of D-plus 2, as well as even greater need for reinforcements ashore, the 21st Marines was again boated in preparation to land at 0800. General Schmidt placed RCT 21 at General Cates' disposal. A corps message to the 4th Division, received at 0915, read in part: "Prepare receive RCT 21 (3d MarDiv) Yellow Beaches, beginning 1130. Assign assembly area your zone. Will be released to you on your request to assist if required in capture of Airfield Number 2." [10] Following landing of the advance command post at 1200, Colonel Withers landed his battalions and supporting units throughout the afternoon. By 1720 all three battalions were ashore and in

[10] *4th MarDiv OpRpt*, Sec IV.

105MM HOWITZER fires north from a position south of Airfield Number 1.

assembly areas near the edge of Airfield Number 1. [11]

Brigadier General Franklin A. Hart, assistant division commander (ADC), 4th Marine Division, had gone ashore at 1245 in order to report on beach conditions and select a site for the division command post. He found Beach Blue 1 under heavy fire and that Japanese shells had scored direct hits on an ammunition dump of the 25th Marines, explosions from which endangered both Blue and Yellow Beaches. Reporting these conditions to General Cates he recommended that division headquarters remain on board the *Bayfield* until the next day.

General Hart also recommended that RCT 21 be used to relieve the 23d Marines before the next day's attack. Although Cates had previously planned to have the fresh unit relieve Lanigan's battered 25th Marines, the ADC pointed out that location of the assembly areas occupied by the 21st and the general congestion of beaches did not favor this action. The commanding general concurred, and at 1654 issued the following order:

This is a warning order. Intend pass 21st through 23d, repeat 23d, tomorrow AM to continue attack present 23d Zone. Elements 4th Tank Bn and 14th Marines, now supporting 23d, will be assigned direct support 21st effective upon relief of 23d. Arrange necessary liaison and reconnaissance prior thereto.[12]

Throughout the day 4th Division elements had made advances of from 50 to 500 yards. The Japanese, although employing every weapon available and using all their cunning, were being forced back yard by yard to positions across the center of the island. But in keeping with past performances, enemy resistance was fanatical and Marine casualties heavy. Combat efficiency for General Cates' division could be rated only 68 percent.

The night of 21–22 February was characterized by enemy harassing fires, local counterattacks, and infiltration in both division zones of action. On the corps' left front, RCT 27

was hit on both flanks at 2100 by a counterattack of undetermined strength, but this was stopped about an hour later without making any penetration. At 0245 the same unit repulsed an attempted infiltration on its left flank.

About the same time, surreptitious activity along the western coast between Brown Beaches 1 and 2 indicated that the enemy might be attempting a counterlanding. The USS *Pasadena* (CL) and the USS *Twiggs* (DD) were ordered to investigate any small-boat activity in that area, and although two strange radar contacts were made, no boats were discovered. General Rockey's division lines were still intact at 0700, but an undetermined number of enemy had been overrun or had infiltrated rearward of Marine lines, which necessitated mopping-up action during the morning of D-plus 3.[13]

In the 4th Division area, about 200 enemy troops formed at Motoyama Airfield Number 2 at 2330 and began moving toward the front lines of 3/23. Naval gunfire and artillery quickly gave this unit assistance, combining to smash the grouped enemy before he neared friendly positions. At 2345 the division requested permission from VAC to use RCT 21, if necessary, to assist in repelling expected counterattacks. General Schmidt approved this request with the provision that another of the 4th Division's regiments be designated VAC reserve as soon as possible after commitment of RCT 21. At 0300 RCT 25 reported that an enemy plane had dropped three bombs behind its lines on the Blue Beach. Along the whole division front small infiltration attempts continued with negligible results. As had become customary, enemy mortar and artillery fire fell on front lines, beaches and rear areas throughout the night.

D-PLUS 3—22 FEBRUARY

Although well tied in, corps front lines bent like a snake across the 3,400-yard front on the morning of D-plus 3. The most acute portion of this bend occurred in the center of the corps' line where elements of RCT 23 were still some 1,200 yards away from the 0-1 line. Combat efficiency of both divisions now suffered seri-

---

[11] The entire 21st Marines landed without incurring casualties in spite of a heavy surf, and suffered no losses during its first night ashore although enemy shells fell in the regiment's assembly area. Ltr LtCol A. Hedesh to CMC, 13Feb53.

[12] *4th MarDiv OpRpt*, Sec IV, 7.

[13] *VAC OpRpt*, 17–19.

ously from heavy casualties, and the Japanese defense showed little indication of weakening. Most assault battalions that came ashore on D-Day had been in the front lines for three days and nights of grueling, nerve shattering action. Troops of these units had little chance to rest or sleep, and their diet consisted solely of K rations and water, occasionally supplemented by unheated C rations. On this morning a cold, drizzling rain did little to improve morale.

The advance on Iwo Jima was progressing more slowly than anticipated. In order to provide impetus for the attack on this fourth day of battle, Generals Rockey and Cates decided to effect relief of some front line units. On the corps' left flank, Colonel Graham's 26th Marines moved out at daybreak with the mission of relieving RCT 27 and continuing the attack northward. Upon the passage of lines, 1/26, already at the front, was to revert to its parent regiment and 2/27, in 27th Marines reserve, would become attached to RCT 26.

The 21st Marines moved out at 0500 to relieve RCT 23 (with 2/24 attached) on the left of the 4th Division. At such time as this relief was completed, the 23d Marines (less mortar platoons of the 1st and 3d Battalions) would take up positions along the northeastern part of Airfield Number 1 as VAC reserve. The mortar platoons were to remain in position to support the attack of RCT 21. The 25th Marines, with 1/24 attached, would remain on the division right while the 24th (less 1/24) continued as division reserve.

With its 1st, 2d, and 3d Battalions abreast from left to right, Colonel Graham's 26th Marines relieved RCT 27. The move was made in a miserable downpour of rain, under extremely heavy enemy fire, and as preparations for continuing the attack began, so did a series of unfortunate events.

As so often happens in battle, the relief of front line units while under heavy fire brought about confusion and disruption. Information concerning adjacent units was insufficient, contact not what it might have been, and attack orders hastily issued. Lieutenant Colonel Tom M. Trotti's 3d Battalion extended 200 yards into the 4th Division's zone and received de-

moralizing fire from a bluff on its right flank. This elevation was 100 feet high in spots and ran down the west center of the island, curving across the 5th Division's front near Airfield Number 2.

Rather than attempt immediate adjustment of lines by lateral movement, Trotti decided to accomplish this move gradually while advancing toward the 0-2 line. But heavy Japanese fire from the dominant ground on the right flank permitted only minor gains and caused many casualties. At about 0940, while attempting to pull his battalion together, Lieutenant Colonel Trotti was killed, as was his operations officer, Major William R. Day. Since the battalion executive officer had previously been wounded and evacuated, Captain Richard M. Cook, commanding Company G, assumed command of the battalion, to be superseded at 1200 by Major Richard Fagan, 5th Division Inspector.

By 1400 the centermost units of RCT 26 had gained about 400 yards, but with flanking units not abreast it was necessary to pull the advanced troops back to more secure positions. Between 1630 and 1800 uncoordinated enemy counterattacks on the left flank, and to a lesser extent in the center, were repulsed by artillery and infantry fire. Heavy fire from the bluff as well as from positions to the front of the regiment continued to fall in RCT 26's zone, but by 1730 the three battalions held good positions for the night.

Units of 2/27 operated in close support of front line units. The other battalions of RCT 27 were deployed to defend the west beach against a counterlanding and at the same time to guard against any Japanese penetration down Motoyama Airfield Number 2.

Although RCT 21 commenced its move to relieve the 23d Marines at 0500, it was not until about 1130 that this relief was reported accomplished. Even then some of RCT 23's units were not entirely disengaged. With the 2d Battalion (Lieutenant Colonel Lowell E. English) on the left, 1st (Lieutenant Colonel Wendall H. Duplantis) in reserve, Colonel Withers' regiment moved against an intricate network of mutually supporting pillboxes emplaced on high ground between Airfields 1 and 2. Because of fortification, plus deeply scarred and pitted

BROACHED LCM is pounded by waves. With its ramp down this landing craft loaded with fuel drums is helpless in the surf. Navy salvage boat and LSM can be seen at left. (Navy Photo)

terrain, any maneuver other than direct frontal assault proved impossible. Tanks and supporting arms operated at extreme disadvantage, if at all. The ground afforded the enemy natural tank barriers while only direct hits by major caliber artillery were sufficient to crack the steel and concrete fortifications housing numerous Japanese guns that fired into assault Marines at point-blank range. For the 21st Regiment progress was costly and exceedingly slow. Actually and figuratively, this unit faced an uphill fight all the way.

The weather turned even worse during the morning, with the rain falling in torrents and visibility becoming extremely poor. Although air support was needed desperately, planes could not help ground troops when visibility dropped almost to zero. Tanks were further handicapped and virtually useless since the drivers could see but a few yards ahead. On the other hand, the well-entrenched Japanese took full advantage of the situation with prearranged fires that covered Marine positions.

Casualties mounted disproportionately to the few yards that were taken.[14] The advance during the morning netted only 50–75 yards.

Because of exceptionally determined resistance in the zone of RCT 21 the 25th Marines, on the right, provided supporting fires across the front of 21's zone of action. Even with this assistance the regiment's gains were limited to 50–250 yards for the entire day. The attack was halted at about 1700 and all units ordered to prepare positions for the night.

The lines of RCT 25 on the morning of D-plus 3 resembled an almost perfect inverted V. The apex was located on the 0–1 line while the left prong stretched back 950 yards southwest

[14] During this day's bitter action 1/21 lost its commander, LtCol M. C. Williams, who was wounded and evacuated. Maj C. M. Murray, executive officer, commanded until the next day when he too was wounded. Maj. R. H. Houser, transferred from regimental weapons company, assumed command on 23Feb and led 1/21 for the duration of the operation. Ltr LtCol R. H. Houser to CMC, 3Apr53; Ltr Col M. C. Williams to CMC, 9Feb53.

ARTILLERY FORWARD OBSERVERS adjust fire from post near Airfield. Wrecked Japanese plane and a shell crater provide concealment and cover for the team.

and the right prong carried 750 yards southeast to the coast. Disposed along this frontage, from left to right, were 1/25, 3/25, 2/25, and 1/24. (See Map IV.)

With 1/24 attached and Companies A and B, 4th Tank Battalion in support, the 25th Marines was directed to make a concerted effort on its left in an attempt to reach the 0–1 line to straighten the division front. Coordinating with RCT 21's advance on its left, 1/25 would attack northward to the regimental left boundary and hold its positions there until pinched out as the 21st Marines advanced across its front. With this action accomplished, the 21st and 25th would launch a coordinated drive to seize the 0–1 line. But with the 21st Marines unable to make any sizable gains in its zone of action the 25th could not launch a full-scale attack.

During the morning, however, a few units had managed to stage attacks in their respective zones. Against moderate resistance, 1/25 on the left jumped off at 0830 and its left advanced 200 yards by 1030, but for the reasons already noted, the 21st Marines had not made comparable gains. Consequently, after making its quick advance, Major Mee's 1st Battalion had a completely exposed left flank. Although Company A was committed to fill the hole, it was unable to stretch the full distance, and the battalion was ordered to hold up until it could tie in firmly with RCT 21.

The 3d and 2d Battalions, in the center of the regimental line, made only local improvements in their positions during the day. While waiting for units on the flank to come abreast, 3/25 requested and received rocket support. Two barrages fired on a hill some 800 yards northwest of the quarry drove over 200 enemy from their emplacements. Well-placed machine guns of 3/25 quickly wiped out one of the largest groups of Japanese yet seen on Iwo.

With morale already at a low ebb because of excessive casualties and the miserably cold rain, troops of the 3d Battalion suffered an additional blow at 1530. Lieutenant Colonel Chambers was severely wounded by enemy machine-gun fire when leaving his forward observation post. Captain James C. Headley, who had replaced Lieutenant Colonel Taul as battalion executive officer, reported to the observation post immediately and assumed command. After apprising himself of the situation, he ordered all companies to begin their preparations for the night. Enemy sniper and mortar fire continued heavy throughout the area.

Colonel Taul's 2d Battalion remained dug in for the greater part of D-plus 3 and made only insignificant gains. The Japanese laid down a heavy mortar barrage about 1100, obviously in preparation for a counterattack, and 2/25 suffered many casualties from bursts along its front lines. Only a small group of enemy formed for the attack, however, and the Marines quickly smashed it. Again at 1830, a body of Japanese was observed moving toward the battalion's front, but quick infantry action with artillery support from the 14th Marines dispersed this formation with little difficulty.

Over on the right of RCT 25 Major Paul Treitel's 1/24 was engaged in mopping up along the coastal area for most of the day. Many pillboxes and caves were destroyed or neutralized, and although units received enemy small arms and knee mortar fire, casualties were comparatively light. Positions were being consolidated and contact established between units by 1700.

There was no indication during late afternoon that the weather would improve in any way. The cold rain continued, and low-hanging fog allowed little visibility. That these conditions were ideal for enemy counterattacks was only too apparent, and both divisions took extreme care in preparing as strong a defense in depth as possible and maintained close contact throughout the night.

Evacuation of casualties became a critical problem during D-plus 3, as mounting surf almost stopped beaching of small craft and amphibious vehicles. The rain, cold, and the coming of darkness made the evacuation stations almost inoperable, so LST 807 volunteered to remain on the beach under fire to act as a hospital ship. Throughout the night doctors operated in the wardroom and the crew assisted in caring for the wounded. Slightly over 200 casualties were treated on this ship and only two of this number died.[15]

During the early morning hours of 23 February a band of Japanese swam ashore on the western beaches and attempted to infiltrate the area of the 27th Marines, in 5th Division reserve. Alert for such action, Marine security elements quickly detected this force but extensive mopping up was necessary.

In the 4th Division zone, an estimated 100 Japanese attempted to penetrate the lines of both 2/25 and 3/25 at about 0500, but again such efforts proved futile. Though possibly not as heavy as on previous nights, Japanese fire continued to hit all along the corps front, inflicting casualties in both divisions.

In preparation for the morning attack, the 4th Division ordered RCT 24 to relieve RCT 25 prior to 0600. The 1st Battalion, 24th Marines would then revert to control of its parent regiment while 2/25 became attached to RCT 24 as regimental reserve. When relieved, Colonel Lanigan's 25th Marines (less 2/25) would pass into division reserve.

Availability of aircraft for direct support of ground troops on Iwo was materially reduced when TF 58 departed during the night of 22/23 February for a second air strike against the Tokyo area of Japan. Admiral Spruance, over-all commander of the Iwo operation, accompanied this fleet northward in the *Indianapolis*. A task group (TG 58.5) of this fast carrier force, composed of the large carrier *Enterprise*, cruisers *Baltimore* and *Flint*, and Destroyer Squadron 54, remained behind at Iwo to provide night fighter protection.

The entire responsibility for providing close air support to Marines ashore now fell on the small (CVE) carriers of Admiral Durgin's carrier support force. These vessels already operated on a full schedule, conducting survivor searches, antisubmarine patrols, combat air patrols and strikes against Chichi Jima. With aircraft of TF 58 gone from the area, the resulting shortage of aircraft for close support

---

[15] *5th Shore Party Rpt*, 6.

would cause delay in meeting some requests for ground attack, thus depriving Marines of much needed assistance.[16]

D-PLUS 4—23 FEBRUARY

The VAC operation order for D-plus 4 (23 February) directed that the attack be continued at 0730 with 0–2 as the objective. The 4th Division was to make its main effort on its left against the second airfield, and the 5th Division was to assist the 4th with fire. Recognizing that the bluffs running north and south along the far left of the 4th Division's zone dominated the entire western side of the island, corps authorized the 5th Division to move across the boundary between divisions if necessary to facilitate its advance and assist the 21st Marines. Units concerned were to be kept advised of all plans and movements.[17]

On the corps left the 26th Marines again found itself stymied by heavy fire from its right front. Colonel Graham had planned to replace 1/26 with 2/27 and then adjust his front to the terrain (high ground on the right, low on the left) by echeloning his advance to the left rear. Although the relief of 1/26 began at 0700 it was not until 0910 that 2/27 was ready to attack. Throughout the day the regiment attempted to advance, but no significant changes in position resulted, and the battalions dug in for the night in approximately the same locations they had held on the previous night.

The serious attrition of leaders continued. About noon a shellburst in the command post of 2/26 wounded the commanding officer, Lieutenant Colonel Joseph P. Sayers, and the executive officer, Major Amedeo Rea, assumed command.

The 1st and 3d Battalions of RCT 27 and Companies A and B, 5th Tank Battalion spent the day re-equipping and performing maintenance. The supply situation ashore was improving, but spare weapons were still at a premium, and 81mm mortar ammunition continued to be a critical item. The men of Company B soon found that their tank park at the northwest corner of Airfield Number 1 was too near the front and too well known to the enemy, so they moved some 500 yards south. At 1100 Company C, which had been supporting RCT 28 in the south, reverted to tank battalion control, moved its bivouac area over to the west side of the first airfield and prepared to join in the northern attack the following day.

In compliance with the corps order, the 4th Division made its main effort against Airfield Number 2 with RCT 21 on the left and RCT 24 on the right. Relief of RCT 25 by the 24th was delayed by the twin obstacles of rugged terrain and enemy fire, and about one hour and 20 minutes elapsed after K-Hour before the division could move out.

The 21st Marines was in position to attack on schedule but could not because of heavy enemy fire, loss of communications, and late arrival of supporting tanks. Troops of this regiment found themselves in a hot corner, unable to advance and taking many casualties. At 1327 another attack failed when the assault company of 2/21 reached its goal but was forced back off the edge of the airfield. No further offensive efforts ensued, and RCT 21 consolidated for the night along the southern edge of the airfield: no gain for the day. On the division right flank RCT 24 pressed forward along its entire front and gained as much as 300 yards in places. Because the left flank did not move during the day, RCT 24 received orders to dig in for the night at about 1500.

Terrain on the right flank where 1/24 was operating limited 4th Division tank activities, as did rough ground, mines, and antitank fire on the left. Tanks from Company C worked up to the southern end of the airfield on RCT 21's front and fired at strong enemy positions across the long (NE-SW) runway. One of these was knocked out by 47mm antitank fire, the third Company C tank destroyed by these high velocity guns in two days.

The 1st and 3d Battalions of the 25th Marines reverted to division reserve when they were relieved by RCT 24, and RCT 23 continued in corps reserve. Mopping up behind the lines kept these units busy, but they also took time

---

[16] VAC AirRpt, Summary, 2; TF 51 Rpt, Pt III, 8.
[17] Disp Landing Force to 5th and 4th MarDivs, 0725, 23Feb45.

to clean and service weapons that had become clogged during the rainy previous day.

The beach situation improved steadily as the work of clearance, construction of exits, and unloading continued. Limited general unloading began on D-plus 4, with LSM's used to ferry the supplies from cargo ships to the shore. Approximately 2,500 rounds of sorely needed 81mm ammunition was unloaded from 3d Division shipping, and LST 646 landed 25 tanks of Major Holly H. Evans' 3d Tank Battalion.[18]

With easterly winds forecast for the next 48 hours the Attack Force Commander requested VAC to commence immediate development of western beaches. These were opposite number one airfield where units of the 5th Division were still mopping up. Since General Rockey's engineer units had all they could handle, the development of these beaches was left to corps engineers.[19]

At 0930, 23 February General Cates closed his command post on board the USS *Bayfield*, and opened at the advance command post location just east of the northwest-southeast runway of Airfield Number 1. With both the 4th and 5th Division headquarters now established on the island, the corps commander landed to appraise the situation and confer with his commanders.

During this meeting the generals decided to

---

[18] Disp CTF 53 to CTF 51, 2126, 23Feb45; Disp LANFOR to EXTROPAC, 2045, 23Feb45.

[19] Disp CTF to CTF 56.1, 2140, 23Feb45; Disp 5th MarDiv to LANFOR, 1824, 24Feb45.

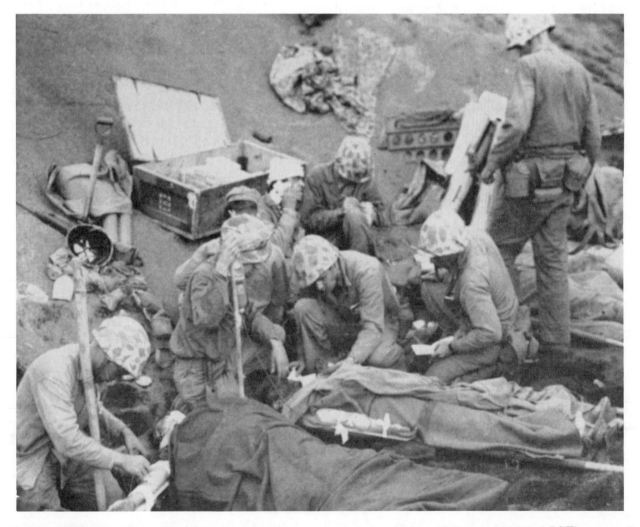

AT AID STATION wounded Marines receive emergency treatment before making the trip to hospital LST's lying off the beaches.

assign an intermediate objective south of the O–2 line. This new line roughly coincided with the O–1 at both ends, but the center bowed out as much as 800 yards to the north to include the second airfield. They planned to continue the attack on the next day (D-plus 5) with the main effort along the line of bluffs that ran almost due north from the southwest end of the airfield. This assault was to be preceded by a heavy preparation by air, naval gunfire, and artillery. Most of the serviceable tanks from three divisions were to be placed in support of the main effort, with the 5th Division Tank Officer (Lieutenant Colonel William R. Collins) responsible for coordination.

D-PLUS 5—24 FEBRUARY

By 0915 (K-Hour), 24 February the Japanese must have known that the Marines planned something special for that morning. During the previous 75 minutes the heavily fortified areas just north of number two airfield had received a tremendous blasting, with lesser preparations all along the front. The mighty *Idaho* lay off the western shore and hurled 14-inch main battery salvos into the critical area above the field, while the *Pensacola* stood off the eastern beaches and fired her heavy guns against positions to the east of the *Idaho's* targets. The howitzers of corps artillery joined in at K-minus 30 minutes, and 15 minutes later the naval guns ceased firing as planes came in from the escort carriers to plaster the same areas with bombs and rockets.[20]

Although wording of the corps attack order for D-plus 5 placed the axis of the main effort in the 5th Division's zone of action,[21] the real punch was to be delivered in RCT 21's zone by tanks operating against the airfield. Once this attack was well underway, the efforts of infantry, tanks, and artillery combined to achieve significant results. But it was slow getting started.

Two taxiways led from the northwest tip of Airfield Number 1 to the second airfield. The original plan for employment of tanks in this attack was for the 5th Division vehicles, followed by those of the 3d Division, to gain access to number two field by proceeding along the western taxiway, while tanks from the 4th used the eastern.[22] However, Company A, 5th Tank Battalion, which led the way along the western route, encountered mines and heavy antitank fire. The first tank struck a mine and was disabled. After continuing a short distance the next one was demolished by a buried aerial torpedo, and heavy fire quickly knocked out three more. Finding their advance effectively blocked, the remaining tanks fought their way back to the bivouac area, and the western approach was abandoned.

All tanks now had to use the eastern taxiway in their push to the second airfield. This route was also mined, and most of the morning was spent in clearance activities and untangling traffic jams along this narrow corridor. Finally about 12 tanks reached the field and opened fire on enemy emplacements north of the strip.

Denied the expected K-Hour armored support, RCT 21 moved out slowly against intense fire of all kinds. During the 4-minute period between 1013 and 1017, Companies I and K lost their commanding officers, but the assault continued despite high casualties. By 1149 the right platoon of Company K had crossed the field and was attacking Japanese positions on a hill just north of the junction of the two runways. Ten minutes later another platoon had made it to the north side of the east-west runway, and the two units joined in a bayonet assault on the high ground. Three times Marines drove the enemy from these positions only to be beaten off themselves by artillery fire. The 3d Battalion was now receiving enfilade fire as it advanced ahead of adjacent units, and shortly after noon the drive ground to a halt.

[20] Although VAC requested the heaviest bombs available for this strike only 26 of the 146 bombs dropped were 500-pounders, the rest were 100-pounders. On this same day the CG, 4thMarDiv complained that air support was inadequate and requested that the Strategic Air Force resume regular flights from the Marianas. Message CG 4th MarDiv to CG VAC, 1240, 24Feb45. On subsequent days the percentage of 500-pound bombs increased. *VAC AirRpt*, Encl A, 2–4.

[21] *VAC OpRpt*, Annex A, Operation Order 4–45, 23Feb45.

[22] *5th TkBn* Periodic Rpt No 5, 1600 23Feb to 1600 24Feb45, (handwritten).

AERIAL VIEW FROM SOUTH TO NORTH shows Airfield Number 1 in foreground and Airfield Number 2 in distance. Charlie-Dog Ridge, Hill 382, and the Amphitheater are numbered 1, 2, and 3 in photo.   (Navy Photo)

By then elements of 3/21 had gained nearly 800 yards in a sustained drive from a line of departure about midway between the airfields. Positions across Airfield Number 2 had been assaulted repeatedly in costly hand-to-hand struggles by infantry employing rifles, hand grenades, picks, entrenching tools, and other makeshift weapons used in place of arms that became clogged with volcanic ash.[23]

The 2d Battalion encountered considerable trouble moving on to the airfield in its zone. When tanks supporting this unit arrived at 1000 they attracted additional heavy artillery and mortar fire that pinned down the assault companies (F and G) of 2/21. As the supporting armor attempted to push along the runway, enemy antitank guns opened up and stopped this movement.[24] Company G on the left finally managed to inch slowly northward around the end of the runway and by 1300 had drawn nearly abreast of RCT 26 on the division's left.[25]

The enemy still clung stubbornly to his positions on the north side of the airfield, but after a second preparation by naval gunfire and artillery, the 21st and 26th Marines launched a coordinated tank-infantry attack at 1330.

Once again Company K of the 21st took possession of the hill north of the center of the air-

[23] Ltr LtCol W. H. Duplantis to Historical Division, HQMC, 1946.

[24] Ltr Maj T. E. Norpell to CMC, 13Feb53.

[25] RCT 26 held up during the morning until RCT 21 could advance on the right to knock out the positions that enfiladed 3/26. *26th Mar SAR*, 7.

strip after a vicious hand-to-hand struggle. At 1415, after driving across the east-west runway, Company I moved on to the high ground and tied in with K. Tanks were now operating on the western half of both runways, pounding gun emplacements and pillboxes. Wherever the Marine armor moved, however, it came under blistering attack by antitank guns and mortar barrages. These latter did little damage to the tanks but were devastating to infantry troops working with them. Horned mines also interfered with movement but alert tankmen detonated many of these with machine-gun fire.

Meanwhile, in the 2d Battalion's zone, Company G tried to work its way north under cover of the west embankment of the field and continue the attack to the day's objective, while Company E crossed the airstrip where the 3d Battalion was going over. At 1415, as it came abreast of the western tip of the east-west runway, Company G was hard hit by a mortar barrage and taken under fire by machine guns and small arms. The attack stopped dead, and Company F was sent up to cover G's withdrawal and reorganization. Company F immediately became engaged in a close-quarter encounter with the enemy that lasted until dusk.

Company E reached the elevation beyond the airfield about 1500 and began a slow attack westward along the east-west runway to make contact with the left assault company. This attempt made little headway, however, and when Company F was unable to make any progress eastward to expedite the junction, this left company withdrew to the south edge of the field for the night. Companies I and K, 3/21 and E, 2/21 stayed in their hard-won positions north of the strip and tied in securely. Desperately needed supplies for these men were carried forward after dark in a trailer drawn by a tank guided across the airfield by two Marines on foot carrying flashlights.

Immediately following the afternoon preparation, RCT 26 moved out with 2/26 and 3/36 attacking abreast. The ground to the immediate front of the regiment was easily taken, but as the advance carried beyond the 21st Marines, 3/26 was once again exposed to flanking fire from the right. Japanese in caves and pillboxes along the bluff line lobbed grenades down

on the Marines. Stretcher bearers suffered heavy casualties as they ran a gauntlet of fire to carry their wounded comrades to the rear. By 1600, 3/26 was about 400 yards ahead of RCT 21 and further advance with an open flank was out of the question, so the regiment began to make preparations for the night. (See Map IV.)

The 1st Battalion moved up out of reserve and took positions along the foot of the ridge line on the division right boundary to tie in with 2/21. Advanced units of 3/26 were ordered to withdraw and make contact with the 2d Battalion on the left and the 1st on the right. Continued enemy pressure made consolidation of the lines extremely difficult, and it was 2200 before Company G was able to break off and move back under the protection of friendly artillery.[26]

Throughout the day artillery support was excellent, with the punch and effect of the 155's massed fires being immediately noted. Corps artillery fired 11 group and 40 battalion missions on D-plus 5.[27] Noteworthy was the coordination between tanks and artillery during the attack. From 1515 to 1545 all artillery on the island was massed in support of the armor. This fire was spotted and adjusted by the commanding officer, 5th Tank Battalion, and control was exercised by the 13th Marines' fire direction center.

Running along the southeast edge of the east-west runway of Airfield Number 2 was a ridge known only as "Charlie-Dog Ridge."[28] In prolongation of this ridge, on a lower level to the southeast, was a semicircular rise of ground that formed the "Amphitheater." In this area Japanese engineers had constructed some of the most formidable defenses on the island. From the south the approach traversed bare flat

---

[26] The CO of Battery G, 13th Marines, personally adjusted fire of several batteries to cover the slow withdrawal of Company G with its many wounded. Ltr Maj R. M. Cook to CMC, 22Jan53.

[27] *VAC ArtyRpt*, 13.

[28] This ridge took its name from the phonetic alphabet designations for the map grid squares in which it was located. This is a common practice in military operations when otherwise insignificant and nameless ground forms assume importance and must be given a name.

ground swept by guns on the ridge. To the east the route led across a weird series of volcanic outcroppings and draws.[29] It was against these positions that the 24th Marines moved out on D-plus 5.

During the morning RCT 24 made good progress on the left where 2/24 and 3/24 attacked abreast of RCT 21 toward the airfield, and by 1100 the 2d Battalion was only 150 yards from the eastern end of the east-west runway.

At 1125 the enemy on Charlie-Dog Ridge opened heavy machine-gun, rifle, and antitank fire into the front lines of the 2d and 3d Battalions at almost point-blank range. To this was added antiaircraft airbursts, mortar, and artillery shells.

Stopped cold by this violent reaction, the Marines called for supporting fires. When air and naval gunfire was refused because of the proximity of front lines to enemy positions, the battalions turned to 105's of the 14th Marines and their own "artillery": the busy little 81mm and 60mm mortars. During the 5-minute preparation fired by these weapons Company G, 2/24 worked four machine guns into positions from which they could bear on some of the enemy emplacements on Charlie-Dog. Hardworking Marines from the weapons company also manhandled a 37mm gun close to the front and succeeded in knocking out six hostile emplacements.

Yard by yard the Marines advanced. Assault squads worked from one strong point to the next, burning and blasting their way to the top of the ridge, followed by the rest of Company G. By 1700 Companies G and I, and one platoon of E, were mopping up the last stubborn defenders. With the elimination of resistance in this area Company F, which had been pinned down in the left of the regimental zone of action, was able to advance and regain contact with the 21st Marines.

Company I, left company of the 3d Battalion, had advanced about 300 yards in cooperation with 2/24, but the other two companies met intense fire from the Amphitheater and suffered heavy casualties. At 1500 the battalion mortars fired 80 white phosphorous smoke shells to screen evacuation of casualties along the front. At 1608 the 3/24 observation post was hit by a mortar barrage. Three men were killed and the commanding officer, Lieutenant Colonel Alexander A. Vandegrift, Jr., was wounded. Major Doyle A. Stout, the executive officer, assumed command when Vandegrift was evacuated.

The 1st Battalion, on RCT 24's right flank, did not engage in the main effort but pushed forward slowly yard by yard over chaotic terrain. The enemy fired machine guns and small arms at short range from cleverly hidden emplacements and cave entrances. Here, as elsewhere along the corps front, Marines caught only fleeting glimpses of the enemy. As the Japanese Naval Headquarters expressed the situation in a report dated 23 February, "At the present time there is the unusual situation in the above [southern sector] area of our [Japanese] troops all being underground, while the enemy troops are above ground." [30]

At 1700, after a day of extremely bitter fighting, Colonel Jordan ordered all units of the 24th to consolidate for the night. Its left flank, participating in the corps' main effort, had advanced about 500 yards to overrun Charlie-Dog Ridge.

Significant progress had been made on D-plus 5. The enemy salient in the center was eliminated and Marines clung to positions along most of the southern edge of the airfield with advance units on high ground north of the runway intersection. On the left the 26th Marines had also pushed northward for another 500 yards. But on the eastern side of the island 4th Division lines remained almost stationary in the face of rugged terrain and a determined enemy.

Behind the front lines, command posts, artillery positions, medical installations, and supply dumps vied for space on the narrow southern end of Iwo. On 24 February two additional important command groups crowded ashore. At 0955 General Schmidt closed his headquarters on board the USS *Auburn* to assume command ashore, and at 1530 General Erskine opened his 3d Division command post on the island.

[29] Capt J. W. Thomason, III, USMCR, "The Fourth Division at Iwo Jima," a manuscript, no date.

[30] 4th MarDiv D-2 Language Section translation, 11Mar45.

Meanwhile, the 3d Division, less RCT 3 and RCT 21 (already ashore), began landing. Surf conditions still precluded the use of small craft, so LCM's were used for the ship-to-shore movement. The northern half of Beach Red 2 and the southern half of Yellow 1 were re-designated Beach Black and assigned to the division. By dark Colonel Howard N. Kenyon's 9th Marines had moved three battalions into assembly areas ready to join in the attack the next day, and the rest of the 3d Tank Battalion landed from LST 477.

Lieutenant Colonel Raymond F. Crist, commanding the 12th Marines (3d Division Artillery), landed just after noon on 24 February and proceeded with his reconnaissance party to the area selected the previous day by his executive officer. The only firing unit to land was Battery B, of Major George B. Thomas' 1/12, which brought in its 75mm pack howitzers late that afternoon.[31] Other 12th Marine units

started landing on the 25th, but it was the first of March before all the pieces were landed and the tactical setup complete.

During their third day in corps reserve, the 23d Marines was strengthened by the arrival of 473 enlisted men and 11 officers from the 24th Replacement Draft. These men were assigned to the battalions in proportion to losses suffered to date in the operation.

By the end of D-plus 5 casualties had risen to 7,758; an increase of 5,338 since the end of D-Day. During the 5-day drive to the second airfield (D-plus 1 through D-plus 5) losses were as follows:

Killed in action	773
Wounded in action	3741
Died of wounds	261
Missing in action	5
Combat fatigue	558
Total	5338

---

[31] This was not according to plan. The regimental executive officer had recommended that 2/12 land first, but due to a misunderstanding the commanding officer of the USS *Knox* ordered Battery B, which was embarked on board his APA, to land. *12th Mar SAR*, 5.

CHAPTER **VI**

Through the Center

(D-plus 6—D-plus 19)

At 0700, 25 February the 3d Division assumed the task of clearing the critical central portion of the Motoyama Plateau. Its route of advance lay across the second airfield and through Motoyama Village to the unfinished Airfield Number 3. On either side of this tableland the ground fell away to the sea in a jumbled series of draws and ridges that obstructed movement and limited observation. By pushing forward in the middle to gain control of the relatively flat ground along the backbone of the island the Marines would gain three advantages: first, they could drive laterally down to the coast attacking along the ridges; second, they could use the routes in the interior for supply and movement of units working the flanks; and third, this would deny the enemy the final positions from which he could place observed fire on the beaches.

While the topography of this center strip made it the best possible route to the north, the terrain was by no means easy. On the plateau the sandy soil of the south gave way to volcanic sandstone that lay in tumbled crevices and jagged outcroppings. Someone has said, aptly, that it might well be used as an illustration for Dante's *Inferno*. Superimposed on this forbidding ground were Japanese defenses of all kinds, and every elevation assumed tactical importance and was bitterly defended. The approaches were protected by mine fields and tank ditches well covered by fire, and mortar and artillery concentrations could be laid on either the forward or reverse slopes.

Despite the advantages of a push through center in the 3d Division's zone, to be followed by thrusts to the flanks to clear the remainder of the island, there were other factors to be considered. One was the problem of supply. To ensure an uninterrupted flow of ammunition from ship to shore, it was considered imperative that the western beaches be opened to receive small craft as soon as possible. The landing force could not afford to depend solely on the cluttered eastern beaches. If the wind shifted strongly to the east, surf conditions would make unloading on that side of the island extremely hazardous. Moreover, General Schmidt had been directed to clear the beaches and airfields and push unloading in order that ships could be made available for the Okinawa Campaign. But before the western shore could be used, the Japanese would have to be cleared from the high ground to the north that dominated those beaches.

Secondly, on either side of the 3d's zone of action, where the plateau jutted into the paths of the other two divisions, high ground menaced General Erskine's flanks.[1] Finally, and perhaps most important, was the fact that

---

[1] J. A. Isely and P. A. Crowl, *The U. S. Marines and Amphibious War* (Princeton, New Jersey, 1951), 495, hereinafter cited as *Isely and Crowl*. Ltr Gen H. Schmidt (Ret) to CMC, 15Jan53.

MAJOR GENERAL ERSKINE commanded the 3d Marine Division on Iwo Jima.

should any one division make any considerable advance beyond the others, there would be the additional task of providing troops for flank support, and the advanced division would find itself being fired upon from every direction.[2] For these reasons the corps continued its struggle to the northeast, attempting simultaneous advances all along the front.[3]

HILLS PETER AND 199 OBOE
(D-Plus 6—D-Plus 8)[4]

At 0930 on D-plus 6, when RCT 9 passed through the 21st Marines to continue the attack, the line of departure skirted the southwest edge of the airfield, bulged across to the high ground immediately north of the center of the field, then picked up again along the

southern edge where the 9th Marines tied in with the 4th Division. The 2d Battalion on the left was confronted by strong positions in the line of bluffs that stretched north from the western end of the airfield and the high ground just north of the east-west runway. On the right, 1/9 faced a low but strategically located hill that later came to be called Hill PETER. (See Map V.)

The preparation for the attack was much the same as on the day before. One battleship and two cruisers fired deliberate main-battery destructive missions from K-minus 50 to K-minus 30. Corps artillery fired a 1,200-round preparation with half of the rounds fired to the front of the 3d Division, and a preattack air strike, using a large number of 500-lb. bombs, was delivered just prior to the jump-off.[5] The corps' main effort was to be in the center.

Enemy fire that swept both runways of the airfield inflicted brutal casualties as the battalions inched ahead. Making its main effort on the left, RCT 9 attached the 26 available tanks from Companies A and B, 3d Tank Battalion to Lieutenant Colonel Robert E. Cushman's 2d Battalion. These vehicles struck out across the fire-swept strip 200 yards ahead of the infantry in an effort to take out the heavy weapons that dominated the field.[6] Even with this support gains were slow and costly for both vehicles and men.

Lieutenant Colonel Carey A. Randall's 1st Battalion forced one platoon to the base of Hill

---

[2] Fresh in General Schmidt's mind was the experience on Saipan where his 4th Division advanced so rapidly that he had a 3,000-yard gap on his flank, which imposed a serious problem of flank security. Ltr Gen. H. Schmidt to Author, 28Oct52.

[3] This chapter deals only with the 3d Division operations in the center of the corps zone of action. The actions of the 5th on the left, and the 4th on the right, are covered individually in Chapters VII and VIII respectively.

[4] The designations "PETER" and "199 OBOE" derived from target grid locations on the island map,

not from elevations. These hills were actually about 360 feet high. Unless otherwise cited, material in the section is based on the following: *3d MarDiv SAR*; 9th Marine Action Report, Iwo Jima Operation, 20Apr45, hereinafter cited as *9th Mar SAR*; *12th Mar SAR*; *21st Mar SAR*; *3d TkBn SAR*; VAC C-3 Periodic Reports, 19Feb45 through 9Apr45, hereinafter cited as *C-3 Periodic Rpt*.

[5] More aircraft were available for close support missions on D-plus 6 than on the previous day when special search missions and refueling operations had placed a serious limitation on air support. TF 56 G-3 Periodic Reports, Iwo Jima Operation, 19Feb45 through 13Mar45, No. 7, hereinafter cited as *TF 56 Periodic Rpt*.

[6] The 2d Battalion considered riding the infantry across the airfield on the tanks, but this idea was abandoned because the height of enemy machine-gun fire was not known and mortar fire against the tanks was intense. *9th Mar SAR*, Encl B, Pt III, 2.

PETER, but the unit was so depleted by then that it could not hold this advanced position. After five hours of fighting the assault had progressed a scant 100 yards; slightly more on the left.

At 1430 the reserve battalion (3/9) was ordered to pass through the 2d Battalion's right and attack to the north until it had bypassed the center of resistance that was holding up 2/9. The battalion would then extend to the left to contact RCT 26, which was some 300 yards ahead at the division boundary. Cushman's battalion was then to attack and eliminate the pocket.

The passage of lines was made at 1510, Company I on the left, K on the right, and Company L prepared to follow the left company to effect contact with the 26th Marines on order. A storm of small-arms and machine-gun fire from the front and flank pinned down the left unit almost immediately, but the rest of the battalion line advanced slowly by fire and movement. Both companies tortuously worked machine guns to forward positions to deliver covering fire, and Company K employed 60mm mortars against close-in targets. With Japanese mortar and artillery fire inflicting heavy losses among the slow moving Marines, the companies were directed to gain protection of the high ground to the front as quickly as possible. The left platoon withdrew from its sector where pillboxes held it up, and maneuvered to the right past the strong point.

FIRE DIRECTION CENTER of 1st Provisional Field Artillery Group. Here fire requests and adjustment corrections are converted into fire commands for the 155mm howitzers in support of the corps.

As the troops crept ahead, the enemy adjusted his artillery to keep pace. The two assault company commanders were killed within a few minutes of one another, and other key personnel, officer and enlisted, fell in rapid succession. Both units faltered and began to draw back from the continuous blast of withering fire, losing contact with adjacent units in the process. Lieutenant Colonel Harold C. Boehm, commanding 3/9, acted quickly to regain control and reestablish contact with friendly elements. He sent his operations officer to take over Company K, which had suffered five officer casualties and was now seriously disorganized. Then he ordered this company to tie in with the 1st Battalion on the right and committed his reserve, Company L, to effect a union with 2/9 on the left. Company I then became the center unit between L and K. By 1915 the situation was stabilized with contact established between

MARINES WARM COFFEE at sulfur pit. The pipe on which canteen cup rests was used in Japanese bath. Water often came to the surface at 160° to 170° **F.**

all units along the regimental front. From left to right were 2/9, 3/9, and 1/9. In addition to infantry losses, nine tanks were knocked out while supporting the 9th Marines on 25 February.

Since only one battery of the 12th Marines was ashore early on D-plus 6, artillery support for RCT 9 was furnished by the 1st Battalion, 14th Marines, in direct support, and the 4th Battalion, 13th Marines, in a reinforcing role. More 3d Division artillery landed during the day, however, and by 1700 Batteries B, D, and E were ready to fire. These units were combined into a provisional battalion under the control of 1/12 and relieved 1/14 in support of the 9th Marines.

The 21st Marines also assisted RCT 9 on its first day in the attack, firing heavy machine guns, 37mm guns, and light mortars over the heads and to the flanks of Colonel Kenyon's men until masked. In addition, the 81mm mortars of RCT 21 were attached to the 9th but reverted to parent control at 1730.

Fighting had been extremely bitter and costly. But by the end of the day RCT 9 was established on the rising ground north of the airfield, except for the far right of the zone where the northeast strip cut through and beyond the lines. The 3d Battalion, 21st Marines, attached to RCT 9 at 1345, manned the regimental reserve line between the airfields during the night of 25/26 February.

By D-plus 7 it was clear that the corps was ramming against the enemy's main battle positions that extended northwest to southeast across the island. In the 3d Division zone this belt included the second airfield and the rising ground to the north. Hill PETER and a second hill, 199 OBOE, 225 yards to the northwest were key terrain features in this area. (See Map V.)

General Schmidt's operation order again directed that General Erskine's division make the main effort with corps artillery delivering 50 percent of its fire in support of this drive, the other 50 percent to be divided equally between the 4th and 5th Divisions.[7]

At 0800 the 9th Marines resumed the attack with the 1st and 2d Battalions abreast, 3/9 and 3/21 (attached) in reserve. Tanks operated with both assault battalions, firing into caves and destroying pillboxes and bunkers. Company C (tanks), assisting 1/9 in the drive against Hill PETER, worked a flame tank around to the reverse side and burned out a tunnel from which enemy troops were emerging. All day long the 9th battled to gain the high ground that blocked its way, but by nightfall there had been no significant gains.

On 27 February (D-plus 8) Colonel Kenyon's regiment continued its bitter struggle to break through to the northeast. During the morning the 2d Battalion made slight gains in the direction of Hill 199 OBOE, and 1/9 on the right reached the top of Hill PETER. However, well-concealed enemy positions on the reverse slope and fire from the vicinity of 199 OBOE prevented any sizable advance in the 1st's zone of action.

Then, in the afternoon, the break came. At 1250, following a 10-minute preparation by division and corps artillery, both battalions struck out in a coordinated attack. The 1st Battalion overran Hill PETER and continued on down the reverse slope and up to the crest of 199 OBOE. On the left the 2d drove ahead to bring its lines abreast of 1/9 for the first time since the attack started.

After three days of seemingly endless uphill battering against these Japanese main-line positions, Airfield Number 2 and the commanding terrain to the north had finally fallen to the exhausted Marines. But although the two key hills were overrun on D-plus 8, many bypassed enemy troops remained in caves to harass the rear. Mopping up in this area continued for the next two days. This had been RCT 9's harsh introduction to the fighting on Iwo. In summarizing the period Colonel Kenyon wrote:

Features of this action were the skill, determination, and aggressiveness displayed by our own troops; the unprecedented tenacity and defensive resourcefulness displayed by the enemy . . . the decisive aid rendered infantry troops by tanks; and finally, the excellent coordination of all supporting units with infantry maneuvers.[8]

[7] VAC OpRpt, Annex A, Operation Order 6–45, 25Feb45.

[8] 9th Mar SAR, 5.

3D DIVISION MARINES man hastily prepared position amid the ruins of Motoyama Village. Sulfur mine and refinery can be seen dimly in background.

MOTOYAMA VILLAGE AND BEYOND

(D-Plus 9—D-plus 14)[9]

As the center and left of the corps line approached the 0–2 objective line, V Corps assigned a new line (0–3) in its operation order for 28 February. Starting on the west coast about 1,000 yards south of Kitano Point this line led eastward, then to the southeast,

[9] Unless otherwise cited, material in this section is based on the following: *3d MarDiv SAR; 9th Mar SAR; 12th Mar SAR; 21st Mar SAR; 3d TkBn SAR; VAC OpRpt,* Annex A, Operation Orders; *3d MarDiv SAR;* Operation Orders; *C–3 Periodic Rpts; VAC OpRpt.*

roughly following the edge of the northern plateau, to join 0–1 at Tachiiwa Point. In the 3d Division's zone of action seizure of this line would place Marines on high ground overlooking the water. It was toward this goal that the division moved out on D-plus 9.

At dawn the 21st Marines started its 1st and 3d Battalions forward to pass through RCT 9. Before these units could reach the line of departure, they became involved in fire fights with enemy snipers and machine gunners, but by 0815 they were ready to pass through.

The attack was preceded by a 30-minute preparation fired by the 12th Marines, reinforced by a majority of the corps 155mm's.

This bombardment was followed at K-Hour by a barrage that lifted 100 yards every seven minutes for a total of 700 yards. On the left the 1st Battalion made only about 150 yards before it was stopped by a heavy concentration of infantry weapons emplaced in the rising ground to its immediate front. On the right of the division's zone, however, where the high ground had already been gained, the 3d Battalion advanced rapidly and moved forward 400 yards by 0930. During this surge by 3/21, elements of Company L became intermingled with a unit of the 4th Division operating on the division boundary. This slowed the attack, and by 1130 units were bogged down all along the 3d Division front.

At 1300 the artillery fired another 5-minute preparation and troops jumped off again behind a lifting barrage. In this afternoon drive, as in the morning, the battalion on the right was able to move ahead at a better pace than the unit on the left. The 3d Battalion swept through the cluster of rocks and pillboxes that had once been Motoyama Village and seized the high ground overlooking Airfield Number 3. This left the 1st Battalion about 400 yards to the rear, still held up by the strong point on the left of the regimental zone of action.

Faced with a wide gap between the two assault battalions, Colonel Withers ordered 2/21 to attack through this hole, bypass the enemy in front of the 1st Battalion, and gain contact with 3/21 near the village. K-Hour was scheduled for 1530, with the artillery firing a preparation and rolling barrage ahead of the advance. Because of the distance (600 yards) and constant enemy fire, 2/21 was late crossing the line of departure and did not derive maximum benefit from the barrage. Only slight progress was made, but at 1700 Company E made contact with the right battalion and Company G tied in with 1/21 to complete a winding but continuous line across the division front. (See Map VI.)

By nightfall it appeared that the 3d Division had finally burned and blasted its way through the center of the enemy's main line. On either side, however, the 4th and 5th Divisions had been held up in costly struggles against Hills 382 and 362A,[10] respectively, two of the most powerful of the Japanese cross-island defenses. The corps order for 1 March (D-plus 10) reflected this change in the situation. The preponderance of supporting fires no longer went to the 3d Division; instead the corps artillery was now to divide its fires equally among the three divisions.

At 0830 the 3d Division resumed its offensive with the 2d and 3d Battalions of the 21st Marines in the assault. The 1st Battalion remained behind on the left flank to clean out the

---

[10] There were three 362-foot hills on Iwo Jima. To avoid confusion they have been designated as A, B, and C. Hill 362A was northwest in the 5th's zone. Hill 362B, also in the 5th zone, was in the north-central portion of the island, and 362C was located to the northeast, in the 3d Division's zone of action.

EVAPORATION VATS AND FURNACES located near the sulfur mines show destruction wrought on surface installations during the fierce fighting. This area is just west of Motoyama Village.

enemy pocket that the regiment had side-stepped the day before. As 2/21 and 3/21 moved out to the northeast the gap between the 1st and 2d Battalions reopened. The 3d Battalion, 9th Marines (attached to RCT 21) was now ordered to attack through this hole across 1/21's front to reach the division boundary and protect the regimental left flank. Attacking at a right angle to the boundary, 3/9 met only light resistance and accomplished its mission by 1500. Meanwhile, the 1st Battalion eliminated the enemy pocket and moved up on the left flank abreast of 3/9 and parallel to the western limit of the 3d Division zone.

As RCT 21 advanced to the northeast and drew away from the 5th Division, the neces-sity of protecting its open left flank seriously overextended the front. To correct this situation two actions were taken. At 1500 corps modified the boundary between the 3d and 5th Divisions so that responsibility for the position held by 1/21 passed to the 5th Division. This shortened the 3d Division front and released 1/21 for other tasks. Then at 1545 the 3d Division split its zone of action down the middle, and ordered an advance with two regiments abreast, RCT 21 on the left, RCT 9 on the right. (See Map VII.)

For this late afternoon attack 3/9 and the tank battalion remained attached to RCT 21, but 3/21 was attached to the 9th Marines. This made unnecessary a time-consuming shift of

MAIL FROM HOME played an important part in sustaining morale on Iwo. The first delivery was made by LST on 24 February. On 1 March an air drop was made. Beginning the next day all mail was flown to the island. (Navy Photo)

units already positioned along the front. The 2d Battalion, 9th Marines was held in division reserve.

At 1640 the 12th Marines, with all battalions now in action and reinforced by 155's from corps artillery, opened up with a pulverizing preparation.[11] Five minutes later the two regiments jumped off abreast, preceded by a rolling barrage. In the zone of RCT 9 the 1st Battalion passed through 3/21, but riddling fire from the front and right flank stopped it after little or no gain. The 3d Battalion, 21st Marines took up a reserve position in the vicinity of Motoyama Village after its relief.

The 21st Marines, with 2/21 on the right and 3/9 on the left, also ran into fierce resistance and made no progress. Meanwhile, however, the 3d Battalion, 26th Marines, completed its relief of 1/21 on the 3d Division's left boundary and that unit reverted to RCT 21 reserve.

Although the afternoon attack (with two regiments abreast) proved futile, progress by RCT 21 during the morning had carried the lines 500 yards forward to deepen the breach in the enemy's heavily fortified defensive line. When the division dug in for the night on 1 March (D-plus 10) with two regiments abreast (the 3d Marines was still afloat in Expeditionary Troops Reserve), it faced northeast from positions approximately 600 yards east of Motoyama, running north across the western portion of Airfield Number 3. (See Map VII.)

On 2 March (D-plus 11) the 9th Marines confronted an enemy strong point of undetermined size but of obvious strength. In the 21st Marine zone of action, however, it appeared that, while there was resistance all along the front, the main obstacle to an advance was the enemy holding high ground just to the north of the division boundary. The principal terrain feature in that area was Hill 362B and the finger-like plateau that extended 400 yards southwest from the hill to the boundary. Since RCT 21 could not advance until this flanking position was in friendly hands, General Erskine received permission from corps to attack north across the boundary to seize Hill 362B. He then shifted the line of demarcation between his regiments to run north from the line of departure, diagonally across the front, to the division boundary. This gave his left regiment a north axis of advance while the 9th Marines was to continue to the northeast in a zone that fanned out on the left beyond RCT 21 to include the entire 3d Division sector. The division main effort was to be made on the left.

K-Hour (0800) was preceded by a 30-minute preparation by the 12th Marines, with 155's and direct support destroyers adding their weight against deep targets. But 155mm fire was limited because the 5th Division was making the corps' main effort and received the preponderance of corps artillery support.

The 2d Battalion, 9th Marines moved up from reserve to jump off on the left, abreast of the 1st Battalion. At first both units made small gains but soon enemy antitank and machine-gun fire checked the advance. Supporting armor engaged bunkers and dug-in enemy tanks, and friendly artillery fire was drawn in close to the lines. But Japanese machine guns, secure and deadly in their emplacements even closer to the front, continued to smother the assault. A second preparation at 1530 and another coordinated attack failed.

The 21st Marines moved out at 0800 with 1/21 and 3/9 in the assault. The 1st Battalion had moved up from the rear to a position on the right of 2/21, and was to attack in column of companies across that unit's front to clear the rest of Airfield Number 3. The 2d Battalion was to support the attack by fire from its present positions until masked, and then revert to regimental reserve. After an advance of about 150 yards the 1st Battalion was held up at the southern edge of the airfield where it remained for the rest of the day.

---

[11] Firing batteries of the 12th Marines came ashore from 24Feb to 1Mar45. All of 1/12 (75mm pack howitzers) was ashore by the end of D-plus 6. LtCol William T. Fairbourn's 2/12 (75mm pack howitzers) completed landing operations the morning of 26Feb. 3/12, LtCol Alpha L. Bowser, Jr., stretched out landing activities from 27Feb to 1Mar, placing the last piece of the 12th Marines in firing position at 1600, D-plus 10. The 4th Bn of Maj J. B. Wallen had its Battery K in firing positions on 27Feb but heavy surf prevented the other two batteries (M and L) from landing until the next day. The 3d and 4th Bns were equipped with heavier 105mm howitzers. *12th Mar SAR*, Encls A, B, C, and D.

The approaches to the plateau and Hill 362B led over flat ground that offered little cover to 3/9 as it moved out in a column of companies. Company L, in the lead, received fire from several large caliber flat-trajectory weapons located in the vicinity of Hill 362B, and it was decided to use tanks to knock them out before resuming the advance. From the battalion commander's observation post at the line of departure, an area was spotted just forward of the lines where tanks could find hull-defilade firing positions. A platoon from Company B (tanks) moved to this location, and, with the commander of Company L directing fire by radio, engaged the enemy guns.

Under cover of this tank fire the infantry resumed its advance. When it became evident that one company so greatly under strength could not cover the zone of action, Company K was thrown in on the right and Company I moved to cover the left. At 1100 the forward elements reached the rising ground in front of the hill where they received greatly intensified small-arms fire. Tanks continued to support the attack, firing over the heads of the Marines at targets on 362B.

The battalion had pulled away from units on the right and left, but was ordered to forge ahead without regard for its flanks. The battalion 81mm mortars and company 60's were used effectively as 3/9 inched ahead up onto the ridge that led to the final objective.

At 1400, 2/21 was ordered to attack and close the gap between the two assault battalions by seizing the high ground beyond the eastern end of the airfield. The battalion commenced its drive at 1600 under almost continuous enemy fire, but by 1700 the lead platoon was slightly ahead of 3/9, which was now near the foot of Hill 362B. At 1730 the commanding officer of 2/21, Lieutenant Colonel Lowell E. English, was wounded, and the executive officer, Major George A. Percy, assumed command. Soon after this Company G, which led the battalion, was ordered to withdraw to tenable positions and tie in with the unit on the left. The other two companies, E and F, echeloned to the right rear to link up with 1/21. However, the fire-swept clearing of the airfield could not be occu-

pied, so physical contact was not established in the center of the regimental zone.

The division main effort on D-plus 11 had been moderately successful, with 3/9 making progress against Hill 362B and 2/21 advancing northeast along the left boundary. The 9th Marines, however, made little progress against the enemy stronghold in the right of the zone.

A captured Japanese map bore out the belief that RCT 9 was up against a powerful well-organized enemy defensive area. Intelligence officers could not determine from this sketch whether or not the line extended completely across the division front, but reports of strong emplacements ahead of the 21st Marines indicated that it might. However, plans for the next phase of attack were postulated on the hope that a soft spot might be found somewhere between the resistance holding up RCT 9 and the positions in the vicinity of Hill 362B.

The corps order for 3 March directed the 5th Division to relieve 3d Division units at Hill 362B by 1000, and General Erskine shifted the boundary line between regiments so that the division zone was again divided equally. This change brought the direction of attack for RCT 21 back to the northeast, paralleling the 9th. He directed that RCT 9's main effort be made on its left and the 21st's on its right. This would channel the bulk of his power through center in an attempt to drive past the stubborn core of resistance that had stymied the division right flank since 1 March. (See Map VII.)

The 1st and 2d Battalions, 9th Marines, battled all day against the maze of caves, pillboxes, dug-in tanks, stone walls, and trenches that blocked their route of advance. These emplacements were cleverly hidden in the chaotic jumble of torn rocks, and the use of smokeless powder by the Japanese further complicated the problem of detection. Enemy mortars and artillery were not as active as on other days, but anti-tank and machine-gun fire was devastating. Marine tanks operated singly or in small groups in close coordination with the infantry, and although they knocked out many emplacements, these machines were unable to breach the hostile line.

The left regiment jumped off toward 0-3 with 2/21 in the attack. The 3d Battalion, 9th (still

SHORE PARTY PERSONNEL used heavy cargo-handling equipment to keep supplies moving forward. This photo, taken from bow of a landing ship, shows cranes and tractors at work. Note Marston matting road at left. Human conveyor belt expedites the unloading of lighter packaged items.

attached to RCT 21), was to remain in position until relieved by 5th Division units, and 1/21 was in division reserve. As Companies F and G advanced, they received high-velocity fire from Hill 362B, but kept moving ahead. By 0900 they had gone nearly 400 yards, and were approaching the elevation around Hill 357 at the eastern edge of the Motoyama Plateau. To cover the flanks of this attack, Company I, 3/9 moved up on the left, and Company E (2/21 reserve) came up along the other side. At 1100 the 2d Battalion gained the top of the hill and began mopping up with the help of flame throwers and demolition teams from Company I.

Although deadly battle was still in progress, it now appeared that no important enemy resistance remained between 2/21 and the sea. Therefore, at 1430 the dividing line between regiments was again changed, and RCT 21 was ordered to swing to the southeast to envelop the

Japanese positions that were holding up the 9th Marines. Hill 362C, in the southeastern portion of the division zone of action, was assigned as the objective.

The 1st Battalion, 21st Marines, was released from division reserve, reverting to parent control for this attack. The shortest route from its reserve assembly area near Motoyama to the line of departure behind 2/21 was across the airfield. But Japanese guns still interdicted the field. As a result, the battalion took a longer but partially protected route that led north around the airstrip into the 5th's zone, then southeast in the shelter of Hills 362B and 357. By 1530, 1/21 was in position, with Company K, 3/9 attached, and ready to jump off.

The attack, which was preceded by a 5-minute preparation by artillery and naval gunfire, made good progress initially but was halted after a 250-yard advance. A platoon of tanks

CRITICAL SUPPLIES are parachuted onto Airfield Number 1. Marine and Army transports delivered 78 tons of equipment by air drop during the operation. (AF Photo)

supported 1/21 from positions near Motoyama Village, placing direct fire on Japanese emplacements in front of the Marines.

At 1800 further attempts to advance were halted, and the division consolidated positions on the best available ground. In the 21st Marines' zone of action 2/21 and 1/21 gained physical contact, but an open flank existed between the right of that regiment and RCT 9. This 250-yard gap was covered by fire. The 9th Marines tied in tightly at approximately the same positions it had held all day.

The significant action on D-plus 12 had all been in the northern half of the zone of action. There the Marines had seized almost all the high ground northeast of the airfield and launched a drive to the southeast to envelop the enemy to the south. (See Map VII.)

Shortly after midnight the Japanese found the gap between the two regiments and began infiltrating along the airfield. After a sharp fight between 2/9 and an estimated 200 enemy troops, this penetration was checked. The 3d Battalion, 21st Marines sent units forward from the reserve assembly area to the airfield where they patrolled until daylight.

The 3d Battalion, 21st Marines, reverted to RCT 21 at 0645 and called in its patrols prior to starting forward to relieve 1/21. It followed a circuitous route to avoid enemy fire, but while crossing the area north of Airfield Number 3, the battalion was taken under fire and considerably delayed.

The corps order for D-plus 13 (4 March) designated 0730 as K-Hour, but General Erskine received permission to hold up until 3/21 was ready to pass through the 1st Battalion. Finally, at 1140, units were ready and the division jumped off following the same scheme of maneuver as on the previous day. On the left of the 21st Marines' zone of action 2/21 continued its efforts to seize the remainder of the high ground overlooking the beaches, with Hill 357 as the immediate objective. On the right, attacking at right angles to the 2d Battalion's front, 3/21 took up where 1/21 left off in its assault against Hill 362C. Company B, 1/21, was sent north to reinforce the seriously depleted 2d Battalion and Company C stayed on line to protect the dangling right flank of 3/21. The rest of the battalion moved back into regimental reserve.

In spite of a 20-minute preparation by division artillery and destroyers, followed by a rolling barrage, the division failed to get its attack rolling. Flanking fire from the 5th Division zone prevented any advance by the 2d Battalion and the 3d made only 100 yards before being stopped by the highly organized and formidable positions around Hill 362C.

The only change in the 9th Marines' zone of action was the return of 3/9, which had been operating with RCT 21. The 1st and 3d Battalions made repeated heartbreaking attempts to advance but were unable to dent the positions to their front. Intermittent rain squalls and low-hanging clouds limited observation and reduced the effectiveness of supporting weapons. Late in the afternoon all divisions received the following dispatch from V Corps:

Consolidate at 1700. Except for limited adjustment of positions plan to utilize tomorrow for reorganization preparatory to attack on a limited front on 6 March. Each div effect necessary reorganization by noon tomorrow to have one RCT less one Bn available for employment 6 March exclusive of regimental reserves for units in the line. General direction of proposed attack to eastward in present zones of action.[12]

Finally, after 14 days of grueling battle the Marines were to take a well-deserved break for reorganization and what little rest the enemy would permit.

On 5 March the 3d Division held the line with four battalions (2/21, 3/21, 1/9, 2/9), while the other two spent the day receiving replacement troops and equipment to strengthen their tired and depleted units for the next attack. Companies B and C, 21st Marines were pulled back from their positions on the line to rejoin their parent 1st Battalion in an assembly area north of Airfield Number 2. The 3d Battalion, 9th Marines remained in position as division reserve between the northeast-southwest runway and Motoyama Village.

No attacks were launched by the Marines and enemy infantry was not aggressive, but the artillery of both sides continued active. Particular attention was given to the Japanese defenses in the vicinity of Hill 362C, with air and naval gunpower cooperating in repeated bombardment against known and suspected positions in that area. Throughout the day artillery officers worked on a fire plan for the support of the assault on 6 March.

PROGRESS BEHIND THE LINES

It took the 3d Division nine punishing days of yard-by-yard advances to move approximately 3,000 yards from positions below Airfield Number 2 to the line it held on D-plus 14. This drive carried General Erskine's 9th and 21st Regiments through the heavily fortified main cross-island defense line and into violent contact with the secondary line of defense. Erskine and his regimental commanders had been constantly on the alert for weak points in the enemy defenses, and when a soft spot was detected the advance was pushed ahead without regard for the progress of adjacent units, with reserves positioned to protect open flanks. Then the breach was widened by launching flank attacks through gaps between assault units and the bypassed enemy left to be mopped up as the division smashed ahead.

The destruction and neutralization effect of supporting weapons was exploited to the fullest extent posible. However, many enemy positions withstood even large-caliber shells from ships' guns. Furthermore, the extensive networks of caves and underground passages made it possible for the Japanese to wait out a barrage secure in subterranean chambers and then come up to the surface to resist from the 200-yard zone immediately to the front of Marines, where heavy supporting weapons could not fire for fear of endangering friendly troops. For these reasons the battle was reduced to a series of close-in engagements between tank-supported Marines with flame throwers and demolitions, and the deeply entrenched, stubbornly resisting enemy.

Such were the tactics and the battle. To support this activity, thousands of men labored unceasingly behind the lines, on the beaches, and on board ships.

On D-plus 6, the day that the 3d Division began its drive up the center of the island, general unloading of cargo ships commenced, with the VAC Shore Party assuming control of all shore party activities. Easterly winds, which rolled up high surf on the eastern beaches, made unloading difficult, but LSM's and LST's plied steadily between cargo ships and the beach and the work progressed rapidly. By D-plus 8 beach exits and roads were constructed on the western side of the island where preliminary surveys showed conditions suitable for beaching LCT's and smaller craft. Enemy fire from northern Iwo, however, frustrated attempts to operate those beaches until D-plus 11 when Purple 2 was opened.[13] All assault shipping had been unloaded and retired from the area by 3 March (D-plus 12), and Garrison Group Zero[14] commenced discharging its cargo the same day.

---

[12] *VAC disp* 1624, 4Mar45.

[13] On D-plus 10 the ammunition resupply ship *Columbia Victory* was ordered to stand off the western beaches to be unloaded. Upon approaching the area she was bracketed by fire from the northwestern end of the island. Near misses caused superficial damage and wounded one man, so she was ordered to withdraw. *CominCh,* 1-9.

[14] Garrison Group Zero consisted of troops of the garrison force that were recommended by type commanders to be present at Iwo during the assault phase

The urgent requirement for a landing strip to handle light observation planes from the Marine observation squadrons caused a revision of the original job assignments for engineer units. On 24 February the 62d Naval Construction Battalion was still on board ship, so the 2d Separate Engineer Battalion (Corps Troops) was given the task of rehabilitating a strip 1,000 feet by 150 feet. By 1600 the following day hard-working men of this unit had filled, scarified, bladed, and rolled 1,500 feet

but could not be carried in assault shipping because of space limitations. The Zero echelon was embarked in additional shipping to arrive at the objective on call after the assault ships but prior to the first echelon garrison ships. *TF 56 TQMRpt, 6.*

of the north-south runway of the southern airfield, and it was ready for use. Two observation planes from Marine Observation Squadron 4 (VMO–4), the first United States aircraft to land on Iwo Jima, flew in from the escort carrier *Wake Island* on 26 February, and by 1 March, 16 light planes of that unit and VMO–5 were based ashore.

With the completion of this partial renovation of Airfield Number 1, general repairs began with the 2d Separate Engineers assigned the reconstruction of the north-south and northwest-southeast strips. The 62d Seabees now assumed responsibility for rebuilding the long northeast-southwest runway. This work

A TEMPORARY CONTROL TOWER was set up in a triangle of the three runways on Airfield Number 1. Marines manned this tower until 7 March when Army Air Force personnel took over for the Island Air Defense Commander. (AF Photo)

FIRST B-29 to land on Iwo, 4 March 1945, and Marine observation plane are pictured together on Airfield Number 1. By 26 March, 36 Superforts had used the emergency facilities on the island. (AF Photo)

proceeded steadily, interrupted only by darkness and occasionally by heavy enemy fire.[15]

On 3 March the first R4D (Sky Train) of Air Evacuation Squadron Two landed and evacuated 12 wounded Marines. Enemy fire on the field prevented further air activity that day, but on subsequent days these flights continued without serious disruption. On 4 March a B-29 made a successful forced landing and took off again after refueling.

Emergency resupply of ammunition (particularly the urgently needed 81mm mortar shells), medical supplies, and radio gear was made by air drop, and mail was also delivered in this manner. The first such mission was flown on 28 February when three planes of the 9th Troop Carrier Squadron (USAAF) dropped 9,215 pounds of supplies along the western beaches. Four 'chutes fell in the water but three of these were recovered by LVT's. Starting on 1 March, the drops were made over Airfield Number 1 and 69 mail bags for the 3d Division were delivered that day by Marine transports of VMR-952.[16] Air drop of supplies and mail continued until 6 March

when air-freight planes began using the airfield.[17]

By D-plus 14, 9,511 casualties had been evacuated to rear areas by transports and hospital ships. Air evacuation, which commenced on D-plus 12, had lifted another 125. The medical companies of the 4th and 5th Divisions, and V Corps Medical Battalion, in support of the 3d Division, had established field hospitals by D-plus 9, and Corps Evacuation Hospital Number 1 as well as the 38th Field Hospital (USA) were functioning ashore by D-plus 12. Only Companies A and B and Headquarters Company of the 3d Medical Battalion (3d Division) were landed on Iwo, but Company D operated medical facilities on the LSV *Ozark*.

These medical installations, all crowded into the narrow southern end of the island, sought shelter from enemy fire by every means possible. Some set up in aircraft revetments, others used Japanese emplacements, and engineers bulldozed large holes for units that found no ready-made protection. Company A, 3d Medical Battalion set up in a revetment and utilized two

---

[15] *VAC EngRpt*, 5-6.

[16] This was not the first mail to arrive on the island. On 24Feb a ship brought mail that was transferred to LST 809, which served as a Fleet Post Office. *VAC Personnel Rpt*, 17.

[17] During the operation Army and Marine air transports (C-47's and C-46's) delivered 78 tons of supplies by air drop and 40 tons by air freight. The last delivery, Mission No. 17, was made on 26Mar45. These cargo planes were from the Army 9th Troop Carrier Squadron and Marine squadrons (VMR's) 253, 353, and 952. *VAC Logistics Rpt*, Encl A, 16-23; *Sherrod*, 349-350.

concrete water storage tanks for surgery and first aid rooms.

The mobile blood bank facility landed on D-plus 8 and opened in the immediate vicinity of Company B, 3d Medical Battalion, in the shelter of a high embankment at the north end of the north-south runway of Airfield Number 1. In this location it was accessible to all medical units operating on the island. The island air evacuation station was also located in the same general area.

Evacuation of casualties from the front was difficult and hazardous. Corpsmen and litter bearers operated under fire over extremely rocky, creviced, and exposed terrain. The courage and devotion of these men was outstanding in the face of the high casualty rate among Marines and naval personnel so engaged. Smoke was sometimes used to conceal the activity of evacuation teams, and tanks also aided in bringing out the wounded.

On D-plus 9 the LST(H)'s, which had been providing emergency treatment for the wounded, were released and left the area carrying full loads of casualties. By that time shore-based medical facilities were able to take over that task, and evacuation was direct from the beach to hospital ships and transports.

Along with care of the wounded went the somber task of collection and burial of the dead. Since no civilian labor was available, service troops were used to gather and inter friendly dead. It was extremely hazardous work because of the close proximity of the dead to enemy positions. Carrying parties were frequently subjected to enemy small-arms and mortar fire.

The Japanese seemed reluctant to leave their own dead on the field, and the slow advance plus rough terrain permitted night movement of enemy carrying parties in search of casualties. When the situation did not permit removal of his dead, the enemy often burned or buried them in pillboxes. thus hiding the true nature of his heavy losses and keeping Marines guessing as to the strength of Japanese forces still manning the island defenses.

As had been expected, the sea proved the sole source of water supply at Iwo Jima. The amount of fresh water carried to the island by assault units was adequate until D-plus 6 when

engineers put water distillation units in operation. Because of subterranean heat, sump pits dug in the beaches furnished water at 137°, but sodium sulphate deposits necessitated frequent cleaning of distillation equipment. On the other hand, if intake lines were placed in the surf to pick up the sea water direct, frequent stoppages occurred when violent wave action washed the lines away. Despite these difficulties, however, water supply never became a serious problem.

The crowded conditions and furious fighting ashore, plus the light enemy air reaction to the landing, caused the landing force commander to delay ordering Colonel Clarence E. Rothgeb's 138th Antiaircraft Artillery Group (Army) ashore. However, two 90mm antiaircraft batteries of the 506th Antiaircraft Artillery Gun Battalion (Army) and units of the 483d Antiaircraft Artillery Automatic Weapons Battalion (Army) landed on D-plus 5. The two remaining 90mm batteries came ashore two days later, and elements of the automatic weapons battalion and group headquarters continued landing until D-plus 11. Three batteries of the 506th were assigned the mission of neutralizing enemy installations on Kama and Kangoku Rocks, which lay off the northwest coast. The 5th Division had been reporting rocket and mortar fire from these rocks, and it was planned to silence the positions by naval gunfire, strafing, and bombing. After considerable working over, light antiaircraft fire was still observed, and the Army 90mm gun units were given blanket authority to fire whenever Kama and Kangoku showed any activity.[18]

Other Army Garrison Force units that were under the operational control of VAC landed during this same period. Major General James E. Chaney, the Commanding General, Army Garrison Forces, and Island Commander, Iwo Jima, landed with his headquarters on 27 February, along with a detachment of the 147th

---

[18] *138th AAA Group SAR*, 1–6. The 138th AAA Group never had occasion to perform antiaircraft missions during the operation since no enemy planes came within range after the guns were ashore. Prior to landing, however, machine guns of Battery B, 506th, mounted on the deck of LST 84, cooperated with 40mm guns of the ship to knock down an enemy plane during the raid of 21 February.

Infantry Regiment and advance elements of the VII Fighter Command. These units immediately commenced reconnaissance and liaison activities in preparation for the subsequent arrival of their complete organizations in the garrison shipping.[19]

General Schmidt achieved coordination of air, naval gunfire, and artillery through Colonel John S. Letcher, his corps artillery officer. Together with representatives of the Landing Force Air Support Control Unit and the corps air and naval gunfire officers, Letcher screened requests for supporting fires, eliminated dupli-

cation of effort, and then forwarded these requests to the proper commands for action. In addition to his close association with those officers, the coordinator worked in continuous communication with liaison officers assigned to the three division artillery regiments.[20] Although the corps headquarters disembarked from the *Auburn* on 24 February, and the ship-to-shore transition of coordination functions began this same day, most of this coordinating group remained on board ship until sufficient communications gear could be landed to

---

[19] Army Garrison Force, Special Action Report, Iwo Jima Campaign, 25Mar45, 3.

[20] *VAC ArtyRpt, Encl P, Annex A to Encl P; Ibid.*, Appendix 2, 38; VAC Operation Plan 3–44, Artillery Annex, Appendix 5; *Isely and Crowl*, 504–505.

AIR EVACUATION of casualties to the Marianas began on D-plus 12. A total of 2,449 patients were evacuated by air. Careful preflight screening prevented any deaths on board planes.

ADMIRAL NIMITZ is greeted on Iwo by Major General Schmidt (shaking hands), Rear Admiral Hill (nearest camera), and Major General Chaney, USA, Garrison Force Commander (on right).

support its activities. Because of delays, Colonel Letcher did not move ashore until 1 March. The Commander, Landing Force Air Support Control Unit (Colonel Vernon E. Megee), came ashore on 24 February, but did not assume control of support aircraft until 1 March, at which time he also became Commander Air, Iwo Jima. The final establishment of these agencies ashore greatly facilitated coordination and control of fire support for the corps.[21]

The battle-tested 3d Marines, which had been held in Expeditionary Troops Reserve since the beginning of the operation, was sent back to Guam on 5 March without having set foot on Iwo Jima. As early as 28 February (D-plus 9) Generals Schmidt and Erskine had requested the use of Colonel James A. Stuart's regiment to give added punch to the slowly moving attack.[22] The landing force had already lost several times the strength of that regiment in casualties, and exhaustion seriously impaired the efficiency of all divisions. These commanders felt strongly that the employment of the 3d Marines would shorten the battle.

Vigorous efforts to obtain the release of the unit to VAC continued, and on the day before the regiment departed General Schmidt informed the Commanding General, Expeditionary Troops that the situation ashore did not justify withdrawal of RCT 3.[23]

General Smith, on the other hand, reasoned that enough troops were already ashore to complete the seizure of Iwo and that another regiment would aggravate already crowded conditions. After consultation with the Commander, Joint Expeditionary Force, (Admiral Turner), he denied the requests and the 3d Marines sailed away.[24]

RESUMING THE OFFENSIVE
(D-plus 15)[25]

The troops resumed the offensive on 6 March in an all-out effort to breach the Japanese final defense line. Eleven battalions of corps and divisional artillery fired the two most intensive preparations of the operation to support first one and then the other of two coordinated

---

[21] *TF 51 Rpt*, Pt V, Sec E, 15; VAC Signal Officer's Report, Iwo Jima Operation, 29Apr45, 114–117, hereinafter cited as *VAC SigRpt*.

[22] Disp CTG 56.1 to CTF 56, 1732, 28Feb45; Interview Gen H. Schmidt with author, 12Mar53.

[23] Disp LANFOR to EXTROPAC, 1239, 4Mar45; Interview Gen H. Schmidt with author, 12Mar53.

[24] *Isely and Crowl*, 528.

[25] Unless otherwise cited, material in this section is based on the following: *VAC OpRpt*, Annex A, Operation Order 13–45, 5Mar45; *3d MarDiv* Operation Order 13–45, 5 Mar45; *3d MarDiv SAR*; *VAC Arty Rpt*.

infantry attacks. These assaults were launched in echelon, one hour apart, so that maximum benefit could be derived from massed fires.

At K-Hour (0800) the 2d Battalion, 21st Marines jumped off in the left of the 3d Division zone of action in conjunction with the 5th Division's attack to the northeast. One hour later the 1st Battalion, 21st Marines, passed through 3/21 to attack with the 9th Marines and the 4th Division to crack the powerful defenses around Hill 362C.

In spite of the massive preassault bombardment by Marine artillery and naval gunfire, 2/21 was greeted by a counterpreparation and received heavy small-arms and automatic weapons fire from the front and left front. The 2d Battalion, 27th Marines, across the division boundary on the left, also met stiff resistance, and the attack in this sector bogged down with no gain.

At 0845 artillery fires shifted to mass in a "time on target" [26] preparation to support the K-plus 60 minute attack. Hill 362C, the objective of this assault, was some 500 yards from the line of departure, and the intervening terrain was an almost incredible confusion of rocks and broken ground in which Kuribayashi's troops had fashioned one of the strongest defenses on Iwo. In this part of the island the pent-up sulfur underground bubbled through fissures and crevices and made the surface so hot that it was almost impossible to live in foxholes.

In five days of deadly struggle Marines had gained almost no ground in this area, and 6 March was no exception. Enemy small-arms, mortar, and antitank fires were heavy despite the tremendous barrage that Marine and naval gunners flung against them.[27]

At 1440 another preparation was fired in an attempt to spark the attack. After two minutes of fire immediately in front of 1/21 and

the 9th Marines, the impact was lifted 100 yards, continuing for five more minutes. Behind this curtain of steel the 1st Battalion was at last able to move out, and the 1st and 2d Battalions of RCT 9 also inched briefly forward. But at 1800 when orders were received to consolidate for the night the greatest gain registered was 150 yards by 1/21, with lesser advances by the 9th Marines.

Meanwhile 2/21, which had been stopped in its tracks at K-Hour, launched a second attack in coordination with 2/27. Company G slashed ahead, clearing the crest and eastern slopes of Hill 357, but the unit on its left could not move and contact between the two was lost. Late in the afternoon, finding it impossible to regain this contact, the company withdrew from its advanced position and tied in along the original line of departure.

The 3d Battalion, 9th Marines, which had been attached to RCT 21 at 0600, spent the day in an assembly area northeast of Airfield Number 3, ready to exploit any gain made by the 21st Marines. After being passed through by 1/21, 3/21 reverted to division reserve and moved back to an assembly area west of Motoyama.

Tanks were of little assistance in this area. Their operations were necessarily limited to existing trails or new routes carved out of the rocks by busy and courageous tankdozers and armored dozers. The trails were mined and covered by antitank guns, and the construction of approaches was time consuming and costly. Company C (tanks) was committed on 6 March in support of the 9th Marines, and two tanks struck mines, suffering damage to their tracks, while a third was hit by 47mm fire. Three tankmen were killed and three wounded as a result.

Although the fighting was dragging terribly, down at the southern end of the island significant developments were taking place. On 6 March Brigadier General Ernest C. Moore, USA, Commanding General, VII Fighter Command, landed on Airfield Number 1 with the Group Commander, 15th Fighter Group and 28 P–51's (Mustangs) and 12 P–61's (Black Widows) of the 47th Fighter and 548th Night Fighter Squadrons respectively. The follow-

---

[26] In a "time on target" (TOT) preparation all weapons are fired on a time schedule so that the first rounds land on the target simultaneously.

[27] The 11 artillery battalions fired about 2,500 rounds of 155mm howitzer ammunition and 20,000 75mm and 105mm shells during the two phases of preparation fires on 6 March. *VAC ArtyRpt*, 14–15.

ing day, the Island Commander, General Chaney, assumed responsibility for base development, air defense, and operation of the airfields. General Moore now relieved Colonel Megee as Commander Air, Iwo Jima, and took over control of island air activities.[28] On 8 and 9 March the forward echelon of Marine VMTB (torpedo bomber squadron) 242 arrived from Tinian to fly antisubmarine patrol around Iwo day and night.[29] These aircraft assumed this task when the escort carriers left Iwo from 9 to 11 March. Support by carrier aircraft continued until 10 March, but Iwo-based planes of the 15th Fighter Group took over combat air patrol duties on 8 March and flew close support missions from that time until 14 March.[30]

PREDAWN ATTACK

(7 March) [31]

At 2055, 6 March the 3d Division received the corps order for continuation of the attack at 0730 the next morning.[32] But General Erskine felt that the old pattern of assault had proved unsuccessful in this sector and should be abandoned in favor of surprise. Therefore, although it was too late for reconnaissance and orientation of units by daylight, he requested and received permission to jump off at 0500.[33] There would be no change in boundaries or objectives. The 21st Marines, using 3/9 (attached) in the assault, was to attack south and seize Hill 362C, while the 9th Marines advanced 200 yards to the east in its zone of action prepared to continue the attack to the coast at daylight. (See Map VIII.)

The chances of this predawn assault being a complete surprise were good. Marine tactics thus far in the Pacific had not included night attacks and, except for a few patrols, Marines on Iwo had not been active in front of their lines after dark. Every precaution was taken to maintain secrecy. No messages concerning the night attack were transmitted over radio nets, and there was to be no special artillery preparation. Troops were cautioned to maintain absolute silence until the bulk of their force had been detected by the enemy.

The 21st Marines had its 1st Battalion already in the line and reasonably well oriented on the terrain, but it was decided to pass the fresher 3d Battalion, 9th, through 1/21 for this attack. Although the night was overcast and rainy, the naval gunfire illumination, which continued until just before the attack, gave sufficient light for assault commanders to pick out necessary intermediate objectives and features of the terrain for determining the direction of attack. Before 3/9 passed through, the company commanders of 1/21 briefed the unit leaders on lay of the land to the front, pointing out the elevation they believed to be Hill 362C, some 250 yards beyond their lines. To establish the direction of attack the commanders of K and L, the two assault companies, were directed to shoot an azimuth to the objective as indicated by officers of 1/21. Any necessary correction in the line of advance was to be made after daylight.

At 0320 the companies left their assembly areas for the line of departure, and jumped off promptly at 0500 with K on the right, L on the left, and I in reserve. The artillery had been using smoke shells liberally in harassing fires throughout the night, and at 0500 smoke was delivered against Hill 362C to screen the attack.

Surprise was complete. The Marines moved stealthily forward without detection until 0535, when an enemy machine gun opened up on the left only to be silenced by a blast from a Company L flame thrower. From then on there was scattered resistance, mainly on the left,

[28] *VAC OpRpt*, 38, 40.

[29] *Sherrod*, 350.

[30] *TF 51 OpRpt*, Pt V, Sec E, 15; *VAC OpRpt*, 38, 40.

[31] Unless otherwise cited, the material in this section is based on the following: *3d MarDiv SAR; 9th Mar SAR; 21st Mar SAR; 3d TkBn SAR;* LtCol H. J. Turton, "A Division Pre-Dawn Attack," Quantico, Va., MCS, AWS (SC), 1946–47; Maj R. D. Heinl, Jr., "Dark Horse on Iwo," *Marine Corps Gazette*, Aug45.

[32] VAC G–3 action message, serial 2131, 6Mar45 (memorandum record, telephonic acknowledgment receipt of VAC OpOrder 14–45); VAC OpOrder 14–45, 6Mar45.

[33] VAC G–3 action message, serial 2143 (record of telephonic conversations, 7Mar45). This document shows VAC authorizing 3d Div to continue attack at 0530, but 3d Div OpOrder 14–15 gives 0500 as K-Hour.

until shortly after 0600 when Company L ran into stiff opposition.

At daybreak (about 0620) the 3/9 commander made a careful check of the ground against a map and photographs and was able to locate definitely the positions of his companies. It was then he learned that the hill company K was in the process of clearing was Hill 331. Hill 362C, which they had hoped to reach under cover of darkness, was still some 250 yards away. Evidently the identification of the objective made prior to the attack had been in error. This was certainly not surprising as even in broad daylight location of position on this rough ground was difficult. Fortunately, however, the direction of attack had been correct, and the companies were contacted by radio and ordered to continue on to 362C at 0715, after a 10-minute artillery preparation on the hill and adjacent high ground.

The Japanese, now fully awake, resisted fiercely and Marines received fire not only from the front, but also from the many positions they had bypassed earlier. Progress was very slow as the many caves and bunkers were eliminated one by one with flame throwers, rockets, and demolition charges. Each position required a separate bit of maneuver by the unit that encountered it.

Finally, however, Company K, which had advanced faster than Company L, seized Hill 362C just prior to 1400 and was ordered to organize positions on the hill and assist L by fire. Since there was no contact with the 9th Marines on the right, Company I was committed to move up on K's right, bending back and facing south to protect the battalion's open flank. Company B, 21st Marines, was attached to 3/9 toward evening to help secure the battalion's other flank.

In summing up his battalion's activities for this day Lieutenant Colonel Boehm wrote:

Most notable in the night attack was the fact that, although nearly all the basic dope was bad, the strategy proved very sound, since it turned out that the open ground taken under cover of darkness was the most heavily fortified of all terrain captured that day, and the enemy occupying this vital ground were taken completely by surprise (actually sleeping in their pillboxes and caves). . . . It should be kept in mind,

however, that a stroke of luck went a long way toward making the attack a success.[34]

The 9th Marines had no more time to prepare for this attack than the 21st, and briefing and orientation had to be done hastily. Fortunately, Major William T. Glass, former executive officer of 2/9, who had been placed in command of 1/9 just before midnight 6 March, was familiar with the terrain and the situation to his immediate front.[35] With the troops already in position the battalions jumped off smoothly.

While the 21st Marines, using 3/9 in the assault, was slipping south under cover of darkness, the 9th Marines moved out to the east. By daylight the 2d Battalion on the left and the 1st Battalion on the right had penetrated 200 yards into the maze of fortifications that had held them so long at bay. But then it happened. The Japanese came suddenly to life and poured devastating fire at the Marines from all directions. Communications to the rear were cut off, and 1/9 had to fight savagely to re-establish freedom of movement behind the lines. The 2d Battalion was even harder hit, and the battle raged confused and terrible.

By 1015 it seemed clear that the 9th Marines could not break through the resistance ahead of it, and General Erskine shifted the boundary between regiments sharply to the south so that the advance of the 21st Marines would pinch out the 9th. By noon the assault companies of 1/9 had recovered sufficiently to launch a coordinated attack. Company C on the left was held up almost immediately, but B on the right moved ahead steadily with Company G, 23d Marines, advancing alongside. This looked like the break that was needed, and Company B was ordered to push ahead toward Hill 362C to make contact with the 3d Battalion, 9th. If this could be accomplished, the Japanese in front of RCT 9 would be cut off. The company gained a foothold on the high ground, but when the 3d Battalion marked its right flank with smoke the distance was too great to fill. Confronted with heavy enemy fire and mounting casualties Company B was

---

[34] *9th Mar SAR*, Encl C, 11.

[35] Ltr LtCol W. T. Glass to CMC, 14Feb53.

withdrawn to tie in with the rest of the 1st Battalion along the line held at dawn. (See Map VIII.)

In the left of the 9th's zone of action Companies E and F of the 2d Battalion were engaged all day in a battle for survival. The reserve company covered the withdrawal of the assault units by fire, and tanks tried desperately to break through to assist. But when the lead tank hit a mine in a defile, the only route to Company F was blocked and the tanks were ordered to support E. With remnants of Company F still pinned down at 1600, a second attempt was made to get tanks through, but rugged terrain also blocked this effort. It was not until the next day that tanks and infantry were finally able to break through to bring out the few remaining riflemen and the company commander.

The 1st and 2d Battalions of the 21st Marines were not involved in the predawn attack. After being passed through, 1/21 made minor adjustments in the lines and faced east but did not advance. The 2d Battalion, however, attacked at 0745 in conjunction with 2/27 on its left and was able to gain easily. But when the 27th Marines was unable to advance, 2/21 withdrew to its former positions around Hill 357. (See Map VIII.)

Major Percy summed up the situation for his battalion in these words:

> It is to be noted at this point that once the battalion had reached the high ground on 3 March, resistance within the battalion zone of action was scattered and easily isolated by assault teams operating on mop-up patrols. But due to the nature of the terrain, the battalion, depleted in strength as it was, was unable to advance more rapidly than the left flank unit, or to hold lines at night in advance of its flanking units.[36]

At 1745 the boundary between regiments was straightened out, again giving Hills 331 and 362C to the 9th Marines, and 3/9 reverted to its parent unit. The predawn attack had been successful where days of daylight assault had failed. The 400-yard advance to Hill 362C by 3/9 placed the Marines in positions from which they could look down on the last enemy stronghold in the 3d Division sector. And although the 1st and 2d Battalions, 9th Marines

had suffered heavy casualties, they had taken a 200-yard bite out of the stubborn core of resistance that had held them stymied since 1 March.

TO THE SEA
(D-plus 17—D-plus 19)[37]

For the next three days 2/21, 1/21, and 3/9 battled to reach the coast, while 3/21 and 2/9 whittled away at the stubborn enemy pocket that had resisted for so long in the 9th Marines zone of action.

On 8 March K-Hour (0750) was preceded by a 10-minute preparation by division and corps artillery and direct support destroyers fired from 0730 to 0800. The 2d Battalion, 21st Marines regulated its advance on the 5th Division and sent patrols out to the front to determine where and in what strength the enemy was located. Whenever Marines tried to move down to the cliffs overlooking the beach they came under flanking fire from the left (north) and right (south). Nine tanks from Company A, 3d Tank Battalion, supported 2/21, firing into caves and pillboxes in the rugged area just ahead of the battalion. On the 2d Battalion's right, however, 1/21 moved slowly ahead and by 1800 had gained 300 yards through the last organized resistance between it and the sea.

In the 9th Marines' zone of action 3/9 attacked east from Hill 362C against bitter but disorganized resistance. The initial objective was the edge of the plateau overlooking the beach with the waters' edge as the final goal. A destroyer executed direct fire into the steep draws that led down to the sea and an air strike was directed against the same area, but for the most part supporting fires were limited to mortars, and the fighting was close-in as the enemy conducted a "last-ditch" stand in the broken terrain. By 1600 the battalion had reached the first objective, but was ordered to hold up on the high ground because any attempt to move down to the beach would bring it under fire from the right flank.

Back in the area of the pocket south of Hill

---

[36] *21st Mar SAR*, Encl B, 8.

[37] Unless otherwise cited, the material in this section is based on the following: *3d MarDiv SAR; 9th Mar SAR; 21st Mar Sar; 3d TkBn SAR.*

CREW OF 75MM HOWITZER takes a break between fire missions. 75mm and 105mm howitzers of the 12th Marines came ashore between D-plus 6 and D-plus 10 to support the 3d Division.

331 the 9th Marines passed the 3d Battalion, 21st Marines (attached) through its 1st Battalion in an effort to flank the resistance from the south, while the 2d Battalion, 9th maintained pressure along its front, consolidating the previous day's gains.

Early in the morning of 9 March General Smith's Expeditionary Troops command post transferred to the *Auburn*, and the *Eldorado*, with Admiral Turner and his staff, departed for Guam. The Joint Expeditionary Force, Amphibious Support Force, Attack Force, Gunfire and Covering Force, and Expeditionary Troops were dissolved as task forces and Admiral Hill assumed the duties of Senior Officer Present Afloat, Iwo Jima, as Commander Task Group 51.21.[38]

[38] *TF 51 Rpt*, Pt III, 23. TG 51.21 consisted of the following: 51.21—SOPA Iwo Jima, 51.22—Garrison Group, 51.23—Service Group, 51.24—Screen Group, 51.25—Gunfire Support Group, 51.26—Carrier Support and Covering Group, 51.28—Minesweeping and Net Laying Group, 51.29—Convoy Group. The Commanding General Expeditionary Troops was designated as TG 51.09 and the Landing Force was designated TG 51.27. The Island Comand Group of the Garrison Force retained its designation as 10.16.

Ashore the action in the 3d Division zone followed the old familiar pattern. An artillery preparation against the pocket did little more than drive the enemy temporarily underground. When infantry and tanks moved in, the Japanese were ready and waiting, conducting a passive but effective defense. Using smoke to cover their operation and air bursts to disperse the infantry, an enemy demolition team knocked out one of the tanks. Neither 2/9 nor 3/21 made any notable gains during the day.

Continuing the drive to the sea, both 3/9 and 1/21 sent patrols down over the cliffs to the beach. Resistance to the front was sporadic and easily overcome. An air strike was called in against one stubborn enemy group, and the 3d Division Naval Gunfire Officer, on board a direct support destroyer, directed its fire into caves and emplacements along the cliffs.

Although Company A (1/21) was the first tactical unit to reach the northeastern beaches, a reconnaissance patrol led by the battalion intelligence officer arrived earlier. This group gleefully scooped up a canteenful of sea water and sent it to the corps commander with the message, "For inspection, not consumption." [39]

The 2d Battalion, 21st Marines, was still unable to push its left (north) flank ahead to the edge of the cliff because of the enemy resistance in the 5th Division zone of action, but on the right it moved forward, keeping contact with 1/21. Although patrol activity all the way to the waters' edge had revealed that enemy resistance was light, all battalions held their positions on the bluffs above the beach for the night.

On 9 March General Schmidt's headquarters announced that carrier planes would not be required any longer for close support, and U. S. S. *Enterprise* left the area at 1800 that evening. No carrier support was furnished the next day and the last of the escort carriers sailed for Ulithi on 11 March. The 15th Fighter Group (USAAF) now flew all troop support missions under control of the Landing Force Air Support Control Unit.

Since the 3d Division was now operating in a restricted area, there was no artillery or naval gunfire preparation for the attack on 10 March. In the zone of action of RCT 9, 3/9 pushed down to the beach and turned south toward the division right boundary. Throughout the day this unit was held up by fire from the high ground on its right flank. The 3d Battalion, 21st and tanks of Company B hacked away at the pocket but made little progress. During the morning one of these tanks was hit by fire from a Marine Sherman that had been abandoned the previous day and was now manned by a Japanese soldier. An infantry bazooka (2.36-inch rocket launcher) was called forward and knocked out the enemy-operated tank.

Farther north, in the 21st Marines' sector, patrols from 1/21 established the fact that there were no enemy on the beach, and that unit swung to the north with its right flank moving along the cliffs. By 1500 all organized resistance had been eliminated in the 1st Battalion's zone of action, and patrols were dispatched to clean out the rear areas. The 2d Battalion, 21st Marines was still unable to advance its left flank, but pivoted to the north to move its right along with the 1st Battalion.

Early in the afternoon the 1st Battalion, 9th was called up from division reserve and moved into the 4th Division zone of action to attack northeast to make a junction with 3/9, thereby localizing the remaining enemy resistance in the 9th Marines' zone. At 1535 the 1st battalion launched its attack, but had not advanced more than 200 yards when nightfall halted the drive. Meanwhile, the 2d Battalion, 9th Marines disengaged from the west side of the pocket and reverted to division reserve. Immediate steps were taken to reequip this unit and integrate and train replacements.

By evening of 10 March, except for the enemy pocket which held out for six more days and scattered resistance in the cliffs overlooking the beach, the 3d Division's zone of action up the center of the island was clear. The bitter fighting to follow could now be reported as "mopping up." (See Map VIII.)

Personnel losses during this 14-day drive up the island were heavy, and the 3d Division's combat efficiency at the end of this period was seriously impaired. Commenting on this situation the Commanding General, 3d Marine Division, wrote:

Infantry battalions were now [9 March] definitely beginning to feel the presence of the large number of replacements, manifested by a sharp drop in combat efficiency. These men were found to be willing but very poorly trained, especially in basic individual conduct. The faulty teamwork, resulting from lack of small unit training, was also a definite hindrance to the operation of the infantry battalions. Many needless casualties occurred in these replacements because of a lack of knowledge of proper use of cover and concealment. [40]

During this period the division suffered 3,563 casualties broken down as follows:

Killed in action	627
Died of wounds	200
Wounded in action	2,241
Missing in action	4
Combat fatigue	491
Total	3,563

[39] Ltr LtCol R. H. Houser to CMC, 3Apr53; 1stLt R. A. Aurthur and 1stLt K. Colhmia, *The Third Marine Division*, (Washington, 1948), 245.

[40] *3d MarDiv SAR*, 16.

CHAPTER VII 5th Marine Division on the Left

(D-plus 6—D-plus 19)[1]

The front occupied by General Rockey's 5th Division on the morning of 25 February formed a 1,200-yard bow. From advanced positions in the center, held by 2/26, the right flank curved back to the south where 3/26 and one company of 1/26 made contact with the 3d Division. On the left, 2/27 bent back a like distance to hold the cliff line near the western beaches. The action of the preceding days made it evident that high ground in the center of the island dominated the 5th Division zone of action, and that no considerable gains could be registered up the west side until the enemy had been cleared from the bluffs along the 3d Division's left boundary.

Since the afternoon attack on D-plus 5 had carried the 5th Division some 400 yards north of the 3d, it was decided that RCT 26 would hold up until the 9th Marines came abreast. On D-plus 6 RCT 9 gained only on its right. Consequently, the bluffs along the left 3d Division boundary remained hostile and Colonel Graham's 26th Marines could not attack. Throughout the day enemy fire from the right front made supply and evacuation difficult. Ac-

curate enemy artillery fire, which fell in command posts that were in defilade from Japanese observers on Iwo, caused the 5th Division to repeat requests for a ground reconnaissance of Kama and Kangoku rocks.[2]

Although the 5th Division did not attack, the 13th Marines fired a 45-minute preparation before K-Hour (0930) and fired on targets of opportunity throughout the day. At 1500 an aerial observer spotted Japanese artillery moving north along a road and adjusted three battalions of the 13th Marines on the target. After the mission was completed the observer reported that three artillery pieces had been destroyed, several prime movers left burning, and an ammunition dump set afire.[3] As the Marine advance began to threaten enemy artillery positions, the Japanese displaced to previously prepared emplacements to the rear. Most of the movement was accomplished at

---

[1] Unless otherwise cited, material in this chapter is based on the following: *5th MarDiv SAR; 26th Mar SAR; 27th Mar SAR; 28th Mar SAR; 13th Mar SAR;* 5th MarDiv War Diaries, Feb-Mar45.

[2] The 13th Marines had also recommended the occupation of these two tiny islets to give United States forces observation posts from which a large portion of the northern part of the island could be seen, and also as a site for sound and flash ranging stations. *13th Mar SAR,* 34, 35.

[3] *Ibid.,* 13. Only three battalions were available for this mission as 4/13 had been assigned to reinforce the fires of the 12th Marines. The three battalions fired 584 rounds on this choice target.

MAJOR GENERAL ROCKEY commanded the 5th Marine Division at Iwo Jima.

night, and this shift on D-plus 6 (25 February) was the only attempt of this sort observed.[4] The Marines' success must have convinced the enemy that it was folly to expose his equipment in daylight, especially with United States airborne observers over the island.

THE SWEEP TO HILL 362A

The 5th Division resumed the attack on 26 February (D-plus 7) in spite of the fact that high ground in the left of the 3d's zone of action had not been cleared. The 26th Marines moved out at 0800 (K-Hour) with the 2d and 3d Battalions and 2/27 in the assault. In the center, Companies D and E of Major Rea's 2d Battalion battled slowly forward against automatic weapons fire from an enemy strong point of pillboxes and caves. In two hours they advanced only 50 yards. Then, at 1000, Company F was committed and passed through Company E, which reverted to battalion reserve. Company F, held in reserve until this day, struck out enthusiastically, reducing the strong point with the aid of tanks from Company B, 5th Tank Battalion. For the first time since landing, Marines of 2/26 could see the enemy they were fighting and close with

him. "The result was a definite upsurge of morale."[5]

On the right, Company A tanks supported 3/26 with overhead fire until rain and low-hanging clouds obscured targets, and that battalion gained about 100 yards. During this action the infantry smashed not only fortifications to the front, but knocked out many enemy guns emplaced in ravines that led down from the plateau, perpendicular to the route of advance. Enfilading fire from these hostile weapons had constituted a menacing thorn in the side to men of the 5th Division. But by D-plus 6 this opposition showed signs of diminishing as Marines pushed to the north. Gains by RCT 9 in the 3d Division sector, and weapons firing in support of that regiment also contributed to progress made in the 3d Battalion zone.

The 2d Battalion, 27th Marines, operating on the left of the 26th Marines, jumped off at K-Hour with two companies abreast. Company D on the right moved rapidly, making 400 yards in the first two hours, and Company E kept pace along the terraces overlooking the beach. After these early gains, however, 2/27 halted to permit 2/26 to come abreast and remained in position for the remainder of the day. Tanks could not be used on the left, but 20 LVT(A)'s from Companies C and D of the 2d Armored Amphibian Battalion supported this attack up the coast from the sea with 75mm fire against enemy-occupied caves. After knocking out three hostile positions, however, the LVT(A)'s were ordered to cease operations because their erratic fire endangered friendly troops.[6]

When the division took up final dispositions for the night on 26 February, the lines still formed a giant bow with elements in the center advanced some 400 yards ahead of the flanks. The day's action had netted about 300 **yards** and pushed the front to within 800 to 1,000 yards of Hill 362A. In addition to being the heavily fortified western anchor of the Jap-

---

[4] *Ibid.*, 39.

[5] *26th Mar SAR*, Appendix 4, 7.

[6] *5th MarDiv SAR*, Annex M, 12, 15. Since these LVT(A)'s had no gyrostabilizer to steady the gun tube, firing from water-borne positions on a choppy sea was extremely difficult.

anese main cross-island defenses, the high ground around 362A gave the Japanese unobstructed observation over the entire southwestern half of the island and most of the Motoyama Plateau. This key terrain feature, dominating the 5th Division's route of advance up the island, became the next major objective. (See Map IX.)

During the night of 26/27 February there were indications that at least some of the defenders might be suffering from a shortage of water. Alert Marines of RCT 26 spotted a large group of enemy soldiers making its way over the cliff line south of Hill 362A toward a well near the coast. Illuminated by bright moonlight, this group made an excellent target; artillery and naval gunfire adjusted on it immediately, putting an abrupt end to this foraging expedition. With the exception of this incident the night was quiet along the division front.

D-plus 8

On D-plus 8 the 27th Marines relieved RCT 26 and attacked at 0800. The 1st and 3d Bat-

talions passed through 2/26 and 3/26 respectively, while 2/27, which had reverted to parent control, continued to operate on the left. The 1st Battalion, 26th was attached to RCT 27 and held in regimental reserve. One battalion of corps artillery reinforced the fires of the 13th Marines during a 30-minute preparation, and naval guns concentrated on Hill 362A from K-minus 30 minutes to K-minus 15 minutes and again for five minutes immediately following K-Hour. Just before the infantry moved out, truck-mounted launchers from the 3d Rocket Detachment plastered the area to the front with a blistering barrage of 4.5-inch rockets, then withdrew quickly to the rear. After naval gunfire lifted from Hill 362A, carrier planes swept in to work over the same area with bombs and rockets.

With commanding terrain on the right, progress along the 5th Division front depended upon the ability of the right flank battalion (3/27) to advance. That unit moved out with two companies abreast, the third company following to fill any gap that might develop between RCT 27 and RCT 9 on its right. The

MACHINE-GUN UNIT takes cover from hostile rifle and mortar fire. With enemy holding high ground on the right, even movement behind the lines was hazardous.

125

advance was rapid during the morning, but about noon contact was lost on the right and 3/27 was held up. The reserve company was committed to regain contact, but by this time enemy resistance had stiffened and only small gains marked the afternoon action.

In the center the 1st Battalion jumped off against sporadic artillery and mortar fire, advancing 200 yards before a stubbornly resisting group of pillboxes stopped the attack. A 75mm halftrack came forward to help in the reduction of this strong point and destroyed one pillbox with direct fire. But when the enemy concentrated intense and accurate machine-gun and small-arms fire against the vulnerable gun crew, this weapon withdrew. There was no suitable position from which the 37mm platoon could engage the hostile emplacements, and tanks were not available, so the infantry resorted to the slow methodical reduction of position after position by assault-demolition teams.

In the afternoon Company C, on the left, ran into a similar fortified area. In this part of the battalion zone terrain allowed limited tank operations, and a request went back for armored support. Two and one-half hours later Shermans from Company B, with one flame tank from Company C attached, arrived on the scene. The flame thrower received a disabling mortar hit before it could get into action, but the other tanks provided effective aid. After giving enemy positions a thorough pounding, these machines led infantry into the

IWO PHONE BOOTH.

pocket, knocking out several more pillboxes and a dug-in Japanese medium tank. With this armor support Company C regained its lost momentum and pushed on another 200 yards before 1915, when reduced visibility halted tank operations.

Meanwhile, Company A continued its advance in the face of mounting casualties. Its more rapid movement carried it ahead of adjacent units, and at 1500 the reserve company moved up as a relief and began to consolidate positions, waiting for Company C to come abreast.

Overlooking the west coast, 2/27 attacked at K-Hour with Company D moving north in contact with the 1st Battalion, and the other two companies driving northwest to fill the battalion zone of action where the island bulged out to the west. In this sector Marines had to fight their way through inland western beach defenses consisting of covered emplacements and caves. Here, too, the terrain and enemy mine fields restricted use of tanks. Gains were slow but steady, and by 1700 the left flank of the regiment had covered 500 yards.

Artillery was active throughout the day on both sides. The enemy used smoke shells to cover his own operations, and white phosphorus air bursts and time fire against the Marines. This last type was not effective, however, as the height of burst was generally too great, and the white phosphorus was more demoralizing than deadly. Japanese artillery did not engage in counterbattery duels, but succeeded in interfering with friendly artillery operations by employing deception. While Marine guns fired a preparation, the enemy often lobbed a few shells into United States front lines. This sometimes caused the belief that supporting fire was falling short on friendly troops and the bombardment was halted or lifted, thus reducing its effectiveness.[7]

The 13th Marines fired many successful counterbattery missions using air spot. From D-plus 1 to D-plus 8 carrier-based observers adjusted this fire. On 27 February (D-plus 8) division ordered VMO–5 to commence operations from Airfield Number 1, and the first OY,

---

[7] *5th MarDiv SAR*, Sec VII, 22; *13th Mar SAR*, 40.

THIS SHERMAN (M4A3) TANK is stalled in Japanese pillbox that crushed as tank rolled over it. Infantrymen stand by waiting for salvage crew to retrieve the vehicle.

flown by the commanding officer of that unit, was launched successfully from the Brodie-equipped LST 776 [8] and landed on the island that afternoon. The second plane was lost overboard before it could be engaged in the launching gear, but after installation of an improvised safety device on D-plus 10 a third VMO–5 plane and two 4th Division OY's were successfully launched and set down on Iwo.

The remaining seven planes of the observation squadron, which had been carried to the objective on escort carriers, were launched without incident on D-plus 9 and based on the island for the rest of the operation. Although these light planes were not equipped for night flying,

30 of the 623 flying hours logged during the campaign were scored during the hours of darkness.[9] These flights by both VMO–5 and VMO–4 were popular with Marines on the ground because with planes overhead enemy activity along the front and hostile mortar and artillery fire was noticeably reduced.[10]

On 27 February the VAC intelligence officer issued a preliminary enemy order of battle that confirmed most of the units previously listed as present on the island. This new estimate, however, increased the number of naval troops by some 5,000 and listed a few additional army units: the 3d Battalion, 17th Independent Mixed Regiment; the 21st Machine Cannon Unit, and the 3d Independent Machine Gun

---

[8] This LST was equipped with booms and cables, called a Brodie device, for launching and recovery of light planes. *CominCh P–0012*, 3–3.

[9] *5th MarDiv SAR*, Annex G, Appendix 2, 1.

[10] *Ibid.*, Appendix 1, 5.

LITTER BEARERS braved enemy fire to carry wounded to aid stations.

Battalion. Total strength of the Japanese on D-Day was now placed at over 20,000; an increase of more than 6,000 men.[11] This document also stated that interrogation of prisoners of war indicated that Lieutenant General Kuribayashi was on the island, but that this had not been confirmed.[12]

D-plus 9

Hill 362A rose sheer and naked above the contorted, rocky terrain ahead as RCT 27 moved out at 0815 on D-plus 9. This formidable looking mass lay squarely in the path of the 3d Battalion, on the right of the 5th Division zone. In the center and left, 1/27 and 1/26, which had relieved 2/27, continued to attack up a slope toward the ridge that led from the ragged edge of the northern plateau to the terraces above the western beaches.

The Japanese resisted fiercely along the entire front, clinging stubbornly to their positions. On the left, the 1st Battalion, 26th Marines sent advance elements far ahead along the beach but could make no general advance until the units on the right overcame enemy resistance in the high ground along the division boundary. (See Map IX.)

---

[11] It is of interest to note that as of 1800, 27Feb, the corps reported enemy dead as 5,483. Of course this figure was only an estimate as it could not accurately account for the large number of Japanese sealed in caves. *C-2 Periodic Rpt*, 27Feb45.

[12] *VAC IntelRpt*, Encl A, "VAC Preliminary Order of Battle, Iwo Jima," 27Feb45.

In the center and on the right the 1st and 3d Battalions of the 27th Marines battled slowly ahead in the face of the most intense small-arms fire they had yet encountered. The 1st Battalion, which had benefited from armored support on the preceding day, again employed tanks with success as it pushed through the highly organized mutually supporting positions of the cross-island defenses. About noon tanks of Company C ran out of ammunition, and Shermans from Company B came forward to continue the attack. Time after time the assault bogged down; then, with infantrymen guiding and designating targets, the tanks forged ahead, blasting bunkers into temporary silence, followed by assault teams that hurried forward to finish the job. During one of these attacks, grenade-throwing Japanese soldiers rushed one of the tanks. Trying to back away from the greenish irritant smoke discharged by these missiles, the vehicle ran into a hole and threw a track. The crew was evacuated safely in another tank, but their disabled Sherman remained abandoned until a later day.

The battalion commander committed his reserve (Company A) to pass through Company C in the left of 1/27's zone at 1630. Perhaps by design, but more likely by coincidence, a Japanese counterattack hit that portion of the Marine lines just as this relief was being accomplished. The attack was not in force, however, and Company A beat off the enemy without any loss of ground. This unit then tried to fight its way forward to tie in for the night with Company B, about 150 yards ahead on the right. This effort proved unsuccessful, and the battalion commander finally ordered Company B to pull back to establish a continuous battalion front.

The 3d Battalion, 27th Marines kept abreast of the 1st throughout the morning and by noon had reached the foot of Hill 362A. While steady pressure was maintained against this hill fortress, elements of Company H on the right and Company I on the left probed for an opening. Company I pushed a patrol up the southwest slopes to the crest of the hill at 1630 after a day of extremely bitter fighting. But this gain was partially nullified when Company I called in its patrol and dropped back nearly a hundred yards to regain contact with 1/27, lost because a small pocket held up the 1st Battalion's right. Company H then pulled back its right flank about 100 yards to make contact with RCT 21, which had replaced RCT 9 on the left of the 3d Division zone of action.

At 1645 Company H bore the brunt of a sharp, savage enemy counterattack against the 3/27 lines. Some 50 to 100 Japanese, driven from their hill positions, engaged in a desperate hand-to-hand struggle with Marines before being driven off with considerable loss. The 3d Battalion prepared its night defenses in the shadow of 362A, but this primary objective remained occupied by the enemy and still formidable. (See Map IX.)

Positions held by RCT 27 during the night of 28 February/1 March were 300 yards ahead of the morning line of departure along a front that ran almost due east and west, passing just south of 362A.

While Colonel Wornham's 27th Marines carried the attack northward, the 26th Marines (less 1/26 attached to RCT 27) made some progress in the salvage and replacement of weapons, and tried to rest and relax as much as possible while in reserve. At 0945 the 2d Battalion was also attached to the 27th Marines, but saw no action until the end of the day when Company F went forward to reinforce the lines of 3/27.

The 28th Marines, in corps reserve since 25 February, was alerted on the 28th for a move to the north. During the afternoon the 2d Battalion, 27th Marines, relieved 2/28 of its patrol and defense responsibilities around Suribachi, and all battalions of RCT 28 moved north to assembly areas while Colonel Liversedge and his commanders reconnoitered routes forward to the front lines.

As the division moved northward, large support landing craft [LCS(L)'s], assigned to work with naval gunfire spotters, peppered caves and ravines along the west coast with their 40mm guns. Experience showed that observers on these craft could distinguish positions of

MARINE TRUCK-MOUNTED 4.5-INCH ROCKET LAUNCHERS in action. After completing the mission these trucks will change position quickly to escape enemy retaliation.

friendly troops near the coast as well, or better, than anyone ashore, and the support vessels were given more and more initiative to fire on targets of opportunity. On 28 February the division took advantage of the observation provided by these support craft by placing observer teams aboard. For the next eight days these teams, composed of an intelligence officer and artillery and naval gunfire spotters, cruised up and down the coast, directing fire against enemy installations and reporting enemy activities.[13]

The night of D-plus 9 was relatively quiet at the front,[14] but about midnight enemy shells

[13] *5th MarDiv IntelRpt*, 39; *5th MarDiv SAR*, Annex H, 7; *TF 51 Rpt*, Pt V, C, 13.

[14] Bn 2/26 established four listening posts along the beach the night of 28Feb/1Mar to assist in night defense measures. One dog from the 6th War Dog Platoon and a small fire group of Marines were

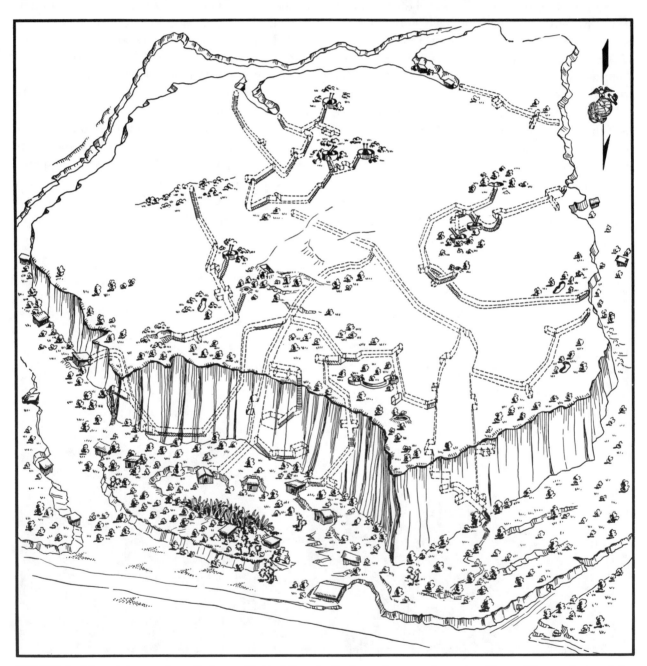

HILL 362A looking at top and north face. Dotted lines indicate underground construction. (Copy of one of five sketches prepared by the 31st U. S. Naval Construction Battalion.)

ADVANCING OVER A RIDGE LINE Marines look for trouble. The Japanese on Iwo conducted vigorous reverse-slope defenses and covered all ridges with mortar fire.

began falling among positions of corps artillery and the 13th Marines. Although this activity by the Japanese artillery was greater than usual, the location of gun flashes in the north revealed that it operated from new position areas. This indicated that Marine counterbattery fire had been effective at least to the extent of forcing the displacement of many opposing field pieces.[15]

During this bombardment, at 0215, the 5th Division ammunition dump was hit and burned fiercely until about 0700 when men of Headquarters and Service Battery of the 13th Marines and bulldozer operators of the 5th Engineer Battalion brought the blaze under control. At least 20 percent of the division's supply of small-arms ammunition was lost, along with corresponding amounts of heavier projectiles.

Two hours after the ammunition was hit a shell landed in the corps artillery fire direction

center.[16] No personnel casualties resulted, but wire lines were knocked out and fire consumed almost all of the telephone wire in the group dump.[17] There were more hits and near misses throughout the congested rear areas, but all installations were well dug in and temporary disruption of communications was the only other damage.[18]

D-plus 10

At 0630 on D-plus 10 RCT 28 started moving forward to pass through RCT 27 and continue the attack against Hill 362A and its supporting positions. The corps' 155mm howitzers and

---

stationed at each post. These elements reported that the only resistance met during the night came from the watch(?) dogs who were kept awake only with great difficulty and constant prodding. *26th Mar SAR,* Appendix 4, 9.

[15] *VAC ArtyRpt,* 14.

[16] This was a friendly 105mm howitzer shell, thrown out from the burning ammunition. Fortunately, this missile did not explode with great force in the FDC. Outside of causing the fire, it did little damage. Ltr BrigGen J. S. Letcher (Ret) to CMC, 13Mar53.

[17] *VAC ArtyRpt,* 14.

[18] At 0238 an air-raid alert was passed, and at 0300 further excitement was added when exploding white phosphorus shells caused someone to sound the gas alarm. This mistake was quickly corrected, however, and the gas alert cancelled at 0310. No enemy planes approached the island, and the "all clear" was given at 0430. *VAC OpRpt,* 28.

BRODIE-EQUIPPED LST 776. Two OY's from the 4th and two from the 5th Division were launched successfully from this specially equipped ship. A fifth plane was lost overboard. (Navy Photo)

5th Division artillery [19] commenced firing a preparation at K-minus 45 minutes (0745). One battleship and two cruisers from the gunfire and covering force added their heavy fires from 0800 to 0830. Aircraft from the support carrier group delivered strikes throughout the day, but did not participate in preparation for the attack.[20]

This proved one of the busiest days for TF 54 since D-Day as fire support ships dueled with enemy shore batteries until late afternoon.

---

[19] The 5th Div now had the use of all four battalions of the 13th Marines, 4/13 having been released from its supporting role with the 12th Marines at 1600, 28Feb45. *13th Mar SAR,* 15.

[20] In this connection the following message from VAC to all divisions is of interest: "In order to effect coordination and to employ available fire power more effectively during King Hour preparations no air strike will be conducted during the period King-minus 45 to King-plus 15 within the zone in which artillery and naval gunfire are shooting." Disp VAC to 3d, 4th, 5th, Divs, 1412, 1Mar45.

Shortly after dawn enemy guns in the northern part of the island opened up, and at 0725 the *Terry* took a direct hit by a 6-inch shell, suffering heavy casualties. The *Nevada* immediately engaged these hostile installations, and after completing their mission in support of the landing force, the *Indianapolis* and *Pensacola* shifted to counterbattery fire. At 1025 the *Calhoun* was hit by a major-caliber projectile, and soon after this enemy shells straddled the *Stembel.* Counterbattery fire continued throughout the day with the *Nevada* destroying one casemated gun and starting a fire in another emplacement, while the *Pensacola's* batteries accounted for a third Japanese gun.[21]

The 28th Marines jumped off with its 1st, 2d, and 3d Battalions in line from right to left. Hill 362A and the ridge that ran east and west from the hill formed the initial objective as on

---

[21] *TF 51 Rpt,* Pt III, 16; *TF 54 OpRpt,* 20.

the day before, and all units gained their first goal quickly. But as they advanced over the crest heavy machine-gun and mortar fire from the next ridge (Nishi) to the North forced them to take cover. Ahead of the center and right battalions the ground fell away sharply into a rocky draw, the sides and bottom of which were covered by fire from small arms, automatic weapons, and well zeroed-in mortars. It soon become evident that breaking through the defenses ahead would be more difficult for the 28th than the short assault to seize the hill and its supporting ridges. Beyond the draw the ground leveled off for about 200 yards, then rose abruptly to form ragged Nishi Ridge.

Faced with almost impassable terrain and an effective reverse-slope defense, the battalion commander of 1/28 tried to maneuver his companies into positions from which they could bring fire to bear against the enemy holed up in the steep northern face of the hill. He sent his reserve (Company A) around the right side of Hill 362A to work down into the draw, but this unit came under such heavy attack by grenades and small arms that the attempt stopped short. During this assault the commander of Company A was killed while leading his men. Company B made a similar short-lived effort to move down off the high ground, but achieved no permanent gain. When the battalion dug in for the night, the left flank was still on top of the hill and the right of the line strung out along the ridge to the east. (See Map X.)

Company C, 5th Tank Battalion served in support of the 2d Battalion, 28th throughout the day. Both flame and regular tanks operated effectively during the morning attack and also mopped up bypassed enemy positions. Even with this help, however, 2/28 could not advance beyond the steep northern slope of the ridge that ran west from 362A. During one of the mop-up actions a tank bellied down in soft ground. The 75's and machine guns of other Shermans could not reach the enemy that fired at this help-less target, so tankmen dismounted and fought along with the infantry to clear the area. The Japanese held out stubbornly, however, making the position too hazardous for salvage operations, and the tank was abandoned after removal of firing mechanisms from the guns.[22]

Despite mortar fire and strong resistance from caves in the right of the battalion zone, the 3d Battalion advanced steadily with two companies abreast, the left flank along the coast and the right unit in contact with the 2d Battalion. Artillery, naval gunfire, mortars, and rockets supported the attack, and engineers blew numerous emplacements as the units moved forward. The battalion gained about 350 yards, but as further movement would have placed the

---

[22] *5th TkBn SAR*, Encl C, 5.

ADVANCING TOWARD NISHI RIDGE Marines move out behind tanks. Hill 362A breaks skyline at far right.

right flank out ahead of the stalled unit on 2/28's left, a halt became necessary.

During the afternoon VAC moved the boundary between the 3d and 5th Divisions about 200 yards to the east, and ordered General Rockey to relieve units of the 3d Division in this new sector of responsibility.[23] To accomplish this, 3/26 was committed on the right of RCT 28 and moved up to replace 1/21. By 1855 the 3d Battalion had established contact with the 3d Battalion, 9th Marines on the right and the 1st Battalion, 28th on the left. The 2d Battalion, 26th Marines then took up a forward position in RCT reserve.[24] When the fighting ended on 1 March, the 5th Division held a 1,000-yard front along the crest of the ridge that ran east and west from Hill 362A. (See Map X.)

---

[23] As noted in Chapter VI.

[24] Disp VAC to 5th and 3d Divisions, 1325, 1Mar45; 5th MarDiv Record of Telephone Conversations, 5th MarDiv to VAC, 1855, 1Mar45.

D-plus 11

While the 5th Division battled slowly through the network of strong positions around Hill 362A, the 3d Division broke out of the Japanese cross-island defense system in the center and struck rapidly to the northeast. Anticipating the development of a gap between his center and left divisions if the 5th did not move out quickly along the boundary to the north and east of 362A, General Schmidt, on 2 March, ordered General Rockey to make his main effort on the right, maintaining contact with the 3d.

As the boundary between divisions swung northeast between Airfield Number 3 and Hill 362B [25] the 5th's zone of action became wider. To meet this situation General Rockey committed RCT 26 on the right of RCT 28, giving it the relatively narrow strip of the Motoyama

---

[25] This was the second Hill 362 that lay at the north end of the plateau.

155MM HOWITZERS were the heaviest artillery available to Marines at Iwo. In general support of the corps, these weapons fired a total of 43,795 rounds. Most of this ammunition was expended in counterbattery and preparatory fire missions.

Plateau included within the division zone. While operating on this short front the 26th Marines could move more rapidly than the 28th, which held a 1,200-yard line, and could commit reserve units to maintain contact with the division on the right. With only the 1st Battalion, 27th Marines as division reserve (2/27 was in corps reserve and 3/27 attached to RCT 28), Rockey also included the following somewhat unusual paragraph in his operation order for 2 March: "A unit creating a gap by advancing will be responsible for filling that gap."[26] This was certainly not intended to slow a coordinated advance by all units, but warned that the division commander had no troops available for plugging holes along his front.

With two regiments in the attack on D-plus 11, the 13th Marines placed its 3d Battalion in direct support of RCT 26 while the 2d Battalion continued in direct support of RCT 28. The 1st and 4th Battalions reinforced the fires of the 3d and 2d Battalions respectively. For the 30-minute preattack preparation, and for the remainder of the day, the 13th Marines was augmented by 50 percent of the corps artillery fires.[27]

The 26th Marines jumped off along the division boundary at 0800 with 3/26 in the assault. As the battalion advanced, a gap opened on the left, and Companies D and F of the 2d Battalion fought forward to regain contact with 1/28 and fill the hole. Slowly Marines gained against the resolute Japanese defense. In this area the enemy depended more on positions cleverly concealed in the numerous crevices and outcroppings scattered throughout the rocky ground than on concrete emplacements, but the natural tank obstacles were extended and strengthened with mines. Kuribayashi's soldiers also crowded the Marine lines, thus further limiting the use of heavy weapons in close support. Although use of armor would be difficult, 3/26 requested and received Company A tanks to spearhead the attack.

The two companies of the 2d Battalion were heavily engaged when the battalion received orders to shift to the right flank to close a new

75MM HALF-TRACKS stand by as demolition team blasts enemy pillbox.

gap that had developed between RCT 26 and the 3d Division (21st Marines). Company E, in battalion reserve, moved out immediately (1400), but D and F had to disengage under heavy fire before they could join the rest of their unit. Lack of information concerning the particular unit of RCT 21 with which contact was to be made further complicated execution of this mission. Mine fields and mortar fire harassed the companies during the shift, but exhausted Marines finally closed the gap just as night fell.

Division engineers attached to the 26th Marines moved right along with the assault elements, clearing mine fields and pushing supply roads forward. Commenting on the road-building activities of these engineers, Colonel Graham wrote, ". . . for the remainder of the operation attached engineers kept usable roads pushed right up to the front lines (and often ahead of front lines)."[28]

The 1st Battalion, 26th Marines was committed to plug the hole on the left of the 3d Battalion when Companies D and F (2/26) pulled out to the northeast. The 3d Battalion, using three companies along its extended lines, carved out a 500-yard gain during the day. (See Map X.)

The 28th Marines, in the left of the division zone of action, jumped off on time with its three battalions in the same positions as on 1 March. The scheme of maneuver called for 1/28 and 2/28 to attack around both sides of Hill 362A and join on the north side for a coordinated assaulted to the first objective: Nishi Ridge.

[26] 5th MarDiv OpOrder 9–45, 1Mar45.
[27] VAC OpOrder 10–45, 1Mar45.

[28] *26th Mar SAR*, 9.

BULLDOZER OPERATORS pushed roads to the front. Sulfur fumes add ghostly appearance to this scene.

This elevation, 200 yards to the north, ran west from the plateau almost to the water's edge, directly across the front. Just beyond it lay what had once been the little cluster of buildings called Nishi. The 3d Battalion would continue up the west coast on 2/28's left flank.

When the 1st and 2d Battalions started forward, they met the same determined resistance as on the day before. Every time Marines moved down into the compartment that crossed the front, they received intense fire from both front and rear. Sherman's from Company B, 5th Tank Battalion, spent the entire morning trying to maneuver into effective supporting positions, but a long antitank ditch running north from Hill 362A interfered with these efforts.

The 13th Marines concentrated on Japanese mortar positions throughout the day, firing both air-spot and forward observer missions with telling effect. But against close-in enemy targets the artillery was useless, so all infantry weapons had to be exploited to the fullest extent. Men from the regimental weapons company managed to set up three .50-caliber machine guns to cover caves that honeycombed the north face of the hill, and friendly mortars blanketed the area ahead.

Finally, with the aid of an engineer armored bulldozer and a tankdozer, the tank trap was filled in enough to permit passage. Leaving one tank behind to cover the reverse slope of the hill, the rest pushed out 200 yards until bottled up by terrain that narrowed down into one small draw. While engaged with the Japanese defenders in this defile, one of the tanks had several demolition charges detonated against its side. These explosives did no damage, however, as the tank was protected by heavy planks so attached that an air space was left between the boards and the armor plate.[29]

Company C tanks came forward at 1400 to relieve those of Company B, which had used up all their ammunition. On the way to the front one platoon of regular mediums and a flame tank blasted and burned hostile positions at the base of Hill 362A that still harassed advancing infantry from the rear. For the rest of the day this company provided a base of fire from stationary positions into the rugged cave-ridden sides of Nishi Ridge.

In the afternoon RCT 28's 1st and 2d Battalions broke the stalemate and pushed units ahead to the Nishi ridge line in spite of heavy casualties incurred while crossing the draw. They clung grimly to these advanced positions despite severe losses and a sharp counterattack by 150 Japanese. At 1400 Lieutenant Colonel Chandler W. Johnson, commanding 2/28, was killed by a high explosive shell while walking from the Company F command post to Company E's, and his executive officer, Major Thomas B. Pearce, Jr., took over command of the battalion. Reserve units mopped up the high ground in the vicinity of Hill 362A, and by nightfall that area was reasonably secure. (See Map X.)

The 3d Battalion, which had been working northeast along the west coast, turned north on 2 March to follow the shoreline within a narrowing zone of action. During the day Company H was squeezed out by the left flank unit of the 2d Battalion and became RCT reserve.[30] The terrain constituted the major obstacle to the advance, but occasional mortar barrages fell on frontlines until late afternoon when the enemy weapons were silenced.[31] At 0900, and again at 1125, a greenish smoke given off by enemy mortar shells caused men to vomit and left them with headaches. This caused a short-lived gas

[29] *5th TKBn SAR*, Encl B, 5.
[30] 28th Mar R–3 Periodic Rpt No 12. 2Mar45.
[31] *28th Mar SAR*, Annex O, 18.

scare, but it was quickly squelched and the men suffered no serious aftereffects.[32]

Attached 37mm guns and 81mm mortars were used extensively and effectively against Japanese positions in the rocky draws, and engineer demolitionists, following close behind the assault, blasted a total of 68 caves during the day.[33]

Corps ordered all divisions to consolidate positions at 1700, but skirmishes continued all along the 5th Division front as Marines fought to reach good defensible ground. By nightfall forward elements were dug in generally along the Nishi Ridge line, and on the far right 2/26 stretched out to the northeast along the division boundary to tie in with 3/9 (attached to RCT 21) just west of Hill 362B.[34] The battle for 362A was over, but the struggle for Nishi Ridge was only beginning, and the 26th Marines faced bloody fighting around Hill 362B and the rocky shambles to the north and east. (See Map X.)

Maps and simple two-dimensional photographs did not adequately portray the broken nature of the ground on Iwo, particularly in the north, and it was only by viewing stereo pairs[35] of photographs that the relief could be visualized. These stereo pairs, while effective, were

---

[32] A report of this incident made by the R–3 (RCT 28) describes the gas as ". . . fairly dense and heavy enough that it went into foxholes. The gas seemed to dissipate quickly. Men did not wear gas masks and it did not affect men unless they were in immediate area of the shell burst. It is the opinion of personnel in [3/28] that the gas is probably picric acid." 28th Mar AR–3 hand written report, 3Mar45.

[33] *28th Mar SAR*, Annex O, 18.

[34] As narrated in the preceding chapter, the 3d Division had received permission to seize Hill 362B, which was located in the 5th Division zone of action but threatened the flank of the advancing 3d. Although 3/9 reached the foot of Hill 362B on 2Mar, corps ordered 5th Division to relieve 3d Division troops in the 5th's zone the following morning.

[35] Two photographs of the same object or area taken from slightly different angle are called stereo pairs. By means of a special viewer the images of two such photos can be merged to make one picture clearly showing depth.

TANKDOZER clears route through rocky defile. Terrain such as this limited tank operations and dozers became an integral part of any tank-infantry team.

difficult to work with, and the 5th Engineer Battalion supplied the division intelligence officer with a total of 6,054 vectograph transparencies of the island for distribution to division staff sections and lower echelons. These vectographs,[36] when used with a special but simple viewer, provided even small unit commanders with an easy means of determining ground contours. In this way, front line observations could be correlated with the terrain as indicated on maps, charts, and photographs of the area. Division operations orders and fire support plans were prepared from a mosaic of vectographs prepared by the intelligence section.

NISHI RIDGE AND HILL 362B

D-plus 12

The 5th Division resumed its attack at 0745 on 3 March with no change in formation. The 28th Marines was to attack north from positions along Nishi Ridge, while the 26th Marines, now up on the Motoyama Plateau, drove north from the division's right boundary and also pushed out northeast to relieve 3d Division units in the vicinity of Hill 362B.

In its narrowing zone of action on the far left, the 3d Battalion, 28th Marines would hold up on the line of departure until the 2d Battalion pinched out Company G. Then Company I on the left was to move out in conjunction with the 2d Battalion. During the morning 3/28 received only light enemy fire as engineer-infantry teams continued mopping up and sealing bypassed caves along the coast.

In the center of the regimental zone the 2d Battalion, supported by 75mm half-tracks, 37mm guns, and a reinforced platoon of tanks, encountered stiff resistance, and Company D, on the right, was halted shortly after 0800 by heavy mortar fire. As Company E advanced

beyond stalled Company D, it was subjected to flanking fire from the right front and the tanks moved into that zone to engage enemy targets designated by the infantry. The action was at close quarters, and Marines frequently exchanged hand grenades with Japanese infantrymen. By 1000 the enemy to the immediate front had been annihilated, and the two assault companies, now reinforced by two platoons from Company F, got underway again.

As 2/28 inched forward it pinched out the right flank company of 3/28, leaving Company I the only unit of the 3d Battalion still in the lines. During the afternoon Companies I and F gained easily against light resistance, but on the right the going was more difficult and units held up for the night 150 to 200 yards forward of the line of departure. (See Map XI.)

Along the boundary between RCT 26 and RCT 28, where the regimental fronts were almost at right angles to each other, 1/28 and 1/26 launched a cordinated attack to clear the enemy facing 1/28 and advance the 28th Marines' right flank to straighten the division line at that point. Casualties mounted fast as they drove through the maze of enemy emplacements hidden in the rugged terrain. Company H, 3/28, attached to 1/28 at daybreak, relieved Company B at 1100, but by 1230 this unit had taken such high casualties that Company B had to move back into the lines. In coordination with 1/26's attack, Company C on 1/28's right flank was successful in overcoming the enemy to its front and rolled forward 500 yards. Companies A and B on the left were unable to keep up, however, and the remnants of Company H were committed late in the day to fill the hole created by this uneven progress. Actually this company was so depleted that it could only cover the gap by fire, but the night passed quietly with no serious consequence.

The line of departure for the 2d and 3d Battalions of the 26th Marines on 3 March resembled a letter "U" with 3/26 on the left and 2/26 on the right. The scheme of maneuver called for straightening and shortening the front by making the main effort in the center, pivoting on the flanks. The 2d Battalion would also try to accomplish the relief of 3d Division troops near Hill 362B by 1000. (See Map XI.)

---

[36] To make vectographs, transparencies from a stereo pair are polarized at right angles to each other and mounted together. Through another polarizing agent, the viewer, the right eye sees the top image only and the left eye the back image only. The effect is the same as normal three-dimensional vision with both eyes. *Impact*, Vol 1, No. 3, August 1943, 45, published by Office of the Assistant Chief of Air Staff, Intelligence, Washington, D. C.; *5th MarDiv IntelRpt*, 9, 36, 37; Ltr LtCol G. A. Roll to CMC, 7Apr53.

WAR DOGS and their handlers stood sentry duty, manned outposts, and accompanied patrols. If an enemy lurks in this cave dog will signal.

The battalions moved out rapidly in one of RCT 26's most successful, but at the same time most costly, attacks of the operation.[37] Tanks of Company B supported the 2d Battalion by covering the left flank of Company F as it smashed forward for a gain of 600 yards. This fire was controlled by the infantry company commander who radioed instructions via a tank liaison man stationed at the 2/26 command post. For the first 300 yards the assault swept across relatively flat and open terrain, but as elements in the center came abreast of the flanks the nature of the ground changed. The "flat land" gave way to sharply cut gorges and jutting outcrops of rock where grimly waiting Japanese slowed the Marine advance. Fierce hand-to-hand struggles raged, and flame throwers, bazookas, and hand grenades were the principal weapons used in this jungle of stone where fields of fire were so limited and surprise encounters frequent. The 5th Division intelligence officer described this area well in his D–2 operation report:

In the final defensive area north of Nishi the increased natural defensive strength of the ground and

[37] The 26th Marines (not including attachments) suffered 8 officer and 273 enlisted casualties on this date, 3Mar45. 26th Mar War Diary, Mar45.

its subterranean defensive features compensated for the reduced amounts of concrete and steel used by the Japs . . . Volcanic eruption has littered the whole northern end of the island with outcrops of sandstone and loose rock. The sandstone outcrops made cave digging easy for the Japs . . . Our troops obtained cover only by defilade or by piling loose rocks on the surface to form rock-reveted positions. A series of irregularly eroded, crisscrossed gorges with precipitous sides resulted in a series of compartments of various shapes. These were usually small but some extended for several hundred yards. The compartments were lined with a labyrinth of natural and artificial caves which covered the approaches from all directions. Fields of fire were usually limited to 25 yards, and a unique or at least unusual characteristic of the Japanese defensive positions in this area was that the reverse slopes were as strongly fortified as were the forward slopes.[38]

---

[38] *5th MarDiv IntelRpt,* 26.

Gains by the 3d Battalion were not so great as those of the 2d, but by the end of the day the dip in the lines had been completely eradicated and the flanks advanced some 200 yards.

While the rest of the regiment fought its way northward, Companies D and E launched an attack to the northeast along the boundary to seize Hill 362B and relieve the 3d Battalion, 9th Marines, in the 5th Division zone of action. By 1430 the two companies of 2/26 had gained positions southwest of the hill and completed the relief of 3/9.

The bloody assault to the crest of rough and craggy 362B was launched at 1600. The two companies burned and blasted their way to the top, using rocket launchers, flame throwers, and demolitions to the fullest extent to overcome the dense network of interconnecting caves

SMALL-UNIT COMMAND POST just behind the lines. Marine standing at center is using SCR 536 radio. Rugged terrain provides excellent protection from all enemy weapons except mortars and grenades.

and pillboxes along the southern and western slopes. Both company commanders (WIA) were among the heavy losses taken in reaching the summit of 362B.

The 5th Division front at the close of D-plus 12 (3 March) traced an irregular line west from the top of Hill 362B along the rugged northern edge of the Motoyama Plateau, then down to the west coast, passing about 200 yards north of Nishi. Gains in some sectors had been as much as 600 yards; as little as 125 yards in others. But the over-all advance by the tired and depleted division on this day was impressive. (See Map XI.)

RCT 28 spent a quiet night, marked only by sporadic mortar fire and minor attempts at infiltration, but an aggressive enemy crowded the 26th Marines throughout the hours of darkness. During the night men of that regiment killed 97 out of an estimated 100 enemy would-be infiltraters in front of the lines.

D-plus 13

The 5th Division met more intensive small-caliber mortar fire on 4 March than experienced previously, and the front, except for the extreme western flank along the coast, was swept throughout the day by machine-gun and rifle fire from caves and underbrush.[39] In this northern area, where the resistance came chiefly from a network of caves in very rugged terrain, front lines were usually in such close proximity to enemy positions that friendly artillery, naval gunfire, air, or even mortars, could not be employed effectively in close support. For this reason flame-throwing tanks and combat engineers with armored dozers and demolitions became the principal supporting arms.[40]

But it was in the narrow lanes and rocky corridors of this contorted northern terrain that the Japanese made their most effective use of mines. The removal of these from constricted areas covered by small-arms and mortar fire constituted a major problem for which no really satisfactory solution ever materialized. The following excerpt from the 5th Engineer

---

[39] *C–2 Periodic Rpt* No 14, 4Mar45.
[40] *26th Mar SAR*, 41.

Battalion report of the operation describes the two methods commonly employed:

"Engineer Tanks" were not available and mines had to be removed by hand, under fire; or equipment had to be run into the minefield until it was blown up, then removed and the process repeated until a path through the minefield was opened. The former method was slow, tedious, and exposed highly trained specialists to high casualties. The latter method was slow, and costly in armored dozers and tanks.[41]

The weather on 4 March was warm (75°), but low-hanging clouds reduced visibility and intermittent showers dampened the spirits as well as the bodies of exhausted troops. An artillery preparation and a rocket barrage[42] preceded the 0730 jump-off, but an air strike scheduled in front of the 5th Division was canceled because of the low ceiling. Attempts to use 75mm half-tracks and 37mm guns of the weapons companies were hampered by the terrain and the vulnerability of gun crews to enemy fire. Tanks provided excellent support, however, particularly the flame tanks, and limited gains made during the day resulted from the coordinated efforts of infantry-tank-engineer teams.

Fighting along the entire front remained much the same and followed a pattern that continued without any great change until the end of the operation. The infantry advanced until pinned down by fire. Then, when hostile positions were located, armored dozers, working ahead of the line under protection of tank and infantry fire, prepared a road over which the Shermans could advance to engage the enemy. After flame tanks had neutralized the area, the infantrymen advanced while demolition teams dealt with bypassed caves and pillboxes. This was a slow and laborious process, but any attempt by the infantry to continue the advance before destruction of enemy positions resulted in excessive casualties. Furthermore, ground thus gained could not be held so long as the enemy controlled firing positions in the rear. The frustration of troops facing an

---

[41] *5th MarDiv SAR*, Annex J, 24.
[42] The sudden and intense concentration of these 4.5-inch barrage rockets, fired from Mk–7 rocket launchers, made this weapon ideal for last-minute preparations. It was often used as a signal for the jump-off in an attack.

enemy who was rarely seen alive is again reflected in this statement from the 26th Marines action report: "Occasionally the tanks flushed out enemy personnel who could be killed by the infantry. This always raised the morale."[43]

In the center of the division zone of action 3/27 passed through RCT 28's right unit (1/28), and by 1800 had also relieved 1/26, which had been operating on RCT 26's left flank. After the passage of lines 1/28 moved south to replace 2/27 in corps reserve. At the eastern end of the line 1/27, now attached to the 26th Marines, took over a 1-company front, relieving the right flank unit of 2/26. Although the division made only minor gains, the fighting on D-plus 13 was bitter and costly, and units were shifted from company to company, and often between battalions, to strengthen the weakened units, most of which were operating at half strength. Headquarters personnel and men from weapons units were sent forward to bolster the rifle companies.

By this time the 26th Marines had been reduced from a D-Day strength of 3,256 officers and men to 2,153 effectives. Of this strength at the end of D-plus 13, 464 were newcomers from the 27th and 31st Replacement Drafts. Faced with similar losses in trained personnel and an influx of 322 replacements, the 28th Marines placed its combat efficiency at 40 percent on 4 March. Alarming as these figures appear, coldly mathematical comparisons do not adequately present the situation. It was the serious loss of key personnel at the company, platoon, and squad level that sorely affected operations. In addition to this, although replacement troops soon became effective and seasoned members of the units they joined, there was always an initial period of inefficiency. Even when these men were well trained and aggressive, they were not yet members of a team. They had to be told and shown what to do and, too often, how to do it.[44]

The Fifteenth Day

During the afternoon of 4 March the 5th Division received the corps order directing that all divisions devote the next day to reorganization, resupply, and preparations for an attack on 6 March. This order further instructed that each division was to ". . . have one RCT, less one battalion, available for employment 6 March, exclusive of regimental reserves for units in the line. General direction of proposed attack to eastward in present zones of action."[45]

To implement this order General Rockey directed RCT 26 to relieve 1/27 with 1/26, and ordered RCT 27, in reserve, to take control of 1/27 and prepare to launch a coordinated attack in the right of the division zone of action. He further directed that RCT 28 have 3/28, operating on a narrow front, expand to take over 2/28's zone of action.[46] This reorganization would leave the division with the 28th Marines holding a two battalion front (3/28 left, 3/27 right), the 26th Marines drawn up with three battalions abreast (3/26, 2/26, 1/26), and the 27th Marines (less 3/27) available in compliance with the corps order.

On 5 March RCT 26 and RCT 28 made only local attacks to straighten the lines, and by 1200 the reorganization was completed. Marine artillery and naval gunfire were active throughout the day, and carrier planes flew 18 missions against enemy positions in the northern part of the island. The tankers spent most of their time in bivouac areas performing sorely needed maintenance work, but a few Shermans operated in the 26th Marines area, reducing caves and strong points in the vicinity of the frontlines. During this limited action one flame tank was disabled by a mine, and one regular tank lost to antitank fire. At the end of the day the 5th Tank Battalion reported 35 machines operational, including three flame throwers.

Enemy infantry remained quiet, but Japanese mortars harassed Marine lines, and high-velocity weapons interdicted Road Junction 338. This junction, in the 3d Division zone a short distance northwest of Motoyama Village, was on the main supply road to the 26th Marines' forward areas.[47] These Japanese weapons, which

[43] *Ibid.*, 41.

[44] *Ibid.*, 37; *27th Mar SAR*, Encl A, 5; *28th Mar SAR*, 30, 51; 26th Mar War Diary, 4Mar45.

[45] Disp VAC to 3d, 4th, 5 Divs, 1624, 4Mar45.

[46] Disp 5th MarDiv to organic units, 1945, 4Mar45.

[47] As the best routes to the north lay in the 3d Div zone of action, the flanking divisions frequently moved

were not silenced until the next day, slowed movement of supplies and knocked out several vehicles.

When relieved by the 1st Battalion, 26th, 1/27 began moving to an assembly area just west of RJ 338, along the division boundary. During this movement, Lieutenant Colonel John A. Butler, the commanding officer, was killed at the road junction when a high-velocity shell hit his jeep. That afternoon Lieutenant Colonel Justin G. Duryea, operations officer of RCT 27, assumed command of 1/27. At 1500, 2/27 moved to an assembly area just north of 1/27, from which it would pass through 1/26 on the division's right flank at daylight.

OF GUNS AND MEN
D-plus 15

K-Hour was 0800. At 0750, 6 March, three battalions of the 13th Marines joined eight other battalions of artillery to fire a smashing, 2-phase preparation for the corps' echeloned, main-effort attack toward the northeast coast.[48] In support of the first phase, a coordinated K-Hour attack to the northeast by RCT's 27 and 21, the massed artillery delivered a 10-minute preparation at a rate of five rounds per gun per minute, followed by a rolling barrage that lifted approximately 100 yards every seven minutes for 21 minutes. The rate of fire for the barrage was two rounds per gun per minute.

The 2d Battalion, 27th Marines started forward at 0500 under cover of darkness and moved to positions just behind 1/26. The actual relief, which began at daylight, was completed by 0730, and the troops were ready to move out as soon as the preparation lifted. But just as the assault was to begin, enemy shells landed in the area of Company E (2/27), on the right, causing 35 casualties and delaying the jump-off for about ten minutes. Company E made little gain and Company F, on the left, advanced only very slowly against strong Japanese positions consisting of pillboxes and the

ever-present caves. One platoon of the reserve company was committed on the left and moved out a short distance, but 2/27 did not make any significant advance on its first day of action in the indescribably rugged northern section of Iwo.

From K-plus 45 minutes to K-plus 81 minutes the 1st, 2d, and 3d Battalions of the 13th Marines shifted their fires to support the second (K-plus 60 minutes) attack launched by the 3d and 4th Divisions. Upon completion of this mission for the corps, 1/13 reverted to a general support role for the 5th Division while 2/13 and 3/13 fired in direct support of RCT's 28 and 26 respectively. The 4th Battalion supported RCT 27 in the division main effort attack throughout the day.

In the 26th's zone of action, the 1st Battalion, which had just been relieved by 2/27, moved to the left and replaced 2/26 in the line. Then at 1245, following an artillery preparation, 1/26 launched an attack. The 3d Battalion, still operating on the left of the regimental front, was to move forward as soon as 1/26 had reduced a strong point that enfiladed its lines. Repeated attempts to break through this resistance failed, however, and neither battalion made an important advance.

On the far left of the division front, RCT 28 maintained generally the same positions throughout the day. The 3d Battalion, 27th Marines (attached to RCT 28) advanced slightly when 3/26 on its right moved ahead a short distance, and 3/28 kept pace along the coast, but no major changes occurred.

In support of the K-Hour attack, one battleship and two cruisers fired 50 rounds of 14-inch and 400 rounds of 8-inch ammunition. These same ships, plus three destroyers and two LCS(L)'s in direct support of the 5th Division, provided call fires throughout the day. In addition to naval gunfire, carrier planes flew 12 very close support missions.[49]

By the end of D-plus 15 it was apparent that all the blasting by artillery, ships guns, and planes had accomplished little to reduce the enemy's ability and will to resist. It was true that his heavy artillery was not very active,

---

troops and equipment through the center to their fighting fronts. Beginning on 2 March the Corps OpOrders specifically authorized this. VAC OpOrder 11–45, 2Mar45.

[48] The roles of the 3d and 4th Divisions in this attack are related in Chapters VI and VIII respectively.

[49] *C–3 Periodic Rpt* No 16, 6Mar45; *TF 51 Rpt*, Pt V, C, 32; *VAC Air Rpt*, Encl A.

but this progressive diminution of fires had been noticed several days prior to this time. It was the light-mortar and automatic-weapons fire that made every yard of advance through this nightmare of stone so costly. Heavy, long-range weapons had not been able to silence this opposition. The fiery streams from infantry and tank flame throwers had, however, proven highly successful against the tough Japanese positions, and with this in mind the 5th Division sent the following message to VAC: "Request close support planes be armed maximum amount napalm for duration operation. Urgent need in ravines along n o r t h e a s t coast. . . ." [50]

D-plus 16

Following the tremendous expenditure of ammunition on D-plus 15, VAC issued orders limiting the use of its own 155mm howitzers to ". . . deliberate destructive fires against known enemy targets," [51] and reduced the divisional artillery units' allowance ". . . to keep ammunition expenditures within limits which will enable a supply to be maintained for emergencies. . . ." The 5th Division was to fire not more than 2,500 rounds of 105mm and 1,500 rounds of 75mm during the 24-hour period beginning at 1800, 6 March.[52] This limitation did not prohibit the granting of any request for fires, but did limit the firing of harassing missions.[53]

The corps operation order for 7 March again directed the 5th Division to make its main effort in the northeast sector of the division zone of action with the high ground overlooking the sea as the objective.[54] General Rockey's order to his three infantry regiments reflected the corps' scheme of maneuver, directing RCT's 26 and 28 to make ". . . minor objective attacks . . ." [55] and RCT 27 to make the main effort in its zone.

K-Hour was 0730, but at 0640, in the presunrise twilight, Colonel Graham's 26th Marines (less 2/26 in corps reserve) jumped off without preparatory fires in a surprise attack to reduce the strong enemy pocket that had blocked the advance on the previous day (6 March).

The 1st Battalion, with Company H attached, moved out rapidly against moderate resistance and overran the objective by 1140, leaving demolition men, aided by tanks, to mop up and seal cave entrances. With this obstacle removed from its flank, the 3d Battalion also moved forward, but after a gain of about 150 yards resistance stiffened all along the regimental front. By the end of the day all six companies were heavily engaged on a thinly held line after an average gain of about 200 yards. (See Map XI.)

The 2d Battalion, 27th Marines, with Company A attached, attacked at K-Hour to make the division main effort. After a 15-minute preparation by 4/13, Company A passed through the right flank of Company E for an assault on a narrow front along the division boundary, while Company G, 21st Marines attacked on the right in the 3d Division zone of action. The objective was a piece of commanding ground from which enemy guns enfiladed Company E's route of advance. The first rush carried leading elements well forward, but as Marines passed into a draw that cut through the first of several ridges to the front, Japanese machine guns opened up from both sides. These hostile positions were difficult to locate and almost impossible to knock out. After considerable heaving and hauling, a 37mm gun was maneuvered into a forward position from which it engaged the opposing weapons. Throughout the day close-range hand grenade battles raged in this area and Marine casualties mounted steadily. Company G, 21st Marines met the same difficult situation, and finally both units withdrew to better positions for night defense.[56] (See Map XI.)

The actions of Companies E and F duplicated the previous day's fighting. Knee mortars,

---

[50] Disp 5th MarDiv to VAC, 1425, 6Mar45.

[51] VAC OpOrder 14–45, 6Mar45.

[52] Disp VAC to division and corps artillery units, 1715, 5Mar45. This dispatch was dated 5 March but the VAC G–3 Journal shows it logged out at 1730, 6Mar45.

[53] *13th Mar SAR*, 17.

[54] VAC OpOrder 14–45, 6Mar45.

[55] 5th MarDiv OpOrder 13–45, 6Mar45.

[56] SSgt Henry Giniger and SSgt Tony Smith, "The Twenty-Seventh Marines in Combat, Iwo Jima," manuscript, undated. Hereafter cited as *Giniger and Smith*.

grenades, and short range rifle fire exacted an exorbitant toll in killed and wounded for a meager gain of 150 yards. Attempts were made to bring up tanks in support, but the terrain proved impassable. About noon one platoon from Company C plugged a gap on the left between RCT 26 and RCT 27. When this platoon advanced ahead of units on either side, it immediately received vicious flanking fire. Grenades and 81mm mortar smoke shells were fired to screen this small unit as it withdrew to a more sheltered line, and at 1330 a second platoon from the same company moved into the line to maintain contact with RCT 26. During the afternoon the grim cave warfare continued but with scant gain.

On the far left, along the northwest coast where enemy resistance in front of RCT 28 had been light, 3/28 and 3/27 sent out combat patrols to develop the situation before moving out in a general attack. With no special preparation fired, the patrols moved out at 0900 and met only scattered groups of the enemy. The main body followed at 1000, impeded only by extremely difficult terrain. The division reconnaissance company, attached to 3/28, was on the left, and Companies H and G extended the line to the east, maintaining contact with 3/27. Only mortars and rockets, firing well to the front, supported the attack. The two battalions pushed 500 yards to the north along the rocky gorge-cut coast by 1530 for one of the longest advances yet made in the 5th Division's zone of action. Further progress would have been possible before dark, but with the lines on ground suitable for defense the Marines halted and dug in for the night. (See Map XI.)

During the day naval gunfire supplemented the limited artillery fires for harassing missions, and all naval gunfire control parties were instructed to expend 500 rounds per ship. Based on information supplied by the corps intelligence section, the division intelligence officer assigned target priorities.[57] Although shrinking enemy-held territory and consequent proximity of friendly troops to targets made close support difficult, the Landing Force Air Support Control Unit authorized ten deliberate,

5TH DIVISION OFFICERS study stereo pairs to orient themselves in the jumbled terrain.

closely coordinated missions, using 119 carrier planes in 147 sorties. Of the 40 napalm bombs carried, however, seven failed to release, and seven of the 33 released did not ignite.[58]

D-plus 17

For the first time since the beginning of the operation the corps order for the attack on 8 March departed from phase-line objectives and directed the divisions ". . . to capture the remainder of the island."[59] The 5th Division was to continue its main effort on the right, with RCT 27 driving to the northeast coast along the division boundary, parallel to the 3d Division advance.

The 2d Battalion, 27th Marines, commenced its attack at K-Hour (0750) but made little progress until tanks arrived. The Shermans had set out from their bivouac area as soon as there was enough light to travel, moving along a route reconnoitered the day before. The rough terrain hampered their progress, and it was not until about 0900 that armor of Company B arrived in position to support the assault. With this aid, Company E finally managed to inch forward through the heavily mined and cave-infested area to the front, grinding out an advance of about 150 yards during the morning.

---

[57] 5th MarDiv D–3 Periodic Rpt No 17, 7Mar45.

[58] *VAC Air Rpt*, Encl A, 5. Other ordnance dropped in these strikes included 67 500-lb bombs, 170 100-lb bombs, and 426 rockets.

[59] VAC OpOrder, 15–45, 7Mar45.

In the left of the battalion zone, where the ground was too rough for employment of tanks, a 15-man crew from Battery B, 13th Marines, wrestled a 75mm pack howitzer and 200 rounds of ammunition up close to the front to provide essential direct fire support. This weapon destroyed several enemy positions, but Japanese resistance in front of Companies D and F remained virtually undiminished and only very limited gains were made.

It was Company E, on the right, that finally broke loose during the afternoon to surge forward in a 300-yard rush to the bluff overlooking the sea. During the morning unrelenting pressure of engineer-tank-infantry teamwork had cracked the Japanese defenses to the immediate front, but this Marine advance appears to have been stimulated by more than just fire superiority. The spark that set off this charge was the fatal wounding of a tremendously popular platoon leader, 1st Lieutenant Jack Lummus.[60] This officer's fearless actions had been an inspiration to his men, and when they saw him fall in battle, fierce anger blazed up to drive them forward.[61]

Although the attack by RCT 28 on the division's left flank was delayed somewhat while the 1st and 2d Battalions passed through 3/27 and 3/28, gains during the day were good. Along the coast 2/28 equalled the 500-yard advance of the previous day, and on that unit's right 1/28 moved ahead 300 yards.

Both battalions jumped off against light opposition and scrambled forward rapidly over the rough ground for at least 100 yards before any serious enemy reaction developed. Then Japanese fire increased along the front, and bypassed positions came to life to harass the rear of assault elements. The attached 75's and 37's of the weapons company were pressed into service, and 81mm mortars fired heavy concentrations in an attempt to neutralize Japanese weapons. Naval gunfire pounded coastal areas ahead of the advance and planes struck

twice at Hill 165, one of the last significant terrain features in the regiment's zone of action.

As enemy resistance stiffened, the infantry requested armor, and 11 regular plus two flame tanks were dispatched to the front. But the only available route forward was heavily mined, and engineer clearance teams were pinned down most of the day by rifle fire with the result that only four rounds of 75mm ammunition and half a load of flame oil were expended in support of the 28th Marines on D-plus 17.

The 26th Marines, with the 1st and 3d Battalions still in the line, tried to advance the division center against the complex maze of pillboxes and interconnected caves in the area that had once been the village of Kita. The plan was for 3/26 to advance only a short distance to a point where 1/26 on the right and 1/28 on the left would pinch that unit out. Neither the 1st nor the 3d Battalion could advance far enough to place this plan in effect, however, and at the close of the day the regimental front remained essentially unchanged. (See Map XI.)

At the end of the day's fighting, the Japanese commander on Iwo made the following report to Tokyo:

Troops at "Tamanayama" and Northern districts are still holding their position thoroughly and continue giving damages to the enemy. Their fighting situation believing their country's victory looks godlike.[62]

Looking certain defeat squarely in the face, however, he added:

I am very sorry that I have let the enemy occupy one part of the Japanese territory, but I am taking comfort in giving heavy damages to the enemy.[63]

LAUNCHING THE FINAL DRIVE
D-plus 18–19

During the next two days the division advanced its left flank about 40 yards across almost impossible terrain. Japanese resistance in this sector was light until the 28th Marines

---

[60] Lieutenant Lummus was awarded the Medal of Honor for his dauntless leadership on 8 March.

[61] 27th Mar SAR, Encl F, 13. In another report this attack was described as ". . . a terrific Marine drive . . . which at times assumed the proportions of an American *banzai* charge." *Giniger and Smith*, 18.

[62] *Horie*, 9. Tamanayama refers to the area east of Airfield No. 2 in the 4th Division zone of action. The "Northern districts" fell in the 5th Division zone.

[63] *Ibid.*

came under intense and accurate fire from high ground that ran southeast from Kitano Point. Slowed by this fire, the drive to the northeast finally came to an abrupt halt against a long, low ridge line that overlooked a deep gorge. In this steep draw the Japanese held out 15 more days to create the final pocket of resistance on Iwo.

Along the remainder of the 5th Division front, however, the 26th and 27th Marines battled north and northeast against the stubborn enemy for meager gains. At 0700 the morning of 9 March 2/26 (released from corps reserve on 8 March) moved up and relieved the left-most units of 1/26. This placed elements of 3/26, 2/26, and 1/26 on line from left to right. The regiment made no advance until the 28th Marines came up on the left. At 1530 the 28th pulled abreast and squeezed out Company I, 3/26. The 26th then jumped off in the attack but made no appreciable gain against extremely heavy and accurate small-arms fire. (See Map XII.)

Early in the morning of 10 March 2/26 completed relieving elements of 3/26 (Company G) and the 26th Marines attacked at 0800 for no gain. A second attack at 1400 netted only 75 yards. The plan for D-plus 19 had called for 2/26 to advance diagonally (northeastward) across the front of the 1st Battalion and pinch out that unit, leaving only the 2d Battalion on line. The day's small gain did not allow execution of this plan, and at 2000 1/26 and its zone passed to control of RCT 27, on the division right flank. The 3d Battalion became corps reserve at about noon, the 10th of March.

Although the 21st Marines, to the southeast, had reached the sea in its zone of action, the 27th made no attempt to occupy the beach physically once it gained the high bluffs overlooking the shore line. Instead, this unit fought to swing the division right flank northward to sweep the remaining enemy up into the narrow northern tip of the island. The 1st and 2d Battalions met extremely stiff resistance when they jumped off on 9 March and registered no gain during the day. (See Map XII.)

In early afternoon the hazard of land mines was forcibly demonstrated when an explosion seriously wounded Lieutenant Colonel Justin G. Duryea, commanding 1/27, and Lieutenant Colonel John W. Antonelli, commanding officer of 2/27. They had met near the front lines with other officers to confer on the situation. The company commander and another officer from Company E, and the intelligence officer of 2/27 were also wounded by this blast. Both battalion commanders and the company commander were evacuated, but the other two officers continued in action. Command of the 1st and 2d Battalions passed to the executive officers, Major William H. Tumbelston and Major Gerald F. Russell, respectively.

The 3d Battalion went into action on the right flank on 10 March with orders to attack northwest along the cliff line above the northeast coast to a point where it could pass across the 2d Battalion front. The 1st Battalion, on the left, was to continue its assault in column of companies to the northeast, squeezing out the left unit of 2/27 and then turning to the northwest along the RCT 26–27 boundary. Enemy fire, mines, and the rugged terrain combined to hold the Marines almost to a standstill, and when units tied in for the night elements of all three battalions were still in the line. (See Map XII.)

The 13th Marines fired preparations and scheduled supporting fires for the attacks on these two days, but its contribution was not limited to this normal function. About noon on 9 March General Rockey ordered his artillery regiment to have ten percent of its personnel stand by on 1-hour notice as infantry replacements. The next day a detail from Headquarters and Service Battery and the 1st and 3d Battalions reported to the 28th Marines, and men from the other two artillery battalions reported to the 26th Marines.

On 9 March Iwo-based P–51's joined carrier planes in strikes against Japanese in the northern tip of the island and continued flying troop-support missions until D-plus 23. After the strikes on 10 March the corps air officer reported, "The precision low-altitude work of the P–51's was particularly pleasing to the ground troops." [64]

[64] VAC Air Rpt, Encl A, 6.

In the 14-day period (25 February–10 March) covered in this chapter, the 5th Division drove 3,000 yards up the west coast from positions abreast of Airfield Number 2 to a line that stretched from sea to sea across the narrow northern end of the island. North of the division front, Kuribayashi and his 109th Division headquarters, elements of the 2d Battalion, 145th Infantry Regiment, the remainder of the 3d Battalion, 17th Independent Mixed Regiment, and a miscellany of stragglers from other units were compressed into an area of less than one square mile. In a dispatch to Tokyo on 10 March, General Kuribayashi summed up the Japanese situation in this manner:

Although the attacks of the enemy against our Northern districts are continuing day and night, our troops are still fighting bravely and holding their positions thoroughly * * * 200 or 300 American infantrymen with several tanks attacked "*Tenzan*" all day. The enemy's bombardments from one battleship (or cruiser), 11 destroyers, and aircraft are very severe, especially the bombing and machine-gun fire against Divisional Headquarters from 30 fighters and bombers are so fierce that I cannot express nor write here.[65]

Not until 15 bloody days later did Marines eliminate the last pocket of organized enemy

---

[65] *Horie*, 10. *Tenzan* was the area east and north of Hill 362B where RCT 27 was attacking.

resistance in the northern end of the island. By D-plus 19 all that remained for the enemy force was to fight and die for the Emperor. In his Periodic Report for 10 March the VAC intelligence officer summed up enemy morale as follows:

The enemy is now disorganized, particularly in the 4th Marine Division's sector, but his will to fight to the death is apparently undiminished.[66]

Evidence of the enemy's determination to resist to the end is found in the number of prisoners of war captured as of the close of this period. Total POW's taken by the corps was 111. Of this figure only 67 were Japanese, the other 44 being Korean labor troops.[67]

During this period the division suffered 4,292 casualties as follows:

Killed in action	830
Died of wounds	263
Wounded in action	2,974
Missing in action	5
Combat fatigue	220
Total	4,292

---

[66] *C–2 Periodic Rpt* No 20, 10Mar45.

[67] *Ibid.* Broken down by divisions the number of POW's taken as of 10 March was: 3d MarDiv—49, 4th MarDiv—28, 5th MarDiv—34.

CHAPTER VIII 4th Division on the Right

(D-plus 6—D-plus 19)[1]

While the 3d and 5th Divisions moved north and then northeast up the center and west coast of the island, General Cates' 4th Division turned to the right to clear the one-third of Iwo lying east of Airfield Number 2 and south of Hill 362C. In this fantastically rugged area the Japanese had strengthened the natural defenses by digging and building, transforming the entire sector into a mighty fortress.

The stoutest defenses in the area were at terrain features called Hill 382 (which the Japanese called *Nidan Iwa*), the Amphitheater, Turkey Knob, and the smashed village of Minami. During the days of desperate fighting required to seize and hold this incredible stronghold, these several closely related positions became known collectively as the "Meat Grinder". *Nidan Iwa*, 382 feet high, was located 250 yards northeast of the east-west runway of the airfield. The top of the hill, surmounted by the stark remains of a Japanese radar station, was hollowed out and rebuilt to contain field pieces and antitank weapons. Each of these concrete gun housings was in turn protected by as many as ten supporting machine-gun emplacements. The rest of the hill was honeycombed with the same elaborate tunneling that characterized other major installations on the island. In addition, crevices and

ridges crisscrossed the entire surrounding area. Light and medium tanks, armed with 57mm and 47mm guns, parked well back in these crevices, commanded the length of the main (northeast-southwest) runway of the airfield and approaches from the southwest.

From Hill 382 the land dropped to the south and east in a semicircular series of ridges and draws leading down from the plateau like giant steps. Six hundred yards south of 382 rose the ugly looking rock that came to be called Turkey Knob. Though not very high it housed a reinforced concrete communication center, and served also as a strong observation post overlooking the entire southern end of the island. (See Map XIII.)

High ground in the vicinity of Turkey Knob fell away sharply to the southwest to form the bowl known as the Amphitheater. The enemy had strengthened the natural defenses in this area by constructing three tiers of heavy concrete emplacements in the south-slope hill faces. He had also installed an extensive communication system and electric light circuits. From these positions, antitank and machine guns swept the southern approaches to the Knob.[2]

---

[1] Unless otherwise cited, material in this chapter is based on the following: *4th MarDiv OpRpt; 14th Mar OpRpt; 23d Mar OpRpt; 24th Mar OpRpt; 25 Mar OpRpt; 4th TkBn OpRpt.*

[2] Capt. J. W. Thomason, III, USMCR, "The Fourth Division at Iwo Jima", a manuscript, 21Aug45; 4th MarDiv D–2 Periodic Rpts; 4th MarDiv Preliminary POW Interrogation Rpt No. 5, 27Feb45. These defenses, prepared by the 2d Mixed Brigade Engineers, were reported by POW's to be the most extensive and powerful on the island. This terrain is also described

MAJOR GENERAL CATES commanded the 4th Marine Division at Iwo Jima.

Between these fortifications and the sea lay a wilderness of rocky, cave-studded terrain. An excellent description of this area is contained in the division intelligence report of 5 March:

> . . . During the period the terrain not under our control to the Div's front was scrupulously observed and studied by D–2 observers from various Bn OP's, close inshore from an LCI(G), and from a VMO–4 OY–1. The volcanic, crevice lined area is a tangled conglomeration of torn trees and blasted rocks. Ground observation is restricted to small areas. While there are sundry ridges, depressions and irregularities, most of the crevices of any moment radiate from the direction of Hill 382 to fan out like spokes generally in a southeasterly direction providing a series of cross corridors to our advance and eminently suitable for the enemy's employment of mortars. The general debris caused by our supporting fires provides perfect concealment for snipers and mortar positions. From the air, caves and tracks are observed everywhere, but the enemy's camouflage discipline is flawless and it is the rarest occasion that an AO [Aerial Observer] can locate troops.[3]

THE MEAT GRINDER

D-plus 6

Early in the morning of 25 February the 21st Marines reverted to the 3d Division, and the

briefly in the account of the 4th MarDiv action on D-plus 5, Chapter V of this monograph.

[3] 4th MarDiv D–2 Periodic Rpt No 62, 5Mar45.

line of demarcation between RCT 21 and RCT 24 became the 4th Division left boundary. Airfield Number 2, except for the eastern one-third of the east-west runway and the northeast tip of the long runway, now lay in the 3d's zone of action, but the entire eastern bulge of the island remained the responsibility of the 4th.

At 0630 the 23d Marines reverted from corps reserve to parent control and prepared to attack abreast of the 24th Marines by passing through that regiment's left unit. The assault was to be made in a column of battalions with 1/23 following 3/23 at 600 yards, and 2/23 in reserve. The 24th Marines, with 2/25 attached, would continue the assault with 3/24 on the left, 1/24 on the right, and 2/24 reverting to regimental reserve when relieved by 3/23. The 25th Marines, less 2/25 remained in division reserve.

The division made its main effort on the left with RCT 23 maintaining contact with the 3d Division, which was making the corps' main effort up the center of the island as related in Chapter V. Since tanks could not operate effectively over rough terrain on the right, most of the armored support went to 3/23. Enemy antitank weapons and mines blocked movement of vehicles to the front through the 4th Division zone of action, so permission was requested and received to send the tanks forward through the 3d Division zone to firing positions along RCT 23's left boundary. Using this approach, the mediums effectively supported infantry troops by destroying enemy antitank guns, pillboxes, and machine-gun emplacements. But not until about 1430 did engineers, working with an armored bulldozer, succeed in clearing a route for tanks to move forward through RCT 23's zone of action.

The 3d Battalion, 23d Marines encountered heavy resistance from small arms and mortars as it fought across its front. All supporting weapons were employed throughout the attack, and finally Company K, on the left, forced its way across the strip and gained a foothold on high ground to the north, while Company L, on the right, pushed eastward along the ridge described in Chapter V as Charlie-Dog. Hostile mortar fire that effectively interdicted the open runways of the airfield made it extremely difficult for 3/23 to maintain contact with RCT 9 on its left.

The 24th Marines jumped off with its 3d Battalion (plus Companies E and G, 25th Marines) on the left, and the 1st Battalion (with Company F, 25th Marines and Company A, 2d Armored Amphibian Battalion attached) on the right. Artillery, naval gunfire, and carrier planes shelled, bombed, and strafed the Amphitheater and Minami areas before the attack. During the air strike battalion 81mm mortars fired a 200-round preparation close to the lines. Armored amphibians from Company A, 2d Armored Amphibian Battalion, tried to support 1/24 from positions off the east coast as on previous days, but choppy seas so limited their effectiveness that they were withdrawn.

Both battalions ran into heavy mortar and automatic-weapons fire as they jumped off. Japanese resistance ahead of the 3d Battalion came from the Amphitheater, while in front of the 1st Battalion enemy troops were strongly emplaced in many caves and folds in the terrain just forward of the Marine lines. About an hour after the attack began five tanks re-

REAR ENTRANCE to Japanese position in high ground north of East Boat Basin in 4th Division zone of action. From this area enemy had unobstructed observation of the eastern beaches. (Navy Photo)

LOOKING SOUTH FROM TOP OF AMPHITHEATER. 4th Division Marines had to cross this relatively flat and open ground to reach the strong enemy positions in the area.

ported to 3/24 to assist that unit, but because of extremely rough ground these proved of little value. After a gain of about 100 yards both battalions were stopped by very heavy and effective fire of all kinds. As usual, key officers and noncommissioned officers were among the casualties taken during this morning attack, including the commander of Company A, 1/24 who was wounded and evacuated. Early in the afternoon an air strike along the high ground in front of 3/24 put a temporary damper on the mortar fire, enabling Marines to inch forward for short gains.

The 2d Battalion, 24th Marines, relieved by 3/23 at K-Hour, spent most of the day in RCT reserve resting and reequipping, but this respite was brief. At 1530, 2/24 received orders to move up and relieve 1/24 on the right of the regimental line. This hasty relief took place without casualties, and the battalion spent a relatively quiet night on position.

Along the rest of the 4th Division front Japanese attempted to infiltrate front lines, and enemy shells fell in both forward and rear areas sporadically throughout the hours of darkness. Fire support ships fired normal night missions,[4] with mortar gunboats providing large area neutralization, and an LCI firing 40mm rounds into enemy mortar and rocket positions along the coast.

D-plus 7

The second day of struggle for Hill 382 and the Amphitheater dawned bright and clear, but during the afternoon light showers and a lowering ceiling interfered with air activities over the island. Bad weather between Iwo and the Marianas prevented bombers of the Seventh Air Force from making scheduled strikes.

General Cates had alerted the 25th Marines to pass through the 24th, and at 0530 the battalions started moving up. The 1st Battalion was to relieve 3/24 on the left, the 2d was to go into the

center of the line, and the 3d would replace 2/24 on the right flank. The 1st and 3d Battalions executed the relief and were ready to attack on time at 0800, but 2/25, which had been attached to RCT 24, experienced difficulty extricating its companies and shifting them to new positions, so the jump-off was delayed until 0820. After being passed through, the 3d Battalion, 24th Marines became attached to RCT 25 as regimental reserve, the rest of the regiment reverting to division reserve. Patrols from 1/24 thoroughly searched all destroyed enemy vessels on Beaches Blue 1 and 2, from which occasional rifle and machine-gun fire had harassed the division's rear along the coast, but most of the day was spent in hasty reorganization and re-equipping.

The three battalions of RCT 25 attacked behind an artillery preparation that pounded the area 250 yards ahead of the Marine lines for 15 minutes, then lifted 100 yards every five minutes for 20 minutes. The assault moved well for the first 100 yards, then 1/25 on the left and 2/25 in the center ran into a wall of extremely heavy machine-gun fire from the Amphitheater and Turkey Knob. Tanks from Company A, 4th Tank Battalion rumbled up to locate and knock out this opposition, but they were unable to do so, and Japanese mortars quickly concentrated on this new threat. Artillery forward observers attempted to direct Marine counterbattery fire, but observation was too limited by the topsy-turvy terrain. Two OY-1's from VMO-4, which had just landed on the island, also joined in the search but could do little to penetrate the skillful and disciplined camouflage in the area north and east of the division front.[5]

---

[4] Bad weather had interfered with ammunition resupply for naval gunfire support ships and caused a limitation on expenditure of illumination and 5-inch shells. But by D-plus 6 the situation had improved, and the allotment was increased from 50 to 75 star shells and from 400 to 500 5-inch shells per ship. *TF 51 Rpt*, Pt V, C, 24, 26, 38.

[5] When the *Bismarck Sea* was sunk and the *Saratoga* damaged on the evening of 21 February, the five tactical air observers and one of two VMO-4 pilots on board the former were rescued, but for the next four days the 4th Division was without tactical air observers and used 5th Division carrier-based observers. With the landing of two VMO-4 planes on 26 February, however, the division resumed its own tactical observation, using secondary and volunteer observers until the return of the regular men. In addition, air spot for 4th Division artillery was provided continuously from 20 Feb to 12 Mar by observers in TBM aircraft from the *Wake Island* (CVE). *4th MarDiv OpRpt*, Annex C, 10, 11, 15.

Company C (1/25) sent one platoon supported by a tank around its right flank to envelop the enemy at Turkey Knob and silence some of the intense opposition. As the platoon worked toward the Knob, Japanese mortars shifted their fire and caught it in a barrage that killed several men, including the platoon leader. With its commander gone and hostile mortar and machine-gun fire increasing, the unit withdrew, using a smoke screen to cover evacuation of casualties.

In the center of the 25th Marines' line 2/25 also met stubborn and constant resistance from countless caves and pillboxes to its front. The chaotic terrain that aided the Japanese defense in this zone of action also prevented the use of tanks, 75mm halftracks, and 37mm guns. Both assault companies suffered heavy casualties and marked up insignificant gains. At 1500 Company E passed through F on the right and the later unit set up a secondary line of defense.

Along the coast Company I, 3d Battalion, 25th, aided by two Shermans and LVT (A)'s, spent the day mopping up the East Boat Basin area, while on the left Company L progressed slowly against stiff resistance. The reserve company cleaned up behind the advance and sent elements to the left to cover the boundary where 2/25 lagged behind the more rapid advance of 3/25.

On the left of the 4th Division zone of action the 23d Marines jumped off at 0800 in a renewal of its assault against Hill 382. Where he had attacked the day before in a column of battalions, Colonel Wensinger now split his zone and committed the 1st Battalion on the left of the 3d, both units in a column of companies.

When the 1st Battalion passed through Company K (3/23) with Company C in the lead, it immediately received a blast of heavy and accurate fire. Japanese weapons on and around Hill 382 poured a deadly barrage against the lead company's front, while other hostile fire struck the left flank from positions in the 3d Division's zone where 1/9 fought for control of the northern portion of the airfield and commanding ground beyond.[6] Successive mine

fields on the taxiway of Airfield Number 2 and in the vicinity of the radio weather station, between the field and Hill 382, limited employment of tanks in close support of the infantry. But Shermans of Company C shuttled back and forth between rearming points and the front lines to blast enemy installations on the hill. Two tanks were destroyed by land mines and a third damaged during this day-long action.

On 1/23's right, 3/23 met the same well-directed fire but moved doggedly ahead, reducing the hill's forward supporting positions with flame, rockets, and demolitions. Advance elements of Company I, spearheading the attack, reached the southwestern slopes of Hill 382 late in the afternoon, but enemy rocket and mortar fire drove them back. After both battalions had returned to tenable positions for the night net gains for the regiment totaled about 200 yards.

With firm contact between regiments finally established at 2100 the division lines resembled a flattened and elongated letter "M", with the center of both regimental fronts advanced beyond the flanks. In the center of the zone, where 1/25 faced the tough Amphitheater and Knob defenses, a re-entrant developed that continued for many days. (See Map XIII.)

Ammunition expenditures throughout the day had been high, and infantry carrying parties worked well into the night to bring replenishment supplies forward across fire-swept areas. Throughout the hours of darkness enemy infantry prodded Marine lines, and hostile mortar fire harassed both front and rear areas. At 0535 Company I, 23d Marines, heard the sound of tanks to its front and reported enemy preparations for a counterattack. Artillery was called down on the general area and the suspicious activity ceased.

In his periodic report for the day, the 4th Division D–2 characterized enemy resistance as "bitter," and stated, "The enemy was determined to deny us Hill 382, and his unusually heavy mortar barrage on it twice forced our troops to retire after having occupied the hill area." Concerning the conduct of the defense in the 25th Marines zone of action, the D–2 reported: "RCT 25 reports that the enemy is now fighting to the death in pillboxes, foxholes and

---

[6] The 3d Division's action during this period is covered in Chapter VI, "Hills PETER and 199 OBOE."

LIGHT JAPANESE TANK dug in to cover approaches to Airfield Number 2. The enemy did not move his tanks but derived maximum benefit of their fire power as stationary high-velocity artillery pieces.

trenches in its area and is not retreating as he apparently formerly had done." [7]

Discussing enemy capabilities and probable courses of action in the same report, the intelligence officer listed as most probable that the Japanese would continue the defense in depth from present positions:

> In spite of the strength of our established beachhead the enemy still holds three-fifths of the Island. The best area for cover and concealment and many excellent OP sites still remain in his hands. With Blue [U. S. forces] in control of air and sea, ultimate defeat must be obvious to the enemy. Balancing these factors it would appear most likely that the enemy will endeavor to conserve his strength and continue his stubborn underground defense to make our securing of this airbase as slow and costly as possible. Such a course of action would be far more beneficial to the Japanese Empire than a *banzai* charge.[8]

Counterattack was placed second in order of probability. The possibility that a water shortage might force the enemy to attack was discounted:

> . . . It is hard to reconcile the meticulous defense arrangements with the thought that the enemy would overlook or neglect dispersed water storage. It is likewise remembered that many elements fought for weeks on Saipan with virtually no water. . . .[9]

D-plus 8–9

The 4th Division continued to attack during the next two days against the powerful, mutually supporting positions of the enemy's main defense line east of the airfield. Five battalions were committed abreast, from left to right: 1/23, 3/23 (relieved by 2/23, D-plus 9), 1/25, 2/25, 3/25. On each day the K-Hour assault was preceded by an intensive 45-minute coordinated preparation by corps and division artillery, with aircraft on station for call missions after K-Hour.[10] (See Map XIII.)

---

[7] The quotes in this paragraph are all taken from 4th MarDiv D-2 Periodic Rpt No 55, 26Feb45.

[8] *Ibid.*

[9] *Ibid.*

[10] As indicated in previous chapters of this monograph, the corps 155's were under orders to give priority of fires to the 3d Division during this period, but reinforced the 14th Marines on D-plus 8 with 300 rounds for the preparation, and fired 25 percent of the general support missions throughout the day for the 4th Div.

In the 23d Marines' zone of action the Japanese again resisted fiercely from Hill 382, repulsing attack after attack from the west. But northwest of the hill, on D-plus 8, the left flank of 1/23 gained 150 yards against diminishing opposition. In its zone of action on the right, 3/23 pushed close to the top of 382. Elements of this battalion engaged in a raging hand-to-hand battle with the enemy around the ruins of the Japanese radar station, only to be driven off the crest by a heavy artillery and mortar barrage. A tank bulldozer and engineers labored most of the day clearing a route forward for Company B tanks, and by late after-

noon the Shermans worked their way forward to support the infantry. When orders were received to consolidate on the most favorable ground with solid contact left and right, 3/23 withdrew its advance elements to approximately the morning line of departure and dug in there.

Intermittent concentrations of light and heavy Japanese mortar fire fell along the front-lines and rear areas during the night. At 0043, although there had been no warning of enemy aircraft in the area, parachutes were seen falling into enemy territory 400 to 600 yards ahead of the 23d's lines. Believing them to be supply 'chutes, Marines concentrated artillery and

SOUTHWEST SLOPES OF HILL 382 pictured after Marines of the 4th Division had secured the area.

naval gunfire against the drop zone to destroy the cargo and enemy troops attempting to recover it.

On the next day, D-plus 9, the boundary between assault battalions of the 23d Marines was shifted to the southeast and the direction of attack for the left unit swung more toward the east, paralleling the 4th Division's left boundary. This change placed Hill 382 in the 1st Battalion's zone, and gave the 2d Battalion, which had relieved 3/23, a direction of attack up to a corridor southeast of the hill. (See Map XIII.)

On the right, 2/23 moved slowly forward up the corridor in column of companies against heavy fire from camouflaged bunkers and pillboxes. By 1200 Company G had pushed forward 200 yards, but then enemy fire hit Marines from both sides and halted the advance. At this time one platoon of Company F was committed on the right to gain the rising ground along the regimental boundary. This maneuver proved only partially successful as 1/25 (on RCT 23's right), was unable to seize and hold the elevation, and the platoon found itself face to face with enemy troops protected in emplacements concealed by heavy brush not more than 15 to 25 yards to the front. This platoon held the ground it gained and remained in these positions on 2/23's right flank.

In addition to the assault on Hill 382, the 1st Battalion, operating in the left of the regimental zone, had the responsibility of maintaining contact with the 9th Marines, now beginning to move out more rapidly northeast of the airfield. This job fell to Company E, 23d Marines,[11] while Company A hammered against the hill. One platoon of Company E became separated from its parent unit and followed RCT 9 several hundred yards into the 9th's zone of action before it could be halted and returned to the company. At 1000, elements of Company B moved up on the left to help maintain contact across the boundary.

Progress on the left advanced Company A around the north side of the hill during the

morning, and at 1415 this unit launched an attack to envelop the rocky elevation's reverse (eastern) slopes. During the assault bazooka men closed in under heavy fire and eliminated two enemy tanks that had previously escaped destruction because of their defiladed positions. With these guns silenced, the rest of the company moved to positions from where it could engage the entrenched enemy on the east slopes of the hill. Although the Marines had virtually surrounded Hill 382 by this time, enemy defenders still resisted savagely with mortar, rocket, and artillery fire from positions in the rocky wilderness to the east.

Antitank weapons, mines, and rough terrain continued to limit the use of tanks in close support of infantry on D-plus 8 and 9, but the tankers pushed forward as far as possible to deliver overhead fire. The 14th Marines fired close-in preparations before the jump-off, then lifted fire ahead of the troops to neutralize enemy small arms and automatic weapons. One of the primary and most difficult tasks of artillery was locating and silencing hostile mortar, artillery, and rocket installations. All corps and division observation and intelligence agencies cooperated in the detection of Japanese weapons, but it was a slow process.

The massed firepower of the 4.5-inch rockets was used repeatedly to neutralize centers of resistance and add punch to preparation efforts prior to attacks. As long as the enemy enjoyed good observation, the rocket trucks of the 1st Provisional Rocket Detachment attracted heavy counterbattery bombardment whenever Marine crews went into action. Therefore, the rocket trucks maneuvered rapidly, fired, and retired with all possible speed to a rear assembly point. When an intensive barrage was desired in a certain area, a section consisting of six trucks and launchers would fire once, reload from ammunition carried on the vehicles, fire again, and then withdraw. This double ripple of 432 rounds took less than five minutes to deliver.[12]

While the 23d Marines attacked Hill 382 on D-plus 8 and 9, RCT 25, with 3/24 attached, continued its frustrating head-on assaults

---

[11] Company E, 2/23 had been attached to 1/23 on the previous day. When 2/23 was committed on D-plus 9, Company E, 24th, was attached to bring the 2d Battalion more nearly up to strength.

[12] 4th MarDiv OpRpt, Annex C, 27.

against the Amphitheater, Turkey Knob, and the Japanese front lines that extended southward from the Knob to the coast just east of the Boat Basin.

On 27 February (D-plus 8) 2/25, in the center, and 3/25, on the right, were to continue the attack straight ahead. The 1st Battalion, on the left, would bypass the strongly held area to its immediate front by moving troops to the left through the zone of RCT 23. That regiment was reported to have advanced its right flank unit (3/23) to a position on the high ground above the Amphitheater bowl. Once 1/25 gained a foothold on the ridge it was to drive southeast from the regiment's left boundary toward 2/25 with the envelopment of Turkey Knob from the north as its main objective. (See Map XIII.)

Companies A and C were ready to move out in the assault at 0800, but 3/23 had not yet advanced far enough in its zone to permit the jump-off by 1/25. The 1st Battalion delayed moving until 1500 when it passed Company A through the elements on its left to launch the assault. This attack was supported by tanks and preceded by an intense rocket barrage. The first 150 yards of the route led across an open area and, as troops and tanks advanced, enemy weapons of all kinds opened up with deadly fire. Two of the tanks were knocked out by 47mm antitank shells, and a third was hit but managed to limp back to the rear. Heavy machine-gun fire from around the Knob raked advancing Marine lines, causing numerous casualties and making positions along high ground above the Amphitheater untenable. At 1715 the battalion commander ordered Company A to fall back to the line held on the previous night, and 1/25 consolidated with A on the left and Companies C, L (3/24), and B extended to the right (southeast) to tie in with 2/25.

The 2d and 3d Battalions, attacking on the 1st Battalion's right, moved out directly forward on D-plus 8. In the center, 2/25 ran into a stubborn enemy strong point in the left of the battalion zone. Company G spent the entire morning trying to overcome this resistance, and about noon Company F relieved G and continued the assault. Two tanks were as-

signed to support that company, but the terrain limited their use and made it impossible to bring regimental 37mm and 75mm guns to bear.

The 3d Battalion, on 2/25's right achieved greater success. Company I secured the East Boat Basin and moved to high ground overlooking the Basin to tie in with Company L's right flank. Companies L and K gained about 200 yards during the day, but held up when further advances would have made it difficult to maintain contact with the slower-moving 2d Battalion on the left. Company K, 3/24, joined 3/25 during the afternoon to help strengthen the lines for night defense.

The employment of three, and sometimes four, companies on line across a single battalion front was common throughout the operation in the 4th Division zone of action. The rugged terrain limited observation and fields of fire to a few yards, making it necessary, particularly at night, to maintain physical contact along the front. It often became necessary to commit two understrength companies on a frontage that, in open terrain with full-strength units, could be covered by one company.

Commenting on this in his action report for the operation, the Commanding General, 4th Marine Division wrote:

. . . Against constant, heavy opposition of the type encountered on Iwo Jima, it is considered that the commitment of fewer troops in the line to allow more rest for reserve units would have resulted in excessive infiltration, disruption of rear area activities, and additional casualties.[13]

The 25th Marines moved out again at 0815 on D-plus 9 with the same scheme of maneuver as the day before. The 1st Battalion passed through the right flank of RCT 23, with Companies A, C, and I (3/24) in column, to attack Turkey Knob from the north, while Company B stayed on the low ground southwest of the Knob to assault eastward around the base of the Amphitheater to contact other elements of the battalion, thus completing a double envelopment.

Following a preparation by artillery and rockets, the lead company advanced rapidly across open ground where it had received such heavy fire the previous day, and penetrated

[13] Ibid., 3.

about 50 yards into a patch of woods just north of the Knob. As Marines reached this point, the enemy loosed a terrific mortar and rocket barrage, and machine guns directed a withering fire from high ground to the battalion's front and exposed left flank. Artillery observers with the 1st Battalion called counterbattery missions, but the Japanese fire did not abate.

By 1200 the situation became critical. Company A and one platoon from Company C had suffered heavy casualties and were unable to advance. But the successful double envelopment of the Knob depended upon the woods being held at any cost to enable Company B to make contact at that point.

At 1215 the rest of Company C moved into the woods followed by Company I, and at the same time Company B, with two tanks attached, jumped off in its attack against the high ground east of Turkey Knob. As Company B moved out, enemy troops, well established and dug in on the high ground, threw mines and grenades down on the Marines, and machine guns enfiladed the entire front. A mine soon disabled one of the tanks, and at 1630 Company B fell back to its former position. During this attack, two other tanks worked forward to the front lines of Company A (northwest of Turkey Knob) and fired against the thick walls of the large concrete communications installation atop the Knob. The 75mm shells had little effect, however, and no further advance was made.

By 1645 it became apparent that there would be no junction between the two enveloping forces and that the advance positions of the three companies above the Amphitheater could not be held during the night. Therefore, using smoke to cover their movement, these units withdrew to the morning line of departure.

On the 1st Battalion's right, the 2d Battalion attempted to extend its left flank to support the attack of Company B and push forward to seize the commanding ground to its immediate front. Once again terrain prevented the use of tanks and half-tracks to support the infantry, and heavy enemy fire, particularly from pillboxes in the left of the battalion zone, held up the advance. At noon the battalion commander requested that a 75mm pack howitzer be sent up to support his assault from positions inaccessible to the Shermans and half-tracks. It was a slow and difficult task, but by 1500 a gun crew from 1/14 had a howitzer set up ready to operate. This piece placed 40 rounds of direct fire against the enemy strong point and, while the position was not destroyed, the shelling neutralized it sufficiently to allow Company F to advance some 75 yards to a position from which it destroyed this installation the next day. The battalion was closely engaged with the enemy until about 1900, but by 2000 the lines were consolidated and the pack howitzer returned to the artillery battalion an hour later.

The 25th Marines' right flank battalion, 3/25, regulated its advance with that of the unit on its left. Early gains were fairly rapid, 100 yards by 1000, but when 2/25 held up so did 3/25, and no further progress was made during the day. It is interesting to note that the largest infiltration attempts against the 4th Division lines the night of D-plus 9 and early morning of D-plus 10 were in the sector of 3/25, which had experienced the lightest resistance during the day. These occurred at 2200 and again at 0230. Both efforts were repulsed with an estimated 200 casualties to the enemy.

Naval gunfire support was normal on D-plus 9 with direct-support destroyers, reinforced by heavier general support ships, firing a 30-minute pre-K-Hour preparation. For the rest of the day call-fire missions were performed, and mortar and gunboat units operated along the coast on the division right flank. In the afternoon one destroyer closed the eastern shore and successfully engaged enemy guns with direct fire up draws that opened to seaward.[14]

Carrier planes struck at enemy installations in front of both the 23d and 25th Marines, but 50 percent of the napalm dropped in front of RCT 25 in the morning strike failed to ignite. The second strike for RCT 23 was long delayed and then failed to hit the target area requested.[15]

At the end of the fighting on D-plus 9 (28 February) the Japanese still held strong positions on Hill 382 and the Amphitheater-Turkey Knob defenses, but Marines had outflanked the

---

[14] 4th MarDiv D–3 Periodic Rpt No 55, 28Feb45.
[15] *Ibid.*

hill north and south and were in position to bypass the Amphitheater and continue the push to the east coast.

In his periodic report for 9 March the D–3, 4th Marine Division, did not attach any particular significance to the day's activity, merely stating:

No change in area of operations. Results obtained from today's operations were possible only by determined close quarter fighting. The Div is prepared to continue the attack.[16]

On the other hand, the division intelligence officer felt that, although gains had been small, the division had finally cracked the central defensive core of resistance. Based on this premise, he reversed his estimate of enemy capabilities and probable courses of action, and listed "counterattack" as most probable. Explaining his revised estimate, the D–2 pointed out that:

POW interrogation reveals general counterattacks are discouraged by Jap commanders as long as gun and mortar positions are intact. [But] After permanent positions have been overrun by Blue troops, counterattacks are to be made at the discretion of unit commanders.[17]

The D–2 believed that because of damage to his communications and consequent loss of control, the enemy was likely to make piecemeal attacks rather than one big coordinated assault. He held further, that the Japanese would be least likely to mount a counterattack of any size in the 4th's zone of action because of the very difficult terrain and the enemy's habit of attacking down a road or cleared area.[18]

D-plus 10

The corps order for D-plus 10 (1 March) directed the 4th Division to continue the attack, maintaining contact with the 3d on its left, but to hold present positions south of grid line 74[19] except as necessary to maintain contact left to right. Since this line ran east and west about 200 yards south of Hill 382, this meant that the

---

[16] *Ibid.*

[17] 4th MarDiv D–2 Periodic Rpt No 57, 28Feb45.

[18] *Ibid.*

[19] Grid line 74 was a line on the gridded map of the island. It ran east and west across the island through the center of Airfield Number 2 and crossed the east coast just north of Tachiiwa Point. (See Map XIV.)

division's main effort would be against the hill and along the boundary with the 3d Division.

Early in the morning RCT 24 began relieving units of RCT 23. The move, and most of the relief, occurred under cover of darkness with small units of RCT 24 taking the place of like-sized units of RCT 23, being careful to avoid engagement with the enemy during the shift. K-Hour (0830) was preceded by a coordinated 45-minute corps artillery and naval gunfire preparation and an intensive bombardment by division artillery from 0820 to 0830 that lifted in successive concentrations after K-Hour.

The 24th Marines moved out with the 1st and 2d Battalions abreast, 2d on the left. Each battalion employed two companies in the assault. Both companies of 2/24 came under heavy artillery and mortar fire immediately, but it was particularly severe in front of Company F on the left. The battalion requested supporting fires to silence the enemy artillery, and at 0935 carrier planes struck hard with napalm about 600 yards ahead of Marine lines. An hour later 155's of corps artillery pounded the same area, followed by a naval gunfire barrage. It took three hours to obtain these deep support fires against enemy weapons that had been registered on front line companies since 0700. When received, however, this support quieted opposition considerably. Company F advanced about 150 yards in the afternoon.

During the morning Company F extended itself across the division boundary to maintain contact with the 3d Division. In the afternoon, although 2/24 gained steadily, the 3d Division moved more rapidly, and a gap developed along the boundary. At 1430 RCT 24 sent two companies of its reserve battalion to regain contact on the left flank.

Company G battled throughout the day to dislodge the tenacious enemy from his shattered positions on Hill 382. Flame throwers, bazookas, and grenades were used in close combat, and assault squads exposed themselves to intense and accurate small-arms fire as they blasted cave entrances in a systematic yard-by-yard advance. The eastern side of the surrounded hill was swept by fire from the next

JAPANESE MEDIUM TANK presents difficult target for Marine guns as it huddles in deep crevice on west slope of Hill 382. This weapon was sited to cover the length of Airfield Number 2.

ridge, and Japanese mortars and artillery pounded the crest and slopes of 382 in desperate barrages, seemingly careless of damage done to the Japanese defenders.

Late in the afternoon the battalion commander of 2/24 and his company commanders made a thorough reconnaissance of Hill 382 to select positions for the night and to plan the next day's attack. During this inspection hand grenade fights were in progress, and assault squads were still blowing cave entrances and using flame throwers on remaining points of resistance.

At this time Company G held a north-south line that passed through the center of Hill 382. Marines controlled the west ridge of the two-ridge crest of the hill, while 100 yards to the east the Japanese still clung unyieldingly to the second ridge. Across the intervening space opposing forces sparred in a bloody duel with

rifles, machine guns, and rifle grenades as the principal weapons.[20]

On the 2d Battalion's right the 1st Battalion tried to advance along the south flank of Hill 382, where Company A tied in with Company G, 2/24, and up on to the high ground at the head of the draw to Company C's front. Company A could not move any great distance because 382 and the surrounding area were under heavy fire. But Company C with two tanks attached fought its way slowly forward against searing machine-gun and rifle fire from a patch of woods to the immediate front and the rising ground beyond. The Shermans provided covering fire as the infantry inched ahead, but the opposition persisted and casualties mounted. Just before noon the company commander was wounded,

---

[20] Interview LtCol R. E. Carey with author, 20Jan53. Then a captain, Carey commanded Company E, 2/24 at Iwo.

and smoke was called in to cover the evacuation of casualties.

The company reorganized quickly under a new commander and at 1300 resumed the attack behind a heavy Marine artillery and mortar barrage. Two minutes after this second jump-off the new commander became a casualty and a second replacement came forward to take over the unit. During the afternoon Company C gained some of the high ground, and at 1700 began consolidation of positions.

On D-plus 10 the regiment made its greatest progress on the left where 2/24 moved about 400 yards to the east along the division left boundary, and on the right flank where 1/24 advanced half that distance to gain a foothold on high ground overlooking Minami. In the center, however, RCT 24 had engaged in a day-long see-saw battle in the labyrinth of miniature canyons on Hill 382 with no noticeable change in the lines.

South of Grid Line 74 the 25th Marines jumped off at 0830 with the 1st Battalion, on the left, making the main effort and another attempt to eliminate the salient around the Amphitheater and Turkey Knob. The 2d and 3d Battalions were to hold their present place on the line until the bulge had been eliminated. (See Map XIV.)

The 1st Battalion's plan of attack was the same as on the previous day: to effect a double envelopment of Turkey Knob by moving three companies along the high ground (from the northwest) above the Amphitheater to attack southeast against the Knob while Company B assaulted from the low ground south of this fortress to make a junction with the other prong of the attack. Company I, 3/24, which had participated in the attack with 1/25 during the last two days, was relieved at 1000, but Companies I and K, 23d Marines reinforced this battalion (1/25) to renew the assault.

HUGE CONCRETE COMMUNICATIONS BLOCKHOUSE near Turkey Knob. This installation withstood days of direct assault by flame and gun tanks. Sherman next to blockhouse is disabled.

Company C led the attack this time, replacing Company A as the spearhead, with I and K (3/23) following in that order. By 1000 these three units had crossed the open area and entered the woods but met the same rain of fire that had mauled them the day before. Artillery forward observers again called counterbattery fire, and air spot was requested. Marine artillery had little immediate effect on the hostile mortars, however, and aerial observers could not locate the origin of the enemy barrage.

Company B jumped off at noon in the face of a steady fusilade from machine guns and rifles, accompanied by frequent volleys of rifle grenades and mortar shells. All afternoon Marines pressed the attack, but Company B failed to gain the elevation to tie in with Company C north of the Knob. As a result, all units were once more ordered to withdraw from their exposed locations to morning positions. As the depleted companies started to pull back the enemy laid down a heavy barrage all along the front, and Marines called for a smoke screen to cover the withdrawal and evacuation of casualties.

The two battalions on the right made only minor improvements in position on the morning of D-plus 10. The 2d advanced its left through machine-gun and knee-mortar fire to straighten the line, but did not attempt to move in the afternoon. Forward observers directed the fire of 1/14's 75mm howitzers against targets to the front, and a tank blasted at enemy installations from a position in the 3d Battalion's zone of action.

D-plus 11

The 4th Division continued the attack on 2 March with no change in formation or plan. Corps had again directed that the main effort be made on the left with units south of Grid Line 74 advancing only enough to maintain contact with elements to the north.[21]

North of the grid line RCT 24 changed boundaries between battalions to swing the direction of attack around toward the southeast so that the regiment would be striking down corridors instead of across them. The 3d Battalion (less Company L in RCT reserve) was to attack on the left (north) flank, while 2/24 in the center continued its efforts to reduce Hill 382 and seize the next ridge to the southeast. The 1st Battalion would drive forward in a narrowing zone of action until pinched out between 2/24 and 1/25.

Although facing stiff opposition and encountering difficulty in keeping contact with 1/9 on the left, the 3d Battalion advanced about 300 yards. In the center, however, the 2d Battalion finally overran Hill 382, in a more significant action.

Four tanks and the 2d Section, 1st Provisional Rocket Detachment, were attached to 2/24 when it jumped off at 0800 following an intensive artillery preparation. Tanks and rocket launchers blasted the area ahead of the Marines with explosives and flame, but the tanks drew so much enemy fire on themselves and the infantry, and were so handicapped by the terrain, that they were withdrawn. As the executive officer of 2/24 later wrote:

Artillery and naval gunfire was paving the way out in front, but the resistance close in had to be dealt with as usual by the attacking companies employing hand grenades, rifles, and automatic rifles, 60mm mortars, flame throwers, demolitions, and bazookas.[22]

At 1100 the battalion commander met with his company commanders at the reserve company command post for a conference. The two assault companies were bogged down and receiving intense machine-gun and large-caliber mortar fire. Something had to be done. It was decided that one platoon of Company E, with two tanks, should move around to the right to outflank the enemy holding up the advance.

The executive officer of Company E, who had just assumed command following the evacuation of the former commander, was issuing orders for the flanking movement when a large mortar shell burst in the command post. One platoon leader died instantly while the executive officer and two other company officers were seriously wounded. The only remaining pla-

---

[21] VAC OpOrder 10–45, 1Mar45.

[22] Maj F. E. Garretson, USMC, "Operation of the 2d Bn., 24th Marines on Iwo Jima, Volcano Islands, 19Feb–18Mar45," Advanced Officer's Course, The Infantry School, Ft. Benning, Ga., 19Feb47, a monograph, 25.

toon leader took over the company and continued the attack, and by 1500 this company, with one out of six officers left to command, had accomplished the mission. The rest of the day was spent in mopping up the objective and consolidating positions. Sealing caves in and around Hill 382, and the elimination of scattered enemy groups that continued to hold out, dragged on for several days. In fact, while the action report of 2/24 states that the hill was secured on D-plus 11, the regimental report does not note the hill as secured until the following day. The division D-3, however, saw the remaining activity around 382 as a mop-up action after D-plus 11 and stated, rather laconically, in his periodic report for the day:

> It appears that there are underground passageways leading into the defenses on Hill 382 and when one occupant of a pillbox is killed another one comes up to take his place. This is a rather lengthy process . . . .[23]

Hoping to catch the enemy off guard, the 1st Battalion, 25th Marines jumped off at K-minus 90 minutes (0630), without normal preparatory fires, to infiltrate and again seize the high ground north of Turkey Knob. With no change in plans, Companies C (1/25) and I (3/23) were to envelop from the northwest while Company B moved up from the south. For the first few minutes things went well. Then, at approximately 0650, the enemy opened up with rocket and mortar barrages and close-in fire from machine guns. Marine retaliation was swift, as friendly artillery and mortars lashed out in reply, and eight tanks rumbled forward to support the attack. One thousand gallons of flame thrower fuel and many 75mm shells were hurled against the large communications blockhouse that dominated Turkey Knob but could not crush enemy resistance.

By 1430 Company B, working north onto the high ground from positions south of the Amphitheater, was only 65 yards from a junction with Company I, and the double envelopment seemed almost completed. But at 1445 the enemy unleashed a crushing barrage, causing Company B to fall back with many casualties. With both flanks now exposed, positions of companies on the high ground became untenable,

and the battalion commander ordered his units to withdraw for the night. At 1730, replacements reached the battalion and were immediately placed in the lines to help the exhausted and depleted battalion cover its assigned sector during the night.

In the center, 2/25 was ordered to extend its left flank to assist the advance of Company B, and Company L, 3/23 was attached for that purpose. But progress on that flank was slow, with F and L making no appreciable gains.

The 25th's 3d Battalion, on the far right, held its positions during most of the day and, although not in the attack, suffered casualties from enemy mortar fire.[24] Late in the afternoon 3/25 and the right unit of 2/25 were given permission to advance to the next commanding ground to the front. This jump of 300 yards occurred without opposition, and troops dug in on new ground for the night. (See Map XIV.)

The irregularity of the lines and the proximity of enemy and friendly troops along most of the front made close support by artillery and direct support ships difficult, but corps and division artillery, with two battleships and one cruiser in general support, were quick to bring down heavy counterbattery fire on active enemy guns. Destroyers and gunboats came close in along the eastern bulge of the island to place well directed fire up rocky draws that led down to the sea.

Carrier planes supported the division on D-plus 11 by executing six strikes against enemy positions around Higashi, about 1,000 yards to the front.[25] Pilots and observers of VMO-4 flew five missions during the day. One of these was a somewhat makeshift photographic mission accomplished from an OY-1 with a division public relations photographer taking the

---

[23] 4th MarDiv D-3 Periodic Rpt No 57, 2Mar45.

[24] The commander of 3/25 notes in his action report: "The failure of 3/25 to advance while suffering casualties . . . had a depressing effect on the morale of the troops in 3/25." *25th Mar OpRpt*, Appendix 8, 11.

[25] The landing force was well pleased with the air support on 2 March: "Performance of air coordinators, air observers, and air strike groups highly satisfactory during today's operations. Many difficult close support missions executed in restricted areas to full satisfaction of front line units. Please pass to all concerned." Disp LANFOR to CTG 52.2, 1952, 2Mar45.

pictures from an altitude of 1,000 feet. These shots, developed and enlarged by the division D-2 section, provided the best means available for study of terrain to the front. The sustained bombardment of Iwo Jima had so torn the face of the land that pre-D-Day maps were by now of little use in terrain appreciation.[26]

D-plus 12

On 3 March the 4th Division jumped off at 0630 without benefit of preparatory fires, hoping to gain at least a temporary advantage through surprise. At 0500 the 23d Marines relieved RCT 25 and passed 1/23 through 1/25 at K-Hour, but 2/25 and 3/25 became attached to RCT 23, retaining their positions in the center and on the right. The 24th Marines continued the assault in the division's left zone of action.

The heaviest opposition now seemed concentrated in high ground northeast of Hill 382 and the Minami area. Having driven beyond the hill, RCT 24 now prepared to assault formidable new defenses in its zone. To the south the Amphitheater and Turkey Knob, although greatly weakened after six days of continuous assault, were still in enemy hands. These two strong points were keys to the Minami defenses and would have to fall before any sizable gains could be made in that area, and it was against this salient that RCT 23 made its main effort on D-plus 12. (See Map XIV.)

Shermans of Company C, 4th Tank Battalion and one platoon of the 4th Engineer Battalion were attached to 1/23 for the regiment's main attack southeastward above the Amphitheater to make contact with the left element of 2/25. This would complete reduction of the Knob and isolate enemy troops in the Amphitheater.

Immediately after the jump-off, corps and division artillery pounded areas forward of the front lines with heavy neutralization fires, and initial gains were encouraging as the enemy seemed taken by surprise.[27] As the right flank

units of 1/23 neared the blockhouse atop Turkey Knob, however, heavy fire stopped the advance. This huge concrete structure had already withstood two days of close assault and still constituted a serious obstacle to further progress. Routes of approach were mined and covered by accurate machine-gun and rifle fire. Engineers courageously weathered this to clear a path to allow a flame tank close access.

The slow and costly assault, which continued until late afternoon, partially reduced the Turkey Knob blockhouse, and Company B, the reserve unit, passed through Company C to continue the attack to make contact with 2/25. Intense enemy fire and antipersonnel mines checked this assault also after only a short advance, and units consolidated for the night with the enemy salient still intact.

The 23d Marines' center and right battalions held their positions while 1/23 attacked. The 3d Battalion regained control of Companies I and L, which had been attached to 2/25 and 3/25, and remained in regimental reserve. Company K, however, with tanks and 75mm half-tracks attached, spent most of the day burning and blasting enemy positions in the southwestern face of the Amphitheater, and Company I was committed toward the end of the day to fill in south of the Amphitheater between 1/23 and 2/25. The 2d Battalion, 23d Marines, still in corps reserve, remained in an assembly area between the first and second airfields, prepared to move to the attack anywhere in the corps zone of action on 2-hour notice.

The 24th Marines also moved out in the attack at 0630, 3 March without preparatory fires. The formation was the same as on the preceding day, with the direction of attack toward the southeast. The terrain consisted of numerous hillocks, mounds, and shallow crosscorridors with nearly vertical sides. Covered reinforced concrete emplacements, with firing ports placed to protect the front and both flanks, were cleverly located in this area, taking maximum advantage of protection afforded by ground formations. Every avenue of approach

---

[26] *4th MarDiv OpRpt*, Sec IV, 32; 4th MarDiv D-2 Periodic Rpt No 59, 2Mar45.

[27] This 0630 attack by the 4th Division was not a predawn jump-off as early morning twilight began at

0541 on 3 March, but it was 27 minutes before official sunrise. *TF 51 OpPlan*, Annex B, Daylight and Dark Tables for Mar45.

was controlled by machine-gun and rifle fire, with enemy mortars and artillery registered to cover defiladed areas. Only with the greatest difficulty could tanks move forward to favorable locations to engage enemy targets in this region, and once they were in position could command only limited fields of fire.

Artillery could be used for close support at ranges over 100 yards, but as the infantry closed on hostile positions, 81mm and 60mm mortars fired within 50 yards of the advancing Marines. As had been true throughout the operation, only through the slow and tedious maneuver of infantry teams employing demolitions, flame throwers, bazookas, and grenades could such a stronghold be reduced. This type of fighting required able and aggressive leadership at the small-unit level, and the high casualty rate among junior officers and noncommissioned officers seriously retarded the progress of the attack.

Despite the difficulties involved, men of Company B (tanks) wrestled their Shermans forward along the narrow, twisting routes of approach and provided effective support whenever possible. Rocket launchers also added their barrages to those of the artillery and mortars, making quick runs to firing positions near the front, then withdrawing hurriedly to escape countering fire from enemy weapons.

The attack inched slowly and painfully ahead, and by 1500 the advance of Company E, 2/24 had pinched out Company A, 1/24 on the right. When the regiment took up final positions for the night it had advanced up to 350 yards in the center. The 1st Battalion now held a narrow front on the right with only Company B in the line. The 2d Battalion in the center had three companies abreast, and the 3d Battalion tied in between G, 2/24 and A, 1/9 with two companies up and one in reserve. (See Map XIV.)

D-plus 13

During the eight days of deadlock and fierce conflict in the Hill 382 and Turkey Knob areas, the weather had been generally favorable. Mild temperatures and fair skies predominated, although early in the morning ground haze combined with smoke to limit observation, and on a few days light showers fell in the afternoon. Night temperatures sometimes went below 60°, and it was then that tired Marines were grateful for the characteristic subterranean heat of the island that warmed their foxholes.[28] The next day, 4 March, dawned gray and sullen, and intermittent showers fell from the overcast skies. Visibility was so limited that all air strikes were canceled and aerial observation seriously curtailed.

The division continued the assault on 4 March with no change in formation or direction of attack. The main effort was on the left with the 24th Marines pushing southeast. On the right 2/25 and 3/25 held their positions while 1/23 attacked in conjunction with RCT 24 on its left. The axis of advance was directed to the southeast so that the Marines could drive down the draws that led from Hill 382 to the coast rather than across those terrain compartments.

Naval gunfire and artillery supported the attack with normal preparatory and supporting fires, but due to lowered visibility most of the missions were controlled by ground observers rather than air spot. One destroyer and a gunboat worked all day along the coast locating and engaging targets in the cliffs and draws.

The infantry battalions made extensive use of the indispensable 60mm and 81mm mortars to give close support. The 81mm ammunition supply situation was still unsatisfactory, however, and expenditures were controlled. The 60mm mortar fire covered areas to within 30 yards of the lines to pin down and neutralize the enemy to the immediate front. Tanks and rocket launchers were used whenever and wherever possible, with flame tanks being particularly valuable in aiding 3/23's mop-up operations against the partially bypassed Amphitheater.

The 23d and 24th Marines launched a second coordinated assault at 1500, following a 15-

---

[28] In the early morning it was frequently possible to locate Marine foxholes in the broken terrain by observing the ghostly columns of steam that hung in the cool air. Interview LtCol F. E. Garretson with author, 23Jan53.

KEEP LOW AND KEEP MOVING. Enemy riflemen proved to be good marksmen in the close fighting on Iwo and Marines had to move quickly from one covered position to another.

minute artillery preparation, but could make only minor gains. Shortly before dark Marines consolidated on positions 150 yards ahead of the morning line of departure at the most advanced point. (See Map XIV.)

The pattern of battle in the 4th Division's zone of action on D-plus 13 differed little from previous days. The enemy defended stubbornly and well from closely integrated positions, exacting a heavy toll for every yard gained. Many cleverly camouflaged positions escaped discovery until advancing troops were so near that heavy supporting weapons could not be used against them. Others, although observed and taken under fire, withstood even the largest shells available on Iwo, and could be silenced only by combined tank-engineer-infantry action. Assault units suffered heavy casualties, and survivors became extremely exhausted with a consequent serious loss of combat efficiency among those who engaged in attack after attack.

But by this time, 4 March, there was some cause for optimism. Although the enemy still clung resolutely to his battered positions in the Amphitheater area, it was felt that the division had finally penetrated the formidable main cross-island defense belt in its zone of action. Furthermore, the unceasing efforts of corps artillery in its counterbattery mission had produced positive results, for enemy artillery, rockets, and heavy mortars offered less and less opposition. The loss of high ground had also adversely affected Japanese artillery operations. Without the excellent observation previously afforded by Hill 382 and Turkey Knob, enemy weapons were confined largely to area fires.[29]

STALEMATE

D-plus 14

Complying with the corps order for 5 March, the 4th Division spent D-plus 14 in reorganiza-

[29] 4th MarDiv D-3 Periodic Rpt No 59, 4Mar45; 4th MarDiv D-2 Periodic Rpt No 61, 4Mar45.

tion and preparation for continuation of the attack on 6 March. By noon the division was to have one regiment, less one battalion, free from any responsibilities and available for an attack the next day.[30]

General Cates selected the 23d Marines for the special attack mission. To free that regiment from all other duties the 25th Marines again took over responsibility for the division's right zone of action. The 2d and 3d Battalions, 25th, which were already in the line, reverted to RCT 25. The 1st Battalion moved back into the line, relieving 1/23 in approximately the same positions held by men of 1/25 on 2 March. These shifts freed RCT 23 from all front line commitments, but that unit's 3d Battalion was still involved in the considerable task of containing and cleaning up the resistance along the southern edge of the Amphitheater-Turkey Knob complex. To take over that job, the 25th Marines organized the Division Reconnaissance Company (attached at 0700, 5 March), and

[30] Disp VAC to 3d, 4th, 5th MarDivs, 1624, 4Mar45. This order is quoted in Chapter VI of this monograph.

EAST OF MINAMI the terrain became even more wild and broken. Japanese mortar positions, concealed and protected by the jumbled rocks, remained active until the area was overrun.

Company L, 3/25 into a provisional battalion commanded by the executive officer of 1/25, Major Edward L. Asbill.

The above shifts comprised the major changes in the 4th Division lineup on 5 March. Minor adjustments along the 24th Marines' front released three companies to form a regimental reserve line in that zone of action.

With reorganization completed by 1200, the remainder of the day was devoted to strengthening defenses, re-equipping, and rest. Artillery, naval gunfire, and air executed call fires throughout the period, paying particular attention to neutralization of enemy mortars that harassed the 4th Division front.

The 2d Battalion, 23d Marines reverted from corps reserve at 1500 and was replaced by 1/23. The day ended with the 24th and 25th Marines in the line, each with three battalions abreast. The new Composite Battalion, 25th Marines contained the enemy salient between 1/25 and 2/25 and the 23d Marines, less 1/23, was in division reserve ready for the attack on 6 March.

D-plus 15

The corps operation order for 6 March called for an all-out artillery and naval gunfire preparation followed by a two-phase assault to the northeast and east by elements of all three divisions.[31] The 4th Division was directed to attack at K-plus 60 minutes (0900), making its main effort on the left in conjunction with the 9th Marines.

The coordinated fires of 12 artillery battalions, reinforced by naval gunfire, shifted to support the second phase of the corps attack at K-plus 45 minutes. In the 4th Division zone of action the barrage was concentrated on the left where RCT 23 was to pass through RCT 24 in a column of battalions to make the main effort in a drive southeastward.

The 2d Battalion, 23d Marines jumped off at 0900 and 3/23 moved up to follow at 400 yards. Assault elements instantly ran into accurate automatic-weapons and rifle fire from the front, and Company F on the right held up after an

advance of only about 50 yards. On the left, however, the terrain was suitable for tanks, and Company G with four supporting Shermans gained 300 yards. When the right unit's attack stopped, Company E (in reserve) was ordered to pass through the gap between Companies G and F. As the reserve company executed this movement, it came under an extremely heavy mortar barrage that wounded the company commander and inflicted numerous other casualties. The executive officer assumed command, reorganized quickly, and pushed on to accomplish the maneuver. Company E continued its attack and by 1500 had forced two platoons abreast of the two flanking assault companies despite constant withering fire from the front.

Forward observers called artillery concentrations to within 100 yards of the front lines in an attempt to neutralize some of this opposition, but although accurate, this fire had little effect. Company K, 3/23 was attached to the 2d Battalion and jumped off at 1600, passing through Company F in an attempt to advance the battalion's right flank to positions abreast of Company E's platoons on the left. This attack lost momentum quickly and netted only 50 yards against determined enemy resistance from the right of the 23d Marines' zone.

At 1800 when the 2d Battalion started digging in for the night, Company G was on the left 350 yards in front of the line of departure, Company K on the right about 150 yards beyond, and Company E filled in the center, making contact with both G and K. Company F was in battalion reserve. (See Map XV.)

Enemy mortars again singled out Company E at 1900. A barrage hit the command post, wounding the new company commander and 22 enlisted men, and killing the executive officer. By now this unit was badly disorganized, having suffered heavy casualties and lost two commanders on the same day. When the battalion intelligence officer arrived to take over the company, he became its seventh commander since D-Day.

On the 23d Marines' right RCT 24 jumped off at 0900 with two battalions abreast. The 2d Battalion attacked on a 3-company front with Company A, 1/24 attached in reserve. The 1st Battalion, less Companies A and C (regi-

---

[31] VAC OpOrder 13–45, 5Mar45. The 3d and 5th Division participation in this attack is covered in Chapter VI and Chapter VII.

mental reserve), moved out with only Company B in the assault. The 3d Battalion reverted to division reserve when relieved by 2/23.

Japanese mortars plus accurate rifle and machine-gun fire hit the Marines as they moved out into the same type of broken terrain as 2/23, on the left. Gunfire support ships assisted the attack by placing fires in the Higashi area, and planes delivered three heavy strikes just southeast of that place, about 1,000 yards ahead of friendly lines. But these supporting fires, as usual, had no effect on the stubborn resistance to the immediate front, and gains by RCT 24 were limited to 150 yards on the left, less than that on the right.

The division operation order for 6 March directed the 25th Marines, with the Division Reconnaissance Company attached, to continue mopping-up operations and hold its positions on the right, conforming to the advance of RCT 24 on the left flank. While the Provisional Battalion hammered at the southern edge of the salient with flame thrower tanks, regular Shermans, and 75mm half-tracks, the 1st Battalion advanced a short distance along the north side to keep pace with the unit on the left.

The greatest progress by the 4th Division (350 yards) was made by RCT 23 on the left, where the terrain was comparatively easy. But along the rest of the front, enemy resistance from prepared fortifications and natural caves in the jagged ridges held the Marines to small gains. Japanese rifle fire was extraordinarily accurate, and hostile artillery, mortar, and rocket fire showed increased activity over that of the preceding two days. The tremendous preparation by Marine artillery and naval gunfire appeared to have had little effect. (See Map XV.)

The cumulative result of fatigue and casualties had affected operations for some time, but by now the situation assumed serious proportions. The division D–3 periodic report for 6 March estimated combat efficiency at 40 percent and went on to say:

. . . The results of fatigue and lack of experienced leaders is very evident in the manner in which the units fight. . . .[32]

----

[32] 4th MarDiv D–3 Periodic Rpt No 61, 6Mar45.

D-plus 16

Sporadic enemy mortar fire and several small-scale infiltration attempts marked the night of 6–7 March. At 2210, 3/25 reported Japanese troops moving across its front toward the ocean in what was thought to be an attempt to attack the battalion right flank. Artillery and mortar fire quickly dissolved this hostile formation. Later in the night 40 to 50 of the enemy worked their way into the positions of 1/25, some of them even jumping into Marine foxholes. In the melee that ensued 13 Marines and 50 Japanese were killed.

The 23d Marines remained in close contact with the enemy throughout the night, and frequent exchanges of rifle fire and hand grenades occurred. Then, at 0502, the Japanese scored one of their infrequent direct hits with a large caliber rocket on the command post of 2/23, with tragic results. The battalion commander, executive officer, operations officer, adjutant, and two clerks were wounded, and the communications chief was killed. All the wounded men were evacuated except the commanding officer, who immediately commenced reorganization of his staff. Shortly after daylight, however, the regimental executive officer, Lieutenant Colonel Edward J. Dillon, went forward to assume command of 2/23, relieving Major Robert H. Davidson, who had been badly shaken by the blast. The temporary reorganization which Davidson had started was completed by Dillon, utilizing a skeleton staff of officers and enlisted personnel from regimental headquarters.

The attack order for 7 March directed the 4th Division to continue the assault with no change in boundaries or formation. K-Hour was to be 0730, but the jump-off was delayed 30 minutes to give 2/23 more time to recover from the early morning disaster in its command post. The division moved out with no preparation, but the artillery directed neutralization fires on all known enemy mortar and artillery positions from 0800 to 0830. The 23d Marines attacked in a column of battalions with 2/23 leading. Company G on the left made a substantial advance against light resistance, but E in the center and K on the right met stiff opposition and gained little.

In accordance with a prearranged plan, Company G pressed the attack to open a sizable gap on its right flank and uncover the battalion reserve, Company F. That unit immediately moved out against the flank of the strong point confronting Companies E and K. This assault succeeded, and Company F took over the center zone from E and continued the attack. On the right, Company K pressed its advance and soon came abreast to straighten the battalion line. This neat little maneuver netted the battalion about 150 yards by 0900.

During the remainder of the day strong opposition held the 23d Marines to negligible gains, with only Company G on the left able to register any important advance. The resistance consisted principally of heavy machine-gun and rifle fire from concealed positions in the rocky ridge formations and draws along the front.

In the center of the division zone of action RCT 24 attacked with 2/24 and 1/24 abreast as on the preceding day. The 2d Battalion fought forward slowly against well-directed automatic-weapons and rifle fire until a gap developed between its left company and the right unit of RCT 23. Hostile fire from that flank became extremely heavy, and at about 1500 the enemy began penetrating the gap.

In order to close the hole and contain the pocket, the battalion commanders of 2/23 and 2/24 arranged to have Company K, 23d Marines echelon one platoon to the rear to contact a platoon of Company G, 2/24's reserve, which moved up along the regimental boundary on RCT 24's left flank. This cooperative action effectively sealed off the salient, and lines were then adjusted and consolidated all along the battalion front on the most defensible ground.

The day's action of 2/24 netted only about 50 yards, but the battalion action report pointed out that resistance in the zone of action had been "notably reduced," except for the pocket on the left flank. The report went on to state that the major portion of the enemy's secondary defensive line appeared to be neutralized, but that units on either flank were still receiving heavy opposition.

The 1st Battalion, 24th, passed Company C through B to continue the assault on D-plus 16.

During execution of this relief the enemy opened up with a mortar barrage that hit Company C, causing numerous casualties. This fire continued to fall in that area, and the company became partially disorganized. But at 0800 it moved out and in 45 minutes had progressed 50 yards. Soon after this initial advance the company commander was killed by a rifle bullet while leading his unit in an attempt to take a bit of high ground on the left flank. The executive officer immediately assumed command and continued the attack.

For the remainder of the day Company C inched forward through crevices and gullies, blowing up caves and working under constant small-arms fire. From a forward observation post, the battalion air officer called two strikes against suspected mortar positions, and heavy artillery concentrations were also delivered in support of 1/24.

Still under orders to advance only in conformance with the regiment on its left, the 25th Marines held its original positions throughout the day. The 1st Battalion, on the left, utilized flame and medium tanks to sear and pound enemy installations close to its front, and the Provisional Battalion continued operations against stubborn resistance in the Amphitheater-Turkey Knob area. The 2d Battalion sent a 6-man patrol from Company G about 200 yards to the front. This group returned at 1300 and reported that it had encountered no enemy resistance.

On the regiment's right flank the 3d Battalion had occupied itself during the previous three days in strengthening its defenses to prevent a breakthrough by enemy troops during the anticipated 4th Division drive southeastward to the coast. During this push the division's left flank and center were to advance almost at a right angle to the front of 3/25, which tied into the coast about 1,000 yards east of the East Boat Basin. (See Map XV.) The attack would thus compress enemy troops into an area bounded by the sea and Marines holding the line on the south: in effect, a hammer and anvil, with the 25th Regiment now acting as the anvil.

The battalion's attached engineers laid an antipersonnel mine field across the front, and two lines of barbed wire about 75 yards apart were also stretched forward of the battalion, with trip flares and booby traps set between them. Three 37mm guns with a supply of canister shells were emplaced in the line, and machine guns were carefully positioned to deliver grazing fire across the front although fields of fire were limited. All 60mm mortars of the battalion were combined in one battery and registered for close defense and the 81's adjusted to fill the gaps in artillery concentrations to the front.

While front line combat held the spotlight of attention at all times, intelligence personnel kept busy behind the lines in constant search for information concerning enemy capabilities and intentions. Early in March a detail from RCT 25 found an undated enemy map of the northern half of the island. It contained no unit identifications but showed enemy and friendly elements in approximately the positions held several days previously. POW's explained that this map had been prepared for a maneuver held in January, proving that the enemy had expected and even rehearsed the situation almost exactly as it developed, and that his plans called for a vigorous defense in the rugged area east of Airfield Number 2 even after the rest of the defenders had been driven into the northern perimeter of the island.[33]

D-plus 17

The division made its main effort in the center on 8 March attacking toward the sea along the east coast. Since corps no longer required that the 4th's main effort be on the left, the division again shifted the direction of attack to the southeast to conform to the character of the terrain. In compliance with corps orders the division jumped off at 0620 (K-minus 90 minutes) without a preparation, but the 14th Marines and corps artillery fired successive concentrations in support of the attack from 0620 to 0650, and division artillery remained on call after 0650.

In the 24th Marines' zone 3/24, and Company A, which had been attached to 2/24 but was holding a critical portion of the enemy salient

along the boundary between RCT's 23 and 24, became attached to the 3d Battalion. The 1st Battalion was ordered to extend to the left to cover a 2-company front, relieving one company of the unit on the left. This battalion would then attack with two companies abreast. Boundaries between the two battalions were adjusted accordingly.

The 23d Marines continued its attack on the division left with the same battalion-column formation used on 7 March. The 2d Battalion, in the lead, replaced Company K (attached) with Company E, but made no other changes.

Operations along the division line differed little from the day before. Heavy resistance continued in front of the left and center regiments with particularly bitter fighting along the RCT 23–24 boundary. Company A (1/24) eliminated the enemy salient in that area during the morning and went into RCT reserve behind 1/24. The strong center of resistance astride the regimental boundary withstood all attempts to crack it, and as small advances were made on either side, a second reentrant developed. This strong point held out all afternoon, and when regiments tied in for the night Company E, 2/23 and Company I, 3/24 held long, difficult lines containing the enemy salient between the two regiments.

COUNTERATTACK [34]

There was a noticeable increase in Japanese activity in front of the 23d and 24th Marines during the early evening, and enemy mortar, rocket, and artillery fire mounted in intensity. At 2300 the 2d Battalion, 23d Marines and the 3d Battalion, 24th reported large-scale infiltration attempts along the regimental boundary in the area of the salient. Then at 2330 a full-scale counterattack hit Company E, 2/23. (See Map XVI.)

Although some of the attackers shouted and screamed, this was no wild *banzai* charge. The Japanese had used the twisted, shell-torn ter-

---

[33] 4th MarDiv D-2 Periodic Rpt No 65, 8Mar45.

[34] Unless otherwise cited, the narrative of the counterattack is based on the following: 4th MarDiv D-2 Periodic Rpt No 66, 9Mar45; 4th MarDiv D-2 Language Section, "Reconstruction of Counterattack Stopped by BLT 2/23 on Morning 9 March;" *23d Mar OpRpt; 24th Mar OpRpt.*

4TH DIVISION POST OFFICE. Nothing did more to lift the spirits of exhausted Marines than a letter. This shipshape and well dug-in installation handled all incoming and outgoing mail for its division.

rain to good advantage as they worked their way close to the lines before commencing the assault. A few even infiltrated through the front lines to the 2/23 command post where they harassed the operations section with hand grenades thrown from ranges of 10 to 15 yards. Some enemy troops carrying stretchers tried to penetrate Marine lines by shouting "Corpsman"! Close-quarter fighting raged throughout the hours of darkness with Company E bearing the brunt of the attack, but heavy fighting also took place in Company L, 3/24's sector and elsewhere along the line.

Shortly after midnight Company E reported a severe ammunition shortage, and a jeep and trailer were dispatched to the front with a load. The route forward was infested with enemy, and the jeep drew hostile fire as it picked its precarious way to the lines. This company alone expended 20 cases of grenades (500), 200 high-explosive 60mm mortar shells, 200 60mm mortar illumination shells, and uncounted quantities of .30-caliber ammunition for machine guns and

rifles. In addition to illumination fired by Company E and other front line units, support ships expended 193 star shells during the night.

By daylight the struggle had nearly died out, but mopping up continued until noon. Approximately 650 enemy dead were counted in the area of the main attack, and reports from other sectors brought the total to nearly 800. But it was impossible to determine the exact numbers involved. Subsequent 4th Division advances uncovered large numbers of dead Japanese who were probably caught in heavy artillery barrages thrown down ahead of Marine lines in support of the defense. Marine casualty figures for this night attack are not available, but the combined casualties for RCT 23 and RCT 24 during the 2-day period 8–9 March were 90 killed and 257 wounded, making it evident that the assault cost the enemy far more dearly than it did the Marines.[35]

---

[35] The 2-day period has been used for comparison because the counterattack began the night of 8 March and continued during the early hours of 9 March.

Maps and documents recovered from the dead revealed the major Japanese unit in the counterattack to be the 1st Company, 310th Independent Infantry Battalion, reinforced by a machine-gun platoon and one infantry platoon. Other identification indicated that elements of the 3d Battalion, 145th Infantry Regiment, the 314th Independent Infantry Battalion, an engineer unit, and naval units had also engaged.

These enemy troops were well-armed and equipped, and many carried demolition charges. The attack was preceded by an all-out artillery preparation augmented by rockets, grenades, machine-gun and rifle fire, demolition charges, and magnetic mines. The Japanese used everything they had. Many of the heavy rockets and mortar shells were duds, however, and fell harmlessly in rear areas.

It is probable that the objective of this attack was to break through and drive south to join forces with other Japanese units. One captured map, which accompanied the 1st Company's attack order, listed the "Airfield" (prob-ably Airfield Number 1), "South Beach" (the landing beach) and "Suribachi" as objectives. In explanation of these objectives that appeared so impossible, the 4th Division D-2 Language Section's reconstruction of the counterattack had this to say:

. . . At first glance these last two entries in the course of the attack [South Beach and Suribachi] may seem puzzling; but in the light of past experience, it must be remembered that Japanese troops usually shoot the works when launching counterattacks and often choose impossible objectives. It is perfectly plausible that these troops (uninformed because of communication breakdowns) hoped to join forces in the area north of Airfield No. 3, sweep down to the beaches originally occupied by BLUE (friendly) forces and eventually capture Mount Suribachi. If so, it would appear the whole scheme was an all-out effort. . . .

TURNING POINT
D-plus 18

The division resumed the attack at 0700 on 9 March, following a 10-minute preparation.

MOPPING UP by-passed enemy soldiers was a continuous operation. These Marines have just thrown a grenade and are standing by with rifles and BAR's at the ready.

In the 23d Marines' zone the 2d Battalion advanced its center and right a considerable distance against fairly light opposition, but the left was held up by fire from a ridge along that flank. South of RCT 23 the 3d Battalion, 24th Marines still encountered determined opposition from the strong point along the RCT 23–24 boundary. The first attack failed to penetrate this core of resistance, but a second assault at 0900 succeeded, and the battalion pushed ahead 300 yards during the remainder of the day.

No gains were registered along the rest of the division front. In contrast to progress on the left, 1/24 and 1/25 could not crack the stubborn resistance to their front, and the right flank units in RCT 25's zone of action held their positions in accordance with division orders. (See Map XVI.)

With all units of the division now decimated by casualties and exhaustion, companies were frequently shifted from one battalion to another to bring assaulting organizations up to effective strength. On 8 and 9 March, however, RCT 24 found it necessary to reorganize its 1st and 2d Battalions, disbanding one company in each and using the men from those units to augment the remaining companies. Now the 1st Battalion included Company A with 135 effectives and Company B with 115. This battalion also changed commanding officers when Lieutenant Colonel Austin R. Brunelli, the regimental executive officer, took over. The 2d Battalion, which ended up with Company F and Company G, each mustering about 150 men, became attached to RCT 25 and was sent to relieve that unit's 3d Battalion on the division right flank.

The Provisional Battalion, which had been operating in the Amphitheater-Turkey Knob area, was disbanded on 9 March and its responsibilities were taken over by 2/25. On the same day, however, another provisional battalion was organized from units of the Division Support Group, and designated the 4th Provisional Battalion. The 4th Division Support Group commander, Lieutenant Colonel Melvin L. Krulewitch, assumed command. This unit, numbering 37 officers and 498 enlisted men, mopped up the division rear areas and made daily sweeps over ground behind the front lines until disbanded on 12 March.[36]

D-plus 19

The 24th Marines (less two battalions) reverted to division reserve on 10 March, and the division attacked with RCT 23 on the left and RCT 25 on the right. The 1st Battalion, 24th Marines was withdrawn from the line and replaced by 3/25, but 3/24 became attached to RCT 23 and continued to operate in its former zone of action. The 2d Battalion, 24th remained attached to RCT 25.

The division attacked at 0800 following the last coordinated corps and divisional artillery preparation of the operation. These fires blasted the area just forward of the lines for 25 minutes before K-Hour, then lifted to move forward in successive concentrations of 100 yards every five minutes until K-plus 15.

The left regiment (RCT 23) moved out with 2/23 and 3/24 in the attack, the latter on the right. Progress was steady against light opposition on the right, but enemy troops holding strong positions in the rocky ridges along the division left boundary directed accurate and effective machine-gun and rifle fire against the left, making gains on that flank difficult and costly. Small pockets of resistance challenged the advance throughout the zone, but assault units bypassed these whenever possible, leaving them to be mopped up by engineer-tank-infantry teams using flame throwers and demolitions.

Marines had moved 700 yards in the 23d's zone of action by 1500 and reached positions approximately 500 yards from the beach along the east coast. The regiment held up on this commanding ground but sent patrols forward to feel out the enemy. Patrols from 2/23 penetrated to the coast near Tachiiwa Point, and men from 3/24 scouted to within 100 yards of the coast in that battalion's zone. Returning at 1700, these units reported no contact with the enemy.

The scheme of maneuver in the 23d Marines' zone of action had been a simple drive to the southeast toward the coast, but on the right, where RCT 25's lines curved around the persist-

---

[36] *4th MarDiv Support Group Rpt*, 17, 18.

ent Amphitheater-Knob salient, the plan was more complicated. Making its main effort on the left with 3/25, 1/25, 2/25, and 2/24 on line, left to right, RCT 25 planned to have its 3d and 1st Battalions attack to the southeast parallel to RCT 23's advance, with 1/25 pivoting on its right flank as the assault moved ahead. When 3/25 had advanced to a point opposite 2/25 the latter would swing its left unit forward to tie in with the right of the 3d, pinching out 1/25, and the attack would continue through to the ocean across 2/24's stationary front. (See Map XVI.)

The 1st and 3d Battalions jumped off at 0800 as ordered and encountered medium to heavy opposition in the high ground to their front where the enemy had held out so stubbornly for nearly two weeks. When it became apparent that the 3d on the left would be able to move faster than the 1st, the former unit was ordered to continue without regard for its flanks. As 3/25 drove to the southeast, 2/25 advanced northeast to meet it. Shortly after noon the center company of 2/25 made contact with the right flank of the 3d Battalion and by 1600 those two units had occupied the controlling ground in the vicinity. In swinging out to join forces with 3/25, however, the 2d Battalion bypassed a small force of enemy troops. This pocket was surrounded by units of 1/25 and 2/25 that had been pinched out as the advance crossed their front.

After a push of 600 yards RCT 25 consolidated for the night with its left flank tied to RCT 23 about 800 yards from the coast, and its stationary right flank still positioned along the beach. During the night the greatest activity occurred around the pocket that had formed during the day's advance. The rest of the front was quiet with only sporadic attempts at infiltration.

Results for the day were gratifying throughout the division zone of action. On the left strong centers of resistance had been overcome, and while the lines did not reach the coast, patrols had investigated to the water's edge and reported no contact along the routes followed. In the center, after almost two weeks of frustration, Marine lines made contact east of Turkey Knob and the infamous salient in that area was

eliminated. It was now evident that the Japanese counterattack had marked the turning point in the battle. Although bitter and costly fighting continued for six more days, particularly in the 25th Regiment's zone, organized resistance was now dying out in the 4th Division area. (See Map XVI.)

During the 14-day period covered in this chapter the 4th Division, in constant head-on assault, fought its bloody way from Charlie-Dog Ridge past Hill 382, the Amphitheater, Turkey Knob, through Minami and formidable defenses northeast of 382, almost to the coast. The slow but relentless movement of this division front can be compared to the closing of a giant door. The right flank, which advanced less than 1,000 yards, acted as a hinge while the rest of the division (the door) turned upon it and attacked northeast, east and southeast to close and sweep trapped enemy forces toward the sea.

The Japanese conducted an astute defense. General Kuribayashi had planned well, but much credit for execution of the plan in the 4th Division zone must go to Major General Senda, who commanded the 2d Mixed Brigade and exercised tactical control during the battle. Enemy weapons and mine fields were well placed to take maximum advantage of terrain features, fire control was excellent when judged by Japanese standards, and camouflage discipline outstanding. Machine-gun positions controlled draws, while mortars were disposed to deliver fire on routes of approach, including the crests, forward, and reverse slopes of ridges.

The following description of the enemy's conduct of the defense, prepared by the intelligence officer, 4th Marine Division, describes the action well:

As a result of a close study of the enemy's recent defensive action, aided by observation from OP's and air reconnaissance, the following explanation is suggested of the enemy's defense in this Div's Z of A. The enemy remains below ground in his maze of communicating tunnels throughout our preliminary arty fires. When the fire ceases he pushes OP's out of entrances not demolished by our fires. Then choosing a suitable exit he moves as many men and weapons to the surface as he can, depending on the cover and concealment of that area, often as close as 75 yards from our front. As our troops advance toward this point he delivers all the fire at his disposal, rifle, machine-gun, and mortar. When he has inflicted sufficient casualties to pin down our advance he then withdraws through his underground tunnels most of his forces, possibly leaving a few machine gunners and mortars. Meanwhile our Bn CO has coordinated his direct support weapons and delivers a concentration of rockets, mortars and artillery. Our tanks then push in, supported by infantry. When the hot spot is overrun we find a handful of dead Japs and few if any enemy weapons. While this is happening, the enemy has repeated the process and another sector of our advance is engaged in a vicious fire fight, and the cycle continues. Supporting indications to these deductions are:

(1) When the hot spot is overrun we find far too few dead enemy to have delivered the fire encountered in overrunning the position;

(2) We find few if any enemy weapons in the position overrun but plenty of empty shell cases;

(3) We find many tunnel entrances, some caved in, all appearing deep and well prepared, some with electric light wires;

(4) During the cycle, close air and OP observation detects *no* enemy surface movement.[37]

The one obvious mistake made by the Japanese in this long, grueling defense to the death was the night counterattack of 8–9 March. This action cost the enemy many lives and gained no advantage. Even this rather hopeless plunge can be somewhat justified, however, when the situation that existed then is seen from the Japanese point of view. By 8 March the enemy was under heavy, constant pressure in an ever-shrinking area where most of the critical terrain features had been captured. He was quickly becoming dispossessed and disorganized, with few courses of action remaining. Because communications were undoubtedly badly disrupted, it is possible that the enemy facing the 4th Division did not realize just how hopeless his cause appeared and therefore harbored some hope that the counterattack might not be in vain.

Against the obstinate enemy defense, 4th Division Marines had no alternative to continuous frontal assault. Constant attempts were made to flank or envelop enemy strong points throughout the operation, but the mutually supporting fortified positions and the restricted areas of operations prevented successful flanking action on a large scale. Not until the latter stages, when the left regiment had advanced to a favorable position on the division's northern flank, was it possible to move down the ravines to the sea.

In the assault on fortified positions the following factors increased the difficulties of the problem and contributed to excessive casualties:

(*a*) Unsuitability of terrain for the employment of heavy direct-fire weapons, such as the tank-mounted 75mm gun and the 75mm half-track.

(*b*) Relative ineffectiveness of artillery, air, and naval gunfire against heavy installations.

(*c*) Lack of a portable direct-fire weapon capable of breaching concrete installations.

(*d*) Mutually supporting nature of the majority of the fortifications, making attack by assault teams more costly than if heavy direct-fire weapons could have been employed.[38]

The 4th Division suffered a total of 4,075 casualties during the 14-day period from 25 February through 10 March.

Killed in action	642
Died of wounds	205
Wounded in action	2,836
Missing in action	1
Combat fatigue	391
Total	4,075

[37] 4th MarDiv D–2 Periodic Rpt No 63, 6Mar45.

[38] *4th MarDiv OpRpt*, Annex C, 3.

CHAPTER IX

The Final Phase

The final phase of the operation began on 11 March. The 3d and 4th Divisions drove rapidly to the east coast in their zones of action, eliminating the last organized resistance, and by 13 March only two stubborn pockets held out in those areas. At the northern end of the island 5th Division troops pushed slowly northward against bitter opposition, but by 16 March the last of the Japanese were bottled up in the western half of Kitano Point and the rocky gorge near the coast 500 yards to the south. In this last desolate, shell-torn draw the enemy held out until 26 March (D-plus 35), ignoring all inducements to surrender.

Artillery, air, and naval gunfire could be used only in the extreme northern end of the island during these last days of the battle. There the Mustangs (P–51's) of the 15th Fighter Group provided effective close support until 14 March, and all Marine artillery battalions combined to fire heavy preparations and harassing fires until withdrawn from the fight on the 16th. Destroyers performed most of the naval gunfire missions but the heavy cruisers *Tuscaloosa* and *Salt Lake City* fired until 12 March. From 17 to 24 March destroyers furnished illumination and then they too were withdrawn. Elsewhere the lines were in such close proximity and the enemy-held areas so small that tanks and half-tracks had to replace these heavy support weapons.

CUSHMAN'S POCKET

(D-plus 20—D-plus 25)[1]

By morning of 11 March the only effective opposition to the 3d Division came from terrain along the right boundary, where the Japanese held a shattered ridge nose overlooking the sea, and the stubborn core of resistance southwest of Hill 362C. This last strong point, which had already withstood several days of attack by 1/9, 2/9, and 3/21, was named "Cushman's Pocket," after the commanding officer of 2/9, Lieutenant Colonel Robert E. Cushman, Jr. (See Map XVII.)

The 1st Battalion, 9th Marines, which had launched an attack northeastward from the 4th Division zone of action on 10 March, continued the assault on 11 March with two companies abreast. This drive was intended to sweep the last hostile troops from the ridge in the southeast corner of the 3d's zone and make contact with 3/9, which was moving south along the coast against the same high ground. Then both battalions would turn west to attack Cushman's Pocket from the rear.

Supporting tanks shielded the 1st Battalion as it moved out across an open field south of the rocky nose and blasted all caves and suspected positions as Marines fought their way up onto

---

[1] Unless otherwise cited, material in this section is based on the following: *3d MarDiv SAR*, Pt III; *9th Mar SAR*; *12th Mar SAR*; *21st Mar SAR*; *3d TkBn SAR*.

the ridge. The 3d Battalion also requested Shermans but not until early afternoon did armor reach the front in that zone of action along a road cut through by an armored dozer. With this support the 1st and 3d Battalions crushed the opposition and made contact at 1515. After the junction these units mopped up along the coast and then organized a defense for the night in high ground just east of Hill 362C and outposted the beach.

About 500 yards westward the 3d Battalion, 21st Marines, attached to RCT 9, continued battering against the southwest edge of Cushman's Pocket. Although this pocket was contained on only one side, the Japanese made no effort to sally forth for offensive operations or to withdraw. Instead they held their ground and conducted a bitter defense in place from caves, spider traps, and dug-in tanks.

Early in the morning a sled-mounted 7.2-inch rocket launcher was attached to 3/21 in the hope that its crushing barrages might shake the enemy from his positions in the pocket. This weapon, designed for mounting on the back of an M4A2 tank, would not fit the new M4A3 tanks in use by VAC. Therefore, the corps ordnance officer had supervised the modification of four of these weapons to operate from sleds. Each sled mount consisted of 20 rocket tubes capable of delivering a dense, shocking explosion of 640 pounds of TNT in a single volley. Towed into action by a tank or dozer, this launcher had a maximum range of 250 yards. Deflection and range were set by moving the entire sled. Ten barrages' smashed the pocket area, and although the effect could not be directly observed it appeared that no miracle had taken place. As the Marines moved in enemy resistance continued undiminished and the men of 3/21 gained little.[2]

Along the division's north (left) boundary high ground dominated the beach area in the 5th Division's zone of action, so RCT 21 (less 3/21) did not try to advance that day. During the morning RCT 27 moved troops in behind the left flank of 2/21 to launch an attack to the north, and by 1030 the 21st Marines was able to withdraw that battalion from combat for a

much needed rest. The 1st Battalion, 21st then extended northward to tie in with the 5th Division. (See Map XVII.)

No artillery fired in support of the 3d Division on 11 March, but the 1st Battalion, 12th Marines was held ready for call fires if needed. The other three battalions of the 12th reinforced the fires of the 13th Marines. Aerial observers maintained surveillance of the 3d Division's zone of action during the day and reported the location of friendly troops.

As the 5th Division's east (right) flank worked slowly northward during the next four days, the 1st Battalion, 21st Marines moved in the same direction across the division boundary to protect the 5th's flank. With its lines tied to Company I, 27th Marines, the battalion held positions along the cliffs overlooking the coast and sent combat patrols out along the beaches below. The advance of the 5th Division governed progress along the bluffs and shorelines.

Marine engineers and infantrymen continued destroying pillboxes and caves during the hours of daylight, but at night the enemy crawled out of other caves and holes to hurl grenades and then dart back into their hideouts. Alert Marines shot and killed many of these night raiders before they could make good a retreat.

By 15 March the 1st Battalion, 21st Marines had extended about 600 yards northwestward into the 5th Division zone and held positions along the bluff and outposts down on the beach. The 2d Battalion, which reverted to RCT 21 reserve on 11 March, spent the daylight hours in reorganization and resupply, but manned a regimental reserve line during the night.

On 12 March the 1st and 3d Battalions attacked west toward Cushman's Pocket while 3/21 acted as a holding force on the opposite side. On the right (north) flank 3/9 had relatively easy going in its zone of action, but 1/9 met stiff opposition and moved slowly. An armored bulldozer cleared a tank road to the 1st Battalion's front, but at no time could more than two Shermans operate together in the rough terrain. Infantrymen worked their way forward among the miniature sandstone buttes to guide tanks and point out the camouflaged enemy emplacements. Most of these positions

[2] *VAC OpRpt*, 60; *3d MarDiv SAR*, 18; *3d TkBn SAR*, Pt III, 9.

were so well concealed that they escaped detection until Marines were almost on top of them. As usual in this type of fighting, the infantry flame throwers and demolitions proved the most successful weapons.

The 3d Battalion, 21st reverted to its parent organization on 13 March and left its position on the west side of the shrinking pocket. The 1st and 3d Battalions, 9th Marines continued pressing the attack from the east. On the north flank 3/9 completed reduction of that portion of the pocket in its zone of action, and 1/9 made substantial gains to compress the enemy-held area to about 250 yards on a side. Regular Shermans and flame tanks operated very effectively on the 13th, neutralizing a number of concrete emplacements. Upon completion of its assignment against the pocket, the 3d Battalion, 9th was ordered to the Hill 362C area where it undertook a systematic mop-up.

NAVAL GUNFIRE caused landslide which partially blocked entrance to this cave in cliffs above northeastern shore. 3d Division units held positions along top of these cliffs and outposted the beaches as they waited for the 5th Division to advance northward.

THE LAST POCKET of enemy defenders in the 4th Division zone of action held out in a jungle of small sandstone buttes and withered vegetation.

The next day, 14 March, operations against Cushman's Pocket entered the last phase. The 1st Battalion pressed the attack during the morning and early afternoon to gain about 100 yards. Then at 1530, the 2d Battalion passed through that unit to finish the job. A large capacity flame-thrower tank, on loan from the 5th Division, and Shermans from the 3d Tank Battalion scorched and pounded the last enemy defenses until only sporadic resistance challenged infantrymen as they moved in to finish the task.

By this stage in the operation a large percentage of infantry troops were replacements who lacked the combat training and experience that prepared and conditioned men for closing with the enemy. Therefore, the skill and efficiency of assault Marines showed marked deterioration after three weeks of personnel attrition of original D-Day troop strength. During the final days of 3d Division efforts to smash remaining pockets armor support made success possible. Gun tanks, armored bulldozers, and flame-throwing Shermans combined their operations to give the exhausted infantry a very effective and much needed assist.[3]

With organized resistance almost at an end in the 3d Division zone of action on 15 March, General Schmidt ordered the 3d to relieve elements of the 5th Division on that unit's right (east) flank and attack to the northwest.[4] Early on the 16th, the 1st and 2d Battalions of RCT 21 relieved 3/27 and 2/26. The 21st Marines assumed responsibility for a zone of action about 800 yards wide on the 5th Division's right. The new boundary between divisions passed northwest from a point approximately 400 yards east of Hill 362B to the northern tip of the island where it bisected Kitano Point. (See Map XVII.)

When RCT 21 jumped off to the north in conjunction with the 5th Division at 0815, 16 March, it moved out behind the last preparation fired for any unit of the 3d Division. Three battalions of the 12th Marines,[5] reinforced by 5th Division artillery and the corps 155's, fired from K-minus 20 minutes to K-plus 10 minutes. Artillery commenced the preparation bombardment as close as 50 yards from friendly

---

[3] *9th Mar SAR*, Encl B, 4.

[4] VAC OpOrder No 23–45 w/changes, 15Mar45.

[5] 3/12 commenced embarkation on 16 March and was not available. 3d MarDiv G–3 Periodic Rpt No 31, 16Mar45.

front lines and moved forward in 100-yard increments as the attack began.[6] The destroyer *Healy* shelled the northern tip of Iwo for 50 minutes and then stood by to deliver call fires. Eight Army P-51's were ready on Airfield Number 1 to give support if needed, but the restricted area of ground operations permitted no air strikes.[7]

The 1st Battalion, 21st encountered light opposition in its zone on the right, but the 2d Battalion met stiff resistance from scattered islands of the enemy. Heavy rifle fire and the jagged ground constituted major obstacles to advance. There were few concrete emplacements in this northern zone but the Japanese defended tenaciously from caves and spider-trap positions in the rough terrain. Occasionally individual enemy soldiers armed with demolition charges and grenades raced out against tanks or groups of Marines but were shot down before they could do any great damage to personnel or equipment. Both battalions reached the coast line at Kitano Point by 1330 and began mopping up. (See Map XVII.)

---

[6] Ltr LtCol T. R. Belzer to CMC, 22Apr53.

[7] 3d MarDiv OpOrder 23-45, 15Mar45; 3d MarDiv G-3 Rpt No 31, 16Mar45.

With the elimination of Cushman's pocket on 16 March and the clearing of this newly acquired zone of action on the same day, the 3d Division announced the end of all enemy resistance in its zone of action.[8]

THE 4TH'S LAST POCKET[9]
(D-plus 20—D-plus 25)

The impressive gains by the 4th Division on 10 March had placed Marines in position to launch a quick drive southeastward to the sea to eliminate the last resistance in the island's eastern bulge. Patrols sent out by the 23d Marines reported little opposition between that unit's front lines and the coast, and the 25th Marines, although encountering stiff resistance at the close of the day, had occupied commanding ground in its zone of action.

The division jumped off at 0730, 11 March with RCT's 23 and 25 abreast, left to right. The 23d pushed rapidly to the coast, overrunning weak enemy resistance to the front and

---

[8] 3d MarDiv G-3 Periodic Rpt No 31, 16Mar45.

[9] Unless otherwise cited, material in this section is based on the following: *4th MarDiv OpRpt*, Sec. IV; *14th Mar OpRpt; 23d Mar OpRpt; 24th Mar OpRpt; 25th Mar OpRpt; 4th TkBn OpRpt.*

TANKS AND INFANTRYMEN make a frontal assault against Japanese positions at the base of a rocky ridge in the 5th Division zone of action.

A PORTION OF CUSHMAN'S POCKET, scene of the last organized Japanese resistance in the 3d Division zone of action.

sending strong patrols to cover all beach areas. Engineers followed close behind the advance, working with the infantry to seal caves and push a road forward in the regimental zone. The 1st Battalion relieved 2/23 on the left at 1700, and the regiment pulled back and settled down on the same positions it held the preceding night. This line, about 400 yards from the coast, provided the best ground for control of the area as terrain to the front was characterized by broken ridges and deep fissures.

The 25th Marines could not duplicate the 23d's speedy drive to the sea. Shortly after the jump-off heavy rocket, mortar, and small-arms fire hit assault units on the division's right, and bitter fighting continued in that area throughout the day. Late in the afternoon a captured Japanese soldier reported that about 300 enemy troops remained in caves and tunnels of the small area of resistance to the front. He told Marine interrogators that this die-hard group had rifles, ammunition, grenades, demolition charges, and plenty of water, but little food. The highlight of this POW's information was that a Japanese major general held out with the troops in the pocket.[10]

By the end of D-plus 20 it became obvious that this small pocket would be a tough nut to crack. The enemy-held terrain consisted of a series of deep crevices and sharp ridges run-

---

[10] 4th MarDiv D–2 Periodic Rpt No 68, 11Mar45.

ning in a generally southeasterly direction toward the coast. Other lesser gullies cut transversely through the area to create a maze of compartments and cross compartments. Rough rocky outcroppings and scrubby vegetation that had survived the fierce bombardments provided excellent cover and concealment to the defenders.[11]

K-Hour was postponed two hours on 12 March to give intelligence personnel an opportunity for broadcasting a surrender appeal to the enemy general, thought to be Major General Senda, commanding the 2d Mixed Brigade. The POW who supplied the information willingly led a detail of Marines forward to a spot on the front lines near the brigade commander's supposed hideout. For the next two hours the power plant operator tried to start the gasoline engine that provided electricity for the amplifier, and when an alternate motor also failed to run the project was called off. During the entire time this group received annoying sniper fire that caused one casualty and some damage to equipment. At 0900 the attack continued.[12]

The 25th Marines jumped off with 2/25, 3/25, and 2/24 on line from left to right. The 2d Battalion, 25th faced southeast across the top of the pocket, and the other two battalions pushed eastward against its west flank. On the opposite side 3/24, attached to RCT 23, contained the enemy along the regimental boundary. (See Map XVIII.)

The plan of attack called for 2/25 to attack down the draws toward the coast while 3/25 and 2/24 supported the attack by firing bazookas, antitank grenades, and 60mm mortars into the area to their front. Following this general scheme, the regiment slugged it out with the Japanese in the pocket for four days. Tanks operated with caution in supporting the attack because of the danger of hitting friendly troops, but both regular and flame throwing mediums contributed in large measure to the eventual success of the infantry. But as in all actions against a deeply entrenched and determined enemy, it took foot troops with flame throwers, bazookas, rifles, grenades, and demolitions to

complete the job. Frequent attempts to persuade the Japanese to give up invariably drew heavy rifle fire, and the fighting went on.

As the operation against the pocket continued the main core of the resistance developed northwest of the "beach road." This road, or what was left of it, paralleled the east coast from the Boat Basin to Tachiiwa Point about 500 yards inland. Plans were made to send tanks out along the road to positions in rear of the pocket to fire north into the draws in an attempt to knock out hostile mortar positions. To accomplish this, 2/24 with engineers attached, pushed forward from positions astride this road to clear it of mines so that the Shermans could proceed. After they had cleared the way infantry and engineers were ordered back as their presence along the road prevented the use of supporting fires by 2/25. The tanks remained and projected streams of flame up the draws with good effect.

On 15 March Colonel Lanigan, commanding RCT 25, shifted the main pressure against the pocket to the south and directed the skeleton companies of the two battalions in the center of the line to attack regardless of contact. This drive gained 200 yards and penetrated deeply into the left flank of the enemy's strongest positions, paving the way for elimination of the stronghold the next day.

During the night enemy troops made several attempts to infiltrate Marine lines from the south, but each time the movement was detected and broken up. When the 25th jumped off at 0630 on 16 March, the Japanese fought back with machine guns, rifles, and grenades, but now, without any real organization left, they resisted only in small isolated groups. By 1030 all battalions had cut through to the beach road, and RCT 25 announced complete destruction of all resistance in the pocket.

Although the original location of General Senda's Brigade Headquarters was just east of Hill 382, there is little doubt that his final command post was in this area where some 1,500 Japanese troops, both army and navy, defended to the end. The torn and battered terrain and the mangled mass of enemy dead bore grim evidence of the bitterness of the struggle for

---

[11] 4th MarDiv D-2 Periodic Rpt No 69, 12Mar45.
[12] *Ibid.*

this last strong point in the 4th Division's zone of action.[13]

TO KITANO POINT
(D-plus 20—D-plus 25)[14]

While the 3d and 4th Divisions were clearing the last defenders from their zones of action, the 5th Division made the corps main effort to the north. On 11 March, following a 50-minute preparation by air, naval gunfire, and the massed fires of 12 artillery battalions, the 28th Marines jumped off on the left with three battalions abreast (2/28, 1/28, and 3/28 left to right), and the 27th, with 1/26 attached, attacked on the right with 1/26, 1/27, 2/27, and 3/27 in line.

Savage resistance forced the fight at point-blank ranges. Heavy supporting weapons were useless as the enemy clung tenaciously to positions close to the front and poured withering machine-gun and rifle fire into the Marine lines. Assault units depended heavily on 37mm guns and 75mm half-tracks of the weapons com-

[13] 4th MarDiv D–2 Periodic Rpt No 73, 16Mar45.

[14] Unless otherwise cited, material in this section is based on the following: *5th MarDiv SAR*, Sec. VIII; *13th Mar SAR; 26th Mar SAR; 27th Mar SAR; 28th Mar SAR; 5th TkBn SAR.*

AMERICAN FLAG FLYING AT NORTH END OF IWO. 5th Division Marines planted the colors on Hill 165 at Kitano Point 25 days after the flag raising on Suribachi.

panies to blast located enemy weapons, and 7.2-inch rockets were again employed to shock the Japanese into silence. But results were negligible. The battalion mortars and attached 4.5-inch rockets, firing almost continuously as close to the lines as possible, actually rendered the most effective aid.

The 28th Marines inched forward about 30 yards up the gradual slope toward the northwest-southeast ridge line overlooking the gorge to its front. Atop this ridge the Japanese held strong fortifications that commanded all approaches from the southwest, and when Marine bombardment became intolerable they took refuge in caves that honeycombed the steep sides of the gorge.

Bitter fighting produced slightly better gains in RCT 27's zone of action. During the morning 2/27 was pinched out and became RCT reserve as the 1st and 3d Battalions moved forward. Actually this unit was so casualty ridden that it could no longer be considered employable and saw no further action as an organized battalion. The 1st Battalion cleaned out a pocket to its front that had been holding up the advance in that zone for five days, and 3/27 seized and held some important high ground after three bloody assaults. On the regiment's left flank 2/26, which had been attached to RCT 28, reverted to parent control and attacked through 1/26 at 1300 for a small gain.

The night was fairly quiet along most of the front, but activity behind the lines of 3/27 became so heavy that company command posts moved up to tie in with their front line platoons for security against grenade-throwing Japanese soldiers who came out of bypassed holes.

The fighting along the division front on 12 March was a repetition of the previous day, with no gains by RCT 28 and only small advances by RCT 27 on the right. The 5th Division intelligence officer estimated that a minimum of 1,000 Japanese troops were defending the northern end of the island, and stated ". . . there is no shortage of manpower, weapons, or ammunition in the area the Japanese have left to defend." The entire northern tip of the island seemed to be honeycombed with caves and passageways. When a 500-pound bomb landed in the mouth of a cave near Kitano Point a big puff of smoke blew out the side of a cliff over 400 yards away, and another bomb landing in a cave entrance in the same area caused a ring of smoke and dust to come up through the ground for a radius of 200 yards around the point of impact.[15]

In the afternoon Company B, Amphibious Reconnaissance Battalion, Fleet Marine Force, Pacific made a water-borne reconnaissance of Kama and Kangoku Rocks off the northwest coast of the island. Platoon leaders and senior noncommissioned officers were carried in 12 vehicles from Company C, 2d Armored Amphibian Battalion, and the company commander and his executive officer made the reconnaissance from an LCI (G). No enemy fire greeted this party as it moved in close to the small islets, and the observers noted no signs of life. When he returned from his mission, the company commander received orders to land on the rocks at 0900, 13 March.[16]

These landings went off as scheduled without a hitch.[17] The landing force consisted of 94 men and six officers divided into ten LCR (landing craft, rubber) teams, and two flame thrower teams that were held in reserve. Fire support was furnished by LVT(A)'s and the LCI(G) with the executive officer of the reconnaissance company acting as gunfire officer. The commander of the company was in over-all command of the operation. Landing first on Kama Rock and then Kangoku, Marines swept the islets without encountering any opposition. Evidence pointed to the fact that Japanese had been on the larger (Kangoku) rock several weeks before. A few barricaded caves and

---

[15] *C-2 Periodic Rpt* No 22, 12Mar45.

[16] Company B, Amphibious Reconnaissance Battalion, FMFPac, Action Report, Iwo Jima Operation, 29Mar45, 3. This unit was attached to VAC for the Iwo operation.

[17] Occupation of Kama and Kangoku received serious consideration both during the planning stage of the operation and after the landing. The rocks were not seized earlier because American troops posted there would have been extremely vulnerable to observed enemy fire from the much higher elevation of northern Iwo Jima. Also, because these islands were low in the water they provided no advantage of observation. Ltr LtGen E. A. Craig (Ret) to CMC, 6Apr53.

stone emplacements were located but no equipment was found. The second rock was declared secure at 1024, and the little landing force returned to its bivouac area on Iwo Jima. The next day Company B was detached from VAC and ordered to report back to the Commanding General, Fleet Marine Force, Pacific.[18]

The 5th Division continued its pressure against the ridge above the gorge and carved out small gains on the right, but with tank support limited by the rough terrain and heavy weapons unable to fire close to the lines, the going was slow and tough. Companies were reduced to platoon size, and the few veteran Marines remaining were exhausted. The majority of experienced and aggressive small unit leaders had long since been evacuated or killed, and while replacements were courageous and willing, they lacked the ability that comes only through experience.

By 14 March it appeared that the slow, tortuous progress of the past three days had carried the 27th Marines through the last strong enemy positions along the northeastern side of the island. The most practical direction of attack was now from east to west paralleling the ridge lines that ran from the center of the island to the coast. Reorienting itself to this new situation the 5th Division ordered RCT 28 to hold in its zone of action while RCT 27, on the right, swung toward the west. In the center of the division line RCT 26 took over a two battalion front and attacked north with 3/26 and 2/26 abreast. (See Map XIX.)

Compared to other days, enemy opposition was light on 14 and 15 March, and RCT 27 and the right battalion (2/26) of the 26th Marines gained up to 1,000 yards during the 2-day period. After armored dozers hacked paths forward, tanks were able to lend support. The flame tanks were particularly effective during this phase and provided "the one weapon that caused the Japanese to leave their caves and rock crevices and run."[19]

Army planes flew the last air support missions of the operation on 14 March when five P-51's dropped fire bombs (gasoline and diesel oil mixture) and strafed in front of 3/27 from 1030 to 1100.[20] From then on the narrow confines of the area of operations prevented use of those planes that had performed so well in supporting ground troops. Artillery and destroyers continued to furnish limited support, firing a preparation for RCT 26 on 15 March and performing night harassing and illumination missions.

The official flag raising on Iwo Jima took place at VAC Headquarters at 0930, 14 March, two days before the island was declared secured. In a short ceremony attended by flag and general officers of the fleet and landing force, U. S. Navy Military Government of the Volcano Islands Proclamation Number 1 was read. The flag that had flown over Suribachi since D-plus 4 was removed when the official flag went up at VAC Headquarters. Following this ceremony the Commander Expeditionary Troops and his staff left Iwo Jima by air.[21]

When the 3d Division passed through RCT 27 on 16 March and took over a zone of action on the 5th's right, the remaining enemy opposition centered in two areas: the steep draw that ran northwest to the sea across the front of RCT 28, and a strong core of resistance in front of RCT 26, just east of that draw. (See Map XIX.)

The 28th Marines (less 3/28), with the 5th Pioneer Battalion attached, was now to hold positions along the ridge southwest of the draw and support RCT 26 (3/28 attached) by fire as that regiment attacked northwest to overcome the strong point to its front and bottle up enemy remnants in the deep ravine.

Following the last artillery preparation of the campaign RCT 26 moved out slowly. Infantrymen advanced cautiously until they drew fire, then armored dozers tore a path through the rocky terrain so that flame tanks could roast hostile positions. As the Shermans neutralized these positions, the infantry inched ahead. Engineers then came up and demolished the battered enemy emplacements. In this area east of the gorge the number of caves encountered diminished as Marines moved north, but the number of cleverly concealed spider foxholes

---

[18] *Ibid.*
[19] *5th MarDiv SAR,* 27.

[20] *VAC Air Rpt,* Appendix 3, 7.
[21] *TF 56 OpRpt,* 10, 11.

THE BATTLE FOR THE GORGE was fought over terrain such as this.   In this picture a Marine light machine-gun squad moves up to join in the final battle.

increased, and Japanese fire from close ranges remained deadly.

Although RCT 26 did not make as great an advance as RCT 21 on its right (that unit pushed all the way to the northern tip of the island in its zone of action), it did gain 400 yards and further compressed the Japanese into the western part of Kitano Point and the deep draw to the southwest. (See Map XIX.)

BATTLE FOR THE GORGE
(D-plus 26—D-plus 34) [22]

At 1800, on 16 March, 26 days and nine hours after the first Marine landed on Iwo Jima, the island was declared secured. The only remaining resistance came from the western half of Kitano Point and the draw to the southwest. In this gorge approximately 500 die-hard enemy troops continued a more or less organized defense for another nine days.

Attacking on 17 March to clear the remaining enemy from Kitano Point, the 26th Marines gained rapidly. The 1st Battalion advanced against moderate rifle fire and reached the north coast at 1230. The battalion then turned its front southwestward to drive against the gorge in front of RCT 28. The 3d Battalion, 26th and the 3d battalion of the 28th registered some slight gains against the northeastern edge of the pocket.

The gorge in which the last resisting Japanese were now cornered was rocky and steep-sided, approximately 700 yards long and between 200 and 500 yards wide. Rock outcrops cut this ravine into other minor draws that constituted major obstacles to all types of movement. The entire area was ideally suited to the type of last ditch defense the enemy had adopted. All routes into the main gorge were swept by heavy and accurate fire from machine guns and rifles concealed in cave positions in the cliffs and outcrops.

The plan for attacking this strong point called for RCT 28, with attached elements of the 5th Pioneer Battalion and Division Reconnaissance Company, to hold the southern rim

[22] This narrative of the battle for the gorge is based on the following: *5th MarDiv SAR*, Sec VIII; *26th Mar SAR; 27th Mar SAR; 28th Mar SAR.*

along the steep cliffs, while RCT 26, with 3/28 and 3/27, worked in from the north and east. For the next nine days exhausted Marines carried out a battle of attrition against the thoroughly entrenched enemy. Advances into the east end of the ravine were measured in yards as each cave had to be sealed off before further progress could be made. Flame-thrower tanks, armored bulldozers, and infantry combined operations to provide the power and teamwork necessary to penetrate the last stronghold.

After its relief by RCT 21 on 16 March, RCT 27 reorganized its depleted units into three battalions of two rifle companies and one headquarters company each. Then at 1700, Companies A and D were attached to the 3d Battalion and that unit was constituted as a composite battalion under Lieutenant Colonel Donn J. Robertson. This consisted of a headquarters and four rifle companies, numbered 470 men, and was attached to RCT 26 on 19 March. The 27th Marines, less the Composite Battalion, remained in division reserve during the remainder of the operation, mopping up rear areas and making preparations to leave the island.

As the Marines drove slowly but relentlessly down the ravine resistance became centered around a huge concrete structure built into a knoll near the eastern end. This igloo-shaped installation was surrounded by mutually supporting caves and absolutely impervious to 75mm tank shelling and demolition attempts with 40-pound shaped charges. After two days of assault during which Marines silenced the supporting positions, engineers with bulldozers sealed a door on the north side and then demolished the structure using five charges totaling 8,500 pounds of explosives.

The battle of attrition continued, and by 1800 on 24 March (D-plus 33) the pocket had been reduced to an area about 50 by 50 yards at the northwest (seacoast) end of the draw. The following morning units of RCT 28, which had assumed full responsibility for the pocket, reached the coastal cliffs to eliminate the last vestige of resistance in the gorge. This had been a weird phase of the campaign, as aptly recounted in the 5th Division's report of the operation:

In attacking these positions, no Japanese were to be seen, all being in caves or crevices in the rocks and so disposed as to give an all-around interlocking, ghost-like defense to each small compartment. Attacking troops were subjected to fire from flanks and rear more than from their front. It was always difficult and often impossible to locate exactly where defensive fires originated. The field of fire of the individual Japanese defender in his cave position was often limited to an arc of 10° or less, conversely he was protected from fire except that coming back on this arc. The Japanese smokeless, flashless powder for small arms, always advantageous, was of particular usefulness here. When the position was overrun or threatened, the enemy retreated further into his caves where he usually was safe from gunfire, only to pop out again as soon as the occasion warranted unless the cave was immediately blown.[23]

[23] *5th MarDiv IntelRpt*, 27.

LAST DAYS

The Japanese defenders fought stubbornly and well to the end, preferring death to surrender, but the Marines made repeated attempts to induce them to give up. Some propaganda leaflets were dropped from planes and fired in artillery shells, but the most frequently used method was voice appeals. Language officers, Nisei (Japanese-Americans), and POW volunteers participated in this last form of persuasion. Out of 65 POW's who had some contact with United States propaganda 53 were influenced and gave themselves up as a direct result. The remaining 12 stated that fear of their own officers and of trickery on the part of the Ma-

SURRENDER APPEAL is made by Japanese-language officer after grenade dropped into cave entrance had no effect.

rines had deterred them. These last did not surrender, but were captured under other circumstances.[24]

Of all Marine propaganda attempts the most elaborate was General Erskine's effort to get a message to Colonel Ikeda. Believing that General Kuribayashi might feel himself personally committed against surrender, the 3d Division Commander addressed an appeal to the commanding officer of the 145th Infantry Regiment, elements of which were known to be defending the Kitano sector.

This message was entrusted to two POW's, former privates in the 145th Regiment, who claimed to know the location of the Japanese colonel's command post. In addition to cigarettes and rations, the two Japanese emissaries were equipped with a walkie-talkie (SCR–536) radio with which they were to maintain contact with "Smith-Chui," the 3d Division Language Section.

The pair of volunteers made several contacts with groups of Japanese soldiers as they picked their way over the rough terrain toward the objective but did not desert their mission. After a few transmissions during the morning, the Japanese couriers discontinued use of the radio for fear it might jeopardize their security. One of them stopped to rest his wounded leg, but the other continued the journey. Six hours after starting the trip the leader of the expedition succeeded in reaching Ikeda's cave where he gave General Erskine's message to one of the headquarters guards for delivery to the colonel. Half an hour later the guard returned with information that he had given the letter to the regimental commander who muttered something about conferring with the general. When the POW heard this he beat a quick retreat from the cave and rejoined his companion.

Breaking radio silence for the first time since morning the two contacted "Smith-Chui," reporting that they were on the way back. They deviated somewhat from the original plan and re-entered the Marine lines in the 5th Division zone of action at 1830. Although they had no trouble surrendering themselves they did experience considerable difficulty in explaining what two Japanese were doing with a walkie-talkie. The set was taken away from them but subsequently returned to the 3d Division.

Nothing ever came of this expedition and whether or not the message ever reached Colonel Ikeda will never be known. But interrogation of the POW's on their return brought out some interesting information. They reported that General Kuribayashi and his staff had joined Ikeda in the latter's cave on March 16. From this cave the enemy still had radio communication with Chichi Jima. They also stated that the troops contacted during their trip realized their hopeless situation, but that the enemy morale was excellent. The POW's believed this was probably due to the presence of high ranking officers in the area.[25]

Interrogation of other POW's corroborated this information and indicated further that Captain Inoue, the Iwo Naval Land Force Commander, had been killed on 8 March near Higashi, and that Major General Senda, the brigade commander, committed suicide at his headquarters on 14 March. The other senior Japanese officers, Kuribayashi, Admiral Ichimaru, and Ikeda were reported alive together in the cave near the southeast end of the gorge on 18 March.[26]

Major Horie, Kuribayashi's Chichi Jima detachment commander, tried to communicate with the general on 17 March to inform him that Japanese Imperial Headquarters had promoted him to full general, but the message was not acknowledged. Then on the 21st Chichi Jima received a message from Iwo, "We have not eaten nor drunk for five days. But our fighting spirit is still running high. We are going to fight bravely till the last."

After a silence of almost three days Hori's radio crackled again and his operator brought him another message, "All officers and men of

[24] VAC IntelRpt, 19, 20.

[25] The foregoing account of Erskine's attempt to communicate with Ikeda is based on the following sources: 3d MarDiv Supplemental Interrogation Rpt of POW No 69, 19Mar45; C–2 Periodic Rpt No 28, 18Mar45.

[26] C–2 Periodic Rpt No 29, 19Mar45; 5th MarDiv Japanese Language Section, Preliminary POW Interrogation Rpt No 36, 18Mar45; 5th MarDiv D–2 Periodic Rpt No 26, 19Mar45; 3d MarDiv POW Identification Card, 21st Mar Prisoner No 83, 20Mar45.

SOLDIERS OF THE 147TH INFANTRY (USA) assumed full responsibility for the ground defense of Iwo on 4 April.   During the months of April and May this unit killed 1,602 Japanese and took 867 prisoners.   (Army Photo)

Chichi Jima, goodbye." This was the last word from the Japanese defenders on Iwo Jima.[27]

It is probable that Kuribayashi died or committed *hara-kiri* in the gorge, but there were reports that he and other senior officers led a Japanese breakout early on 26 March. This attack was not a *banzai* charge; instead it appeared to have been a well-laid plan aimed at creating maximum confusion and destruction. About 0515, 200 to 300 Japanese moved down

from the north along the west side of the island and attacked Marine and Army bivouacs near the western beaches.   A confused battled raged for three hours with VII Fighter Command units hard hit but recovering from their initial surprise to fight back.   The 5th Pioneer Battalion formed a hasty battle line and stopped the attack, accounting for 196 of the enemy. This force was well armed with both Japanese and United States weapons.   Forty carried swords, indicating that a high percentage were officers and senior noncommissioned officers, but

[27] *Horie,* 12.

192

examination of bodies and documents failed to support the rumor that Kuribayashi was among them.[28]

As soon as Marine units could be released, they commenced re-embarkation. The 4th Division was first to load out, beginning on 14 March, completing the happy task on the 19th, and sailing for Maui the same day. Units of the 5th Division began loading on 18 March and departed Iwo, in convoy with corps units, on 27 March, headed for Hawaii.

The 3d Marine Division (less 3d Marines) took over patrol and defense responsibilities from the other divisions as they moved out and conducted patrols and established night ambushes throughout the island. The patrols varied in size from one squad to a reinforced platoon and used tanks and, on one occasion, naval gunfire provided by a destroyer to support their operations.

The 147th Infantry (USA), which was to take over the defense of Iwo, arrived from New Caledonia on 20 March and was attached to the 3d Division for operational control. By the 24th, units of Colonel Robert F. Johnson's regiment had taken over responsibility for the 21st Marines' sector and were providing most of the ambushes and patrols elsewhere.

The capture and occupation phase of the Iwo Jima operation was announced completed at 0800, 26 March and the Commander Forward Area, Central Pacific, assumed responsibility for the defense and development of Iwo Jima. At the same time Major General James E. Chaney, USA, took over operational control of all units stationed on the island, and Brigadier General Ernest Moore, USA, assumed the designation of Air Defense Commander. General Schmidt, who had commanded the largest Marine tactical force ever to engage an enemy,

closed his command post and left Iwo by air at 1330. The VAC Headquarters embarked on the USS *President Monroe*.

Units of the 3d Division began loading out on 27 March when the 21st Marines and the division command post moved on board ship. Other units of the division embarked as ships carrying garrison elements to Iwo became available. On 4 April the 147th assumed full responsibility for ground defense and the 9th Marines moved down to White Beach, ready for loading out. The last unit left on 12 April, arriving at Guam on 18 April.

That the Japanese defense continued stubborn and effective until the end is evident from the casualty figures. During 16 days of the final phase (11–26 March) and the eight additional days while 3d Division units were mopping up and patrolling, Marine losses increased by 3,885 to bring the total for the operation to 25,851.[29] A breakdown of these figures for the final phase is shown below:

	Third	Fourth	Fifth
Killed in action.........	147	139	467
Died of wounds.........	60	87	168
Wounded in action......	505	442	1,640
Missing in action........	....	....	3
Combat fatigue.........	53	52	122
Total............	765	720	2,400
Grand total.......		3,885	

Just what percentage of the Japanese defense force had become casualties by this time is not known, but as of 26 March only 216 prisoners of war had been taken.[30] In April and May, however, aggressive patrol and ambush activity by the 147th Infantry netted 867 prisoners and 1,602 Japanese killed.[31]

---

[28] The 5th Pioneers suffered nine killed and 31 wounded in this action and VII Fighter Command units lost 44 killed and 88 wounded. *C–3 Periodic Rpt* No. 35, 26Mar45; *5th MarDiv SAR*, Annex W, 2.

[29] For more detailed casualty figures see Appendix III.
[30] *C–2 Periodic Rpt* No 35, 9Apr45.
[31] Headquarters 147th Infantry Regiment, Report of Operations Against the Enemy, Iwo Jima, 11Jun45.

CHAPTER **X**

Recapitulation

MEDICAL ASPECTS

The extremely bitter and protracted assault on Iwo Jima imposed a tremendous burden on supporting medical units. From the first bloody days, when doctors and corpsmen clung grimly to fireswept beaches, to the end of the battle, a stream of wounded men passed along the chain of evacuation to receive excellent medical attention in spite of the difficult military and supply situation.

Hospital LST's lying 2,000 yards offshore played an important part during the first nine days, receiving casualties from the beaches and distributing them to APA's and hospital ships for further treatment. Initially, casualties were carried from the beach to LST (H)'s in landing craft, LVT's, and DUKW's, but as surf conditions grew worse and small landing craft could no longer approach the beaches, amphibian vehicles assumed the entire burden. The DUKW's proved most satisfactory as they handled well in the surf and alongside ships and provided greater comfort for the patients than the wet, bouncing LVT.[1]

The LSV *Ozark* operated efficiently as an auxiliary hospital ship, augmenting facilities of the *Bountiful*, *Samaritan*, and *Solace* (hospital ships) and the *Pinkney* (hospital transport). Together with departing transports, these ships evacuated a total of 13,737 casualties from Iwo Jima.[2] Another 2,449 patients were air lifted to the Marianas. The wounded were examined by flight surgeons before take-off to make sure that they could stand air travel, and corpsmen or naval nurses accompanied each flight. This preflight screening was an improvement over previous operations, and its effectiveness can be judged by the fact that no deaths occurred on board the planes.[3]

Distances from front lines to battalion aid stations were short at Iwo, but the difficult terrain and heavy enemy fire made evacuation activities extremely hazardous. Weasels and LVT's were initially most valuable for transportation of casualties to the beaches, but when roads were pushed forward jeep ambulances carried the bulk of thousands of wounded men.

The prolonged enemy use of artillery, mortars, and rockets resulted in a high percentage of especially severe wounds, accompanied by extensive loss of blood and great shock. The availability of whole blood for treatment of such casualties undoubtedly saved many lives. Landing force medical facilities alone used 5,406 pints, and the total used for care of Iwo Jima patients up to D-plus 25 reached 12,600, or slightly less than one pint per man evacuated.[4]

---

[1] *TF 56 MedRpt*, 8, 9.

[2] *TF 53 OpRpt*, Pt VI, 5, 12.

[3] *TF 56 MedRpt* 6. *TF 51 Rpt*, Pt V, H, 9; Report of the (Army) Surgeon General, Monthly Progress Report, Sec 7, Health for June, 1945.

[4] *VAC MedRpt*, 12; *TF 56 MedRpt* 19.

Congestion ashore delayed the setting up of hospitals. Airfields, gun positions, supply dumps, and command posts competed with medical installations for the limited space available, but by dispersing into allotted areas these facilities "literally dug themselves a place on the island" [5] with the help of hard-working bulldozers. Ward tents went up in airplane revetments or simply in long trenches. Engineers converted empty Japanese cisterns into excellent operating rooms by building roofs over them, and portable plywood operating rooms were set up in large holes covered with tarpaulins to keep out dust and cold. Engineers also installed lighting to make possible around-the-clock treatment.[6]

In contrast to the heavy battle casualties, other medical problems were slight at Iwo Jima. Early application of DDT solution by hand spray and later by carrier-based TBM's and Iwo- and Marianas-based C–47's measurably controlled flies and other pests. No diseases occurred among the troops that could be attributed to insects.[7]

Medical personnel serving with front line units and beach evacuation stations suffered very high casualties. They were subjected to intense enemy fire as they moved about caring for the wounded and were frequently shot down alongside men they sought to help. Acts of heroism and self-sacrifice were common among these men as they worked tirelessly to administer first aid. Casualties among doctors and corpsmen totaled 738, including 197 killed.[8]

SUPPLY

Enemy fire, deep volcanic ash, heavy surf, and congested beaches combined to make the supply problem at Iwo Jima singularly difficult. Marine shore parties, Navy beach parties, and ships' crews labored hard and courageously to surmount the many obstacles that made the early phase a nightmare. And then followed more days of grueling effort once general unloading commenced.

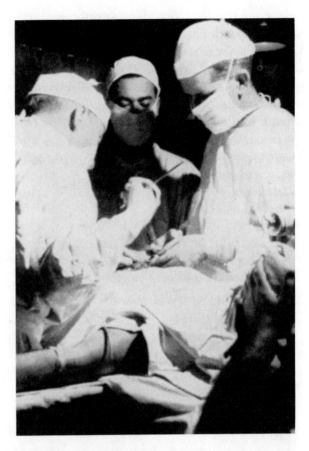

NAVY SURGEONS worked round-the-clock to save lives. This is a portable plywood operating room.

The first supplies to reach shore were standard loads of approximately 700 pounds of small-arms and mortar ammunition, rations, and water carried in each of the assault LVT's. After discharging troops and this initial load of supplies, the amphibian tractors returned to designated LST's to take on balanced loads of ammunition, water, rations, and medical supplies to be landed on order of the division logistical control officers in response to requests from ashore.[9] The Clever-Brooks 3½-ton amphibian trailers, towed by LVT's, also carried preloaded emergency supplies ashore on D-Day. But these unwieldy carriers proved to be "one-time shippers" and were seldom used again after the initial trip to the beach.[10] Floating dumps of signal gear and other high priority cargo were also established in landing craft for early call to the beach.

---

[5] *Ibid.*, 21.

[6] *Ibid.*

[7] *4th MarDiv Logistics Rpt*, Appendix 2, 30.

[8] U. S. Navy Bureau of Medicine, Statistics Division, "World War II Casualties" 1Aug52.

[9] VAC Rpt, Annex C, Appendix 6, 3; *4th MarDiv Logistics Rpt*, 12.

[10] *VAC Logistics Rpt*, 47–49.

During the first few days supply was on a hand-to-mouth basis, with all efforts directed at keeping up with urgent needs of the troops. Supplies landed in LVT's and DUKW's frequently went directly inland without rehandling on the beach. These vehicles and the agile little weasels handled most of the transportation from the beach to inland dumps and front lines until about D-plus 4 when roads became passable for wheeled traffic.[11]

---

[11] VAC Rpt, Annex C, Appendix 10, 33.

The Iwo Jima operation saw the introduction of new uses for Marston matting and armored bulldozers on the landing beaches. The hinged sections of pierced plank matting were carried to the objective in anticipation of soft sand and proved of tremendous value in providing the only usable roadways over the beaches early in the operation. The armored bulldozer, covered with steel plate to protect both driver and machine, operated on the beaches to level sand terraces and cut routes of exit inland. Late in the operation the 5th Division borrowed several

CASUALTIES BEING HOISTED ABOARD SHIP. Hospital ships and transports evacuated a total of 13,737 men from Iwo. (AF Photo)

of these machines from the shore parties to use in clearing routes through the rock-filled, scrub-covered gorges just south of Kitano Point. Here they performed as well as on the beaches as the operators were protected from the still-heavy fire of last-ditch Japanese defenders.

In the opinion of the Attack Force Beach Party Group Commander, Captain Carl E. Anderson, USNR, the Marston matting and armored bulldozers ". . . contributed materially to the success of the landing and the moving of heavy equipment off the beaches, which could not have otherwise been accomplished without almost insurmountable hardship."[12]

Cranes also played an important part in movement of supplies across the beaches. Navy commands proved more than willing to furnish

shipping to lift any equipment that would expedite unloading so that cargo vessels could be released for other tasks. The vast logistical experience of Admiral Hill, whose Task Force 53 transported and landed the Marines and their equipment, was invaluable. He had an exact knowledge of requirements, and his recommendations covered ample cargo-handling equipment for the operation.[13]

The pioneer battalions comprised the basic component of their respective division shore parties, with the 133d and 31st Naval Construction Battalions providing equipment operators and cargo handlers for the 4th and 5th divisions. In addition, two Army port companies and Marine service and supply units performed special missions as part of the shore party organizations.

---

[12] *Ibid.*; ltr RAdm C. E. Anderson, USNR (Ret) to CMC, 26Nov52.

[13] Ltr BrigGen L. S. Swindler (Ret) to CMC, 14May53, hereinafter cited as *Swindler.*

LST RIDES HIGH IN THE WATER after discharging its cargo. Beaches were still littered with wrecked landing craft and vehicles when this photo was taken on D-plus 9. Amphibian trailer in foreground was an unwieldy onetime shipper. (Navy Photo)

ORDER CAME OUT OF CHAOS and Iwo Jima became a busy seaport as tons of supplies poured across the beaches. Note the large number of cranes on this small strip of beach.

The largest sources of labor for ships platoons and shore details, however, were the replacement drafts. The use of these men as a labor pool providing strong backs and willing hands to handle cargo was generally very satisfactory from the standpoint of those responsible for keeping supplies moving.[14] But troop commanders who depended upon these same men to replace battle casualties were disappointed. Having arrived too late for thorough integration into divisions before the operation, these replacements were thrown into battle lacking experience and without even a nodding acquaintance with the leaders of units to which assigned.[15]

Liaison teams from the 8th Field Depot, which functioned as the corps shore party, accompanied the 4th and 5th Divisions in the initial landing and rendered such assistance as they were able. Beginning on D-plus 3 units of the field depot began landing and were assigned to assist the divisional shore parties, both of which suffered from severe casualties and fatigue. When control of landing operations passed to the corps on D-plus 5, the field depot took over smoothly and unloading continued without interruption. Enemy fire still harassed beach areas, causing temporary stoppages of beach activities, and the turbulent surf continued, but by D-plus 6, when general unloading began, conditions were approaching "normal." After west coast beaches were opened to small landing craft on D-plus 11 the tight sup-

---

[14] VAC Shore Party Commander, *Special Action Report, Iwo Jima Campaign,* 30Apr45, 9, hereinafter cited as *VAC Shore Party SAR; 5th Shore Party Rpt,* Encl A, 21, Encl B, 33. The 4th MarDiv Shore Party was not as well satisfied as the others, however, and its report states, "The problem of organizing, disposing of, and applying the efforts of such disjointed units combined with the immediate requirements for them by RCT's precluded efficient application of replacement personnel in shore party activities ashore." *4th MarDiv Logistics Rpt,* Appendix 1, 42.

[15] CG VAC 1st endorsement Ser 02/162, 24May45 on 4th MarDiv ltr Ser 01971 over 156/nhb, 18May45: *Isely and Crowl,* 457, 458.

ply situation eased somewhat as cargo vessels moved from coast to coast to meet variable weather conditions. At no time during the assault was there heavy surf on both beaches at the same time, and the vital ship-to-shore movement of supplies continued.[16]

Despite many difficulties involved in moving cargo ashore, the only serious shortage that developed was in ammunition.[17] The unusually heavy demands placed on artillery and mortars to support the attack consumed the seven units of fire carried in the assault shipping as fast as it could be landed, and by the time resupply ships arrived these initial stocks were seriously depleted.[18]

Unloading of ammunition resupply ships proceeded very slowly because of heavy seas and the fact that the cargo was not loaded for selective discharge. In many cases much valuable time was lost shifting noncritical items in order to gain access to the vitally needed types (mainly 105mm artillery and 81mm mortar shells.)[19] There were days when division am-

munition dumps contained as little as 300 rounds per artillery battalion after completion of pre-K-Hour firing, and after D-plus 7 it became impossible to maintain a really adequate supply at the artillery regimental dumps. On several days the artillery battalions fired more ammunition than was unloaded during the same period.[20] Following the campaign, logistics officers recommended that the allowance of ammunition carried in assault shipping be increased from seven to ten units of fire for artillery and mortars, or that the unit for those weapons be increased.[21]

Minor temporary shortages of ordnance spare parts, 60mm mortar illumination shells, grenades, and CO_2 cylinders for charging flamethrowers were made up by efficient air delivery from Saipan. This marked the first extensive use of air resupply by the Marine Corps.[22]

The Iwo Jima operation provided the first test of the newly formed permanent control organization of the Amphibious Forces, U. S. Pacific Fleet. This agency was established following the Marianas campaign to provide

[16] *TF 53 OpRpt*, Pt III, B; *VAC Shore Party SAR* 15; *Swindler*.

[17] *TF 56 Logistics Rept*, 13.

[18] *VAC Logistics Rpt*, 10, 11; *4th MarDiv Logistics Rpt*, 22.

[19] *Ibid.*

[20] *Ibid.*, Appendix 4, 3.

[21] *VAC Logistics Rpt*, 13; *TF 56 Logistics Rept*, 19.

[22] *VAC Logistics Rpt*, 12, 16.

WEASELS were used to haul supplies to forward positions, carry wounded Marines, string communication wire, and perform many other useful tasks. Here Marines unload 81mm mortar shells from weasel-drawn trailer.

trained personnel and specially equipped control vessels for the 24-hour-a-day task of directing the ship-to-shore movement. In this control group, officers representing the transport division and squadron commanders and CTF 53 paralleled the echelons of the beach and shore parties.

On D-Day the first five waves were dispatched as directed by the central control officer to insure a simultaneous landing on all beaches, but then transport squadron representatives took over with central control assuming a supervisory role.[23]

Rough seas, cluttered beaches, and a shortage of lighterage threw almost insurmountable obstacles in the way of this well-conceived control organization after the well-regulated early assault.[24] Some beaches were crowded with unloading craft and ships while at the same time others did not support enough activity to keep the shore party busy. At times supply vessels were held off shore for long periods when they might have been unloaded. Control personnel and beach parties often learned the nature of the cargo in landing craft only after the vessel had beached.

The Marine divisions felt that transport squadron commanders were too reluctant to decentralize control and that transport division control officers should have been permitted to direct all traffic for their own beaches.[25] The Navy, on the other hand, complained that troop requests for supplies were not channeled through the control vessels and that there was a marked tendency for commanders ashore to send requests direct to the ships concerned or to higher echelons without notifying the beach control officer and embarked troop representative.[26]

Under the circumstances, however, the wonder is not that things were confused but that the vast quantities of supplies actually crossed the beaches so quickly. Expertly handled ship-to-shore communications and a high degree of coordination between Navy and Marine logistical control personnel afloat and ashore did much to overcome the difficulties inherent in the situation.[27]

In his summary of the operation, Admiral Hill paid fitting tribute to men of his command:

> This operation was an extremely difficult one, not only for the troops ashore, but for the ships afloat, and particularly for the small craft and personnel engaged in the ship-to-shore movement. . . . It is with great pride that I pay tribute not only to the FIFTH Amphibious Corps for its heroic assault . . . but to the officers and men of this task force who, although many of them were engaged in their first operation, accomplished their tasks with determination, resourcefulness, and disregard of personal danger that was an inspiration to behold.[28]

ENGINEERS

The VAC received excellent engineer support during the operation. Marine engineers and their skilled Seabee partners accomplished the routine and, to some, colorless, but highly important tasks of road building, operation of water points, and miscellaneous command post, hospital, and supply dump construction jobs. But other missions were far from monotonous and required courage and determination while in close and violent contact with the enemy.

Division engineers working in support of Marine tanks exposed themselves to heavy fire as they removed mines and punched tank trails through the rocky terrain of northern Iwo. Although infantry battalions were equipped and trained to use assault demolitions against enemy emplacements, the unusually large number of caves and fortifications encountered necessitated extensive use of engineer demolitionists with assault units.

Quarries yielded excellent sand-clay fill that greatly facilitated the construction of roads. This material required little mechanical stabilization, and a daily motor patrol, shaping and filling where necessary and sprinkling with water, sufficed to keep the roads in usable condition.[29] This same material was also used in the rehabilitation and extension of Airfield Number 1 and made possible the early completion of a short strip for land-based observation planes. After the 2d Separate Engineer Bat-

---

[23] *CominCh P-0012*, 5-2, 5-3.

[24] *VAC Shore Party SAR*, 18.

[25] *5th MarDiv SAR*, Annex D (Suppply), Iwo Jima Operation, 31Mar45, 2; *4th MarDiv OpRpt*, Pt III, 16.

[26] CTF 53 ltr Ser 046, 2Apr45.

[27] *Isely and Crowl*, 519, 520.

[28] CTF 53 ltr Serial 046, 2Apr45.

[29] *4th MarDiv Logistics Rpt*, 24.

REHABILITATION AND EXTENSION OF THE AIRFIELDS was given high priority. Seabees are shown operating rollers, graders, and huge front-dumping scrapers as they lengthen the east-west runway of Airfield Number 2.   (AF Photo)

talion (Marine) had met this first urgent requirement for an OY strip, complete rehabilitation of the field commenced with Marines and the 62d Seabees sharing the work. Men of the 2d Bomb Disposal Company (Marine) cleared duds and mines ahead of the heavy construction equipment and work progressed rapidly. The two short runways were completed on 4 March, and by 12 March the long, 5,800-foot strip was handling heavy traffic although emergency landings had been made on it as early as 4 March.

NAVAL GUNFIRE

Iwo Jima was the desperate answer of the Japanese to the crushing amphibious might of the U. S. Navy and Marine Corps. On this tiny isolated island General Kuribayashi did everything in his power to devise a defense to stymie the great naval juggernaut that he knew would strike. Realizing that naval guns and aircraft would quickly destroy fortifications in the vulnerable waist of the island the general avoided exposing any large part of his force there. Most

of the weapons were emplaced in the more rugged and dominating terrain to the north and around the base of Suribachi in the south. The Japanese commander insisted that positions be deep, and when necessary he sacrificed fields of fire in favor of protection; measures made possible by the large number of guns available for defending the small island. All positions were well camouflaged and cleverly positioned to avoid detection from air or sea.

Against these defenses United States naval guns were only partially successful. Area fire did little damage, and long or medium range bombardment was not effective. Targets were so heavily reinforced by earthworks that extremely close-range fire was required to uncover them before the essential job of destruction could begin. Admiral Blandy's report on the preliminary bombardment summarizes the problem in this way:

. . . It was not until after fire support ships, their spotting planes, and the support aircraft had worked at the objective for two days, had become familiar with the location and appearance of the defenses, and had accurately attacked them with close-range gunfire and low-altitude air strikes, that substantial results were achieved.[30]

Granted that Japanese ingenuity had developed Iwo Jima into the most difficult target yet encountered by United States Forces in their progress across the Pacific, none of the problems was entirely new. Previous amphibious assaults had amply demonstrated that against such defenses only deliberate, short-range destructive fire would be effective. And both Marine and Navy commanders knew that even under the most favorable conditions this method of bombardment was extremely time consuming.

With this knowledge Marine officers made repeated requests for an extended period of preliminary bombardment. In the light of the

---

[30] *TF 52 SAR*, 10.

same experience naval commanders denied the requests and made the unfortunate decision to limit the softening-up period to three days. The strategic considerations that prompted the Navy to turn down Marine pleas for more preparation are presented in Chapter II of this monograph and need not be repeated here. Suffice it to say that the Navy had not allowed itself sufficient time to perform its mission adequately.

Considering the difficult schedule to be met, the gunfire support ships turned in a very creditable performance. As Kuribayashi had predicted, impressive damage was inflicted on weapons and installations in the relatively exposed areas on and adjacent to the east coast landing beaches. Almost all the blockhouses and pillboxes in that area were knocked out prior to the assault, and the light antiaircraft

TELEPHONE WIRES were overheaded to keep them out of the way of vehicles. A large stock of poles was carried to Iwo for this purpose.

guns around the airfields all received some damage.

The most spectacular and perhaps important accomplishment prior to D-Day was the destruction of the threatening coast-defense guns concealed in the cliffs above the quarry. But this came as a gift. Had these guns not disclosed their positions on D-minus 2 by opening up prematurely on the LCI(G)'s they would probably have survived to oppose the landing. The tragic damage inflicted on the converted landing craft by these quarry guns and those at the foot of Suribachi was only a sample of what they could have done to assault shipping and boat waves on D-Day. As it was, they marked themselves for certain destruction.[31]

The Navy had known about the guns located at the base of Suribachi; therefore, disclosure of previously unknown enemy weapons on D-minus 2 was limited to three guns near the quarry. Admiral W. H. P. Blandy, CTF 52 at Iwo, furnishes the following information relative to the location and destruction of these powerful positions:

". . . that the destruction of the heavy coast defense guns was due to their opening fire . . . upon the LCI(G)'s . . . should be confined to the guns in the cliffs above the quarry. In that position the photographic intelligence available to my task force showed only one gun, whereas the battery actually contained four guns. But at the base of Mount Suribachi, our photographs had shown the entire battery of four guns, and we had these earmarked for destruction before D-Day. However, it is true that the stark necessity for destroying all eight of these coast defense guns was more strongly impressed than ever upon all of us after observing the heavy damage inflicted upon the gunboats. And I am positive that every one of these guns was destroyed by my force.[32]

With the silencing of these coast-defense batteries the Navy succeeded in eliminating all high-velocity weapons capable of delivering direct fire on boats or landing beaches.

The Amphibious Support Force accomplished its primary mission, but other installations that could have been knocked out prior to D-Day remained virtually untouched. Such targets included pillboxes and covered emplace-

ments between Airfields 1 and 2, and those east and west of Airfield Number 2. The ground here did not resemble the rough, jumbled topography of southern approaches to the Motoyama Plateau. It was largely accessible to direct fire at relatively short ranges from vessels standing off the southern coasts. Eight days of slow, costly infantry action passed before Marines cleared this terrain. With additional time available for pre-D-Day firing naval guns might have accomplished much in this area to facilitate its capture.[33]

Once troops were ashore, naval gunfire performed the usual scheduled and call-fire missions by day, and conducted harassing and counterbattery firing at night to the satisfaction of the Marines. The cooperation of these vessels, from the largest battleship to the small, specialized gunboats, was excellent. The nature of the terrain continued to limit their effectiveness, however, and in most instances only neutralization was obtained. Supporting ships and craft were quick to observe enemy activity and take it under fire after first checking with units ashore to determine that the shelling would not endanger friendly troops.

Shore fire control parties of the joint assault signal companies (JASCO's) worked well with firing ships, obtaining maximum results under trying circumstances. Since ground observation was poor these naval gunfire teams had to refer many of their missions to airborne observers for spotting, and a large percentage of the call missions were controlled in this way. Excellent results were also achieved by placing naval gunfire officers on board gunboats or destroyers working along the coasts to observe and direct fire from those vantage points.

Expenditures of naval ammunition at Iwo were enormous, greater than in any previous operation in the Pacific. Troop requests for illumination and close-support missions were so great during the early phase of the fighting ashore that on D-plus 3 the Navy imposed limitations on the number of 5-inch common and 5-inch star shells to be fired per day. To meet this reduction in availability of stars, the divisions employed various methods of coordination

---

[31] See Chap II of this monograph for the narrative of this incident.

[32] Ltr Adm W. H. P. Blandy, USN (Ret) to CMC, 6May53.

[33] *VAC NGF Rpt*, 21–22.

to achieve more efficient illumination across the front.

The daily allowances of 5-inch bombardment ammunition proved to be adequate in all but a few instances, when permission was granted to exceed the quota. No serious disadvantage appears to have resulted in either case. During the period D-minus 3 to D-plus 35 support ships fired 152,000 rounds of 5-inch common and 17,000 rounds of star shells. When expenditures of all other types larger than 40mm are added to the above, the total reaches a staggering 291,300 rounds with a combined weight of 14,250 tons, 3,000 tons greater than the total used at Saipan.[34]

Perhaps the best analysis of the effectiveness of naval gunfire at Iwo Jima is found in the following extract from "Instructions of War" telegraphed from Kuribayashi to the Chief of the General Staff in Tokyo during the operation:

We need to reconsider the power of bombardment from ships. The beach positions we made on this island by using many materials, days and great efforts, were destroyed within three days so that they were nearly unable to be used again. . . .

Power of the American warships and aircraft makes every landing operation possible to whatever beachhead they like, and preventing them from landing means nothing but great damages. . . .[35]

AIR SUPPORT

During the three days of preparation bombardment aircraft operations were hampered by the same factors that limited the success of naval gunfire. The high-level bombing by Marianas-based B–24's over a period of several months did little more than disrupt airfield operations on the island, the primary mission of these flights. Admiral Durgin's escort carrier pilots, on the other hand, worked on all defenses that would interfere with the landing or oppose the assault once troops were ashore. The combination of bad weather, excellent camouflage, and extremely heavy fortifications created tremendous problems for the escort carrier planes.

In addition, the armament used by these support aircraft proved entirely inadequate.

Bombs were far too small to smash the massive buried blockhouses even when located and subjected to pinpoint attack. And napalm, sorely needed to burn off extensive camouflage, failed to ignite in many cases. The 5-inch rocket proved the most effective aerial weapon, but only because of its accuracy, not destructive power. Carrier units probably made their greatest contribution to preliminary bombardment operations by furnishing combat air and antisubmarine patrols and performing spotting missions for naval gunfire.

Carrier pilots accomplished more on the third day of preparation fires than during the previous two days combined. With clear sky and increased familiarization with terrain and targets, Navy flyers struck enemy fortifications with greater accuracy and deliberation. Concentrating on specific objectives on the slopes of Suribachi and emplacements overlooking the East Boat Basin, carrier aircraft struck repeatedly with bombs and rockets throughout the day of D-minus 1. But even these persistent attacks elicited only a very reserved comment from the advance commander, air support control unit, who felt that the attacks ". . . conceivably weakened the areas commanding the landing beaches."[36]

The first Tokyo raid (16–17Feb) by the Fast Carrier Force (TF 58) prevented the enemy from taking any large counteraction to pre-D-Day operations at Iwo, and thus contributed substantially to the preparation effort. But the magnificent neutralization strike against the landing beaches on D-Day by Marine and Navy pilots from TF 58 was an assist more readily appreciated by assault Marines watching and waiting to head into those beaches. Until their departure three days later for a second strike against Empire targets, planes from this unit were a powerful supplement to the support force carrier squadrons. During this time air was able to comply with all requests for ground support.

On D-plus 4, after the large flat-tops had withdrawn northward, a shortage of ground support aircraft developed. Air-sea rescue operations, strikes against the Bonin Islands,

---

[34] *TF 51 Rpt*, Pt V, C, 39; *VAC NGF Rpt*, 45.

[35] As quoted in *Horie*, Appendix, 1.

[36] *TF 52 SAR*, Encl D, 4.

TOP OF SURIBACHI two months after D-Day. A lookout station and Air Force radar equipment have replaced Japanese guns. (AF Photo)

antisubmarine patrols, and other special tasks used planes that should have been available for ground-attack missions. This short supply of aircraft became even more critical when escort carriers retired a considerable distance from the island for refueling. This last condition improved later through assignment of oilers to carrier operation areas closer to Iwo Jima.[37]

When pilots were on station and targets easy to identify from the air, planes responded quickly to ground requests. A number of strikes were completed within 15 minutes after initiation of the request, but, unfortunately, in most cases troops had to wait more than an hour for this valuable aid. Time was wasted while air liaison teams tried to break in on the overcrowded Support Air Request Net (SAR), and more minutes passed in long briefings, target location, and dummy runs for vertification. Liaison parties with the infantry were seldom cleared to coach close support aircraft on to targets during the operation. They limited themselves for the most part, to passing observations over the SAR net to the support air director, who in turn relayed this information to the air coordinator directing the strike.

With reference to this weak link in the functioning of supporting arms, some postoperation suggestions evolved. The three Marine divisions agreed that in the future air liaison parties (ALP's) should be given more direct control over strike aircraft in execution of close support missions. These teams carried radio gear with which to establish air-ground communication, and air officers exposed themselves repeatedly to move up to positions from which they had good observation of enemy positions.[38]

Performance of pilots and control personnel improved as the operation progressed, and it was possible to continue troop support beyond the point when constriction of enemy-held territory and the consequent proximity of friendly forces would normally have caused termination of such activities. Even after the escort carriers withdrew, Army P–51's carried out a few carefully planned and coordinated attacks against hostile positions at the northern tip of the island.

During the 25 days from D-Day through D-plus 24, aircraft flew 341 missions against Iwo targets, expending approximately 1,315 tons of bombs, 12,148 rockets, and 456 napalm bombs.

---

[37] *TF 51 Rpt*, Pt V, E, 7.

[38] *4th MarDiv OpRpt*, Annex C, 6–7; *5th MarDiv SAR*, Annex G, Appendix 1, 3; *3d MarDiv SAR*, 49.

When the napalm ignited its effect was good, but it failed so often to do so that results were disappointing. Ground officers were also dissatisfied with the performance of the 500-pound bombs against heavy emplacements. Even with delayed-action fuses, which were not available until late in the campaign, these ¼-ton bombs were inadequate for the job.

Destruction of enemy emplacements is not the only way that air supports ground action, however, and aerial observers played an important role throughout the battle. This was the first time in the Pacific that extensive use was made of fighter-type aircraft for spotting assignments. These planes, flown by specially trained pilots of VOC–1, performed well and proved to be a valuable augmentation to the float planes normally used to spot naval gunfire. Marine artillery and tactical observers from the divisions operated in torpedo bombers from carriers until the light observation planes of the VMO squadrons became shore based.

For night tactical observation over the island, the three divisions had embarked officers on the carrier *Saratoga*, and during the first two nights of the operation they performed five flights totaling 25 hours. But when that carrier retired after suffering severe damage during the Japanese air attack on 21 February, those valuable missions ceased. It was noticed that the mere presence of a plane overhead had considerable effect in holding down enemy mortar and artillery fire. This was particularly apparent at dusk and dawn when carrier aircraft were not available but the OY's were operating. In an attempt to extend this dampening effect through the hours of darkness, VMO pilots flew several successful night missions from the unlighted airfields.[39]

Enemy antiaircraft fire was "moderate to intense" during the early part of the operation, diminishing to sporadic outbursts from blockhouses and concealed positions as the ground advance overran the larger concentrations of automatic weapons around the airfields and at Nishi, Minami, and Higashi. Japanese gunners scored numerous hits, accounting for 26 planes lost and nine seriously damaged. In ad-

dition many returned to base with holes in wings and fuselage to attest the accuracy of these guns. Total casualties to pilots and crewmen were 36, with 32 killed or missing. The figures given above do not include losses from operational failures or as a result of flights over Chichi Jima.[40]

Generally speaking the performance of all personnel connected with air support was excellent and much improved over past operations. This was a result of the accumulated training and experience, and the increased emphasis placed on air support of ground troops by all echelons of command, both Navy and Marine Corps.[41]

ARTILLERY

Standard artillery tactics and doctrine proved sound at Iwo, but the organic weapons were inadequate for the task of destroying the type of emplacements encountered. The 105mm and 75mm howitzers of the divisional artillery battalions were completely unsuited for this work. Even the much heavier 155mm shells of corps units required ten to 12 hits, all in the same place, to inflict major damages on many of the imposing Japanese fortifications.[42]

Like air and naval gunfire, artillery was severely handicapped by limited observation. Forward observers could seldom see more than 200 yards to the front, and in the more rugged areas, particularly in the 4th Division zone of action, this visibility was often reduced to 100 yards. As a result, although forward observers controlled the majority of the missions, a greater dependence had to be placed on airborne spotters, especially for counterbattery and destruction missions.

The divisional artillery battalions landed under control of their respective artillery regiments and remained in that status during the entire operation. Normal employment placed one battalion in direct support of each assault regiment with the others in general support or reinforcing the direct support units. The 155's, in general support, employed their fires in ac-

---

[39] *4th MarDiv OpRpt*, Annex C, 11.

[40] *TF 56 IntelRpt*, 13; *TF 51 Rpt*, Pt IV, 9–23.
[41] *Ibid.*, Pt V, E, 40.
[42] *VAC ArtyRpt*, 29.

cordance with the corps scheme of maneuver, allotting the bulk of such reinforcement to the division making the main effort. At times throughout the campaign heavy concentrations were accomplished in a particular zone by shifting the efforts of corps and some divisional units from one front to another ahead of echeloned attacks. The commanding officer, 1st Provisional Field Artillery Group, exercised overall coordination in his capacity as corps artillery officer.

The majority of the missions fired by corps 155's were counterbattery. Considering the difficult conditions of observation and detection and the rugged construction of enemy gun positions, these weapons performed well in their primary role. The lighter division howitzers also expended large quantities of ammunition in counterbattery fire but gained more neutralization than destruction. Only when an alert and lucky forward observer caught a hostile gun in the open could the 105's and 75's cause any considerable damage.

Failure to detect and engage vital targets before the close proximity of infantry precluded use of the 155's proved a serious obstacle to efficient utilization of the corps howitzers. Commenting on this after the battle, the corps commander wrote:

It is considered that the major lesson learned relative to the employment of artillery capable of destroying enemy fixed installations is the necessity for anticipating such requirements and taking all possible measures to effect such destruction before our front lines are so close as to make firing of heavy calibers impracticable. This can be effected by a more intensive utilization of deep support fires combined with low-level aerial photography to discover such installations before our troops are so close as to prevent the utilization of medium artillery and naval gunfire in the destruction.[43]

In some areas barrages that lifted progressively on a time schedule ahead of the troops were successful. This was especially true in the 3d Division zone between the second and third airfields, but in other areas where the ground was more broken this technique accomplished little.

Ammunition expenditures by the 168 howitzers of the 14 battalions on Iwo were fabulous.

---

[43] CG, VAC endorsement to *VAC ArtyRpt.*

A breakdown of the 450,156 rounds fired is shown below : [44]

Number and type of weapon:	Number rounds fired
48 75mm howitzers	181,510
96 105mm howitzers	224,851
24 155mm howitzers	43,795

SUPPORTING ARMS COORDINATION

Three basic ingredients contributed to the successful coordination of supporting arms at Iwo Jima : Close personal liaison at all levels, good communications, and a mutual understanding of the special capabilities and limitations of each weapon. Coordination started at the battalion level with the commander or his representative discussing the plan of attack with his liaison officers and drawing up a request for supporting fires. This process was repeated at regiment where the requests from subordinate units were reviewed and modified when necessary or desirable.

On division levels, final coordination was achieved by the commander or his representative and the division air, naval gunfire, and artillery officers. These officers acted upon regimental requests and, after adding other missions based on the over-all scheme of maneuver, molded them into a consolidated fire plan.

The systems of coordination employed at the three division headquarters were basically the same, but the more formalized technique of the 3d Division, with a special installation known as the "supporting arms tent," worked particularly well. The following extract from that unit's action report best serves to describe the method:

The basic method of coordination between supporting arms was to achieve close personal liaison on all levels. Targets were freely interchanged according to the method of attack best suited, and, whenever operations were in progress or prospect, the artillery, naval gunfire, and air officers were together or readily accessible to each other by wire. Plans for scheduled fires or pre-King-Hour preparations were habitually prepared jointly, and so presented to the G–3, Chief of Staff, and the Commanding General. Much of the success achieved may be traced to the separate maintenance of a "supporting arms tent," so-called, adjacent

---

[44] *VAC ArtyRpt,* Encl F; *14th Mar OpRpt,* 35; *12th Mar SAR,* 21; *13th Mar SAR,* 56.

to the G–3 Section. In this center, wire communications converged from the division switchboard, from the similar 5th Amphibious Corps establishment, from the division artillery fire direction center, and from the naval gunfire and air radio centrals. It was thus possible to establish any sort of communications necessary, and to plan without interruption, while being within a few steps of the G–3 Section.[45]

The concept governing use of supporting arms at the corps level was that aircraft and naval gunfire vessels performing troop support missions are in effect additional artillery with the corps. Accordingly the corps commander designated his corps artillery officer as coordinating agent.[46] Coordination was accomplished by close liaison between the corps artillery air, and naval gunfire officers and the Commander, Landing Force Air Support Control Unit, in the Joint Operations Rooms on board the *Auburn* (AGC) and later through facilities of the supporting arms tent at corps headquarters ashore.[47]

During the 10 days of the operation when air support was under the Expeditionary Force Air Support Control Unit on board the *Eldorado* (AGC), coordination between air and artillery was difficult because of slow communications. Fortunately there was little high-ordinate gunfire, and support air directors could send planes on missions without a detailed check on artillery.[48] When control of support air passed to the Landing Force Air Support Control Unit ashore, which set up in close proximity to the corps supporting arms tent, this difficulty was largely eliminated.[49]

Corps coordinators determined when artillery fires would have to be restricted to permit air strikes and passed the information to the various commands for action. In addition, the general support missions of ships and corps artillery were planned in the supporting arms center. Since a majority of the ships were assigned to direct support of the divisions, most of the coordination between naval gunfire and artillery

---

[45] *3d MarDiv SAR*, 53.
[46] *VAC OpPlan* No 3–44, Annex H, Appendix 5.
[47] *VAC NGF Rpt*, 38.

[48] *TF 51 Rpt*, Pt V, E, 34.
[49] *ASCU Rpt*, 4.

AFTER THE BATTLE twisted steel reinforcing rods form laticework through which B–29's and P–51s' are viewed from inside demolished Japanese blockhouse. (AF Photo)

A VALUABLE AIR FACILITY only 660 miles from Tokyo appeared on Iwo Jima after only a few short months of American hard work and know-how.

took place at divisional level. No effort was made to rearrange division plans because changes would have arrived too late for proper execution.[50]

The functioning of the supporting arms center was never completely effective owing to lack of enough qualified personnel for continuous operation. Furthermore, coordination at all echelons was handicapped by a lack of time. But the over-all effect was good. Subordinate units planned the use of supporting weapons as best they could, and in general duplication of effort was eliminated before requests reached the implementing agencies.[51]

COMMUNICATIONS

Without highly efficient communications Iwo Jima could never have been taken. Control, coordination, and supply all depended on the hundreds of radio and wire nets that connected ships to shore, air to ground, and headquarters to headquarters ashore or afloat. This is, of course, an obvious truth, but it is too often overlooked. The communication personnel of all echelons and services involved in the operation

deserve high praise and due credit for their excellent performance of duty.

There were cases of enemy jamming and interference from other friendly sets, but operators learned to communicate through the jamming in most cases, and interference between units of the assault force was corrected by juggling channels. Some nets, such as the Support Air Request Net, were overcrowded, and only by enforcing strict radio discipline could they function adequately.

The terrain was favorable for voice radio transmission, and full use was made of the "walkie-talkie" (SCR–300) and the lighter "spam can" (SCR–536) radios by platoons, companies, and battalions. Artillery forward observers using the much heavier and bulky SCR–610 radios recommended that more SCR–300 channels be made available so that they too could use the easily carried "walkie-talkie."

The short distances involved and the slow movement of the front lines permitted compact but elaborate wire nets. Important lines were duplicated to minimize the effects of enemy fire, and where possible wires were overheaded, using two-by-four poles brought along for that purpose. Lines on the ground suffered frequent

---

[50] *VAC ArtyRpt*, Encl P, 4.
[51] *Ibid.*

209

damage from vehicles, especially tanks and tractors, and wiremen worked long hours trouble shooting and repairing breaks.

Navajo Indian talkers were used extensively in the transmission of secret messages by voice radio. With the corps and division headquarters afloat for the first several days, this was the only available means for sending highly classified traffic over the air. Their complicated Navajo language was completely unintelligible to anyone not of the same tribe and security was assured. The military vocabularies of the Indians were so different that each division had to assign two of its own talkers to corps headquarters to insure understanding.[52]

CONCLUSION

In the savage struggle at Iwo Jima the amphibious forces of the U. S. Navy and Marine Corps proved that, given control of the surrounding seas and skies, they could seize any objective, no matter how powerful its guns and emplacements or how stubborn and skillful the defenders.

But the 6,821 Marines, soldiers, and sailors who lost their lives did not die to prove the soundness of existing amphibious doctrine. The operation was planned and executed in accordance with the grim necessities of the air war against Japan. Strategically located Iwo Jima had to be taken.

The urgency of their mission was impressed on Marines assaulting the island defenses long before the fighting ended. The first distressed B–29 Superfort made an emergency landing on Airfield Number 1 on 4 March (D-plus 13) and by 26 March, 35 other Twentieth Air Force bombers were saved by now-friendly Iwo. Development of the air facilities progressed rapidly under Major General James E. Chaney, USA. Sand-clay strips rapidly gave way to an elaborate system of black-top runways and dispersal areas, and fuel storage tanks and repair shops mushroomed to support the bustling air activities.

Mustangs of the VII Fighter Command began their escort duties on 7 April when 108 P–51's made the long flight from Iwo to cover a daylight B–29 attack on Tokyo. This mission was followed by other similar trips and fighter sweeps against ground targets in the main islands. It had been expected that these long-range fighter activities would be Iwo's major contribution to the air war. But when the big bombers from the Marianas shifted to night incendiary raids, without escort, the island became more important as an intermediate base that greatly increased the efficiency of B–29 operations against the Empire.

By the end of the war a total of 2,251 Superforts carrying 24,761 crewmen landed on the island. A large number of these would have been lost if Iwo had not been available. An excerpt from *Impact*, a wartime publication of the Army Air Force, describes what Iwo Jima meant to the men who made the long, dangerous run to Japan:[53]

. . . Located about midway between Guam and Japan, Iwo broke the long stretch, both going and coming. If you had engine trouble, you held out for Iwo. If you were shot up over Japan and had wounded aboard, you held out for Iwo. If the weather was too rough, you held out for Iwo. Formations assembled over Iwo, and gassed up at Iwo for extra-long missions. If you needed fighter escort, it usually came from Iwo. If you had to ditch or bail out, you knew that air-sea rescue units were sent from Iwo. Even if you never used Iwo as an emergency base, it was a psychological benefit. It was there to fall back on.

In the final analysis battles are won not by machines but by men trained to fight, wanting to live, but unafraid to die. Iwo Jima has come to symbolize the courage and offensive spirit that brought victory to the Armed Forces of the United States in World War II. The 24 Medals of Honor awarded for valor during the campaign reflect the high level of individual and collective heroism characteristic of that action. Countless other acts of selfless bravery went unnoted in the holocaust of Iwo, but the then Secretary of the Navy, James V. Forrestal, expressed his "tremendous admiration and reverence for the guy who walks up beaches and takes enemy positions with a rifle and grenades or his bare hands."[54]

---

[52] *VAC SigRpt*, 5.

[53] Office of the Assistant Chief of Air Staff, Intelligence, Washington, D. C. "Iwo, B–29 Haven and Fighter Springboard," *Impact*, Vol III, No 9, Sep–Oct45, 64.

[54] As quoted in the *New York Times*, 26Feb45, 1, col 6.

APPENDIX I Bibliography

This historical monograph is based upon an evaluation and examination of many sources. These include action reports, unit diaries and journals, operation plans and orders, dispatches, letters, and preoperation studies by units participating in the campaign. The narrative in general depends upon reports of lower echelon units to provide details of specific actions. In all cases source material supporting any particular event or action comes from records of the organization most directly concerned at the time. Operation reports of higher echelon commands served to present the over-all picture and aid in the integration of various complex activities into the complete story of Iwo Jima.

Approximately 175 participants in the campaign from operation commander to platoon leaders, contributed to the finished product through written comments or personal interview. Information thus gained served either to supplement or corroborate the hundreds of documents consulted during preparation of the monograph. Also, in this manner valuable information was received that never found its way into official records, although many of the personal recollections and anecdotes were used primarily to verify or clarify material contained in the official action reports.

Many documents studied while conducting research actually had only an indirect bearing on the operation; such records are not listed in the bibliography. Only the most useful and pertinent sources, including all those cited in the text, appear among the items included in the list below. Unless otherwise noted, all sources given here are filed in the archives of the Historical Branch, G–3, Headquarters, U. S. Marine Corps, Washington, D. C.

DOCUMENTS

Joint War Planning Committee Plan 91/D, 13Sep43, "Seizure of the Bonins."

Joint War Planning Committee Study 244, 24Jan44, "Immediate Occupation of Iwo Jima."

Joint Chiefs of Staff Directives 713 and 713/4, 12Mar44, called for an acceleration of the Pacific War through assigning new objectives and canceling others.

Assistant Chief of Air Staff, Operations, Commitments and Requirements PD 384.3, Japan (11–9–43) Sec. 3, 17May44, "Paper on Long Range Fighter Groups."

Joint Chiefs of Staff Paper 924, 30Jun44, "Operations Against Japan Subsequent to Formosa," suggested a drive into the Bonins after the Formosa Operation.

Army Air Force Memorandum for the Joint Planning Staff, 21Jul44, "Fighter Escort for VLR Bombers," informed the JPS that Iwo Jima could be used to base fighter planes for escorting bombers to Tokyo.

Joint War Planning Committee Plan 91/3, 12Aug44, "Plan for the Seizure of the Bonins," notes from the Joint Planning Staff's 163d meeting, 16Aug44, Iwo Jima singled out as the only practical objective in the Bonin Group.

Joint Logistics Committee Study 67/4/m, 23Aug44, "Memorandum of Request, Naval Personnel Requirements for Pacific Theater through 3 June 1945," three divisions specified for projected Volcano-Bonin Operation in April 1945.

Joint Chiefs of Staff Paper 713/19, 3Oct44, "Future Operations in the Pacific," CinCPOA directed to occupy positions in the Nanpo Shoto (Volcano-Bonins), target date 20Jan45.

Joint Planning Staff Paper 404/15, 18Oct44, "Operations for the Defeat of Japan," a Joint War Plans Committee outline of projected operations to defeat Japan, including Iwo Jima.

Joint Chiefs of Staff Paper 713/18, 2Oct44, "Future Operations in the Pacific," Admiral King's proposed directive for future Pacific operations to include occupation of positions in the Volcano-Bonin Group.

Joint Intelligence Committee Report (44) 491 (0) Final, London, 8 December 44, "Possibility of Japanese Withdrawal from the Outer Zone," a paper by the Joint Intelligence Subcommittee of the Combined Chiefs of Staff that deals with the effect of the Japanese naval defeat in the Philippines on Japan's war plans and potential.[1]

CominCh P–0012, Commander in Chief United States Fleet report of amphibious operations to capture Iwo Jima, 17Jul45.

CinCPOA Joint Staff Study DETACHMENT, 7Oct44, plan for assault on Iwo Jima; forces to be used and information regarding enemy defenses and strength on the island.

CinCPOA Campaign Plan GRANITE II, 3Jun44, outlines conduct of future Pacific operations and objectives for 1944 and 1945.

CinCPac-CinCPOA Intelligence Items and Translations.

CinCPac-CinCPOA Bulletins, Numbers 126–44, 9–45 (4th Supplement), 9–45, 75–45, 79–45, 122–45, 124–45, 140–45, 152–45, 170–45, 161–45, and 2–46.

Headquarters U. S. Army Forces, Pacific Ocean Areas, Office of Assistant Chief of Staff, G–2, "Study of Iwo Jima," undated.

Commander, Amphibious Forces, U. S. Pacific Fleet (CTF 51), Operation Plan A25–44, 27Dec44, over-all operation plan for capture and occupation of Iwo Jima.

Commander, Amphibious Forces, U. S. Pacific Fleet, Report on the Capture of Iwo Jima, 19May45.

Intelligence Section, Amphibious Forces, U. S. Pacific Fleet, "Information on Iwo Jima (Kazan Retto)," undated.

Commander, Fast Carrier Force (CTF 58), U. S. Fifth Fleet, Report of Combat Operations from 10Feb45 to 4Mar45, 13Mar45, includes accounts of operations in support of Iwo Jima assault and diversionary raids against Japan.

Task Force 56 Report on Iwo Jima Operation, contains reports on planning, intelligence, operations, logistics, personnel, and special staff functions, 27Mar45.

Task Force 53 Iwo Jima Operation Report, 2Apr45.

Task Force 52 Iwo Jima Special Action Report, 22Feb45.

U. S. S. *Makin Island* (CVE 93) Action Report, Occupation of Iwo Jima, 10Feb45 to 11Mar45, undated.

Composite Spotting Squadron One, Participation of VOC–1 in Iwo Jima Operation, 18Mar45.

---

[1] Aforementioned documents are in custody of Records Branch, Assistant Chief of Staff, G–3, Department of the Army, Washington, D. C.

Task Force 54 Report of Operations in the Iwo Jima Campaign, 10Mar45.

V Amphibious Corps Operation Orders 4–45, 10–45, 11–45, 13–45, 14–45, 15–45, 23–45.

V Amphibious Corps Special Action Report, Iwo Jima, contains individual reports of planning, operations, intelligence, logistics, personnel, air, naval gunfire, ordnance, signal, medical, artillery, and air support control unit officers, dated separately by report.

V Amphibious Corps, Assistant Chief of Staff, G–1, Special Action Report, Iwo Jima Campaign, 1May45 (Personnel).

V Amphibious Corps, Assistant Chief of Staff, G–2, Special Action Report, Iwo Jima Campaign, 20Apr45 (Intelligence).

V Amphibious Corps, C–2 Study of Enemy Situation.

V Amphibious Corps C–2 Periodic Reports 1 through 35, 19Feb45 through 9Apr45.

V Amphibious Corps C–2 Special Interrogation Report of Major Hara, Mitsuaki, commanding officer of 1st Bn, 145th Infantry Regiment [IJA], 22Mar45.

V Amphibious Corps, Assistant Chief of Staff, G–3, Special Action Report, Iwo Jima Campaign, 31Mar45, (Operations).

V Amphibious Corps C–3 Periodic Reports, 19Feb45 through 9Apr45.

V Amphibious Corps, Assistant Chief of Staff, G–4, Special Action Report, Iwo Jima Campaign, 30Apr45 (Logistics).

V Amphibious Corps Transport Quartermaster Special Action Report, Iwo Jima Campaign, 27Mar45.

V Amphibious Corps Operation Plan 3–44, Annex M (Engineer Plan), 23Dec44.

V Amphibious Corps Engineer Special Action Report, Iwo Jima Campaign, 17Apr45.

V Amphibious Corps Artillery Special Action Report, Iwo Jima Campaign, 18Mar45.

V Amphibious Corps Naval Gunfire Special Action Report, Iwo Jima Campaign, 30May45.

V Amphibious Corps Air Special Action Report, Iwo Jima Campaign, 30Apr45.

V Amphibious Corps Signal (Communications) Report, Iwo Jima Campaign, 29Apr45.

V Amphibious Corps Surgeon's Report, Iwo Jima Campaign, 24Mar45.

V Amphibious Corps Landing Force Air Support Control Unit Special Action Report, Iwo Jima Campaign, 17Mar45.

V Amphibious Corps LVT Special Action Report, Iwo Jima Campaign, 30Apr45.

V Amphibious Corps Headquarters Commandant Special Action Report, Iwo Jima Campaign, 30Mar45.

Company B, Amphibious Reconnaissance Battalion, Fleet Marine Force, Pacific (attached to V Corps), Special Action Report, Iwo Jima Operation, 29Mar45.

3d Marine Division Operation Order 23–45.

3d Marine Division Special Action Report, Iwo Jima Operation, 30Apr45, contains enclosed individual reports of administration, personnel, intelligence, operations, logistics, and supporting arms components.

3d Marine Division Periodic Report No 31, 16Mar45.

3d Marine Division G–2 Language Section, Aggregate Report from POW's who worked on Communications Center Pillbox and Tunnels leading thereto from Various Units. 2Mar45.

3d Marine Division Supplemental Interrogation Report of POW No 69, 19Mar45.

3d Marine Division POW Identification Card, 21st Mar Prisoner No 83, 20Mar45.

9th Marines Special Action Report, Iwo Jima Operation, 20Apr45, contains reports from R–1, R–2, R–3, and R–4 sections, plus action reports from the individual organic battalions.

12th Marines Special Action Report, Iwo Jima Operation, undated, contains reports from R–1, R–2, R–3, and R–4 sections, plus action reports from individual organic battalions.

21st Marines Special Action Report, Iwo Jima Operation, 10Apr45, contains reports from R–1, R–2, R–3, and R–4 sections, plus action reports from individual organic battalions.

3d Tank Battalion Special Action Report, Iwo Jima Operation, 9Apr45, contains reports from organic companies.

3d Engineer Battalion Special Action Report, Iwo Jima Operation, 17Apr45.

4th Marine Division Operation Report, Iwo Jima, 19 February to 16 March 1945, 18May45, contains basic report of five sections covering plans and preparations, movement to objectives, ship-to-shore movement, narrative of the operation, comments and recommendations, plus individual administration, intelligence, operations, logistics, and communications annexes.

4th Marine Division D–2 Periodic Reports, 19 February to 16 March 1945.

4th Marine Division D–2 Language Section Translations, 9Mar45, "Reconstruction of Counterattack Stopped by BLT 2/23 on Morning 9 March."

4th Marine Division D–2 Language Section Translations, 10Mar45, "TAN OpOrder A, No. 43, Iwo Jima, 1Dec44."

4th Marine Division D–2 Language Section Translations, 11Mar45, Japanese Naval Headquarters Report of 23Feb45.

4th Marine Division D–2 Language Section Preliminary POW Report No. 13, 8Mar45.

4th Marine Division D–2 Language Section Translations, 26Feb45, "Instructions From Chief of Staff, 17Feb45," [Japanese 109th Division Chief of Staff].

4th Marine Division D–2 Language Section Translations, 28Feb45, translation of captured enemy diary.

4th Marine Division D–3 Periodic Reports, 19 February to 16 March 1945.

14th Marines Operation Report, Iwo Jima, 13Apr45, contains reports from R–1, R–2, R–3, and R–4 sections, plus action reports from individual organic battalions.

23d Marines Operation Report, Iwo Jima, 9Apr45, contains reports from R–1, R–2, R–3, and R–4 sections, plus action reports from individual organic battalions.

24th Marines Operation Report, Iwo Jima, 20Apr45, contains reports from R–1, R–2, R–3, and R–4 sections, plus action reports from individual organic battalions.

25th Marines Operation Report, Iwo Jima, 15Apr45, contains reports from R–1, R–2, R–3, and R–4 sections, plus action reports from individual organic battalions.

4th Tank Battalion Operation Report, Iwo Jima, 18Apr45, contains reports from organic companies.

4th Engineer Battalion Operation Report, Iwo Jima, undated.

4th Medical Battalion Operation Report, Iwo Jima, undated.

4th Marine Division Support Group Operation Report, Iwo Jima, 4Apr45.

5th Marine Division Special Action Report, Iwo Jima Operation, 19 February to 26 March 1945, 28Apr45, contains basic report of nine sections covering a summary, planning, task organization, training and rehearsals, embarkation, movement to objective, ship-to-shore movement, operations ashore, and special comments and recommendations, plus individual administration, intelligence, operations, supply, transport quartermaster, shore party, air support, naval gunfire support, and communications annexes.

5th Marine Division Operation Orders 9–45 and 13–45.

5th Marine Division D–3 Journal, Iwo Jima.

5th Marine Division War Diary, February 1945.

5th Marine Division War Diary, March 1945.

5th Marine Division D–2 Periodic Report No 26, 19Mar45.

5th Marine Division Japanese Language Section, Preliminary POW Interrogation Report No 36, 18Mar45.

13th Marines Special Action Report, Iwo Jima Operation, 7Apr45, contains reports from R–1, R–2, R–3, and R–4 sections, plus action reports from individual organic battalions.

26th Marines Special Action Report, Iwo Jima Operation, 20Apr45, contains reports from R–1, R–2, R–3, and R–4 sections, plus action reports from individual organic battalions.

26th Marines War Diary, March 1945.

27th Marines Special Action Report, Iwo Jima Operation, 17Apr45, contains reports from R–1, R–2, R–3, and R–4 sections, plus action reports from individual organic battalions.

28th Marines Special Action Report, Iwo Jima Operation, undated, contains reports from R–1, R–2, R–3, and R–4 sections, plus action reports from individual organic battalions.

5th Tank Battalion Special Action Report, Iwo Jima Operation, 24Apr45, contains reports from organic companies.

5th Tank Battalion Periodic Report No 5, 24Feb45.

5th Shore Party Regiment Special Action Report, Iwo Jima Operation, undated.

Army Air Forces, Pacific Ocean Areas, Report of Participation in the Iwo Jima Operation, 1945, contains reports of VII Bomber Command units and Seventh Air Force fighter groups. Filed at the Air University, Maxwell Field, Alabama.

Headquarters, 147th Infantry Regiment, Report of Operations Against the Enemy, Iwo Jima, 11Jun45. Filed at the Adjutant General's Office, Kansas City Records Administration Center, Kansas City 24, Missouri.

Army Garrison Force, Special Action Report, Iwo Jima Campaign, 25Mar45.

138th Antiaircraft Artillery Group, Special Action Report, Iwo Jima Campaign, 17Mar45.

BOOKS AND PERIODICALS

Aurthur, 1stLt Robert A. and Cohlmia, 1stLt Kenneth, *The Third Marine Division*. Washington: Infantry Journal Press, 1948.

Assistant Chief of Air Staff, Intelligence, Washington, D. C., *Impact*, Vol I, No. 3, August 1943.

Assistant Chief of Air Staff, Intelligence, Washington, D. C., "Iwo, B–29 Haven and Fighter Springboard," *Impact*, Vol. III, No. 9, September–October 1945.

Boggs, Maj Charles W., *Marine Aviation in the Philippines*, Marine Corps Historical Monograph. Washington: Government Printing Office, 1951.

Conner, Howard M., *The Spearhead, The World War II History of the 5th Marine Division*. Washington: Infantry Journal Press, 1950.

Dulles, Foster R., *America in the Pacific*. New York: Houghton-Mifflin Company, 1932.

Fahey, James C., *The Ships and Aircraft of the United States Fleet*. Washington: Ships and Aircraft, Publishers, 1950.

Halsey, Fleet Admiral William F. and Bryan, LtCdr J., III, *Admiral Halsey's Story*. New York: McGraw-Hill Book Company, 1947.

Heinl, Maj Robert D., Jr., "Dark Horse on Iwo," *Marine Corps Gazette*, August 1945.

Hoffman, Maj Carl W., *Saipan: The Beginning of the End*, Marine Corps Historical Monograph. Washington: Government Printing Office, 1950.

Hoffman, Maj Carl W., *The Seizure of Tinian*, Marine Corps Historical Monograph. Washington: Government Printing Office, 1951.

Hough, Maj Frank O., *The Assault on Peleliu*, Marine Corps Historical Monograph. Washington: Government Printing Office, 1950.

Hough, Maj Frank O., *The Island War*. Philadelphia and New York: J. B. Lippincott Company, 1947.

Isely, Jeter A. and Crowl, Philip A., *The U. S. Marines and Amphibious War*. Princeton: Princeton University Press, 1951.

Lodge, Maj O. R., *The Recapture of Guam*, Marine Corps Historical Monograph. Washington: Government Printing Office, 1954.

Military Intelligence Service, War Department, *Tactical and Technical Trends*, No 58, May 1945. Washington: Government Printing Office, 1945.

Osborn, Fairfield, ed., *The Pacific World*. New York: W. W. Norton & Company, Inc., 1944.

Price, Willard, *Japan's Islands of Mystery*. New York: John Day Company, 1944.

Sherrod, Robert, *History of Marine Corps Aviation in World War II*. Washington: Combat Forces Press, 1952.

Smith, General Holland M., *Coral and Brass*. New York: Charles Scribner's Sons, 1949.

Terry, Philip T., *Terry's Japanese Empire*. Boston and New York: Houghton-Mifflin Company, 1914.

Williams, LtCol Robert H., "Up the Rock on Iwo the Hard Way," *Marine Corps Gazette*, August 1945.

MISCELLANEOUS

Chief of Staff of the United States Army, Biennial Report, 1 July 1943 to 30 June 1945.

Encyclopedia Britannica, articles, "Ogasawara Jima," and "Volcano Islands."

Garretson, Maj Frank E., "Operation of the 2d Bn., 24th Marines on Iwo Jima, Volcano Islands, 19Feb–18Mar45," an unpublished monograph prepared for the Advanced Officers Course, The Infantry School, Fort Benning, Georgia, 19Feb47.

Giniger, SSgt Henry and Smith, SSgt Tony, "The Twenty-Seventh Marines in Combat, Iwo Jima," an unpublished manuscript, undated.

Horie, Maj Yoshitaka, "Explanation of Japanese Defense Plan and Battle of Iwo Jima," 25Jan46.

Japanese Studies in World War II: "Air Operations on Iwo and the Ryukyus," No 57; and "Operations on Iwo Jima," No 61. On file at the Office of the Chief of Military History, United States Army.

Navy Department Press and Radio Release, medals, citation and unit commendation awarded to officers and crews of LCI(G) Group Eight and LCI(G) Flotilla Three [for Iwo Jima action], 5Sep45.

The New York Times, "Forrestal Pays Tribute to Marines," 26Feb45.

The New York Times, "Japanese Chief on Iwo Praised by Tokyo Radio," 3Mar45.

Thomason, Capt John W., III, "The Fourth Division at Iwo Jima," an unpublished manuscript, undated.

Turton, LtCol Howard J., "A Division Pre-Dawn Attack," Historical Study, Marine Corps Schools Senior Course (1946–47). Filed at Records Section, Marine Corps Schools, Quantico, Virginia.

U. S. Army Surgeon General, Monthly Progress Report, Section 7, Health for June, 1945.

U. S. Navy Bureau of Medicine, Statistics Division, "World War II Casualties," 1Aug45.

U. S. Ships' Histories: USS *Pensacola*, USS *Petrof Bay*, USS *Steamer Bay*, USS *Wake Island*. Filed at Office of Naval Records and Library, Ships' Histories Branch, Navy Department.

APPENDIX II

Chronology

1944

31 January–7 February
U. S. forces invade and capture Majuro and Kwajalein Atolls, Marshall Islands in first offensive against Japanese territory.

17–22 February
U. S. forces invade and occupy Eniwetok Atoll, Marshall Islands.

29 February–28 March
Admiralties invaded and main islands captured by U. S. Army troops.

22 April
U. S. troops land at Aitape and Hollandia in northern New Guinea.

15 June
China-based B–29's bomb Kyushu Island in first Superfort attack on Japan.

15 June–9 July
U. S. Marines and Army troops invade and capture Saipan in the Marianas.

15 June
U. S. Navy carrier task force strikes Volcano-Bonin Islands in first raid on these groups.

19–20 June
First Battle of the Philippine Sea: Japanese Navy suffers severe losses.

24 June and 4 July
U. S. Navy carrier task force again bombards Volcano-Bonin Islands, including Iwo Jima.

21 July–10 August
U. S. Marines and Army troops invade and recapture Guam, Marianas Islands.

23 July–1 August
U. S. Marines assault and seize Tinian, Marianas Islands.

15 September
U. S. Army troops land on Morotai, Netherlands East Indies, and capture airfield on that island.

15–17 September
U. S. Marines and Army troops assault Peleliu and Angaur in the Palau Islands.

23 September
U. S. Army troops seize Ulithi as advance naval base.

3 October
JCS directive orders occupation of one or more positions in the Nanpo Shoto (Volcano-Bonins).

9 October
Admiral Nimitz informs General Smith that Iwo Jima is to be the Nanpo Shoto objective.

20 October
U. S. Army troops invade Leyte to open the Philippines Campaign.

23–26 October
Second Battle of the Philippine Sea (Battle for Leyte Gulf).

11–12 November
U. S. Navy surface forces rock Iwo Jima with heavy bombardment.

24 November	B–29's conduct first Marianas-based attack on Tokyo; first raid by land-based aircraft on Japanese capital.	23 February	American Flag raised atop Mount Suribachi by the 28th Marines.
8 December	U. S. Navy surface units shell Iwo Jima.	25 February	The 3d Marine Division (less 3d Marines) committed in battle for Iwo.
15 December	U. S. Army units land on Mindoro Island, Philippine Islands.		General unloading of cargo begins.
24–27 December	U. S. Navy surface units bombard Volcano-Bonin Islands, including Iwo Jima.	27 February	The 3d Division overruns Airfield Number 2, Hills PETER and 199–OBOE.

1945

		28 February	American Army troops invade Palawan, Philippine Islands.
5 January	U. S. Navy vessels shell Iwo Jima.	2 March	Marines of the 5th Division overrun Hill 362A.
9 January	U. S. Sixth Army invades Luzon.	3 March	Marines of the 3d Division clear Airfield Number 3.
24 January	Powerful U. S. naval surface force bombards Iwo Jima.		5th Division captures Hill 362B.
3 February	American troops re-enter Manila.	4 March	First B–29 lands on Iwo Jima.
15–16 February	V Amphibious Corps Landing Force departs Marianas after final rehearsals for assault on Iwo Jima.	6 March	15th Fighter Group (USAAF) arrives on Iwo Jima with P–51's and P–61's.
16 February	Admiral Mitscher's Fast Carrier Force (TF 58) launches 2-day air strike against Honshu to divert attention from Iwo Jima operation.	7 March	Major General James E. Chaney (USA), Island Commander, assumes responsibility for island base development, air defense, and airfield operation.
16–18 February	Amphibious Support Force (TF 52) conducts preparation bombardment of Iwo Jima with aircraft and gunfire.		3d Division makes predawn attack against Hill 362C. Hill captured later in the day.
19 February	The 4th and 5th Marine Divisions assault Iwo Jima and gain foothold.	8 March	Japanese night counterattack (night of 8–9 March) repulsed by 4th Division.
21 February	The 21st Marines (VAC Reserve) committed in 4th Division zone of action.	9 March	General Holland M. Smith's Expeditionary Troops (TF 56) Command Post transfers from *Eldorado* to *Auburn* and Admiral Turner and staff on board *Eldorado* leave for Guam. Task Forces 51, 52, 53, 54, and 56 all disbanded. Rear Admiral Harry W. Hill
	Japanese *Kamikaze* air attack made on support ships off Iwo Jima.		

	assumes duties of Senior Officer Present Afloat, Iwo Jima.
	3d Division patrols reach northeast coast.
10 March	4th Division troops break through to the east coast, pinch out enemy salient around Amphitheater and Turkey Knob.
	Americans land on Mindanao, Philippine Islands.
11 March	Iwo-based Army fighter planes assume responsibility for providing air defense and ground support missions when last Navy escort carriers leave.
14 March	Official flag raising ceremony marks proclamation of U. S. Navy Military Government in Volcano Islands. Commander, Expeditionary Troops departs for Guam.
	First Marine units commence loading out for departure from Iwo.
16 March	Last enemy opposition crushed in 3d Division zone with elimination of Cushman's Pocket.
	Final Japanese resistance destroyed in 4th Division zone as last enemy-held pocket is wiped out.
	Iwo Jima declared secured at 1800 after 26 days of bitter assault.
20 March	147th Infantry Regiment (USA) arrives for garrison duty.
25 March	Final Japanese pocket of resistance on Iwo Jima eliminated by 5th Division.
26 March	Japanese survivors launch desperate early morning attack in 5th Division zone against Marine and Army

	bivouac areas near the west coast.
	Capture and occupation phase announced completed at 0800.
	Commander Forward Area, Central Pacific, Vice Admiral John H. Hoover, assumes responsibility for the defense and development of Iwo Jima.
	Major General Chaney assumes operational control of all units on the island.
	Major General Harry Schmidt closes VAC Command Post ashore and departs by air, leaving the 9th Marines to assist in mop-up activities.
1 April	American troops land on Cebu Island, Philippine Islands.
	U. S. Tenth Army (including the 1st and 6th Marine Divisions) lands on Okinawa, Ryukyu Islands.
4 April	147th Infantry assumes full responsibility for ground defense and mopping up on Iwo Jima and the 9th Marines prepares to leave.
7 April	Eighty P-51's flying from Iwo Jima escort B-29's over Japan in first of U. S. land-based fighter aircraft flights to the enemy home islands.
18 April	Last Marines leave Iwo Jima.
22 June	Japanese resistance ceases on Okinawa.
5 July	Philippine Islands Campaign ends.
6 August	B-29 flying from Marianas drops atomic bomb on Hiroshima, Japan.
9 August	Second atomic bomb hits Nagasaki, Japan.
10 August	Japan sues for peace.

217

APPENDIX III

Casualties[1]

UNIT	Killed in Action		Died of Wounds		Wounded in Action		Total	
	Off	Enl	Off	Enl	Off	Enl	Off	Enl
V Corps[2]	1	25	0	14	22	212	23	249
3d Marine Division								
Division Troops[3]	6	151	2	41	25	573	33	775
9th Marines								
H&S and Weapons......	0	15	0	5	7	74	7	94
1st Bn................	5	124	1	34	14	423	20	581
2d Bn................	4	170	2	41	20	389	26	600
3d Bn................	32	104	3	24	19	326	54	454
21st Marines								
H&S and Weapons......	0	2	0	0	1	0	1	2
1st Bn................	3	69	1	51	16	396	20	516
2d Bn................	8	95	0	20	20	441	28	556
3d Bn................	5	89	1	26	18	383	24	498
12th Marines								
H&S Btry.............	0	0	0	0	0	4	0	4
1st Bn................	0	6	1	2	8	38	9	46
2d Bn................	1	3	1	4	3	38	5	45
3d Bn................	0	0	0	0	1	9	1	9
4th Bn................	1	2	0	0	3	18	4	20
3d Tank Bn.............	0	23	0	2	8	85	8	110
3d Engineer Bn..........	0	5	0	4	3	92	3	101

[1] Marine Corps casualty figures furnished by Personnel Accounting Section, Records Branch, Personnel Department, HQMC. These figures were certified and released in August 1952.

[2] V Corps category includes: VAC Hq Bn, 1st Prov Fld Arty Gp, 8th Fld Dpt, 2d Arm Amph Trac Bn, 2d Sep Engr Bn, VAC Sig Bn, VAC Med Bn, 2d Bomb Disp Co, Co B of FMFPac Amph Recon Bn, 2d Sep Topo Co, and other Corps Hq Troops.

[3] 3d Division Troops category includes: H&S Co, Recon Co, MP Co, Sig Co, 3d JASCO, Special Wpns Bn, elements of 3d Marines attached, 28th, 30th, and 34th Repl Drafts.

UNIT	Killed in Action		Died of Wounds		Wounded in Action		Total	
	Off	Enl	Off	Enl	Off	Enl	Off	Enl
3rd Marine Division—Con.								
3d Pioneer Bn............	0	3	0	0	1	8	1	11
3d Service Bn.............	0	0	0	1	3	13	3	14
3d MT Bn...............	0	0	0	0	1	7	1	7
3d Medical Bn...........	0	0	0	0	0	12	0	12
4th Marine Division								
Division Troops [4]........	16	105	2	24	23	504	41	633
23d Marines								
H&S and Weapons......	0	24	0	3	5	81	5	108
1st Bn................	8	142	1	33	20	417	29	592
2d Bn................	5	125	3	30	26	538	34	693
3d Bn................	6	101	1	22	22	443	29	566
24th Marines								
H&S and Weapons......	0	5	0	0	1	53	1	58
1st Bn................	4	112	5	27	18	460	27	599
2d Bn................	9	138	1	31	20	516	30	685
3d Bn................	1	141	0	33	27	558	28	732
25th Marines								
H&S and Weapons......	2	9	0	6	12	79	14	94
1st Bn................	6	111	0	31	16	446	22	588
2d Bn................	8	196	0	51	19	540	27	787
3d Bn................	10	184	0	38	26	502	36	724
14th Marines								
H&S Btry.............	0	0	0	0	1	1	1	1
1st Bn................	2	14	0	8	4	75	6	97
2d Bn................	1	10	0	0	7	45	8	55
3d Bn................	3	11	1	2	7	51	11	64
4th Bn................	1	2	0	1	2	31	3	24
4th Tank Bn............	0	20	2	3	12	86	14	109
4th Engineer Bn..........	4	51	1	9	22	244	27	304
4th Pioneer Bn...........	2	24	1	4	15	143	18	171
4th Service Bn...........	0	0	0	0	1	18	1	18
4th MT Bn..............	0	1	0	0	0	7	0	8
4th Medical Bn..........	0	0	0	0	0	5	0	5
5th Amph Trac Bn........	2	8	0	0	0	35	2	43
10th Amph Trac Bn.......	0	7	0	1	0	27	0	35
5th Marine Division								
Division Troops [5]..........	22	393	2	107	32	941	56	1,441

[4] 4th Division Troops category includes: H&S Co, Recon Co, MP Co, Sig Co, 1st JASCO, Co D (Scouts) of Hq Bn, 7th War Dog Plt, 1st Prov Rkt Det, VMO–4, Amph Trk Co, 24th and 30th Repl Drafts.

[5] 5th Division Troops category includes: H&S Co, Recon Co, MP Co, Sig Co, 5th JASCO, 6th War Dog Plt, 3d Prov Rkt Det, VMO–5, 25th, 27th, 31st, and 37th Repl Drafts.

UNIT	Killed in Action		Died of Wounds		Wounded in Action		Total	
	Off	Enl	Off	Enl	Off	Enl	Off	Enl
5th Marine Division—Con.								
26th Marines								
H&S and Weapons......	1	19	2	6	9	109	12	134
1st Bn.................	4	177	2	64	30	748	36	989
2d Bn.................	2	125	4	54	28	570	34	749
3d Bn.................	5	150	2	33	24	507	31	690
27th Marines								
H&S and Weapons......	4	19	1	8	8	111	13	138
1st Bn...............	6	161	5	61	27	530	38	752
2d Bn................	2	85	2	35	22	481	26	601
3d Bn................	5	118	1	53	15	509	21	680
28th Marines								
H&S and Weapons......	1	23	0	7	3	92	4	122
1st Bn................	4	134	3	40	25	573	32	747
2d Bn................	6	138	0	34	25	586	31	758
3d Bn................	5	162	1	34	16	464	22	660
13th Marines								
H&S Btry.............	0	4	0	1	0	11	0	16
1st Bn................	4	27	2	7	5	58	11	92
2d Bn................	1	9	0	3	2	50	3	62
3d Bn................	2	22	2	6	9	78	13	106
4th Bn................	0	18	0	3	1	55	1	76
5th Tank Bn.............	1	12	0	5	8	52	9	69
5th Engineer Bn..........	1	30	0	24	11	187	12	241
5th Pioneer Bn...........	5	25	0	11	10	168	15	204
5th Service Bn............	1	5	0	2	0	41	1	48
5th MT Bn...............	0	7	1	0	4	53	5	60
5th Medical Bn...........	0	1	0	0	0	2	0	3
3d Amph Trac Bn.........	0	3	0	5	0	17	0	25
11th Amph Trac Bn.......	0	1	0	1	6	28	6	30
Marine air units and ships' detachments [6]...........	2	23	0	0	5	28	7	51
Total Marine Casualties [7]...............	215	4,339	60	1,271	826	16,446	1,101	22,056

[6] These include: Marine detachments on board the following naval vessels—*Chester, Nevada, Saratoga, Zeilon, Franklin, Randolph, Indianapolis, Boston,* and in these Marine air units—VMF 214, VMF 311, VMB 612, VMTB 131, VMTB 134, VMTB 242, VMR 052, VMR 343, VMR 353.

[7] These totals do not include 3 officers and 43 enlisted men still listed as missing, presumed dead, or the 46 officers and 2,602 enlisted men that were combat fatigue casualties during the operation.

NAVY UNITS	Killed in Action	Died of Wounds	Wounded in Action	Missing, Presumed Dead	Total
Hospital Corpsmen serving with Marine units [8]	176	19	529	0	724
Medical and Dental Officers serving with Marine Units	2	0	12	0	14
31st, 62d, and 133d Naval Construction Battalions	42	7	218	2	269
Ships, craft, and air units [9]	143	44	1,158	446	1,791
Total Navy Casualties	363	70	1,917	448	2,798

ARMY UNITS					
Units attached to V Corps Landing Force [10]	7	1	28	1	37

[8] Navy Hospital Corpsmen, Medical and Dental Officer casualty figures furnished by U. S. Navy Bureau of Medicine and Surgery, Statistics Division, "World War II Casualties," 1Aug52.

[9] Navy ships, craft, air units, and construction bn casualty figures furnished by Navy Bureau of Personnel, Personal Affairs Division, Casualty Branch. These figures were compiled and released in 1948. They include all gunfire support ships, landing ships and craft, fire support craft, carriers, transports, mine sweepers, cargo vessels, air units, UDT's, and shore-based units exclusive of medical personnel and naval construction bns attached to Marine units during the operation. Under U. S. Navy casualty accounting procedure the casualties included in the above missing, presumed dead column are broken down into four categories: presumed dead, determined dead, reported dead, and declared dead.

[10] Casualty figures taken from VAC OpRpt, Annex G; 5th MarDiv SAR, Annex A. Casualty figures are for: 138th AAA Gp (USA); 568 SAW Bn; 726th SAW Co; 49th Sig Construction Bn; 442d and 592d Port Cos; 471st, 473d, and 476th Amph Truck Cos.

APPENDIX IV

Command and Staff List

EXPEDITIONARY TROOPS (TF 56)

Commanding General..LtGen Holland M. Smith
Chief of Staff.........Col Dudley S. Brown
G–1.................Col Russell N. Jordahl
G–2.................Col Edmond J. Buckley
G–3.................Col Kenneth H. Weir
G–4.................Col George R. Rowan

V AMPHIBIOUS CORPS (VACLF)

Commanding General..MajGen Harry Schmidt
Chief of Staff.........BrigGen William W. Rogers
G–1.................Col David A. Stafford
G–2.................Col Thomas R. Yancey (USA)
G–3.................Col Edward A. Craig
G–4.................Col William F. Brown

3D MARINE DIVISION

Commanding General.MajGen Graves B. Erskine
Asst Division Com-
    mander...........Col John B. Wilson
Chief of Staff........Col Robert E. Hogaboom
D–1................Maj Irving R. Kriendler
D–2................LtCol Howard J. Turton
D–3................Col Arthur H. Butler
D–4................LtCol James D. Hittle
Headquarters Bat-
    talion............LtCol Jack F. Warner (until 14
        March)
        LtCol Carey A. Randall (after
        14 March)

3d Marines [1]

Commanding Officer..Col James A. Stuart
Executive Officer.....LtCol Newton B. Barkley
R–3................Capt Paul H. Groth

[1] This regiment did not land on Iwo Jima and did not actively participate in that operation. The 3d Marines remained in the area as ExTrpPac Reserve until 5Mar45, when it returned to Guam.

1st Battalion, 3d Marines

Battalion Commander.LtCol Ronald R. Van Stockum
Executive Officer.....Maj Leyton M. Rogers
Bn–3...............Capt Joseph V. Millerick

2d Battalion, 3d Marines

Battalion Commander.LtCol Thomas R. Stokes
Executive Officer.....Maj Howard J. Smith
Bn–3...............Capt French R. Fogle

3d Battalion, 3d Marines

Battalion Commander.LtCol Ralph L. Houser
Executive Officer.....Maj Royal R. Bastian
Bn–3...............Capt William R. Bradley

9th Marines

Commanding Officer..Col Howard N. Kenyon
Executive Officer.....LtCol Paul W. Russell
R–3................Maj Calvin W. Kunz

1st Battalion, 9th Marines

Battalion Commander.LtCol Carey A. Randall (until 6
        March)
        Maj William T. Glass (6–14
        March)
        LtCol Jack F. Warner (after 14
        March)
Executive Officer.....Capt Frank K. Finneran
Bn–3...............Capt James R. Harper (until 27
        February)
        Capt Robert R. Fairburn (after
        27 February)

2d Battalion, 9th Marines

Battalion Commander.LtCol Robert E. Cushman, Jr.
Executive Officer.....Maj William T. Glass (until 6
        March, again from 15 March)
Bn–3...............Capt Laurance W. Cracroft

3d Battalion, 9th Marines
Battalion Commander . LtCol Harold C. Boehm
Executive Officer . . . . . Maj Donald B. Hubbard
Bn-3 . . . . Capt Joseph T. McFadden

21st Marines
Commanding Officer . . Col Hartnoll J. Withers
Executive Officer . . . . . LtCol Eustace R. Smoak
R-3 . . . . Capt Andrew Hedesh

1st Battalion, 21st Marines
Battalion Commander . LtCol Marlowe C. Williams (until 22 February, WIA)
   Maj Clay M. Murray (22 February, WIA)
   Maj Robert H. Houser (after 22 February)
Executive Officer . . . . . Maj Clay M. Murray (until 22 February)
   Maj George D. Flood, Jr. (after 22 February)
Bn-3 . . . . Maj George D. Flood, Jr.

2d Battalion, 21st Marines
Battalion Commander . LtCol Lowell E. English (until 2 March, WIA)
   Maj George A. Percy (after 2 March)
Executive Officer . . . . . Maj George A. Percy (until 2 March)
   Maj Michael V. DiVita (after 2 March)
Bn-3 . . . . Capt Thomas E. Norpell

3d Battalion, 21st Marines
Battalion Commander . LtCol Wendell H. Duplantis
Executive Officer . . . . . Maj Paul M. Jones
Bn-3 . . . . 1stLt James C. Corman

12th Marines
Commanding Officer . . LtCol Raymond F. Crist, Jr.
Executive Officer . . . . . LtCol Bernard H. Kirk
R-3 . . . . LtCol Thomas R. Belzer

1st Battalion, 12th Marines
Battalion Commander . Maj George B. Thomas
Executive Officer . . . . . Maj William P. Pala
Bn-3 . . . . Maj Clarence E. Brissenden

2d Battalion, 12th Marines
Battalion Commander . LtCol William T. Fairbourn
Executive Officer . . . . . Maj Oliver E. Robinett
Bn-3 . . . . Capt Joseph F. Fogg

3d Battalion, 12th Marines
Battalion Commander . LtCol Alpha L. Bowser, Jr.
Executive Officer . . . . . Maj Claude S. Sanders, Jr.
Bn-3 . . . . Maj Wilbur R. Helmer

4th Battalion, 12th Marines
Battalion Commander . Maj Joe B. Wallen (until 20 March)
   LtCol Thomas R. Belzer (after 20 March)

4th Battalion, 12th Marines—Continued
Executive Officer . . . . . Maj David S. Randall (until 20 March)
Bn-3 . . . . Capt Lewis E. Poggemeyer

3d Tank Battalion
Battalion Commander . Maj Holly H. Evans
Executive Officer . . . . . Capt Gerald P. Foster
Bn-3 . . . . Capt Bertram A. Yaffe

3d Engineer Battalion
Battalion Commander . LtCol Walter S. Campbell
Executive Officer . . . . . Maj Eldon J. C. Rogers
Bn-3 . . . . Capt Arthur J. Wardrep, Jr.

3d Pioneer Battalion
Battalion Commander . LtCol Edmund M. Williams
Executive Officer . . . . . Maj Howard A. Hurst
Bn-3 . . . . Capt Jack R. Edwards

Service Troops, 3d Division [2]
Commanding Officer . . Col James O. Brauer (until 6 March)
   Col Lewis A. Hohn (after 6 March)
Executive Officer . . . . . Maj Reginald G. Sauls, III

3d Service Battalion
Battalion Commander . LtCol Paul G. Chandler
Executive Officer . . . . . Maj William E. Cullen
Bn-3 . . . . Capt Warren E. Smith

3d Motor Transport Battalion
Battalion Commander . LtCol Ernest W. Fry, Jr.
Executive Officer . . . . . Maj Ira E. Harrod, Jr.
Bn-3 . . . . Maj Ira E. Harrod, Jr.

3d Medical Battalion
Battalion Commander . Cdr Anthony E. Reymont (USNR)
Executive Officer . . . . . Cdr Owen Deuby (USN)

4TH MARINE DIVISION
Commanding General . MajGen Clifton B. Cates
Asst Division Commander . . . . BrigGen Franklin A. Hart
Chief of Staff . . . . Col Merton J. Batchelder
D-1 . . . . Col Orin H. Wheeler
D-2 . . . . LtCol Gooderham L. McCormick
D-3 . . . . Col Edwin A. Pollock
D-4 . . . . Col Matthew C. Horner
Headquarters Battalion . . . . Col Bertrand T. Fay
Commander Support Group [3] . . . . LtCol Melvin L. Krulewitch

[2] This command was superimposed upon and coordinated the activities of the Service, Motor Transport, and Medical Bns.

[3] The 4th MarDiv Support Group task organization for Iwo Jima as follows: HqBn (less dets); 4th MT Bn (less Cos A, B, and C); 4th Tank Bn (less Cos A, B, and C plus Main Plt, Ord Co, 4th Serv Bn); 4th Serv

23d Marines

Commanding Officer. . Col Walter W. Wensinger
Executive Officer. . . . . LtCol Edward J. Dillon
R–3. . . . . Maj Henry S. Campbell

1st Battalion, 23d Marines

Battalion Commander. LtCol Ralph Haas (until 20 February, KIA)
Lt Col Louis B. Blissard (after 20 February)
Executive Officer. . . . . LtCol Louis B. Blissard (until 20 February)
Bn–3. . . . . Capt Fred C. Eberhardt (until 20 February, KIA)
Maj James W. Sperry (after 20 February)

2d Battalion, 23d Marines

Battalion Commander. Maj Robert H. Davidson (until 7 March, WIA, and again from 11 March)
Lt Col Edward J. Dillon (7–11 March)
Executive Officer. . . . . Maj John J. Padley (until 7 March, WIA)
Capt Carl O. J. Grussendorf (after 7 March)
Bn–3. . . . . Capt Edward J. Schofield (until 7 March, WIA)

3d Battalion, 23d Marines

Battalion Commander. Maj James S. Scales
Executive Officer. . . . . Maj Philip J. Maloney
Bn–3. . . . . Maj William H. Cushing

24th Marines

Commanding Officer. . Col Walter I. Jordan
Executive Officer. . . . . LtCol Austin R. Brunelli (until 8 March)
R–3. . . . . Maj Webb D. Sawyer

1st Battalion, 24th Marines

Battalion Commander. Maj Paul S. Treitel (until 8 March)
LtCol Austin R. Brunelli (after 8 March)
Executive Officer. . . . . Maj Horace C. Parks
Bn–3. . . . . Maj Irving Schechter (until 8 March)
Maj George D. Webster (after 8 March)

Bn (less dets); 4th Med Bn (less Cos A, B, and C); 4th Engr Bn (less Cos A, B, and C); 2d Arm Amph Bn (less Cos A, B, C, D, and det of Bn Hq); Div Rcn Co; 1st JASCO (less dets); 1st Prov Rocket Det (less 1st and 2d Secs); Det 726th SAW Co); JICPOA Int Team; Det Sig Bn, VAC; Corps Ln Gp. After the landing the following groups were also attached: 5th Amph Trac Bn; 10th Amph Trac Bn; 24th and 30th Repl Drafts.

2d Battalion, 24th Marines

Battalion Commander. LtCol Richard Rothwell
Executive Officer. . . . . Maj Frank E. Garretson
Bn–3. . . . . Capt John F. Ross, Jr. (until 20 February, WIA)
Maj Charles C. Berkeley, Jr. (after 20 February)

3d Battalion, 24th Marines

Battalion Commander. LtCol Alexander A. Vandegrift, Jr. (until 23 February, WIA)
Maj Doyle A. Stout (after 23 February)
Executive Officer. . . . . Maj Doyle A. Stout (until 23 February)
Maj Albert Arsenault (after 23 February)
Bn–3. . . . . Maj Albert Arsenault (until 23 February)
Maj William C. Esterline (after 25 February)

25th Marines

Commanding Officer. . Col John R. Lanigan
Executive Officer. . . . . LtCol Clarence J. O'Donnell
R–3. . . . . Maj John H. Jones

1st Battalion, 25th Marines

Battalion Commander. LtCol Hollis U. Mustain (until 21 February, KIA)
Maj Fenton J. Mee (after 21 February)
Executive Officer. . . . . Maj Henry D. Strunk (until 19 February WIA)
Maj Fenton J. Mee (from 19–21 February)
Maj Edward L. Asbill (after 21 February)
Bn–3. . . . . Maj Fenton J. Mee (until 21 February)
Capt William J. Weinstein (after 21 February)

2d Battalion, 25th Marines

Battalion Commander. LtCol Lewis C. Hudson, Jr. (until 20 February, WIA)
LtCol James Taul (after 20 February)
Executive Officer. . . . . Maj William P. Kaempfer (until 20 February, WIA)
Bn–3. . . . . Maj Donald K. Ellis (until 20 February, WIA)
Capt Edward H. Birkenmeier, Jr. (after 26 February)

3d Battalion, 25th Marines

Battalion Commander. LtCol Justice M. Chambers (until 22 February, WIA)
Capt James C. Headley (after 22 February)

3d Battalion, 25th Marines—Continued

Executive Officer.....LtCol James Taul (until 20 February)
Capt James Antink (after 22 February)
Bn-3...............Maj Lawrence M. Rulison (until 19 February, WIA)
Capt Elwyn W. Woods (after 12 March)

14th Marines

Commanding Officer..Col Louis G. De Haven
Executive Officer.....LtCol Randall M. Victory
R-3..................Maj Frederick J. Karch

1st Battalion, 14th Marines

Battalion Commander.Maj John B. Edgar, Jr.
Executive Officer.....Maj Charles V. Watson
Bn-3...............Capt Raymond Jenkins

2d Battalion, 14th Marines

Battalion Commander.Maj Clifford B. Drake
Executive Officer.....Maj Donald E. Noll
Bn-3...............Maj Ralph W. Boyer

3d Battalion, 14th Marines

Battalion Commander.LtCol Robert E. MacFarlane (until 19 February, WIA)
Maj Harvey A. Feehan (19–23 February, after 10 March)
LtCol Carl A. Youngdale (23 February until 10 March)
Executive Officer.....Maj Harvey A. Feehan (until 19 February, again 23 February until 10 March)
Bn-3...............1stLt Bernard J. Diggs

4th Battalion, 14th Marines

Battalion Commander.LtCol Carl A. Youngdale (until 23 February, again after 10 March)
Maj Roland J. Spritzen (23 February until 10 March)
Executive Officer.....Maj Roland J. Spritzen
Bn-3...............Capt Russell F. Schoenbeck

4th Tank Battalion

Battalion Commander.LtCol Richard K. Schmidt
Executive Officer.....Maj Francis L. Orgain
Bn-3...............Maj Leo B. Case

4th Engineer Battalion

Battalion Commander.LtCol Nelson K. Brown
Executive Officer.....Maj Melvin D. Henderson
Bn-3...............Maj Melvin D. Henderson

4th Pioneer Battalion

Battalion Commander.LtCol Richard G. Ruby
Executive Officer.....Maj John H. Partridge
Bn-3...............Capt George A. Smith

4th Service Battalion

Battalion Commander.LtCol John E. Fondahl
Executive Officer.....Maj Henry P. Welton
Bn-3...............1stLt James T. Willis

4th Motor Transport Battalion

Battalion Commander.LtCol Ralph L. Schiesswohl
Executive Officer.....Maj Michael J. Danneker
Bn-3...............(Not shown)

4th Medical Battalion

Battalion Commander.Cdr Reuben L. Sharp (USNR)
Executive Officer.....LCdr Eugene G. McCarthy (USNR)

5th Amphibian Tractor Battalion

Battalion Commander.Maj George L. Shead
Executive Officer.....Capt William C. Stoll, Jr.
Bn-3...............Capt William S. Clark

10th Amphibian Tractor Battalion

Battalion Commander.Maj Victor J. Croizat
Executive Officer.....Maj Harry T. Marshall, Jr.
Bn-3...............Capt George A. Vradenburg, Jr.

5TH MARINE DIVISION

Commanding General.MajGen Keller E. Rockey
Asst Division Commander..........BrigGen Leo D. Hermle
Chief of Staff........Col Ray A. Robinson
D-1.................Col John W. Beckett
D-2..............LtCol George A. Roll
D-3.................Col James F. Shaw, Jr.
D-4.................Col Earl S. Piper
D-5...............LtCol Frederick R. Dowsett
Headquarters Battalion............Maj John Ayrault, Jr.

26th Marines

Commanding Officer..Col Chester B. Graham
Executive Officer.....Col Lester S. Hamel
R-3...............LtCol William K. Davenport, Jr.

1st Battalion, 26th Marines

Battalion Commander.LtCol Daniel C. Pollock (until 19 March, WIA)
Maj Albert V. K. Gary (after 19 March)
Executive Officer.....Maj Albert V. K. Gary (until 19 March)
Bn-3...............Capt Aram S. Rejebian

2d Battalion, 26th Marines

Battalion Commander.LtCol Joseph P. Sayers (until 23 February, WIA)
Maj Amedeo Rea (after 23 February)
Executive Officer.....Maj Amedeo Rea (until 23 February)
Capt Thomas M. Fields (after 23 February)
Bn-3...............1stLt Royer G. Warren (until 26 February, WIA)
2dLt William M. Adams, Jr. (after 26 February)

3d Battalion, 26th Marines

Battalion Commander . LtCol Tom M. Trotti (until 22 February, KIA)

Capt Richard M. Cook (22 February only)

Maj Richard Fagan (after 22 February)

Executive Officer . . . . . Maj George F. Waters, Jr. (until 20 February, WIA)

Maj Chester E. Bennett (after 6 March)

Bn–3 . . . . Maj William R. Day (until 22 February, KIA)

Capt Conrad A. Pearson (after 22 February)

27th Marines

Commanding Officer . . Col Thomas A. Wornham

Executive Officer . . . . . Col Louis C. Plain (WIA 19 February)

LtCol James P. Berkeley (after 15 March)

R–3 . . . . LtCol Justin G. Duryea (until 5 March)

Capt Franklin L. Smith (after 5 March)

1st Battalion, 27th Marines

Battalion Commander . LtCol John A. Butler (until 5 March, KIA)

LtCol Justin G. Duryea (5 until 9 March, WIA)

Maj William H. Tumbelston (9 until 14 March, WIA)

Maj William H. Kennedy, Jr. (after 14 March)

Executive Officer . . . . . Maj William H. Tumbelston (until 9 March)

Maj William H. Kennedy, Jr. (9–14 March)

Maj Ronald F. Adams (after 14 March)

Bn–3 . . . . Capt Thomas R. Shepard (until 14 March, WIA)

2d Battalion, 27th Marines

Battalion Commander . Maj John W. Antonelli (until 9 March, WIA)

Maj Gerald F. Russell (after 9 March)

Executive Officer . . . . . Maj Gerald F. Russell (until 9 March)

Bn–3 . . . . Maj C. J. Chandler, Jr.

3d Battalion, 27th Marines

Battalion Commander . LtCol Donn J. Robertson

Executive Officer . . . . . Maj Frederick J. Mix, Jr.

Bn–3 . . . . Maj William H. Kennedy, Jr. (until 9 March)

Maj Frederick J. Mix, Jr. (after 9 March)

28th Marines

Commanding Officer . . Col Harry B. Liversedge

Executive Officer . . . . . LtCol Robert H. Williams

R–3 . . . . Maj Oscar F. Peatross (until 14 March)

LtCol Charles E. Shepard, Jr. (15–25 March)

1st Battalion, 28th Marines

Battalion Commander . LtCol Jackson B. Butterfield

Executive Officer . . . . . Maj William A. Wood

Bn–3 . . . . 1stLt William R. Henderson

2d Battalion, 28th Marines

Battalion Commander . LtCol Chandler W. Johnson (until 2 March, KIA)

Maj Thomas B. Pearce, Jr. (after 2 March)

Executive Officer . . . . . Maj Thomas B. Pearce, Jr. (until 2 March)

Maj James H. Finch (after 2 March)

Bn–3 . . . . Capt Martin W. Reinemann

3d Battalion, 28th Marines

Battalion Commander . LtCol Charles E. Shepard, Jr. (until 14 March and from 25 March)

Maj. Tolson A. Smoak (14–25 March)

Executive Officer . . . . . Maj Tolson A. Smoak (until 14 March and from 25 March)

Maj Oscar F. Peatross (14–25 March)

Bn–3 . . . . Capt. Robert N. Spangler

13th Marines

Commanding Officer . . Col James D. Waller

Executive Officer . . . . . LtCol Kenyth A. Damke

R–3 . . . . LtCol Jack Tabor

1st Battalion, 13th Marines

Battalion Commander . LtCol John S. Oldfield

Executive Officer . . . . . Maj Edward O. Cerf

Bn–3 . . . . Maj James R. Crockett

2d Battalion, 13th Marines

Battalion Commander . Maj Carl W. Hjerpe

Executive Officer . . . . . Maj Olin W. Jones, Jr.

Bn–3 . . . . Maj George E. Moore

3d Battalion, 13th Marines

Battalion Commander . LtCol Henry T. Waller

Executive Officer . . . . . Maj William M. Miller

Bn–3 . . . . Maj Edwin N. Kittrell, Jr.

4th Battalion, 13th Marines

Battalion Commander . Maj James F. Coady

Executive Officer . . . . . Maj William W. Mitchell

Bn–3 . . . . Capt. Jackson C. Turnacliff

Service Troops [4]

Commanding Officer..Col Benjamin W. Gally
Executive Officer.....LtCol Robert L. Cooper

5th Tank Battalion

Battalion Commander.LtCol William R. Collins
Executive Officer.....Maj Gardelle Lewis (until 26 February)
　　　　　　　　　Maj John L. Frothingham (after 26 February)
Bn–3...............1stLt George C. Moore

5th Engineer Battalion

Battalion Commander.LtCol Clifford H. Shuey
Executive Officer.....Maj Herbert I. McCoy
Bn–3...............Capt Richard J. MacLaury

5th Pioneer Battalion

Battalion Commander.Maj Robert S. Riddell
Executive Officer.....Maj Rupert C. Henley
Bn–3...............Capt Harold A. Hayes, Jr.

5th Service Battalion

Battalion Commander.Maj Francis P. Daly (until 22 February, KIA)
　　　　　　　　　Maj Gardelle Lewis (after 26 February)
Battalion Adjutant...1stLt William A. Brokaw

5th Motor Transport Battalion

Battalion Commander.Maj Arthur F. Torgler, Jr.
Executive Officer.....Capt Herbert E. Pierce
Bn–3...............Capt William Montagna

5th Medical Battalion

Battalion Commander.LCdr William W. Ayres (USN)
Executive Officer.....LCdr John E. Gorman (USN)

3d Amphibian Tractor Battalion

Battalion Commander.LtCol Sylvester L. Stephan
Executive Officer.....Maj Erwin F. Wann, Jr.
Bn–3...............Maj George M. Foote

11th Amphibian Tractor Battalion

Battalion Commander.LtCol Albert J. Roose
Executive Officer.....Maj Robert W. Dyer
Bn–3...............Capt Leopold Fiske

V AMPHIBIOUS CORPS (and major attached units)

Corps Troops

Commanding Officer...Col Alton A. Gladden

Hq and Serv Bn, VAC

Commanding Officer...Capt Cyril M. Milbrath

[4] The Service Troops command controlled and coordinated the activities of the following units of the 5th Division: Hq Co, Hq Bn; Recon Co; Sig Co; MP Co; 5th Serv Bn; 5th MT Bn; 5th Tk Bn; 5th Engr Bn; 5th Pion Bn; and 5th Med Bn.

1st Provisional Field Artillery Group

Group Commander...Col John S. Letcher
Executive Officer.....LtCol Marvin H. Floom
Gp–3..............Maj William G. Winters, Jr.

2d 155mm Howitzer Battalion (1st Prov FA Group)

Battalion Commander.Maj Earl J. Rowse
Executive Officer.....Maj Alexander A. Elder
Bn–3...............Capt Earl N. Lewis

4th 155mm Howitzer Battalion (1st Prov FA Group)

Battalion Commander.LtCol Douglas E. Reeve
Executive Officer.....Maj Marvin R. Burditt
Bn–3...............Maj Joe H. Daniel

138th AA Group (USA)

Group Commander...Col Clarence E. Rothgeb

506th AA Gun Battalion (138th AA Group, USA)

Battalion Commander.LtCol D. M. White

483d AAAW Battalion (138th AA Group, USA)

Battalion Commander.LtCol A. Roth

8th Field Depot

Commanding Officer..Col Leland S. Swindler

Landing Force Air Support Control Unit

Commanding Officer..Col Vernon E. Megee

VAC Signal Battalion

Commanding Officer..LtCol Alfred F. Robertshaw

VAC Medical Battalion

Commanding Officer..LCdr William B. Clapp (USNR)

Provisional Signal Group

Commanding Officer..LtCol Harry W. G. Vadnais

Hq, Provisional LVT Group

Commanding Officer..Maj Henry G. Lawrence, Jr.

2d Separate Engineer Battalion

Commanding Officer..LtCol Charles O. Clark

2d Armored Amphibian Battalion

Commanding Officer..LtCol Reed M. Fawell, Jr.

23d Naval Construction Battalion (Cos A and B)

Commanding Officer..Cdr H. W. Heuer (USN)

31st Naval Construction Battalion

Commanding Officer..LCdr D. J. Ermilio (USNR)

62d Naval Construction Battalion

Commanding Officer..LCdr F. B. Campbell (USNR)

133d Naval Construction Battalion

Commanding Officer..LCdr R. P. Murphy (USNR)

Corps Evacuation Hospital Number 1

Commanding Officer..Capt H. G. Young (USN)

38th Field Hospital, Reinforced (USA)

Commanding Officer..Maj Samuel S. Kirkland

APPENDIX V — Task Organization

EXPEDITIONARY TROOPS—Lieutenant General Holland M. Smith

Corps Troops

Headquarters and Service Battalion, V Amphibious Corps (less detachments)

Medical Battalion, V Amphibious Corps

Motor Transport Company, V Amphibious Corps

Provisional Signal Group, V Amphibious Corps

    Landing Force Headquarters Signal Section

    Signal Battalion, V Amphibious Corps (less detachments)

    Shore Party Communication Unit

    Detachment, Signal Company, 8th Field Depot

    Detachment, 1st Separate Reconnaissance and Intelligence Platoon

    Detachment, Signal Headquarters Company, VII Fighter Command (USA)

    Detachment, 568th Signal Air Warning Battalion (USA)

    Detachment, 726th Signal Air Warning Company (USA)

    Detachment, 49th Signal Construction Battalion (USA)

    Detachment 44, 70th Army Airways Communications System (USA)

    Detachment, Communications Unit 434

Landing Force Air Support Control Unit

Headquarters, Provisional LVT Group

2d Separate Engineer Battalion

62d Naval Construction Battalion (less detachments)

23d Naval Construction Battalion (Cos A and B)

8th Field Depot (less detachments, plus VAC Shore Party Headquarters)

Corps Evacuation Hospital No. 1

2d Bomb Disposal Company, plus 156th Bomb Disposal Squad

Company B, Amphibious Reconnaissance Battalion (FMFPac)

38th Field Hospital, Reinforced (USA)

Medical Section, Civil Affairs

Joint Intelligence Center Pacific Ocean Areas Intelligence Team

Joint Intelligence Center Pacific Ocean Areas Enemy Materiel and Salvage Platoon

Corps Artillery

1st Provisional Field Artillery Group

    Headquarters Battery

    2d 155mm Howitzer Battalion

    4th 155mm Howitzer Battalion

    473d Amphibian Truck Company (USA)

Antiaircraft Artillery

138th AAA Group (less detachments) (USA)

    Headquarters Battery, 138th AAA Group (USA)

    506th AA Gun Battalion (USA)

    483d AA Automatic Weapons Battalion (USA)

a. *4th Marine Division* (Reinforced)—Major General Clifton B. Cates

    4th Marine Division

    Companies A and B, plus Detachment, Battalion Headquarters, 2d Armored Amphibian Battalion

    5th Amphibian Tractor Battalion

    10th Amphibian Tractor Battalion

    1st Joint Assault Signal Company

    Marine Observation Squadron 4

    133d Naval Construction Battalion

    4th Marine Amphibian Truck Company

    476th Amphibian Truck Company (USA)

    7th War Dog Platoon

    1st Provisional Rocket Detachment

Detachment, 8th Field Depot
Detachment, 726th Signal Air Warning Company (USA)
Detachment, Signal Battalion, V Amphibious Corps
442d Port Company (USA)
Joint Intelligence Center Pacific Ocean Areas Intelligence Team
24th Replacement Draft
30th Replacement Draft

b. *5th Marine Division* (Reinforced)—Major General Keller E. Rockey
5th Marine Division
5th Marine Amphibian Truck Company
5th Joint Assault Signal Company
471st Amphibian Truck Company (USA)
11th Amphibian Tractor Battalion
3d Amphibian Tractor Battalion
Companies C and D and Detachment, Headquarters Battalion, 2d Armored Amphibian Battalion
Marine Observation Squadron 5
3d Provisional Rocket Detachment
6th Marine War Dog Platoon
592d Port Company (USA)
31st Naval Construction Battalion
27th Replacement Draft
31st Replacement Draft
Detachment, 726th Signal Air Warning Company (USA)
Joint Intelligence Center Pacific Ocean Areas Intelligence Team
Detachment, Signal Battalion, V Amphibious Corps
Detachment, 8th Field Depot
Liaison Group, V Amphibious Corps
Liaison Group, Fleet Marine Force, Pacific V Amphibious Corps Reserve

c. *21st Marines*

d. *3d Marine Division* (Reinforced)—Major General Graves B. Erskine [1]
3d Marine Division (less 21st Marines)
3d Joint Assault Signal Company
Marine Observation Squadron 1
3d Marine War Dog Platoon
Joint Intelligence Center Pacific Ocean Areas Intelligence Team
Detachment, Signal Battalion, V Amphibious Corps
28th Replacement Draft
34th Replacement Draft

e. *Garrison Forces* (Assault Echelon)—Major General James E. Chaney, USA [2]
Detachment, Island Command Headquarters
Detachment, 147th Army Infantry Regiment
Detachment, Headquarters, VII Fighter Command
Detachment, Headquarters, 15th Fighter Group
47th Fighter Squadron
78th Fighter Squadron
548th Night Fighter Service
386th Air Service Group, Special
1st Platoon, 604th Quartermaster Graves Registration Company
223d Radar Maintenance Unit (Type C)
Detachment, Administrative Unit, Group Pacific 11
Port Directors Detachment
Garrison Beach Party

---

[1] The 3d Marine Division (Expeditionary Troops Reserve) was released, less the 3d Marines, to V Amphibious Corps Landing Force control on 23Feb45. *VAC Personnel Rpt*, 4.

[2] These Army units were attached to assault elements of V Corps for transportation and/or employment in the assault phase. Additional Army units were attached to divisions and were listed with the task organization of those commands. *VAC Personnel Rpt*, 1.

APPENDIX VI   Japanese Order of Battle

ESTIMATED ENEMY STRENGTH AT IWO JIMA ON 19 FEBRUARY 1945

Army Units

109th Division—Lieutenant General Tadamichi Kuribayashi [1]

109th Division Headquarters and Signal Company. .300

109th Division Antiaircraft Artillery Battalion—Major Azuma..........................310–340

2d Mixed Brigade—Major General Senda. .5,100–5,200

    309th Independent Infantry Battalion—Captain Awatsu

    310th Independent Infantry Battalion—Major Iwatani

    311th Independent Infantry Battalion—Major Tatsumi

    312th Independent Infantry Battalion—Captain Osada

    314th Independent Infantry Battalion—Captain Hakuda

    Artillery Battalion, 2d Mixed Brigade—Major Maeda

    Engineer Battalion, 2d Mixed Brigade—Major Maekawa

    Field Hospital, 2d Mixed Brigade—commander not shown

145th Infantry Regiment—Colonel Ikeda . 2,200–2,400

    1st Battalion, 145th Regiment—Major Hara

    2d Battalion, 145th Regiment—Major Yasutake

    3d Battalion, 145th Regiment—Major Anso

    Artillery Battalion, 145th Regiment—Captain Masuda

    Engineer Company, 145th Regiment—commander not shown

    Field Hospital, 145th Regiment—commander not shown

---

[1] General Kuribayashi also commanded the Ogasawara Army Group and held over-all command of the defense of Iwo Jima.

3d Battalion, 17th Independent Mixed Regiment—Captain Shimotsuma..................550

26th Tank Regiment—Lieutenant Colonel Nishi 500–600

20th Independent Artillery Mortar Battalion (Reinforced)—Captain Mizuashi..............800

2d Medium Mortar Battalion (Reinforced)—Major Nakao..............................700

3d Medium Mortar Battalion (Reinforced)—Major Kobayashi..........................500

1st and 2d Independent Machine Gun Battalions. .600

    1st Independent Machine Gun Battalion—Captain Kawana

    2d Independent Machine Gun Battalion—Captain Kawasaki

Independent Antitank Battalions..............1, 250

    8th Independent Antitank Battalion—Captain Shimizu

    9th Independent Antitank Battalion—Major Okubo

    10th Independent Antitank Battalion—Major Matsushita

    11th Independent Antitank Battalion—Captain Node

    12th Independent Antitank Battalion—Captain Hayauchi

Army Rocket Unit (three companies)........150–220

1st Company, 1st Mixed Brigade Engineer Unit; 5th Fortress Construction Duty Company; 21st Well Drilling Unit; Detachment, Shipping Engineers 300

Special Machine Cannon Units..............250–300

    20th Special Machine Cannon Unit (with Naval Guard Force)—2dLt Momozaki

    21st Special Machine Cannon Unit (with Naval Guard Force)—2dLt Kondo

    43d Special Machine Cannon Unit (with 109th Division AA Artillery)—1stLt Tamara

    44th Special Machine Cannon Unit (with 109th Division AA Artillery)—commander not shown

Navy Units

Naval Forces on Iwo Jima (over-all command)—
  Rear Admiral Ichimaru
27th Air Flotilla and 2d Air Attack Force—
  Rear Admiral Ichimaru
Iwo Jima Naval Guard Force—Captain Inoue
Naval Guard Force Antiaircraft Batteries [2]......2,400
  125th Antiaircraft Defense Unit—Lt(jg)
    Tamura
  132d Antiaircraft Defense Unit—Ensign
    Okumura
  149th Antiaircraft Defense Unit—commander
    not known
  141st Antiaircraft Defense Unit—Lt(jg) Doi

---

[2] The 125th, 132d, 141st, 149th Naval Antiaircraft Defense Units were disbanded and reorganized into the

Naval Guard Force Coast Defense Batteries......640
Nanpo Air Group Naval Land Force—
  Captain Inoue
  Southern Air Group (Naval Guard Force
    troops, construction personnel, technicians).2,250
  204th Naval Construction Battalion—Lt Iida..1,410
  Technical Air Personnel......................320
                                        _____

  Total Japanese troops on Iwo
    Jima, 19Feb45 [3]............20,530–21,060

Iwo Jima Naval Guard Force prior to 19Feb45. *VAC IntelRpt*, Encl A.

[3] *Ibid.*, 14.

APPENDIX VII Task Force Organization and Command Relationship

In over-all command of the Iwo Jima operation was Admiral Raymond A. Spruance commanding Task Force 50 (Fifth Fleet). Subordinate task organizations participating in the assault on the Volcano-Bonins were:

TASK FORCE 51 (Joint Expeditionary Force), commanded by Vice Admiral Richmond K. Turner, Commander Amphibious Forces, U. S. Pacific Fleet. Task Forces functioning under Joint Expeditionary Force command were as follows:

TASK FORCE 52 (Amphibious Support Force), commanded by Rear Admiral William H. P. Blandy, included an Air Support Control Unit, Support Carrier Group, Mine Group, Underwater Demolitions Group, Gunboat Support Group, Mortar Support Group, and a Rocket Support Group. The mission of this force was to furnish preliminary (pre-D-Day) gunfire and air support including preparation fires, mine sweeping, net laying, beach reconnaissance, and underwater demolition. At 0600 D-Day, TF 52 passed to the direct command of Vice Admiral Turner. Rear Admiral Blandy then assumed command of TG 51.19 (Night Retirement Groups).

TASK FORCE 53 (Attack Force), commanded by Rear Admiral Harry W. Hill. This force was comprised of an air support control unit, embarked assault troops, two transport squadrons, tractor groups, LSM groups, control group, beach party group, and a pontoon barge, causeway, and LCT group. Its mission was to transport and land the Expeditionary Troops.

TASK FORCE 54 (Gunfire and Covering Force), commanded by Rear Admiral Bertram J. Rodgers. This force was composed of three battleship divisions, one cruiser division, three destroyer divisions, and was reinforced on D-Day by an additional two destroyer divisions from Task Force 58. On D-plus 1 two cruiser divisions and two more destroyer divisions from TF 58 joined the Gunfire and Covering Force off Iwo Jima. The potent aggregation thus assembled combined their power to furnish shore bombardment and protect the vulnerable invasion shipping from enemy surface attack.

TASK FORCE 56 (Expeditionary Troops), commanded by Lieutenant General Holland M. Smith. Under this command were all assault troops and certain assigned garrison troops. Units under General Smith's command were responsible for executing all ground attacks and, in the later stages, certain shore-based air operations during the effort to capture, occupy, and defend Iwo Jima. Subordinate units of TF 56 were as follows:

TASK GROUP 56.1 (Landing Force), commanded by Major General Harry Schmidt. General Schmidt's Landing Force Headquarters provided over-all command and coordination of all troops ashore, including shore-based air units, during the attack.

TASK GROUP 56.2 (Assault Troops), 4th and 5th Marine Divisions commanded by Major Generals Clifton B. Cates and Keller E. Rockey, respectively, plus Corps Troops.

TASK GROUP 10.16 (Army Garrison Force), commanded by Major General James E. Chaney, USA.

TASK GROUP 56.3 (Expeditionary Troops Reserve), the 3d Marine Division (Reinforced) commanded by Major General Graves B. Erskine.

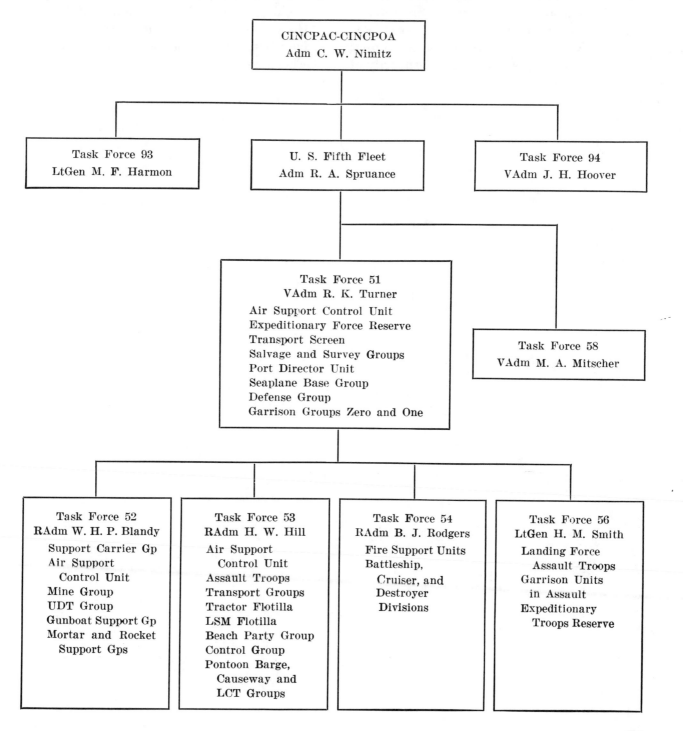

Other task forces supporting the Iwo Jima assault included:

TASK FORCE 58 (Fast Carrier Force of Admiral Spruance's Fifth Fleet), commanded by Vice Admiral Marc A. Mitscher. Carrier aircraft of TF 58 supported the Iwo operation through diversionary strikes on the enemy homeland and supplied close air support at the objective. Fire support vessels of TF 58 also provided valuable firepower at Iwo for several days commencing on D-Day.

TASK FORCE 93 (Strategic Air Force, Pacific Ocean Areas), composed primarily of land-based heavy bombers flying from airfields in the Marianas. These planes, predominantly B-24's of the Seventh USAAF, helped soften the target for assault and, beginning on D-Day, delivered several deep support air strikes on the objective and night harrassing and destructive air strikes on the Bonin Islands.

TASK FORCE 94 (Forward Area, Central Pacific), under Vice Admiral John H. Hoover, provided assault forces with base facilities, logistical support and various rear echelon services.

APPENDIX VIII Medal of Honor Winners

CORPORAL CHARLES J. BERRY, 1st Battalion, 26th Marines. During a nighttime hand-grenade duel with infiltrating Japanese he threw himself to cover an exploding enemy missile with his body saving his comrades from serious injury. (3 March 1945)*

PRIVATE FIRST CLASS WILLIAM R. CADDY, 3d Battalion, 26th Marines. When an enemy grenade fell in a shell hole he occupied with two other Marines he smothered the explosion with his body protecting his comrades from serious injury. (3 March 1945)*

*Indicates posthumous award.

LIEUTENANT COLONEL JUSTICE M. CHAMBERS, 3d Battalion, 25th Marines. Exposing himself repeatedly to enemy fire he inspired his men by fearless example and aggressive leadership during the first bloody days until, seriously wounded, he was evacuated. (19–22 February 1945)

CAPTAIN ROBERT H. DUNLAP, 1st Battalion, 26th Marines. Crawling 200 yards ahead of his lines he located the source of intense enemy fire. He then manned an exposed vantage point without respite for two days and nights to direct fire against the positions. (20–21 February 1945)

SERGEANT DARRELL S. COLE, 1st Battalion, 23d Marines. When his unit was held up by five enemy pillboxes he made a daring attack armed only with a pistol and hand grenades singlehandedly destroying the hostile positions before he was killed by an enemy grenade. (19 February 1945)*

SERGEANT ROSS F. GRAY, 1st Battalion, 25th Marines. When his platoon was held up by pillboxes and a mine field he singlehandedly cleared a path through the mines, attacking and destroying six positions and more than 25 enemy soldiers. (21 February 1945)

SERGEANT WILLIAM G. HARRELL, 1st Battalion, 28th Marines. During a night infiltration he ordered his wounded comrades to safety and despite his own serious wounds waged a lone battle against a determined enemy until evacuated at dawn. (3 March 1945)

PRIVATE FIRST CLASS DOUGLAS T. JACOBSON, 3d Battalion, 23d Marines. Employing his bazooka with deadly accuracy he braved heavy enemy fire to singlehandedly destroy 16 positions and kill approximately 75 Japanese. (26 February 1945)

LIEUTENANT RUFUS G. HERRING, USNR, LCI(G) 449. Thrice wounded and suffering from loss of blood, he propped himself against empty shell cases to direct aid for the wounded and steered his shattered and burning gunboat to safety. (17 February 1945)

PLATOON SERGEANT JOSEPH R. JULIAN, 1st Battalion, 27th Marines. When his company was halted by fire from a series of mutually supporting pillboxes he executed a fearless one-man assault knocking out several positions before he fell. (9 March 1945)*

PRIVATE FIRST CLASS JAMES D. LA BELLE, 27th Marines. Occupying a foxhole with two other Marines he saw a grenade fall beyond his reach in the hole. Shouting a warning, he leaped to cover the missile protecting the others from serious injury. (8 March 1945)*

PRIVATE FIRST CLASS JACKLYN H. LUCAS, 1st Battalion, 26th Marines. When two grenades landed in front of a group of Marines he leaped over the others landing on one and sweeping the other under him to smother both missiles protecting his comrades from serious injury. (20 February 1945)

SECOND LIEUTENANT JOHN H. LEIMS, 1st Battalion, 9th Marines. Having extricated his company from precarious advanced positions he made two trips forward through darkness and withering machine-gun fire to rescue wounded men from a death trap. (7 March 1945)

FIRST LIEUTENANT JACK LUMMUS, 2d Battalion, 27th Marines. Advancing with his platoon against a network of hostile positions he moved boldly ahead single-handedly destroying three pillboxes. Ignoring serious wounds he led his men until killed by a land mine. (8 March 1945)*

238

CAPTAIN JOSEPH J. McCARTHY, 2d Battalion, 24th Marines. Leading a picked assault group against a heavily fortified ridge he exposed himself repeatedly to hurl grenades into enemy emplacements. Then rallying the rest of his company he led a full scale attack capturing the ridge. (21 February 1945)

PRIVATE GEORGE PHILLIPS, 2d Battalion, 28th Marines. Shouting a warning to his comrades when a grenade landed in their midst he threw himself to cover the explosion protecting them from serious injury. (14 March 1945)*

FIRST LIEUTENANT HARRY L. MARTIN, 5th Pioneer Battalion. When Japanese infiltrated his unit's bivouac he organized a defense and, despite severe wounds, led a counterattack assaulting an enemy position alone, armed with a pistol, killing all its occupants before he fell mortally wounded. (26 March 1945)*

PRIVATE FIRST CLASS DONALD J. RUHL, 2d Battalion, 28th Marines. Climaxing three days of aggressive and heroic action against the enemy he covered a Japanese grenade with his body protecting his comrades from serious injury. (19–21 February 1945)*

PRIVATE FRANKLIN E SIGLER, 2d Battalion, 26th Marines. Taking command of his leaderless squad he led a bold charge, then, disregarding his own wounds, he carried three comrades to safety returning to fight on until ordered to retire for treatment. (14 March 1945)

PHARMACIST'S MATE SECOND CLASS GEORGE E. WAHLEN, 2d Battalion, 26th Marines. Painfully wounded on three days he disregarded injuries and enemy fire to aid numerous casualties. Unable to walk after his third wound he crawled 50 yards to care for still another fallen Marine. (3 March 1945)

CORPORAL TONY STEIN, 1st Battalion, 28th Marines. Armed with a personally improvised rapid-fire weapon he charged pillboxes one by one killing 20 enemy in his singlehanded assault. Exposing himself constantly to deliver effective fire against the enemy. (19 February 1945)

GUNNERY SERGEANT WILLIAM G. WALSH, 3d Battalion, 27th Marines. After leading his platoon in two daring assaults he smothered an exploding grenade with his body to save the men around him from serious injury. (27 February 1945)*

PRIVATE WILSON D. WATSON, 2d Battalion, 9th Marines. After a singlehanded assault in which he destroyed a pillbox he scaled a ridge line and standing erect fired his automatic rifle against attacking Japanese killing 60 enemy before expending all his ammunition. (26 and 27 February 1945)

CORPORAL HERSHEL W. WILLIAMS, 21st Marines. Covered by four riflemen he fought a lone 4-hour battle to wipe out one pillbox after another neutralizing one of the most stubborn strong points encountered by his regiment. (23 February 1945)

APPENDIX IX Navy Unit Commendation

The Secretary of the Navy takes pleasure in commending the

SUPPORT UNITS OF THE FIFTH AMPHIBIOUS CORPS
UNITED STATES FLEET MARINE FORCE

for service as follows:

"For outstanding heroism in support of Military Operations during the seizure of enemy Japanese-held Iwo Jima, Volcano Islands, February 19 to 28, 1945. Landing against resistance which rapidly increased in fury as the Japanese pounded the beaches with artillery, rocket and mortar fire, the Support Units of the FIFTH Amphibious Corps surmounted the obstacles of chaotic disorganization, loss of equipment, supplies and key personnel to develop and maintain a continuous link between thousands of assault troops and supply ships. Resourceful and daring whether fighting in the front line of combat, or serving in rear areas or on the wreck-obstructed beaches, they were responsible for the administration of operations and personnel; they rendered effective fire support where Japanese pressure was greatest; they constructed roads and facilities and maintained communications under the most difficult and discouraging conditions of weather and rugged terrain; they salvaged vital supplies from craft lying crippled in the surf or broached on the beaches; and they ministered to the wounded under fire and provided prompt evacuation to hospital ships. By their individual initiative and heroism and their ingenious teamwork, they provided the unfailing support vital to the conquest of Iwo Jima, a powerful defense of the Japanese Empire."

All personnel attached to and serving with the following Support Units of the FIFTH Amphibious Corps, United States Fleet Marine Force, during the Iwo Jima Operation from February 19 to 28, 1945, are authorized to wear the NAVY UNIT COMMENDATION Ribbon.

Headquarters & Service Battalion; Medical Battalion; Signal Battalion; Motor Transport Company; Detachment, 1st Separate Radio Intelligence Platoon; Detachment, Signal, Headquarters, Air Warning Squadron 7—Army Fighter Command; Detachment, 568th Signal Air Warning Battalion—Army; Detachment, 726th Signal Air Warning Company—Army; Detachment, 49th Signal Construction Battalion—Army; Detachment 44—70th Army Airways Communications Service—Army; Detachment, Communication Unit 434 (Group Pacific 11); Landing Force Air

Support Control Unit No. 1; 2nd Separate Engineer Battalion; 62nd Naval Construction Battalion; 2nd Separate Topographical Company; Detachment, 23rd Naval Construction Battalion (Special); 8th Field Depot (plus Headquarters Shore Party); 33rd Marine Depot Company; 34th Marine Depot Company; 36th Marine Depot Company; 8th Marine Ammunition Company; Detachment, 8th Naval Construction Regiment; Corps Evacuation Hospital No. 1; 2nd Bomb Disposal Company; 156th Bomb Disposal Squad—Army; Company B, Amphibious Reconnaissance Battalion, Fleet Marine Force; A and C Platoons, 38th Field Hospital—Army; Joint Intelligence Corps, Pacific Ocean Area, Intelligence Teams No. 22, 23, 24, and 25; Detachment, Joint Intelligence Corps, Pacific Ocean Area, Enemy Materiel and Salvage Platoon; Detachment, 1st Platoon, 239th Quartermaster Salvage and Collection Company—Army; Detachment, Headquarters, Army Garrison Forces, APO 86; Detachment, Headquarters, 147th Infantry—Army; Detachment, Headquarters, 7th Fighter Command—Army; Detachment, 47th Fighter Squadron—Army; Detachment, 548th Night Fighter Squadron—Army; Detachment, 386th Air Service Group (Special)—Army; Detachment, Group Pacific 11; Detachment, Port Director; Detachment, Garrison Beach Party; Headquarters & Service Battery, 1st Provisional Artillery Group; 2nd 155-mm. Howitzer Battalion; 4th 155-mm. Howitzer Battalion; 473rd Amphibian Truck Company—Army; Detachment, Headquarters & Headquarters Battery, 138th Antiaircraft Artillery Group—Army; Detachment, 506th Antiaircraft Gun Battalion—Army; Detachment, 483rd Antiaircraft Air Warning Battalion—Army; 28th and 34th Replacement Drafts (less Advance Groups and those assigned assault units); Headquarters Battalion, THIRD Marine Division (less Reconnaissance Company); 3rd Marine War Dog Platoon; 3rd Service Battalion (less detachment); 3rd Pioneer Battalion (less 2nd Platoon, Company C); 3rd Medical Battalion (less Company C); 3rd Motor Transport Battalion (less Company C); 12th Marines (less detachment); Marine Observation Squadron 1 (less detachment); Headquarters Battalion, FOURTH Marine Division (less Reconnaissance Company and 1st, 2nd, and 3rd Platoons, Military Police Company); 4th Motor Transport Battalion; 4th Medical Battalion; 133rd Naval Construction Battalion; 4th Tank Battalion (less Companies A, B, and C); 4th Engineer Battalion (less Companies A, B, and C); 4th Service Battalion; 4th Pioneer Battalion (less Companies A, B, and C); 442nd Port Company—Army; 14th Marines (less detachment); 4th Marine Amphibian Truck Company; 476th Amphibian Truck Company—Army; Marine Observation Squadron 4 (less detachment); Detachment, 726th Signal Air Warning Company—Army (FOURTH Marine Division—Reinf.); 24th and 30th Replacement Drafts (less Advance Groups and those assigned assault units); Headquarters Battalion, FIFTH Marine Division (less Reconnaissance Company and 1st, 2nd, and 3rd Platoons, Military Police Company); 5th Medical Battalion; 13th Marines (less detachment); 5th Marine Amphibian Truck Company; 471st Amphibian Truck Company—Army; Marine Observation Squadron 5 (less detachment); Detachment, 726th Signal Air Warning Company—Army (FIFTH Marine Division—Reinf.); 5th Pioneer Battalion (less Companies A, B, and C); 31st Naval Construction Battalion; 592nd Port Company—Army; 5th Motor Transport Battalion; 5th Service Battalion; 27th and 31st Replacement Drafts (less Advance Groups and those assigned assault units).

JOHN L. SULLIVAN
Secretary of the Navy

Index

Luzon operation, 23
Maalea Bay, 35, 36
MacArthur, Gen Douglas, 1, 23, 41
MacFarlane, LtCol Robert E., 6
Mail, U. S., 113, 113*n*
Makin Islands, USS, 44
Manchuria, 7, 8
Marianas, 1, 2, 6, 19, 19*n*, 20, 21, 23, 25, 31, 34, 36, 36*n*,
    39, 42, 51, 94*n*, 153, 210
Marine Aviation units
    Bomber Squadron 612, 39
    Observation Squadron 4, 112, 126, 150, 153, 153*n*,
        164
    Observation Squadron 5, 112, 126
    Torpedo bombing Squadron 242, 119
    Transport Squadron 353, 113
    Transport Squadron 952, 113, 113*n*
Marine units
    Fleet Marine Force, Pacific, 24, 25, 28, 31, 32, 35
    Supply Service, Fleet Marine Force, Pacific, 32
    Amphibious Corps, V. *See* Amphibious Corps, V.
    Division, 2d, 20
    Division, 3d, 20, 24, 24*n*, 25, 26, 28, 32, 33, 35–37,
        39, 58, 75, 93, 94, 97, 99, 100, 100*n*, 103–105, 105*n*,
        106–108, 111, 113, 117, 118, 120–124, 129, 134,
        135, 137, 138, 142, 143, 143*n*, 144, 145, 148*n*, 149,
        150, 154, 155*n*, 160, 169*n*, 178, 179, 181, 182, 185,
        187, 191, 193, 207
    Division, 4th, 24–27, 27*n*, 28, 33, 35, 37, 51–53, 60,
        63–65, 80, 83–88, 91, 92, 94, 97, 100, 100*n*, 103,
        105, 113, 117, 126, 143, 146*n*, 148, 148*n*, 149, 150,
        153, 153*n*, 154, 155, 155*n*, 157–160, 163, 165, 165*n*,
        168–174, 176–178, 182, 184, 185, 193, 206
    Division, 5th, 24–26, 26*n*, 27, 28, 33, 35–37, 51–53, 57,
        58, 60, 67, 80, 83–85, 88, 91–94, 100, 100*n*, 103,
        105–110, 105*n*, 113, 114, 117, 120, 122–125, 128,
        131, 132, 132*n*, 134, 137–149, 137*n*, 146*n*, 148*n*,
        169*n*, 178, 179, 181, 185–187, 189, 191, 193, 197
    Infantry Regiment, 3d, 26, 39, 97, 107, 116
    Infantry Regiment, 9th, 26, 39, 98, 100, 103, 104, 106–
        111, 117–120, 122–125, 129, 150, 157, 169, 179, 193
    Infantry Regiment, 21st, 26, 37, 39, 58, 70, 83, 86, 87,
        87*n*, 88–90, 92, 94–97, 100, 103–111, 117–120, 122,
        129, 135, 137, 143, 144, 147, 150, 179, 181, 193
    Infantry Regiment, 23d, 26, 27, 53, 60, 61, 64, 65, 80,
        85–88, 92, 98, 119, 150, 154–160, 165, 166, 168–176,
        182–184
    Infantry Regiment, 24th, 26, 27, 61, 63, 88, 91, 92, 97,
        150, 153, 160, 162, 163, 165, 166, 168–173, 175
    Infantry Regiment, 25th, 26, 27, 27*n*, 53, 61, 62, 63*n*,
        64, 65, 67, 80–82, 85, 87–92, 150, 151, 153, 154,
        157–159, 162, 165, 168–172, 175, 176, 182–184.
    Infantry Regiment, 26th, 25–27, 26*n*, 58, 80, 88, 92,
        95–97, 95*n*, 101, 123–125, 134, 135, 137–139, 139*n*,
        141–147, 187, 189
    Infantry Regiment, 27th, 26, 27*n*, 53, 56–59, 58*n*,
        65, 80, 81, 85, 87, 88, 91, 92, 120, 125, 128,
        129, 131, 142–145, 147, 148*n*, 179, 185–187, 189
    Infantry Regiment, 28th, 26, 35, 53–56, 58, 69, 75–79,
        92, 129, 131–135, 138, 141–147, 185–187, 189

Marine units—Continued
    Artillery Regiment, 12th, 98, 103, 104, 107, 107*n*,
        123*n*, 132*n*, 181
    Artillery Regiment, 13th, 58, 64, 65, 70, 83, 84, 96, 96*n*,
        123, 123*n*, 125, 126, 131, 132, 132*n*, 135, 136, 143,
        145, 147, 179
    Artillery Regiment, 14th, 27, 64, 65*n*, 83, 87, 91, 97,
        155*n*, 157, 172
    Field Artillery Group, 1st Provisional, 26, 36, 107
    Base Depot, 6th, 32
    Field Depot, 5th, 32
    Field Depot, 7th, 32
    Field Depot, 8th, 32 34, 198
    Infantry Battalion, 1/9, 100, 102, 103, 107, 108, 111,
        117, 119, 122, 154, 163, 166, 178–181
    Infantry Battalion, 1/21, 88, 89, 89*n*, 104–111, 117,
        118, 120–122, 134, 179, 181
    Infantry Battalion, 1/23, 54, 60, 61, 65, 67, 85, 150, 154,
        155, 157, 157*n*, 165, 166, 168, 169, 183
    Infantry Battalion, 1/24, 61, 63, 63*n*, 79, 81–83, 85, 88,
        90, 92, 97, 150, 151, 153, 161, 162, 166, 169, 171,
        172, 175
    Infantry Battalion, 1/25, 54, 61, 62, 79, 81, 82, 85, 86,
        90, 153–155, 157–159, 162–165, 168–171, 175, 176
    Infantry Battalion, 1/26, 26, 26*n*, 58, 58*n*, 79, 80, 85,
        88, 92, 96, 123, 125, 128, 129, 135, 138, 142–144,
        146, 147, 185, 186, 189
    Infantry Battalion, 1/27, 54, 56, 57, 65, 80, 85, 92,
        126, 128, 129, 135, 142, 143, 147, 185, 186
    Infantry Battalion, 1/28, 54, 56, 65, 69, 70, 75–77,
        132–135, 138, 142, 146, 185
    Infantry Battalion, 2/9, 100–103, 101*n*, 108, 110,
        111, 117, 119–122, 178, 181
    Infantry Battalion, 2/21, 88, 92, 95, 96, 105, 107–111,
        117, 120, 122, 179, 181, 182
    Infantry Battalion, 2/23, 54, 61, 85, 150, 155, 157,
        165, 169–172, 175, 183
    Infantry Battalion, 2/24, 61, 79, 80, 85, 88, 97, 150,
        153, 160–164, 166, 169, 171, 172, 175, 184
    Infantry Battalion, 2/25, 62, 63, 79, 81, 85, 86, 90, 91,
        150, 153–155, 157–159, 162–166, 168, 169, 171, 175,
        176, 184
    Infantry Battalion, 2/26, 88, 92, 96, 123–125, 129,
        134, 135, 137, 139, 140, 142–144, 147, 181, 186, 187
    Infantry Battalion, 2/27, 54, 56–58, 80, 88, 92, 117,
        120, 123–126, 128, 129, 135, 142–145, 147, 185, 186
    Infantry Battalion, 2/28, 54–56, 58, 69, 72, 75–77, 129,
        132–136, 138, 142, 146, 185
    Infantry Battalion, 3/9, 100–103, 106–111, 117–122,
        134, 137, 140, 178, 180
    Infantry Battalion, 3/21, 94, 96, 103–107, 107*n*, 110,
        111, 117, 120–122, 178–180
    Infantry Battalion, 3/23, 61, 79, 85, 150, 153–158,
        162, 164–166, 168, 169
    Infantry Battalion, 3/24, 63, 97, 150, 151, 153, 157,
        158, 162, 163, 166, 172–175, 184
    Infantry Battalion, 3/25, 54, 61, 62, 67, 79, 81, 85, 86,
        90, 91, 154, 155, 158, 159, 162, 163, 163*n*, 164,
        164*n*, 165, 166, 168, 170, 171, 175, 176, 184

Transport Squadron 15, 39
Transport Squadron 16, 39
Treitel, Maj Paul S., 63, 91
Trotti, LtCol Tom M., 88
Truk, 6
Tumbelston, Maj William H., 147
Turkey Knob, 149, 153, 154, 157–159, 162, 164–166, 168, 171, 175, 176
Turner, VAdm Richmond K., 24, 26, 28, 40, 40n, 49, 116, 121
Turton, LtCol H. J., 118, 118n
Tuscaloosa, USS, 41n, 42n, 178
Twiggs, USS, 87
Ulithi, 1, 31, 37n, 41n, 42, 122
Underwater Demolition Team operations, 18n, 31, 44, 44n, 47
Underwater Demolition Team 15, 48
Vandegrift, LtCol A. A., Jr., 63, 97
Vectographs, *see* Intelligence.
Vehicles. *See* Amphibian vehicles; Equipment.
Vicksburg, USS, 41n, 42, 47
Victory, LtCol Randall M., 65, 65n
Volcano Islands, 2, 3, 19, 38, 42, 69n
Volcano-Bonin Islands, 5, 6, 16, 19, 20, 27, 30, 31, 39, 41n, 44
Volcanic ash, 4
Wake Island, USS, 42, 44, 112, 153n
Wallen, Maj J. B., 107n
Waller, LtCol Henry T., 58
Waller, Col James D., 27, 58, 85
War dogs, 131
Washington, USS, 41, 49
Weapons
  American
    flame throwers, 70, 72, 76, 109, 111, 118, 119, 139, 140, 142, 144, 154, 160, 161, 163, 166, 175, 180, 184, 199
    60mm mortars, 97, 101, 103, 108, 163, 166, 171, 184
    81mm mortars, 61, 67n, 74, 76, 88, 97, 103, 108, 133, 137, 145, 146, 151, 166, 171
    4.2-inch mortars, 83n
    37mm guns, 70, 72, 97, 103, 126, 137, 138, 141, 144, 146, 154, 158, 171, 185
    75mm half-tracks, 72, 126, 138, 141, 146, 154, 159, 165, 170, 177, 178, 185

Weapons—Continued
  American—Continued
    75mm pack howitzer, 59, 64, 98, 107, 124, 146, 158, 159, 163, 206, 207
    105mm howitzers, 27, 58–60, 64, 83, 97, 107, 206, 207
    155mm howitzers, 26, 96, 104, 107, 132, 144, 155, 160, 181, 206, 207
    2.36-inch rocket launcher, 122, 139, 140, 154, 157, 160 163, 166, 184
    4.5-inch rockets, 56n, 90, 133, 141, 141n, 145, 157, 158, 163, 166
    7.2-inch rocket, 179
    tank, 33, 36, 56, 57, 57n, 60n, 61, 62, 62n, 65, 65n, 69–72, 75, 76, 78, 80, 81, 85, 89, 92–96, 100, 101, 103, 107–109, 117, 120–122, 124, 126, 128, 133, 135, 136, 138, 139, 141, 142, 144, 145, 150, 151, 153, 154, 156–159, 161, 163–166, 169–171, 177, 178–182, 184, 187, 193, 210
    tanks, flame, 56, 103, 126, 133, 136, 141, 142, 144, 146, 165, 166, 170, 171, 180, 181, 184, 187, 189
    tankdozers, 56, 62, 117, 136, 156
  Japanese
    antiaircraft, 6, 13
    antitank, 13, 29, 56, 61, 92, 94, 95, 96, 107, 108, 117, 142, 149, 150, 157
    coast defense, 6, 13, 47, 48, 203
    demolitions, 121, 173
    mines, 15, 47, 53, 56, 61, 62, 77, 78, 80, 85, 92, 94, 96, 117, 120, 126, 135, 141, 142, 146, 147, 150, 154, 157, 159, 165, 174, 176
    mortar, 13, 53, 95, 96, 108, 144, 153, 156–158, 170, 176
    rockets, 157, 158, 170
    tanks, 7, 13, 30, 107, 126, 149, 157, 179
Weller, LtCol Donald M., 42
Wensinger, Col Walter W., 27, 53, 61, 80, 85, 154
Williams, LtCol M. C., 89n
Williams, LtCol R. H, 69n
Withers, Col Hartnoll J., 83, 86, 88, 105
Wornham, Col Thomas A., 26, 53, 80, 85, 129
Wood, Lt(jg) Alan S., 76n
Yap, 1
Yokohama, 7
Yokosuka, 75n
Yokosuka Naval Base, 6
Youngdale, LtCol Carl A., 65

253

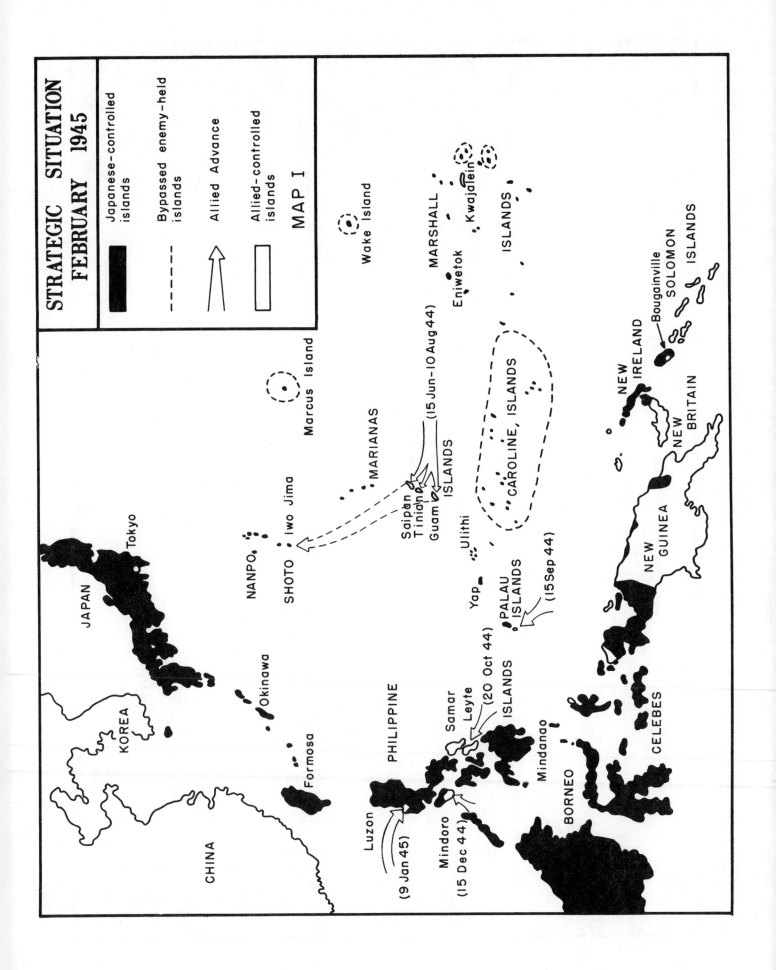

STRATEGIC SITUATION
FEBRUARY 1945

Japanese-controlled
islands

Bypassed enemy-held
islands

Allied Advance

Allied-controlled
islands

MAP I

CHINA

JAPAN

Tokyo

KOREA

Okinawa

Formosa

PHILIPPINE

Luzon

(9 Jan 45)

Mindoro
(15 Dec 44)

Samar
Leyte
(20 Oct 44)

ISLANDS

Mindanao

BORNEO

CELEBES

NANPO

SHOTO

Iwo Jima

Marcus Island

Wake Island

MARIANAS

Saipan
Tinian
Guam

(15 Jun-10 Aug 44)

ISLANDS

Ulithi

Yap

PALAU
ISLANDS

(15 Sep 44)

CAROLINE ISLANDS

MARSHALL

Eniwetok

Kwajalein

ISLANDS

NEW GUINEA

NEW
IRELAND

NEW
BRITAIN

Bougainville
SOLOMON

ISLANDS

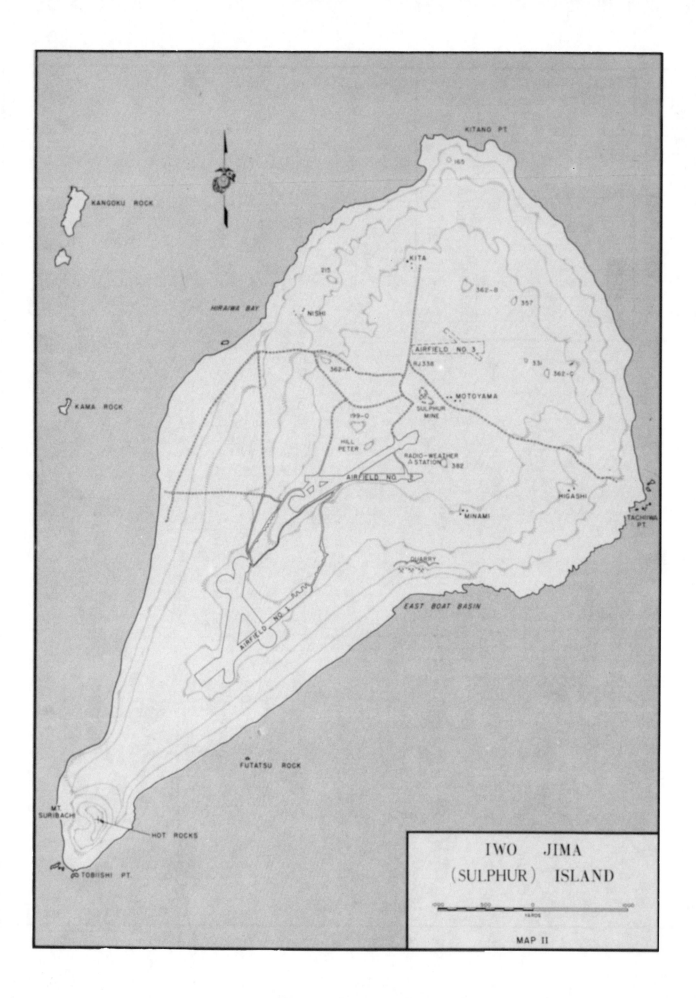

KITANO PT.

165

KANGOKU ROCK

215

KITA

362-B

357

HIRAIWA BAY

NISHI

AIRFIELD NO. 3

RJ 338

362-A

331

362-C

KAMA ROCK

MOTOYAMA

SULPHUR
MINE

199-O

HILL
PETER

RADIO-WEATHER
△ STATION   362

HIGASHI

AIRFIELD NO. 2

MINAMI

TACHIWA
PT.

QUARRY

EAST BOAT BASIN

AIRFIELD NO. 1

FUTATSU ROCK

MT.
SURIBACHI

HOT ROCKS

TOBIISHI PT.

IWO   JIMA
(SULPHUR) ISLAND

1000   500   0   1000
YARDS

MAP II

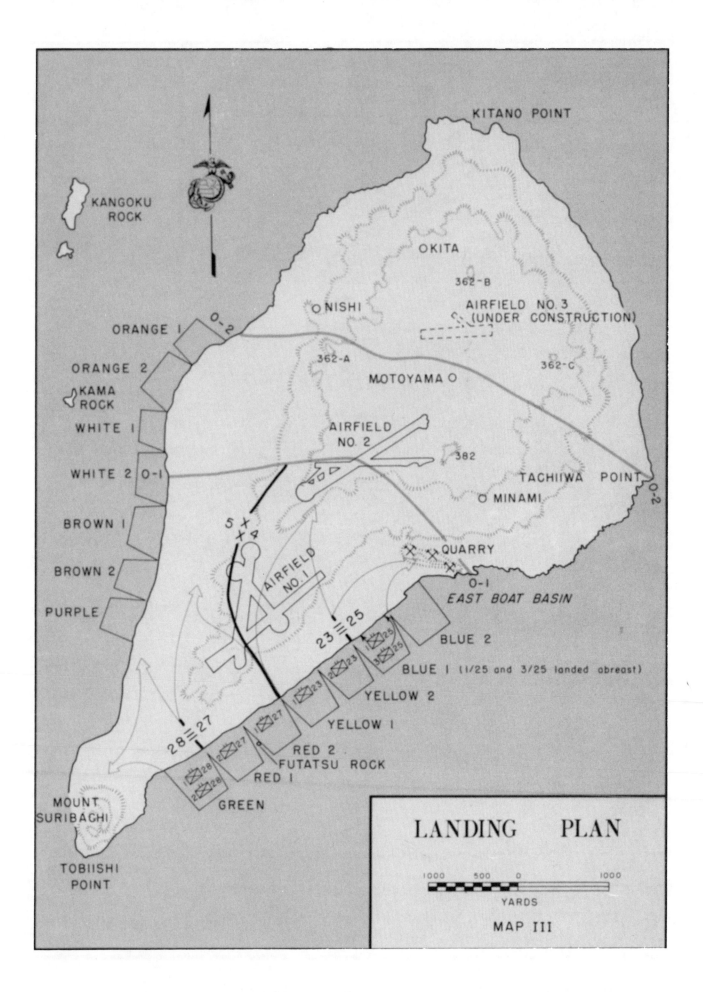

KITANO POINT

KANGOKU ROCK

OKITA

362-B

O NISHI

AIRFIELD NO. 3
(UNDER CONSTRUCTION)

ORANGE 1   O-2

ORANGE 2

362-A

KAMA ROCK

MOTOYAMA O

362-C

WHITE 1

AIRFIELD NO. 2

382

WHITE 2 O-1

TACHIIWA POINT   O-2

O MINAMI

BROWN 1

5 ×
× 4

BROWN 2

× × QUARRY
× ×

AIRFIELD NO. 1

PURPLE

O-1
EAST BOAT BASIN

23 ≡ 25

BLUE 2

3 × 25

BLUE 1 (1/25 and 3/25 landed abreast)

3 × 23

1 × 25

YELLOW 2

1 × 23

YELLOW 1

28 ≡ 27

1 × 27

RED 2

2 × 27

FUTATSU ROCK

RED 1

1 × 28

2 × 27

GREEN

2 × 28

MOUNT SURIBACHI

TOBIISHI POINT

LANDING PLAN

1000   500   0   1000
YARDS

MAP III

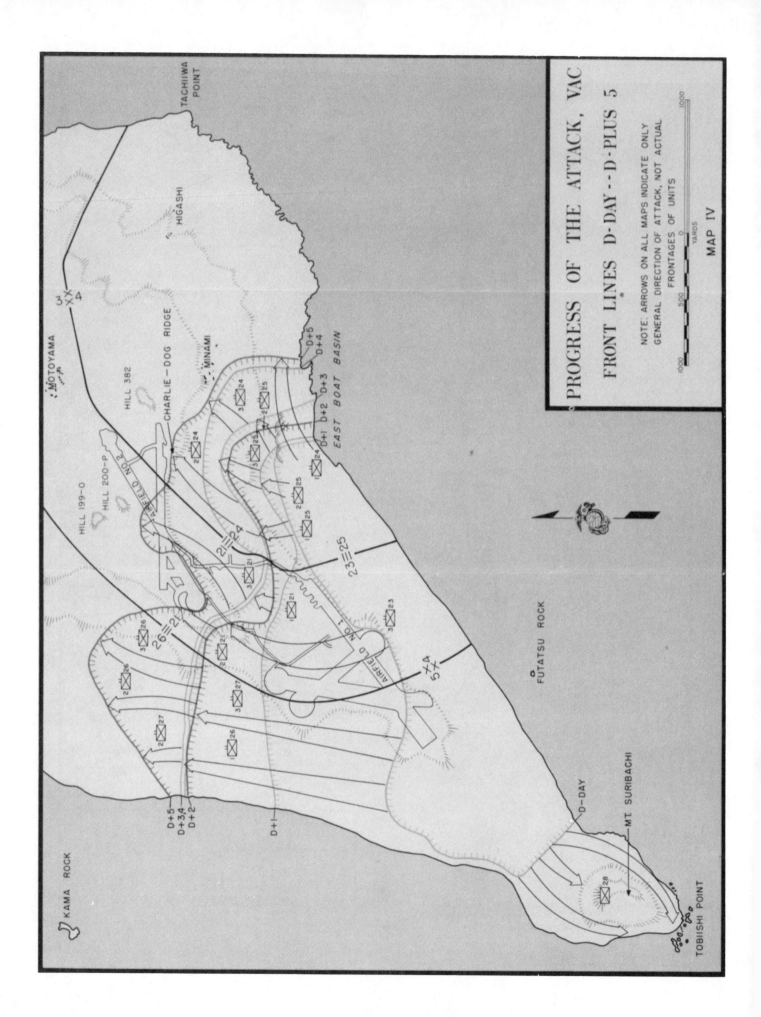

PROGRESS OF THE ATTACK, VAC
FRONT LINES D-DAY--D-PLUS 5

NOTE: ARROWS ON ALL MAPS INDICATE ONLY
GENERAL DIRECTION OF ATTACK, NOT ACTUAL
FRONTAGES OF UNITS

MAP IV

YARDS

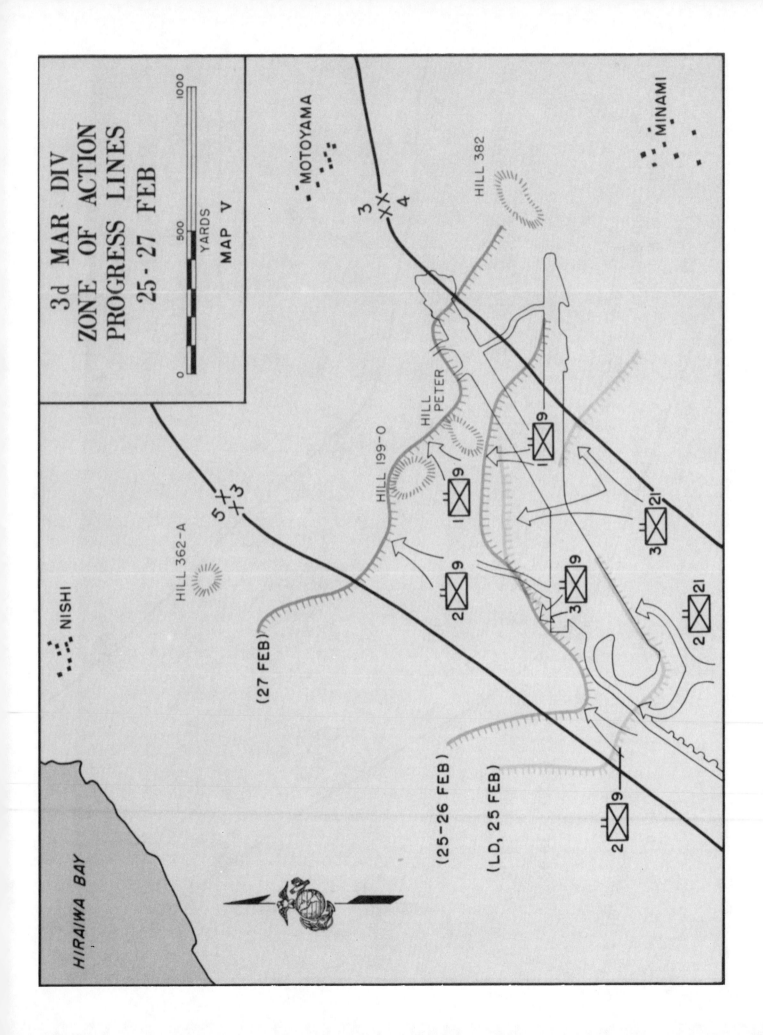

HIRAIWA BAY

3d MAR DIV
ZONE OF ACTION
PROGRESS LINES
25 - 27 FEB

0   500   1000
YARDS
MAP V

NISHI

MOTOYAMA

MINAMI

HILL 362-A

HILL 382

HILL 199-O

HILL PETER

5 ⅹⅹ 3

3 ⅹⅹ 4

(27 FEB)

(25-26 FEB)

(LD, 25 FEB)

2 ⌧ 9

2 ⌧ 9

1 ⌧ 9

1 ⌧ 9

3 ⌧ 9

2 ⌧ 21

3 ⌧ 21

1 ⌧ 9

2 ⌧ 9

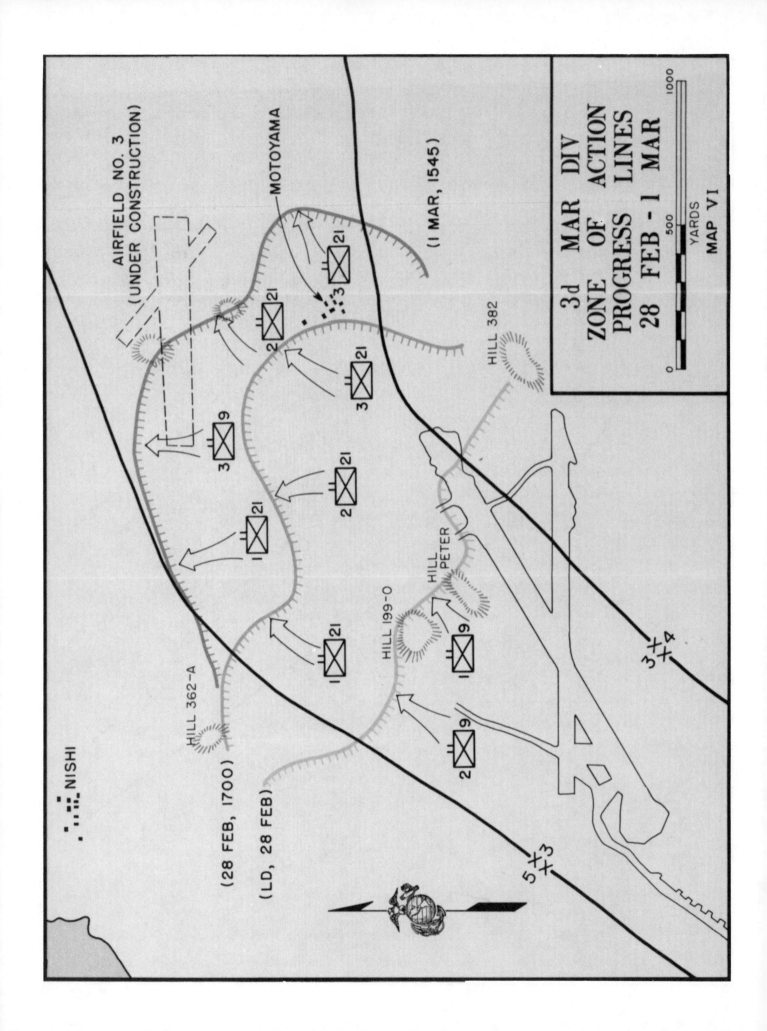

NISHI

AIRFIELD NO. 3
(UNDER CONSTRUCTION)

MOTOYAMA

HILL 362-A

HILL 199-O

HILL PETER

HILL 382

3 9

1 21

3 21

2 21

2 21

2 9

1 9

1 21

2 21

3 3

(28 FEB, 1700)

(LD, 28 FEB)

(1 MAR, 1545)

5 XX 3

3 XX 4

3d MAR DIV
ZONE OF ACTION
PROGRESS LINES
28 FEB - 1 MAR

YARDS

0   500   1000

MAP VI

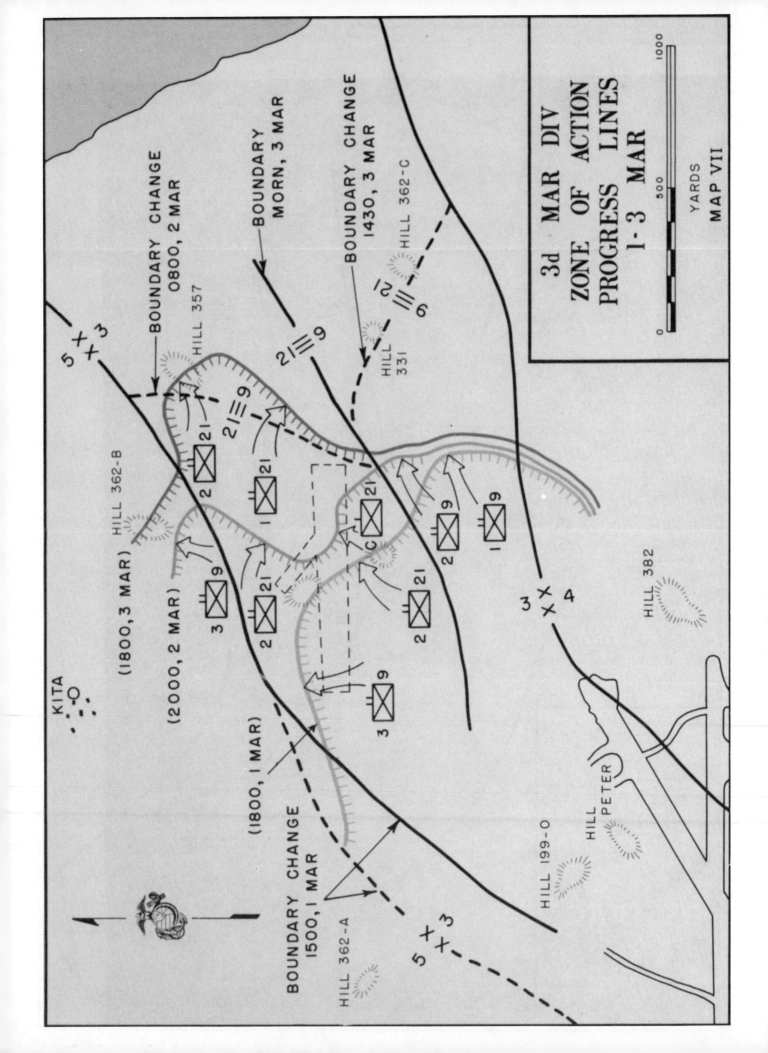

3d MAR DIV
ZONE OF ACTION
PROGRESS LINES
1-3 MAR

YARDS

MAP VII

BOUNDARY CHANGE 0800, 2 MAR

BOUNDARY MORN, 3 MAR

BOUNDARY CHANGE 1430, 3 MAR

HILL 362-C

HILL 331

HILL 357

HILL 362-B

(1800, 3 MAR)

(2000, 2 MAR)

(1800, 1 MAR)

KITA

BOUNDARY CHANGE 1500, 1 MAR

HILL 362-A

HILL 382

HILL 199-O

HILL PETER

5 XX 3

3 XX 4

5 XX 3

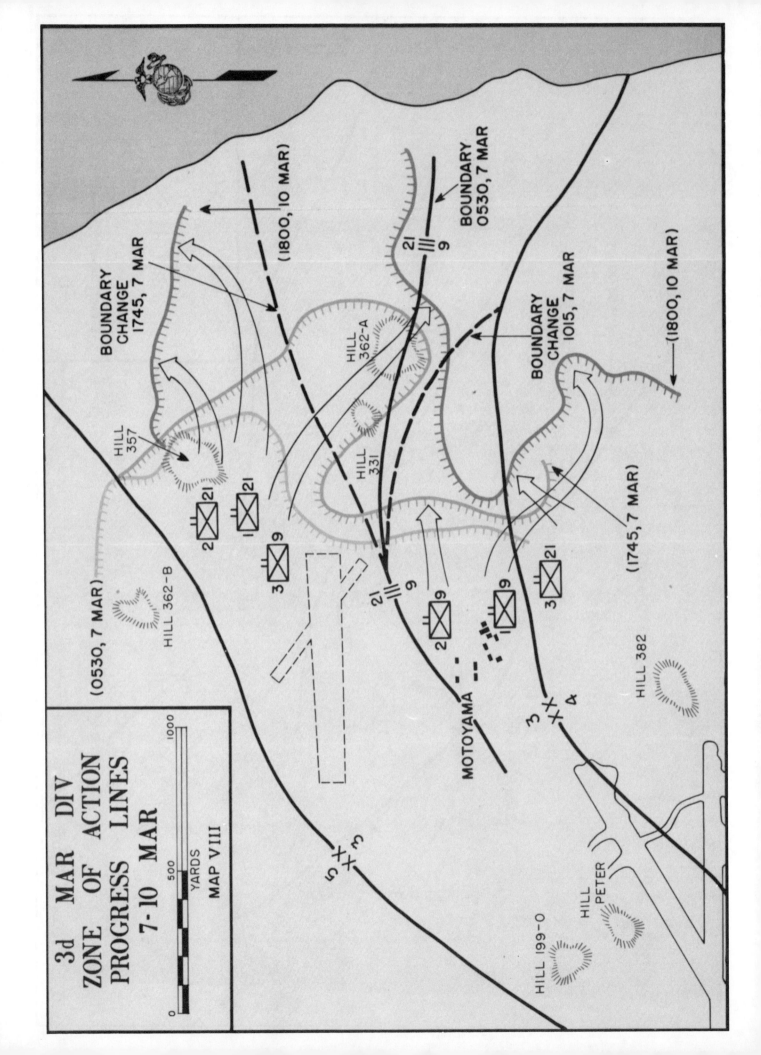

3d MAR DIV
ZONE OF ACTION
PROGRESS LINES
7-10 MAR

YARDS

MAP VIII

(0530, 7 MAR)

BOUNDARY CHANGE 1745, 7 MAR

BOUNDARY 0530, 7 MAR

(1800, 10 MAR)

BOUNDARY CHANGE 1015, 7 MAR

(1800, 10 MAR)

(1745, 7 MAR)

HILL 357

HILL 362-A

HILL 331

HILL 362-B

HILL 382

MOTOYAMA

HILL 199-O

HILL PETER

2 21

1 21

3 9

21 9

2 9

1 9

3 21

21 9

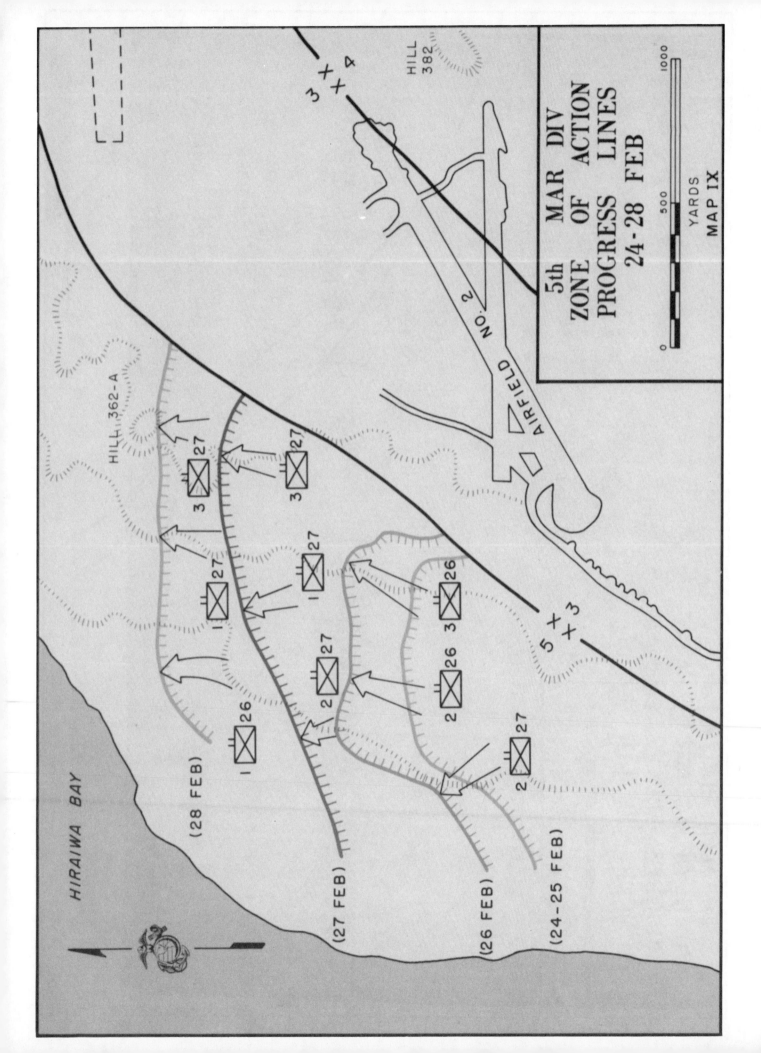

HIRAIWA BAY

HILL 362-A

HILL 382

AIRFIELD NO. 2

(28 FEB)

(27 FEB)

(26 FEB)

(24-25 FEB)

3 X 4

5 X 3

3 X 3

1 26

3 27

3 27

1 27

1 27

2 27

3 26

2 26

2 27

5th MAR DIV
ZONE OF ACTION
PROGRESS LINES
24-28 FEB

YARDS

0   500   1000

MAP IX

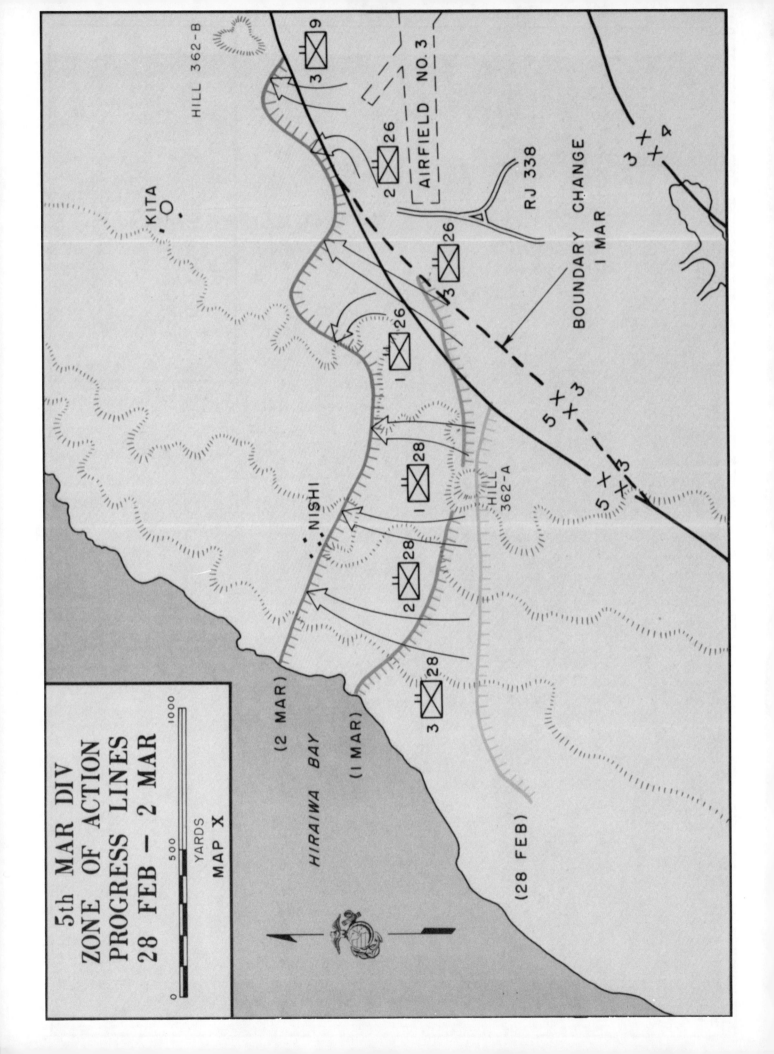

5th MAR DIV
ZONE OF ACTION
PROGRESS LINES
28 FEB — 2 MAR

MAP X

YARDS

0   500   1000

HILL 362-B

KITA

AIRFIELD NO. 3

RJ 338

BOUNDARY CHANGE
1 MAR

3 XX 4

5 XX 3

5 XX 3

3 9

2 26

2 26

3 26

1 26

1 28

2 28

3 28

HILL
362-A

NISHI

HIRAIWA BAY

(1 MAR)

(2 MAR)

(28 FEB)

(28 FEB)

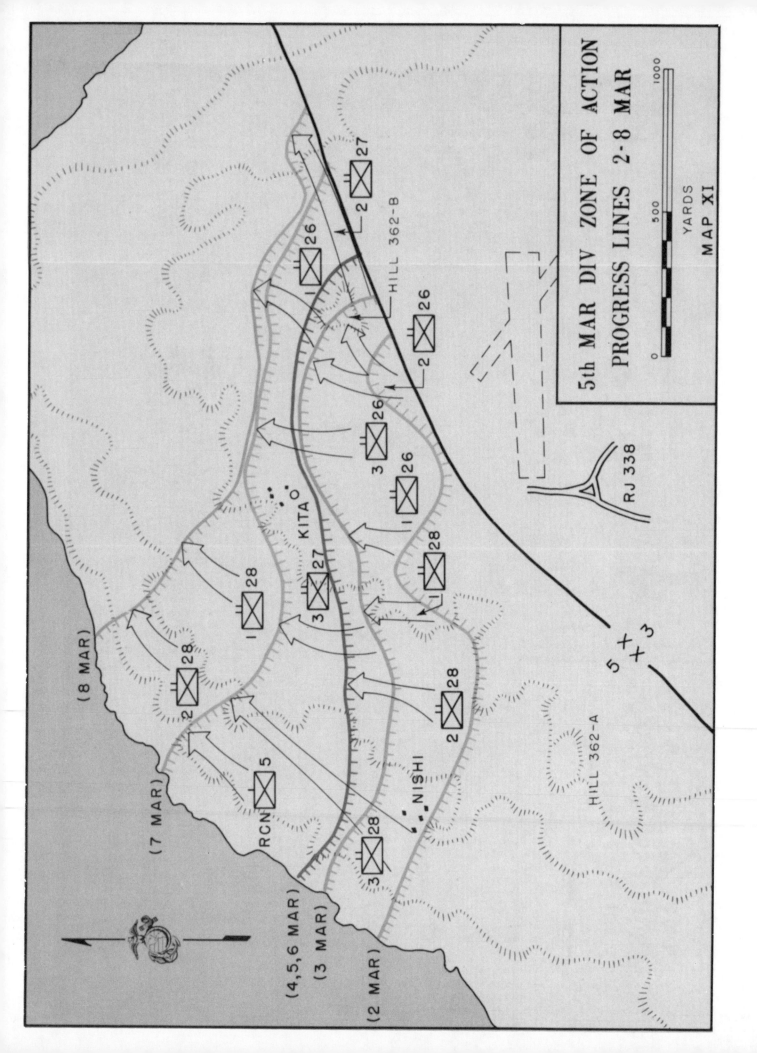

5th MAR DIV ZONE OF ACTION
PROGRESS LINES 2-8 MAR

YARDS

MAP XI

RJ 338

HILL 362-A

HILL 362-B

NISHI

KITA

RCN 5

3 28

2 28

1 28

3 27

2 28

1 28

3 26

1 26

2 26

1 26

2 27

(8 MAR)
(7 MAR)
(4,5,6 MAR)
(3 MAR)
(2 MAR)

5 X 3

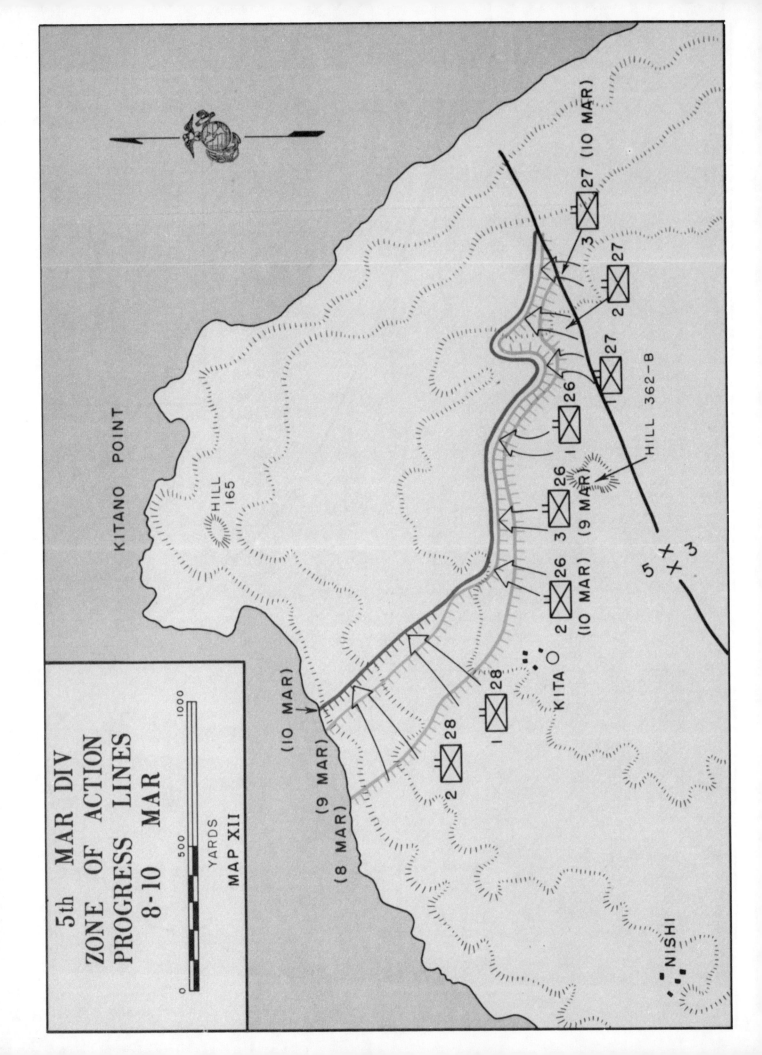

5th MAR DIV
ZONE OF ACTION
PROGRESS LINES
8-10 MAR

YARDS
MAP XII

0   500   1000

KITANO POINT

HILL 165

(8 MAR)

(9 MAR)

(10 MAR)

(10 MAR)

2 28

1 28

KITA

2 26 (10 MAR)

3 26 (9 MAR)

1 26

2 27

27

3 27 (10 MAR)

HILL 362-B

5 XX 3

NISHI

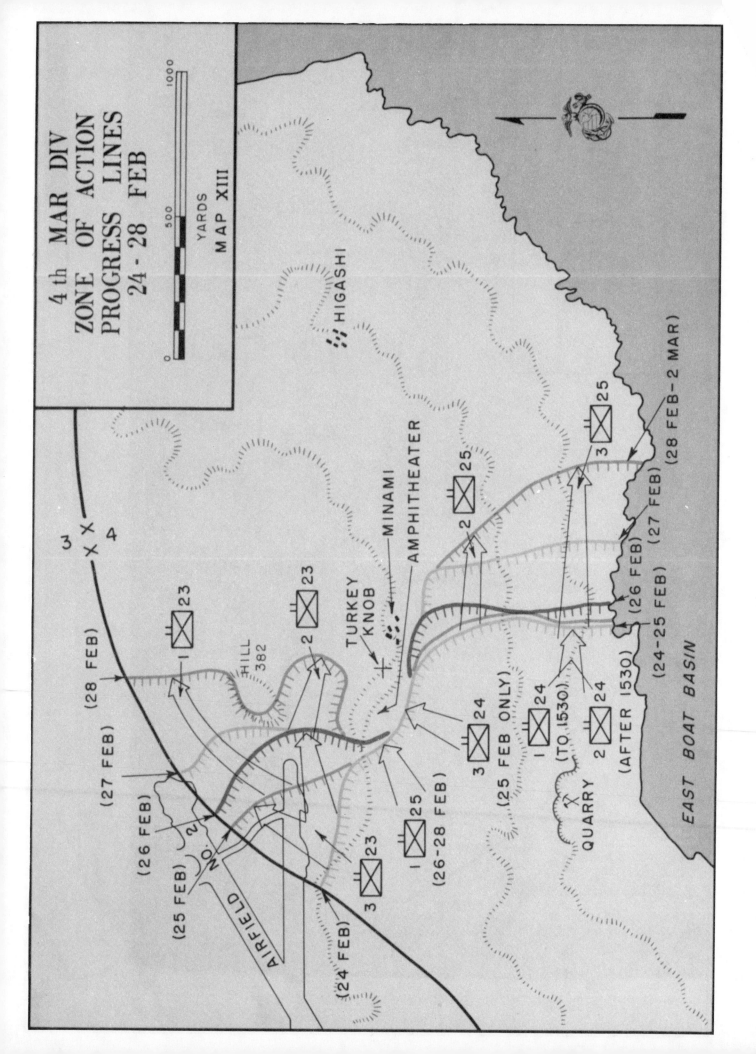

4th MAR DIV
ZONE OF ACTION
PROGRESS LINES
24-28 FEB

YARDS
MAP XIII

0   500   1000

HIGASHI

3 X X 4

1 ☒ 23

2 ☒ 23

MINAMI

AMPHITHEATER

HILL
382

2 ☒ 25

3 ☒ 25

(28 FEB-2 MAR)

(28 FEB)

TURKEY
KNOB

(27 FEB)

(26 FEB)

(25 FEB)

NO. 2

3 ☒ 23

1 ☒ 25
(26-28 FEB)

3 ☒ 24
(25 FEB ONLY)

1 ☒ 24
(TO 1530)

2 ☒ 24
(AFTER 1530)

☒
QUARRY

(24-25 FEB)   (26 FEB)   (27 FEB)

(24 FEB)

AIRFIELD

EAST BOAT BASIN

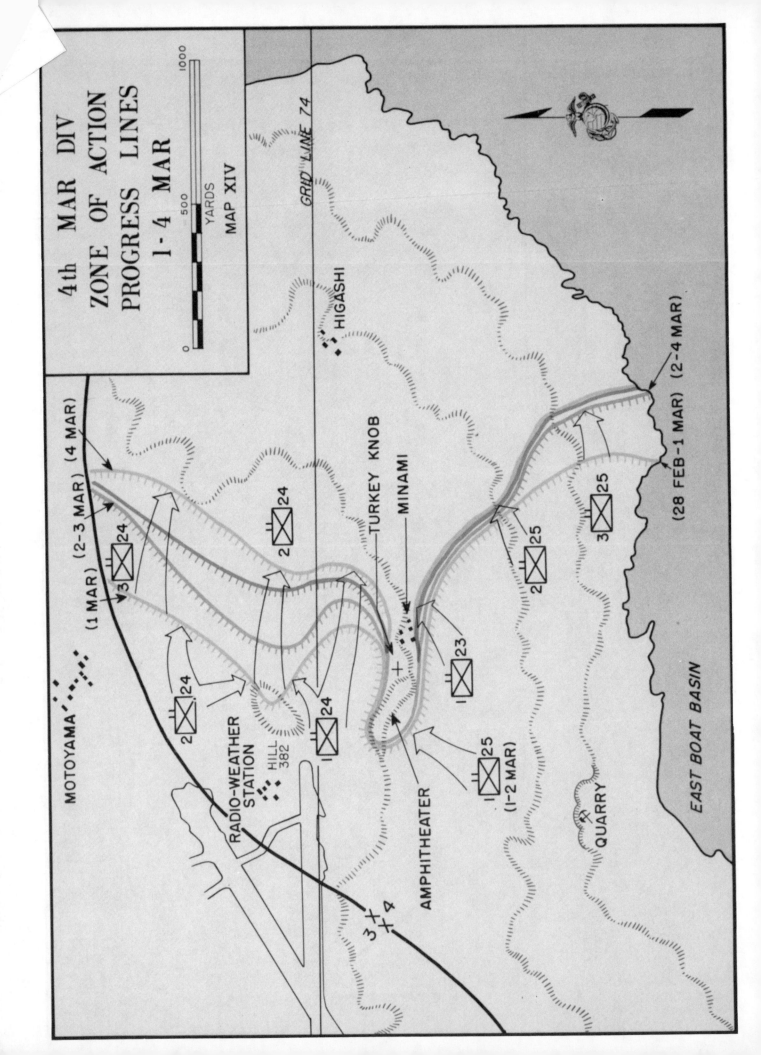

4th MAR DIV
ZONE OF ACTION
PROGRESS LINES
1-4 MAR

MAP XIV

YARDS
0 500 1000

MOTOYAMA

(1 MAR) (2-3 MAR) (4 MAR)

RADIO-WEATHER STATION

HILL 382

3│X│24

2│X│24

1│X│24

2│X│24

HIGASHI

GRID LINE 74

TURKEY KNOB

MINAMI

AMPHITHEATER

1│X│23

1│X│25
(1-2 MAR)

2│X│25

3│X│25

(28 FEB-1 MAR) (2-4 MAR)

QUARRY

EAST BOAT BASIN

3│X│4

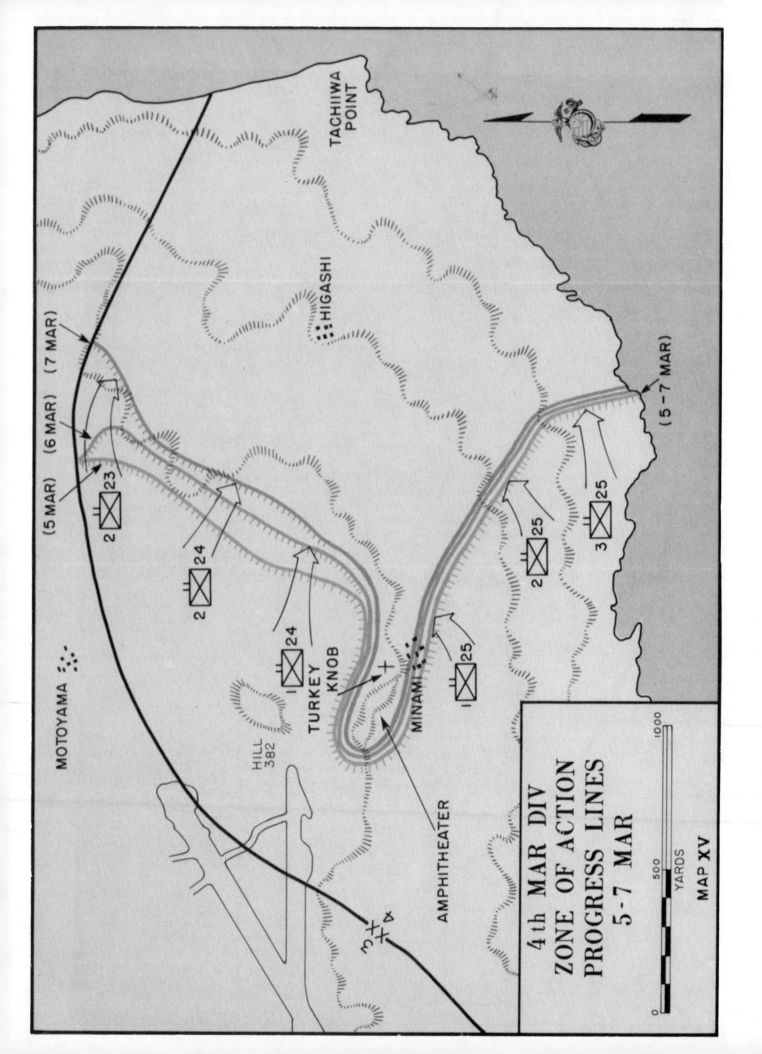

MOTOYAMA

HILL 382

TURKEY KNOB

AMPHITHEATER

MINAMI

HIGASHI

TACHIIWA POINT

(5 MAR) (6 MAR) (7 MAR)

(5–7 MAR)

2 ⊠ 23

2 ⊠ 24

1 ⊠ 24

1 ⊠ 25

2 ⊠ 25

3 ⊠ 25

XX
4
3

4th MAR DIV
ZONE OF ACTION
PROGRESS LINES
5–7 MAR

MAP XV

YARDS

0   500   1000

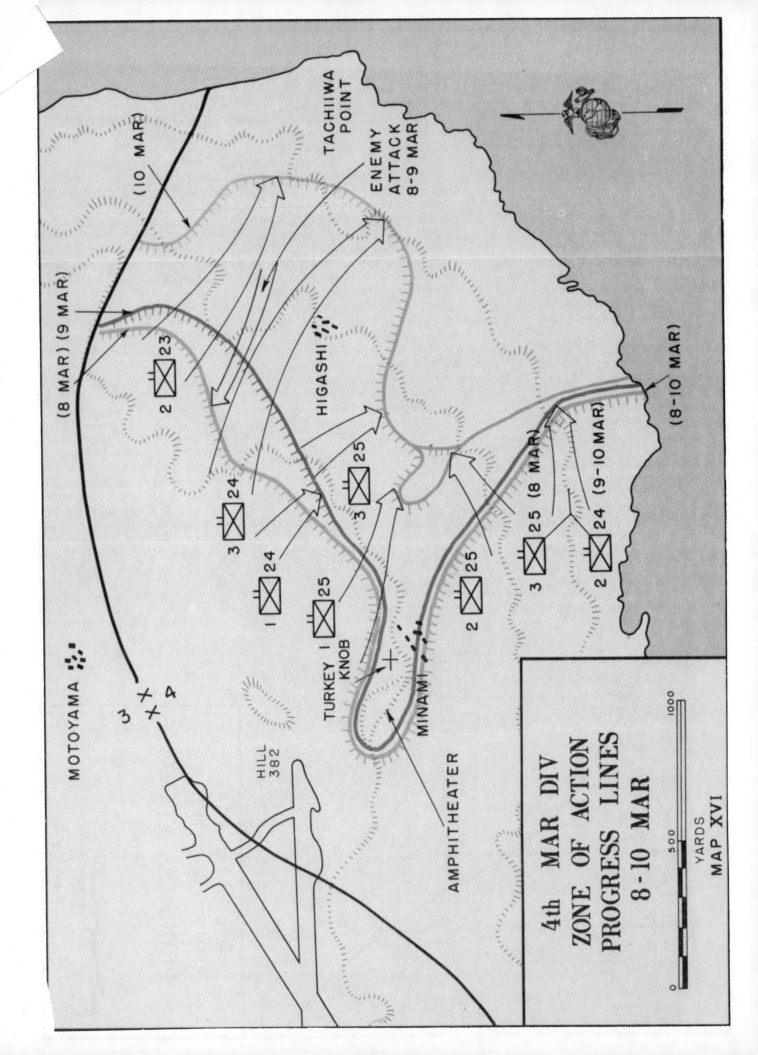

4th MAR DIV
ZONE OF ACTION
PROGRESS LINES
8-10 MAR

YARDS
MAP XVI

MOTOYAMA

HILL 382

3 ✕ 4

AMPHITHEATER

TURKEY KNOB

MINAMI

HIGASHI

TACHIIWA POINT

ENEMY ATTACK 8-9 MAR

(10 MAR)

(8 MAR) (9 MAR)

(8-10 MAR)

(9-10 MAR)

2 | 23

3 | 24

1 | 24

1 | 25

3 | 25

3 | 25

2 | 25

3 | 25 (8 MAR)

2 | 24 (9-10 MAR)

0   500   1000

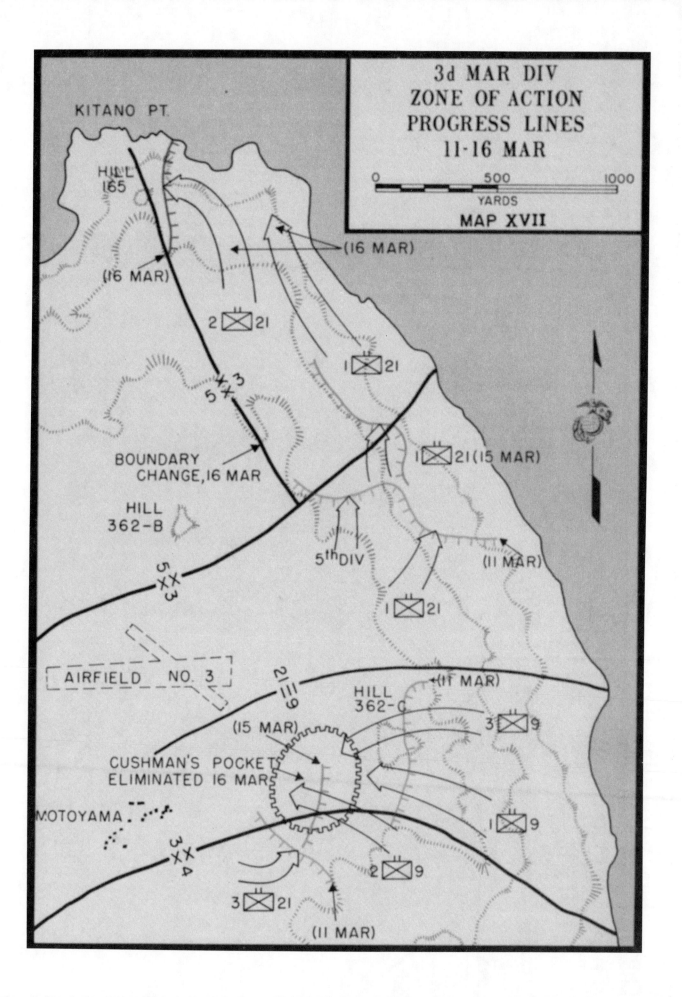

KITANO PT.

HILL 165

3d MAR DIV
ZONE OF ACTION
PROGRESS LINES
11-16 MAR

0   500   1000
YARDS

MAP XVII

(16 MAR)

(16 MAR)

2 ☒ 21

1 ☒ 21

XX 3
5 XX

1 ☒ 21 (15 MAR)

BOUNDARY
CHANGE, 16 MAR

HILL
362-B

5 XX 3

5th DIV

(11 MAR)

1 ☒ 21

AIRFIELD   NO. 3

21 ‖ 9

HILL
362-C

(11 MAR)

(15 MAR)

3 ☒ 9

CUSHMAN'S POCKET
ELIMINATED 16 MAR

MOTOYAMA

1 ☒ 9

3 XX 4

2 ☒ 9

3 ☒ 21

(11 MAR)

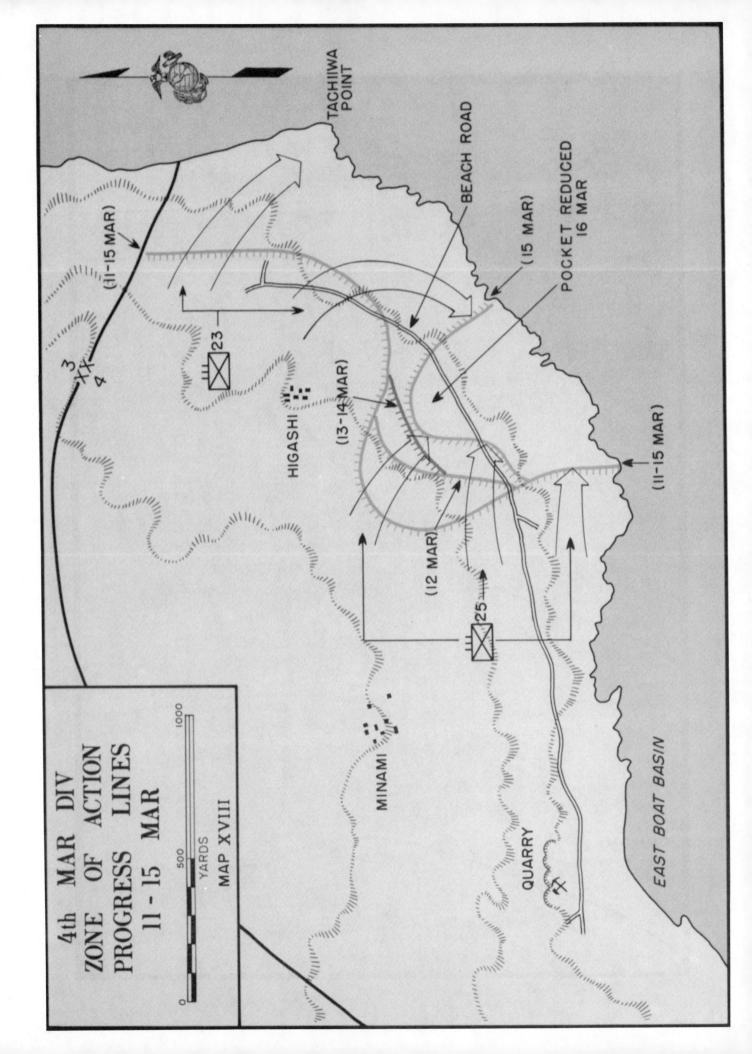

4th MAR DIV
ZONE OF ACTION
PROGRESS LINES
11 - 15 MAR

MAP XVIII

YARDS

0   500   1000

TACHIIWA POINT

BEACH ROAD

POCKET REDUCED
16 MAR

(15 MAR)

(11-15 MAR)

(11-15 MAR)

(13-14 MAR)

(12 MAR)

HIGASHI

MINAMI

QUARRY

EAST BOAT BASIN

XX
3
4

23

25

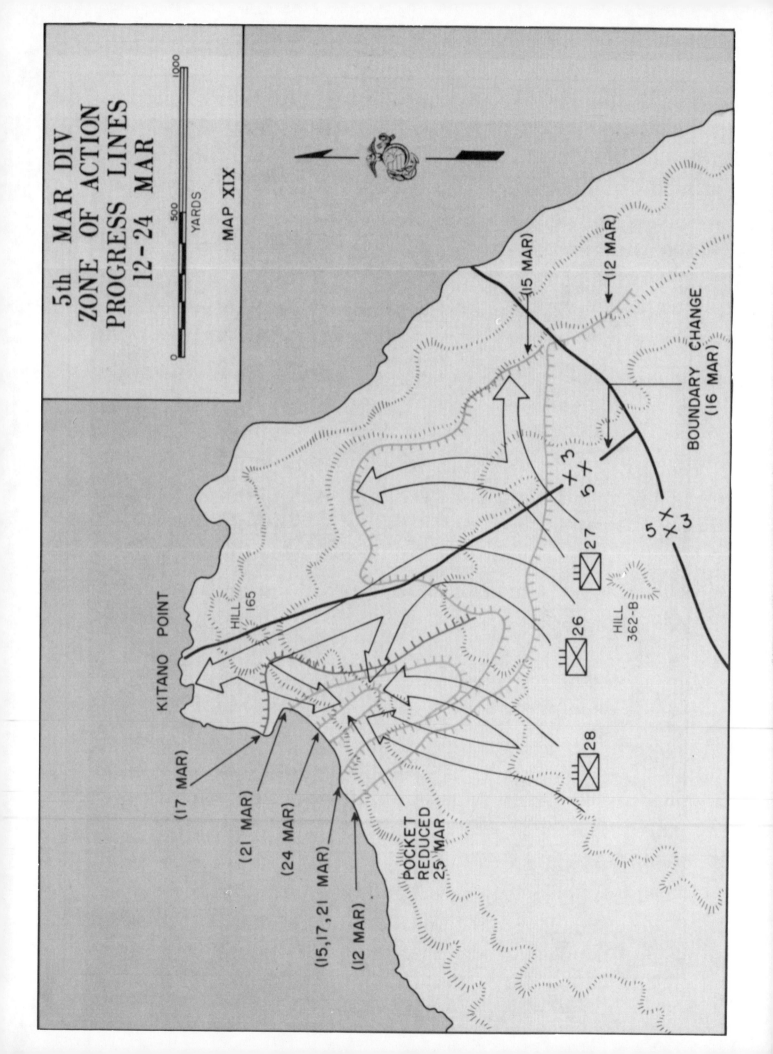

5th MAR DIV
ZONE OF ACTION
PROGRESS LINES
12-24 MAR

YARDS.

MAP XIX

KITANO POINT

HILL 165

(17 MAR)

(21 MAR)

(24 MAR)

(15,17,21 MAR)

(12 MAR)

POCKET REDUCED 25 MAR

27

26

28

HILL 362-B

5 X X 3

5 X X 3

(15 MAR)

(12 MAR)

BOUNDARY CHANGE (16 MAR)

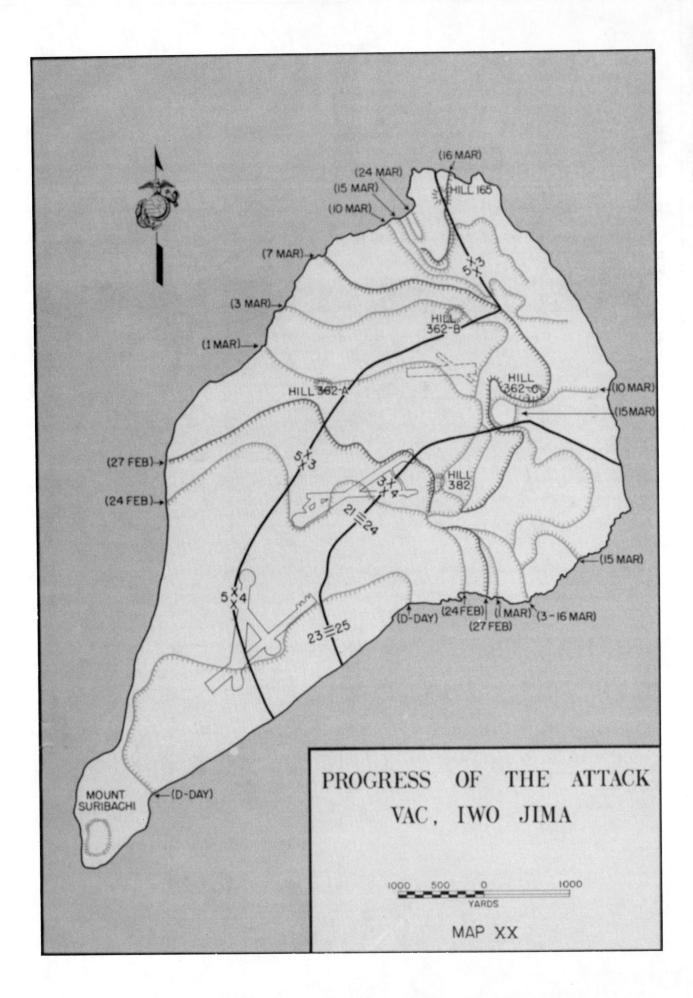

(16 MAR)
(24 MAR)
(15 MAR)
(10 MAR)
HILL 165
(7 MAR)
5 X 3
(3 MAR)
HILL 362-B
(1 MAR)
HILL 362-C
(10 MAR)
HILL 362-A
(15 MAR)
(27 FEB)
5 X 3
(24 FEB)
3 X 8
HILL 382
21 ≡ 24
(15 MAR)
5 X 4
(D-DAY)
(24 FEB)
(1 MAR)
(3 - 16 MAR)
(27 FEB)
23 ≡ 25
MOUNT SURIBACHI
(D-DAY)

PROGRESS OF THE ATTACK
VAC, IWO JIMA

1000   500   0   1000
YARDS

MAP XX

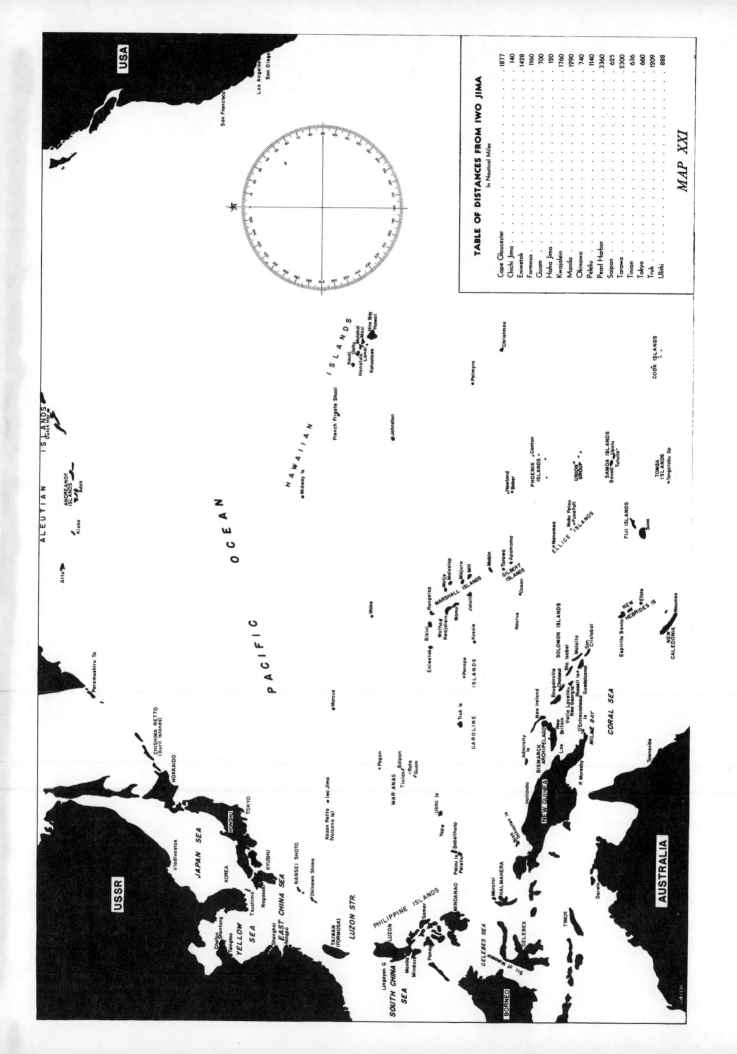

TABLE OF DISTANCES FROM IWO JIMA
In Nautical Miles

Cape Gloucester	1877
Chichi Jima	140
Eniwetok	1428
Formosa	1160
Guam	700
Haha Jima	120
Kwajalein	1760
Manila	1290
Okinawa	740
Peleliu	1140
Pearl Harbor	3360
Saipan	625
Tarawa	2300
Tinian	636
Tokyo	660
Truk	1209
Ulithi	888

MAP XXI